The Political Legacy of
King Hussein

The Political Legacy of
King Hussein

ALEXANDER BLIGH

sussex
ACADEMIC
PRESS

BRIGHTON • *PORTLAND*

Copyright © Alexander Bligh 2002, 2007

The right of Alexander Bligh to be identified as editor of this work has been asserted in accordance with the Copyright, Designs and Patents Act 1988.

2 4 6 8 10 9 7 5 3

First published in 2002; transferred to digital printing 2007, in Great Britain by
SUSSEX ACADEMIC PRESS
PO Box 139
Eastbourne BN24 9BP

and in the United States of America by
SUSSEX ACADEMIC PRESS
920 NE 58th Ave   Suite 300
Portland, Oregon 97213-3786

British Library Cataloguing in Publication Data
A CIP catalogue record for this book is available from the British Library.

Library of Congress Cataloging-in-Publication Data
Bligh, Alexander, 1949.
    The political legacy of King Hussein / Alexander Bligh.
    p. cm.
    Includes bibliographical references and index.
    ISBN-13: 978-1-84519-237-2 (pbk : alk. paper)
    ISBN-10: 1-902210-72-7 (pbk : alk. paper)
    1. Jordan—Politics and government—1952–1999.
    2. Hussein, King of Jordan, 1935–
    I. Title: King Hussein. II. Title.

    DS154.55 .B55 2002
    956.9504'3—dc21
                                                    2002018731

Cover photograph of the late King Hussein is by courtesy of Zoharab Zoharab (Jordan).

Typeset & designed by G&G Editorial, Brighton.
Transferred to Digital Printing 2007.
This book is printed on acid-free paper.

Contents

Foreword by Robert B. Satloff

For the last generation, the Middle East has been characterized as a region in which leaders enjoy longevity though their countries lack stability. While a small handful of regional states have historical legitimacy, most are latter-day creations whose demographic, geographic, and religious divisions are only barely hidden by the long tenure of leaders and regimes whose survival is owed to various mixes of coercion and cooptation. Thanks to the wisdom, ingenuity and uncanny political instincts of the late King Hussein bin Talal, the Hashemite Kingdom of Jordan may be evolving into the exceptional case – a country notable more for its development of national identity and political legitimacy than just the long tenure of its leader.

Given the anti-Hashemite enmity of Jordan's Arab neighbors and the deep ideological and demographic divisions within the country, that the kingdom even exists today, at the opening of the twenty-first century, is a fascinating story of perseverance, courage and luck. That it might be a model for political development for other regional states is truly remarkable. In this exhaustively researched and insightful study, historian Alexander Bligh tells how Hussein not only survived nearly a half-century on the throne of his small, weak, resource-poor country but how Hussein left his country more stable, secure, and cohesive than when he inherited the mantle of leadership.

Conventional wisdom holds that Hussein looked for political guidance to the legacy of his grandfather, the founder of modern Jordan, Emir (and later King) Abdullah. So often did Hussein cite the memory of his grandfather, Abdullah's tireless efforts to achieve a noble peace, and the pain of standing beside Abdullah when the latter was murdered in Jerusalem in 1951, that it is natural to infer that Hussein's world-view was a continuation of Abdullah's. As Dr. Bligh correctly points out, that is not the case. Indeed, Hussein's historic success and Jordan's progress in recent decades is precisely due to the fact that Hussein understood the lessons for Jordan and the Hashemite family of Abdullah's lifelong quest at territorial and political aggrandizement. Rather than risk the patrimony to satisfy ambition, Hussein opted instead to secure what he had, forging a new national identity around what Dr. Bligh calls a "smaller Jordan," i.e., the kingdom on the East Bank of the River Jordan. From that basic strategy, argues Dr. Bligh provocatively, flowed a decision to jettison the West Bank (and, especially, its anti-Hashemite population) to save the East Bank as well as a strategic relationship with Israel founded on convergence of interests and eventually resulting in full bilateral peace.

Today, with dangers on both Jordan's eastern and western borders and with the process of political development at home still far from complete, the kingdom is facing another pivotal and uncertain moment. The coming period of change will prove a supreme test to the abilities of the new king, Abdullah II. In his brief tenure, he has so far shown himself to understand well the priorities that animated his father's rule. If he, his advisors, and the kingdom's leaders apply those lessons with the right formula of discretion and boldness, stealth and statesmanship, then Jordan will truly become, as Dr. Bligh writes, "a nation-state no longer concerned with its existence but rather with the quality of its existence."

Executive Director
The Washington Institute for Near East Policy
Washington, DC

"I hope they [history books] will judge in my favor, not against me. I have aspired to that all my life, and as a man who has done his best, I hope history will judge me favorably."
Interview, October 30, 1992, *FBIS*, November 5, 1992

"Annexing the West Bank in 1948 was a mistake."
Interview with the Lebanese *al-Hawadith*, January 4, 1974

"Israel, after its occupation of the West Bank in 1967, began to depict the 1950 union of the two banks as an annexation of this territory to Jordan."
Speech to the Algiers Arab summit conference, June 8, 1988, quoted in *al-Dustur*, June 9

Introduction

After a long battle with cancer King Hussein passed away in early 1999. The monarch, so long the target of potential assassins, eventually gave up his own struggle with his illness. The grief and sorrow demonstrated by the citizens of Jordan and elsewhere were very genuine. During his life King Hussein (1935–99; ruled 1953–99) had become a father figure to his own people and a world leader to the rest of the nations. Upon his death the late monarch left a clear political legacy: the existence of the Hashemite Kingdom as a legitimate nation-state within the Middle Eastern family of nations.

This book speaks of the actions and ideology which made Hussein the creator of modern-day Jordan, a nation-state that has demonstrated its resilience and inner strength during a succession of crises over 50 years. The emergence of that Jordan, an East Bank country, along the lines outlined by King Hussein, is the result of a process which saw its very hesitant initial steps in 1963 and was completed with the signing of the 1994 Israeli–Jordanian peace accord – an instrument signed by two independent countries, and not agreed as one element of a larger formal Arab–Israeli reconciliation. This critical process was supplemented by the beginning of the democratization process in the late 1980s, which continued until the last days of the monarch.

This book is a tribute to a courageous leader who led his country and the Middle East into a new era. His careful yet innovative policies secured the continued existence of the Hashemite Kingdom and served many times as a major frontier in the face of expansionist and aggressive policies in the region.

Recent literature in the field of Middle Eastern studies recognizes that over a generation the region has undergone a major change. It is no longer a single geopolitical unit, but rather a mosaic of nation-states. Within this framework, the Hashemite Kingdom of Jordan stands as an example of transformation from the vision and ideology of Hussein's great-grandfather Sharif Hussein (1852–1931), of one Arab nation, into a nation-state in many ways resembling other such entities. The continued existence of the kingdom, and its emergence as a legitimate nation-state among the Arab nations, is the result of the far-sighted policies of Hussein. During the final part of his long rule the king made the Jordanian nation-state and the East Bank that remained in the hands of the Hashemite dynasty after the armed confrontation of June 1967 synonymous. That country, "Smaller Jordan," under the leadership of the king, developed patterns of political behavior typical of a national entity dealing mainly with its own domestic and regional interests. Calmly, often behind the scenes, Hussein moved away from the larger pan-Arab interests. In the 1960s he was the first to do so; today, heads of all Middle Eastern countries, while paying their dues to the general Arab cause, operate as leaders of national entities.

The main thesis of this book is that contrary to common belief and in spite of his image as a weak leader, Hussein was one of the main figures shaping the fate of the Middle East since the 1960s. He realized in the early 1960s the need to redefine his kingdom and make it a Jordanian, and not a Jordanian–Palestinian, nation-state in order to guarantee its survival in a hostile environment led until 1970 by President Nasser of Egypt. Nasser's intentions, probably with some Palestinian collaboration, might have transformed the kingdom into another Middle Eastern republic without the Hashemites. This picture of relations with Egypt (until 1971, the UAR – United Arab Republic) and the constant friction between Jordan, the Palestinians, and Israel has produced the particular identity of Jordan. This book analyzes a series of critical crises, mainly involving those players that helped shape the strategic decisions of the king and led him to his final desti-nation: an independent country under the Hashemite dynasty, operating under a set of national priorities that represent the consensus of the Jordanian people.

The book examines, *inter alia*, the emergence of Jordanian nationalism, in practice and in ideology, from 1960 to 1999. The analysis will begin with the 1960 crisis, which found Israel and Jordan on the same side, confronting the United Arab Republic (a union of Egypt and Syria, 1958–61). The king found an added source of danger in that situation: his own West Bank Palestinian citizens. The realization that West Bank Palestinians were a major threat to the social and political fabric of the kingdom led the king in 1960 to resume secret relations with Israel – this, in spite of his developing belief that the final price for such an alliance might be the giving away of the Palestinian West Bank. The result of later crises in 1963 and 1966 was Hussein's elaborate decision to turn over the West Bank to Israel in 1967, without losing any Arab credibility and without making Israel aware that the option of a return of territories to Jordan, usually referred to as the "Jordanian Option," never existed. However, Israel's mistaken belief in the existence of that option contributed to their support for the continued survival of the kingdom.[1] The chapters that follow will offer in this context a whole new interpretation regarding Jordan's participation in the 1967 war, and using hitherto unresearched documents, will describe and analyze the stages between 1960 and 1967 leading to this outcome.

The initial premise is that the process of building a Jordanian non-Palestinian entity started spontaneously as a reaction to a threatening geopolitical situation in the 1960s and the evolving sense of siege. This impression led the king to try and minimize the number of hostile actors encircling Jordan. Within this assessment Israel emerged as a potential and later an actual ally, whereas the Palestinians on the West Bank acted in a way that threatened the Hashemite Kingdom. The process was later carefully picked up by Hussein, leading inevitably to a non-Palestinian Jordanian nation-state making public peace with Israel in 1994 without demanding or getting back any of the West Bank.

Israel and Jordan began their dialogue in the summer of 1960 with top-level negotiations between military officers in the wake of a major Israeli intelligence failure early in the year and the assassination of the Jordanian prime minister in August 1960. In both cases the United Arab Republic was the clear winner. The similarity of Israeli and Jordanian interests, and later the link resulting from the common threat, developed into a secret, regular forum between the king and Israeli prime ministers which survived two wars and numerous political challenges. The two countries developed a powerful sense of common aims, present interests, and the realization that any future threat to either of them might in turn change the fate of the other. Thus, in assessing the components of this association I shall examine the national interests of Jordan to see Israeli intentions through Jordanian eyes, looking at the sphere of mutual interests, and finally, how these common interests came to play a role in a series of regional crises.

In September 1963 Hussein established his own direct link to Israel in addition to the top military channel of communication that had been created in 1960, a decision resulting from a painful trade-off between on one hand, his Palestinian citizens, hostile, subversive and exposed to foreign agitation, and on the other hand, Israel, which had its own designs on the West Bank, and was looking for ways to correct past military failures, but manifesting a strong interest in the continued existence of the kingdom. The king opted for the lesser of the two evils. Clearly, his decision was sparked by the crisis in April 1963, which stemmed from riots following the declaration of a new Arab union between Egypt, Syria and Iraq. This led to a wider conflagration in April and May 1963 that threatened the existence of the kingdom and led all players to reassess their regional policies. Hussein's analysis of these circumstances led him to believe that the Hashemites' meeting of interests with Israel might be to his advantage. Clearly, in resuming top-level negotiations with Israel he was aware of what he perceived as Israeli designs on the West Bank, and yet he believed that even this threat would present an acceptable risk to his kingdom rather than it being left without any strategic partners. In Lukac's words: "[that cooperation] was not directed at conflict resolution but at conflict management."[2]

Although the present volume aims to concentrate on the strategic junctures, it deviates from time to time to a more tactical and detailed study of specific moves, because some of the information used for the analysis has either been unpublished so far or significantly adds to the understanding of the processes interpreted, in a way different from the approach so far suggested. Sometimes it is necessary to explain ingredients of the "creative ambiguity" used by Hussein in order to distinguish between his proclaimed positions and his true interests.

Several key processes are studied. First, there is the emerging conflict between the two banks of the river in the 1960s and the way this led Hussein to give up a part of the kingdom in order to save the rest of it. I shall provide the facts and an interpretation of the courageous yet futile war in 1967 – a war that was intended not to keep the West Bank in Jordanian hands but to ensure that "Smaller Jordan" would have fewer subversive elements in the form of the Palestinians.

Secondly, I shall define the ingredients of the Jordanian national interest as different from the Arab interest as a result of the need to clarify relations with Israel and the Palestinians. Undoubtedly, one element of the making of a Jordanian nation-state has to do with the deviation from pan-Arab policies. During the period under discussion the king gradually moved away from concern with the potential threat from other Arab countries, presented as underlying inter-Arab considerations, to openly stress Jordanian interests. His on-and-off flirtation with the PLO and to a lesser extent his relations with Syria, Iraq and Saudi Arabia will be viewed through the prism of Jordanian national interests in action. What should be added in this context is Hussein's constant struggle against the siege laid by a succession of Jordan's neighbors. Hussein's concern with hostile moves by these countries led him to devise a rotating foreign policy. While relations with Israel, most of the time secret, served as a constant in his regional policy, he moved from one Arab country to another in forming *ad hoc* coalitions, always careful to keep his regional policies non-aligned in spite of the pro-Western orientation of his regime. Hussein's regional policies, along with his domestic Jordanization, eventually secured the existence of his kingdom. It is notable in this context that on many occasions Hussein professed his admiration and love for his grandfather, King Abdullah, who was assassinated in July 1951. However, even though Hussein managed to follow in the footsteps of Abdullah in making peace with Israel, the path taken with regard to Arab nationalism was rather different. Whereas Abdullah, the son of the great champion of Arab nationalism during World War I, Sharif Hussein, took upon himself to reconstruct an Arab kingdom, Hussein left behind a nation-state based on Jordanian nationalism, limited to a small part of the Arab lands of the Middle East.

Thirdly, there was the urgent need to devise Jordanian nationalism in the face of Palestinian nationalism, and thus build up the basic legitimacy for the existence of a distinct Hashemite Kingdom on part of the former Mandatory Palestine. A slow and very careful process of unveiling the king's true intentions in regard to the Palestinian West Bank accompanied the formation of this unique national approach. Time and again the gradual process of gaining international recognition by the PLO forced major changes of policy on the king. Even though, as discussed in the following pages, Hussein wanted to rid himself of the West Bank as of 1966, and succeeded in doing so in 1967, it took him until the signing of the peace treaty with Israel in 1994 to publicly demonstrate this by his actions.

Many political analysts have tried to answer the secret of the survival of King Hussein of Jordan, a king so often described as lacking in legitimacy within his own country and the Arab world at large. Yet, at the time of his death he was the longest serving Middle Eastern leader. One element of any new attempt to decipher this political and historical enigma should concentrate on studying the combination of his uniquely developed nationalism, with a realistic approach and carefully changing tactics, alongside a solid ideological foundation. The nationalism he promoted was intended to serve as the cornerstone of a continued process of providing legitimacy for the kingdom, along with ideology and political philosophy to support his actions. It is not merely that "social and political ideology has always been an important driving force in [Jordan's] history."[3] It is much more than that: the king provided his people and the outside world with a comprehensive national framework. His version of nationalism as a provider of ideological support for his political moves, especially on Palestinian–Jordanian relations, will be analyzed in the following pages. The main working assumption in this regard is that unlike most national ideologies elsewhere, which spring out spontaneously, the Middle East included, the Jordanian national ideology was imposed from above by the king as a necessary tool in creating cohesion and a center of identity among his own citizens. This book is, then, a study of the transformation of political views into a full-scale political agenda, and its implementation.

Finally, it is the process of creating and later operating political institutions that would carry the Jordanian democratic message to the individual Jordanian citizen. This is probably the last contribution of Hussein to his people between the late 1980s and his death. Perhaps the most important accomplishment of Hussein in this context is the one he could not live to see: a smooth transition from him to his son and successor, King Abdullah II. The transfer of power, impossible by all accounts until not long ago, is a testimony to the robust Jordanian political system and the loyalty of its citizens. The centerpiece of that system is the recognition that there is one single Jordanian entity, which can no longer be threatened with being taken over by enemies, domestic or external. This process is not yet complete; after all, certain elements in the making of Jordanian policy cannot be changed even with the change of guard, even though efforts are constantly being made. The large Palestinian population does not relate to the history and values of the original East Bankers, and the scarcity of natural resources have made Jordan subject to outside economic and political fluctuations and deprived it of a large degree of foreign policy independence.

This study makes use of primary sources in Arabic, English and Hebrew. The Arabic material is mainly from the Jordanian press and the compilation of the king's speeches to local audiences and interviews with foreign media, usually in connection with major events in Jordan and the region, since 1967. Western diplomatic archival sources usually give a fairly accurate picture. After all, Hussein spoke fluent English and "knew every nuance"[4] of the language, and also developed friendly relations with a succession of Western representatives. Accordingly, Hussein's remarks as recorded by Israeli leaders who saw him on a sporadic basis and by US diplomats who met him regularly serve as a reliable primary source. Obviously, no one person was ever given the whole picture by the king. That is, therefore, the role this political historian has taken upon himself. Regarding Hebrew sources, it should be noted that the friendly relations between Israel and the Hashemite Kingdom enabled Jordanian officials to follow very closely every word in the Israeli media regarding their country. It is therefore possible to resort to the Israeli press and past secret records of Israeli internal meetings to verify the exact Israeli public position on related Jordanian issues. On many occasions even if details of secret meetings were not conveyed to Hussein in their entirety their main essence found its way to the Israeli–Jordanian negotiations. These expressions formed the basis for many internal Jordanian assessments regarding Israel's positions.

This book concentrates on primary sources now available to the researcher in order to compare notes and gather the parts together into the larger Hashemite puzzle. It is the intention to present Hussein as a leader with a vision. This vision, the establishment of his kingdom as a nation-state and its defense, was the mission of this brave king up to his last moment.

The author wishes to thank several individuals and organizations whose help was significant in making the ideas behind this book into a monograph. Hopefully it will contribute to a better understanding of the

Hashemite Kingdom of Jordan. First and foremost, Professor Gabriel Sheffer, of the Hebrew University, Jerusalem. Although his effort in securing seed money for a study of the political worldview of King Hussein did not materialize in its intended study, it enabled the much improved version – as it appears in chapter 4 of this book. Other academic institutions also contributed to the funding of this book: the colleges of Jezereel Valley and Judea and Samaria, both in Israel. It is my sad debt of honor to thank the late Mr Moshe Zak, whose book on Israeli–Jordanian relations served as my inspiration, and who later agreed to read this book in draft form. Unfortunately he did not complete this undertaking. I also wish to thank my assistant, the late Avi Shabat, whose untimely death came as such a shock during the writing of this book. Other people, most of whom wish to remain anonymous, helped me in various ways and served as a source of constant intellectual challenge. I thank them all, especially the senior official whose draft manuscript written in Amman during and after the Gulf crisis, "The Temptation of Mecca: King Hussein and the Gulf Crisis," served me in shaping some of the concepts regarding this event. I wish to emphasize that the ideas in the book are original and only I am responsible for anything appearing here.

1

The Hashemite–Palestinian Crisis of April 1963

The assassination of King Abdullah in Jerusalem in July 1951 opened a new era in Jordan. His son Talal, though becoming the legal successor, did not rule owing to a mental illness. Talal's son, Hussein bin Talal, was proclaimed the minor King of Jordan in August 1952. Later, in May 1953, he became the full King of the Hashemite Kingdom. Jordanian politicians used the year following the assassination to put together a constitution, which, with several modifications, continues to serve as the basis for Jordanian political life. The years between 1952 and 1963, which are not covered by this book, contributed tremendously to the political worldview of Hussein. In a nutshell, those years saw *inter alia* an anti-Hashemite prime minister using the Jordanian constitution and its freedom of party activity to try to operate against Hussein. That activity is a reflection of the more threatening enemy until 1967: President Nasser of Egypt, who did not give up until the war his wish to see the monarchy turned into a pro-Nasserite republic. Within this context of subversion and confrontation the 1957 Zarka conspiracy, along with the dispatch of British troops in 1958 to protect the regime in the face of an aggressive regional pro-Nasserite wave, stand out as two examples of the potentially short life expectancy of Hussein, and the kingdom along with him. These crises resulted in a pause in the Jordanian movement towards a Western style of politics, which resumed only in the late 1980s. The picture of aggressive domestic opposition and of being surrounded by hostile forces, coupled with the realization that the best supporters of the kingdom – first the British and later the Americans – were far away, served as the basis for a policy of survival that would lead Hussein in the years ahead to some creative policy guidelines that eventually would not only guarantee the existence of the kingdom but would make Hussein one of the leading political figures in the Middle East.

Several crises occurred in the short history of Jordanian rule over the West Bank (1948–67), which may be viewed as triggering a redefinition of relations between the Hashemite government of the kingdom and its

Palestinian citizens in the West Bank. Of these, the events of April 1963 constitute a major watershed, for they marked the first time that the Hashemite dynasty had to contend with a combined domestic and regional challenge on its own without Western support. This sense of isolation ultimately led Hussein to develop a strategic alliance with Israel, thereby acknowledging the Palestinian population of the West Bank as the most dangerous single threat to the survival of the dynasty. His decision was also the result of a personal sense of being alone: as the last remaining ruling descendant of the Hashemite dynasty, Hussein bore the full burden of preserving the kingdom. Surrounded by hostile neighbors, he had to make all political and policy decisions alone, with no confidants to consult. Only some years later would he begin to groom his eldest brother, Hassan, as crown prince.

The crisis of April–May 1963 is unique even in the context of successive crises, since it led all players to reassess their regional policies. It prompted Hussein to expand military contacts with Israel, which had been initiated in 1960,[1] into a full-scale political dialogue which has shaped relations between the two countries to this day. Israel, for its part, was forced by the crisis to consider the possibility of the seizure of the West Bank as a necessary strategic goal separate from the question of whether or not the Hashemite Kingdom of Jordan survived. The trigger for the crisis was the declaration of a new Arab union between Egypt, Syria and Iraq, provoking riots in the West Bank to pressure the king to join it. This led to a wider Israeli–Jordanian–West Bank conflagration that threatened the existence of the kingdom and led to unexpected political consequences.

The events of April–May 1963 were to be replayed in the Israeli–Jordanian–West Bank crisis of November 1966, and would come to a head before and during the Middle Eastern military conflict in May–June 1967. In the wake of the crisis, Hussein and his government arrived at a realistic assessment of both Palestinian and Israeli intentions, leading him to abandon hopes of reconciliation with the West Bank Palestinians, if indeed he had had any, and to raise the level of negotiations with Israel. The widespread conviction by East and West Bankers that the 1950 union of the two banks of the Jordan under Hashemite rule was unworkable,[2] evidenced by ongoing riots, unrest and abortive coups against the king culminating in the episode in April–May 1963, left no doubt about the seriousness of the subversive threat posed by the West Bank Palestinians. The king was aware that this instability had engendered the formulation of a clear-cut Israeli policy on the West Bank, especially after the events of 1963. Conveyed to the king by Israeli leaders both directly and indirectly, it called for Israel's occupation of the West Bank at the slightest indication of change in the strategic status quo of the kingdom. This policy was fully applied in June 1967 and again in a different format during Jordan's civil war crisis in 1970.

Its aim was the preservation of the kingdom at all costs (including reducing the Palestinian risk to the king by taking over the West Bank – a central tenet of Israeli security thinking). What were the main components of the king's trade-off of his desire to see the integration of the Palestinians into his kingdom, for stability with Israel, and how was this strategic shift a direct result of the crisis of April 1963?

As had happened in the past, it was Egypt that ignited the tinder that was to flare up into the conflagration of 1963. Anxious to re-establish a new pan-Arab union following the 1961 collapse of the United Arab Republic, Egypt found the right opportunity following the two Ba'th revolutions in Iraq and Syria in early 1963, failing to recognize the animosity between these two wings of the party. These uprisings sparked fears among policy makers in both Israel and Jordan that their respective countries would be encircled by regimes capable of unified aggression against them. The US response to these new realities was cautious, with Secretary of State Dean Rusk stating that the US was "very much interested in the independence and security of our friends in Jordan and Saudi Arabia."[3] Israeli officials, however, discussed the possibility of a Ba'th revolution in Jordan.[4]

Although initially the Israelis ruled out an immediate crisis,[5] events soon proved otherwise. The two new regimes, along with Egypt publicly embracing the idea of pan-Arab unity, conducted a series of negotiations that culminated on April 17, 1963, with the proclamation of a new union. In the event, this new political framework never materialized, but the declaration itself was enough to send shock waves throughout the Middle East, felt especially acutely in Israel and Jordan.

In many respects these regional developments paralleled those of 1958. Then, however, the outbursts of revolutionary violence had elicited Western military support for the Hashemite regime, including the deployment of British troops on Jordanian soil. This time,[6] the Western powers were reluctant to come to the aid of any of their allies in the region.

The Jordanian–West Bank–Israeli crisis flared up[7] as an immediate reaction to the unity proclamation on April 17, manifesting itself mainly in three arenas: on the streets of the towns on the West Bank and Palestinian centers of population on the East Bank; at the governmental and parliamentary level in both Jordan and Israel; and along Jordan's borders with Syria and Israel. Hours after the new union was announced, demonstrations broke out in the Jordanian sector of Jerusalem and in the rest of the West Bank, several fatalities occurred, and the Jordanian authorities imposed a curfew on all West Bank towns. Reactions on the West Bank to violent incidents involving the army were hostile[8] and it was commonly believed that the fatalities were the result of a premeditated policy. Demonstrators raised a four-star flag – three stars symbolizing the three uniting powers, and the fourth representing their wish to see Jordan incorporated into this union. Preachers in mosques spoke against the regime. Demonstrations, sometimes violent, continued throughout the West Bank for days, and general unrest lasted for several weeks. Quiet was restored to the Palestinian areas of the kingdom only after the king ordered his army to intervene, which included posting snipers on the walls of the old city of Jerusalem.

Outspoken anti-Hashemite sentiment and open contempt for Jordanian sovereignty was voiced in the Jordanian parliament by Palestinian delegates on April 20. In a move that exceeded the political action against Hussein in 1956, a majority in parliament voted no confidence in Prime Minister Samir al-Rifa'i,[9] leading to the dissolution of parliament and the appointment of a new prime minister by the king.

Meanwhile, Israel beefed up its military forces, especially in Jerusalem. However, with the continuation of tension in Jordan, the Israeli prime minister David Ben-Gurion sent a letter to President John F. Kennedy on May 12 asking the US to take action in order to preserve the Hashemite regime.[10] Although the US and other Western powers came to the conclusion, some six weeks after the start of the crisis, that the regime could indeed collapse at any moment, the Israeli impression then, in spite of some movements of the US Sixth Fleet, was that unlike in 1958, the US would let the political process play out and would not intervene in order to salvage the Jordanian regime.[11]

The crisis was over approximately eight weeks after it began. The West Bank Arabs resumed their political stance of suppressed hostility to the regime, awaiting a more fortuitous opportunity to rid themselves of the Hashemites. From a Jordanian perspective, growing Palestinian nationalism and the momentum of the concept of a Palestinian entity, especially on the West Bank, meant more tension between the East and West Banks. A rumor in November 1963, well after the passing of the April storm, concerned the formation of a "Kingdom of Palestine"[12] on both sides of the Jordan River. Whether this was a tribal balloon floated by the Hashemites or by the Palestinians and for what purpose was unclear. Either way it was yet another indication of the active forces at play on both banks of the river.

Jordan's Perspective: growing Hashemite isolation

Ever since he became king on his own in 1953, Hussein had attempted to build up an independent monarchy with full political rights for its citizens. However, he inherited two heavy liabilities that jeopardized these goals: the history of secret relations between his grandfather, King Abdullah, and Jordan's neighbor to the west, Israel; and the 1950 decree annexing the

West Bank and declaring all its people full Jordanian citizens. The history of relations with Israel, and the takeover of the West Bank in the context of the 1948 conflict, hounded Hussein and made him constantly suspected of holding secret talks with Israel. Even the removal of the British chief-of-staff of the Arab Legion in 1956 failed to add to the Arab standing of the king, for when danger arose in the wake of the 1958 revolution in Iraq, British military forces interceded on his behalf. Additionally, the gap in educational and economic development between the West and the East Banks constituted a divisive domestic element, exacerbated by political hostility to the monarchy's control in the West Bank.

Of all the players in the region, Jordan was in the most precarious position during the 1960s, exposed to growing risks to its regime and to the king personally not only from within but from outside as well. Hussein had reason to fear the pro-Nasserite regime in Syria, which had brought it into the UAR in 1958, and added to Jordan's encirclement by anti-monarchy regimes. He also felt threatened by the republican regime in Iraq. Surrounded by hostile republican regimes, Hussein was forced into an uneasy alliance with his perennial enemy, the dynasty that had robbed his family of the Muslim holy places in the mid-1920s – the Saudi kingdom.

The secession of Syria in 1961 from the short-lived UAR did not alter Jordan's geopolitical standing among its Arab neighbors. UAR President Nasser continued to single out the two monarchies of Jordan and Saudi Arabia as targets for subversion aimed at toppling their regimes and replacing them with pro-Egyptian leaders. A series of attempts were made on the king's life during the tenure of the UAR and thereafter, and the Jordanian prime minister, Hazza' al-Majali, was assassinated by a bomb planted at his office in August 1960.

Nasser was greatly assisted in his anti-Hashemite activity by Palestinians in the West Bank. The zone became an open field for the recruitment of young Palestinians, reminiscent of similar enlistment efforts for the *fidayin* by Egyptian agents in the 1950s. Consequently, the presence of Jordanian security forces in the West Bank was strongly felt in contrast to the East Bank, an area generally loyal to the regime. Palestinian resentment of the Hashemites was expressed by periodic demonstrations and by sermons in the mosques. Hostility was reinforced by the announcement by Iraq in 1959 of the notion of a Palestinian entity, and thereafter by an Arab summit resolution establishing the Palestine Liberation Organization (PLO) in 1964 in defiance of the king's objections. These developments, along with the resumption of Palestinian guerrilla activity against Israel from Jordanian territory in 1965, compounded the vulnerability of the regime. The crises of 1963 and 1966 activated a growing awareness by the king that he must reassess his overall strategic position and bring about a set of conditions that would relieve him of the Palestinian burden.

Quelling the April 1963 crisis presented Hussein with a series of grave challenges: on the domestic level, the possibility of a revolution instigated by the army, and the prospect of a major confrontation between the West and the East Banks; on the regional level, the possibility of an Israeli invasion and the deterioration of relations with Egypt, the main instigator of subversion against the kingdom; and on the international level, the desire to extract some sort of guarantee from the Western superpowers for the future of the kingdom.

Ten days into the crisis the king was informed[13] by the US of the possibility of a conspiracy within the army, stemming apparently from a group of officers under the influence of republicanism who might try to join forces with Palestinian troops. However, the Jordanian monarch had structured his army[14] to prevent such an eventuality, assigning mostly non-Palestinian officers to combat units and Palestinian troops so as to preclude any disobedience in situations that required firing at Palestinian demonstrators, and eliminating the possibility of a pro-Palestinian coup attempt.[15] The army proved its loyalty throughout the crisis, and would play a major role in maintaining the stability of the monarchy during the two major crises to follow in 1966 and 1967.

The most serious security risk for Jordan in 1963, as during the entire period from 1948 to 1967, was the Palestinian population of the West Bank, a perception held not only by Jordanian leaders but by Western foreign ministries[16] as well. The explicitly anti-Hashemite tenor of the parliamentary debate on April 20 and the vote of no confidence in Prime Minister Rifa'i, the first of its kind in Jordanian history, plainly justified this assessment. Moreover, it prompted certain unorthodox moves by the king. In an unusual meeting at 1:30 a.m. on April 21 with a US representative he voiced[17] disappointment in and criticism of many of the Palestinian members of parliament. That night, several of the parliamentary deputies who had voted against Rifa'i, most of them from the West Bank, were arrested.[18] Although the king did not volunteer any details regarding further deterioration he saw coming, clearly he perceived it as an East Bank–West Bank clash.

What was equally evident to the king and his government was that Egypt was the sponsor of the subversion in Jordan,[19] both financially and militarily. This patronage went beyond the hanging of pictures of Nasser throughout the West Bank and the hailing of him as the people's true leader. Sizable Palestinian pro-Nasserite elements felt they were coming closer to accomplishing their political goals, which were the overthrow of the Hashemite regime and the establishment of a republican pro-Nasserite government. The Jordanian assessment at the beginning of the crisis was that Egypt would be satisfied with nothing less than this political goal. Still, the Jordanian leadership believed that Egypt was not anxious to become involved in a new round of regional hostilities. In reality, Egypt would have settled for any republican regime in Jordan so long as the hated monarchist, reactionary Hashemites were removed. Hussein mounted a combined public and behind-the-scenes diplomatic campaign *vis-à-vis* Egypt. Speaking before a variety of domestic audiences during the early stages of the crisis, he consistently refrained from any reference to Egypt's disruptive role.[20] At the same time, Jordan desperately tried to obtain UN political intervention aimed at persuading Egypt to refrain from continued subversion in Jordan, reflecting a conviction by Jordan's leaders that the very existence of the kingdom was in danger.

The fear of an Israeli invasion in the event of instability in the West Bank was shared by both the Western powers and Jordan long before the 1963 crisis,[21] yet the prospect of sending Western soldiers over to defend Jordan was never discussed with Jordan, or even in closed Western forums, after 1958. Hussein thus lacked a component of Jordanian survival that had been traditional since the establishment of the kingdom until the late 1950s: a Western security umbrella.

Domestically, the crisis illuminated the deep rift between the West and East Banks once again. Even more worrisome for the Hashemite regime was the widespread conviction that relations between the two banks could not improve and that rather, they would continue to generate more crises in the future. The southern Hebron mountain area in particular stood out as a hotbed of anti-regime activity,[22] followed in intensity by Jerusalem, Nablus and Irbid, which had a large Palestinian population.

The king's reaction to the outbreak of the crisis was ideologically noteworthy for it marked the start of a long process undertaken by him to define the terms "Jordan" and "Jordanian." In a landmark speech[23] on April 22, Hussein, the great-grandson of the champion of the 1916 Arab revolt against the Ottomans, referred to the term "Jordanian Arab" in the context of a warning that to raise a hand against the king was tantamount to resisting true Arab unity. In light of his distrust of the West Bank Palestinians, and the public accusations he directed at them, this statement may be viewed as the first indication of a new conceptual approach, namely that Jordan in reality consisted of the East Bank only, and that the West Bankers, as evidenced by their political behavior, were in the process of removing themselves from it.

One of the most important lessons of the crisis for Hussein was the necessity to distinguish between rhetoric and hard facts in Jordan's relationship with the US, and the conclusion that the American commitment to Jordan's survival was doubtful. Though US officials referred to Jordan at times as the "Rock of Gibraltar," indicating their confidence in the continued survival of the kingdom, the overall feeling of Washington was that Hussein's regime was not too strong and stood the risk of being toppled. A series of US expressions of support, culminating in an ostensibly reassuring letter received from President Kennedy,[24] caused more concern than encouragement, reminiscent of a similar letter that the Saudi acting king, Faysal, had received from the president a year previously. That letter too conveyed assurances, yet shortly thereafter, in December 1962, the US recognized the pro-Nasserite Yemen Arab Republic, causing grave concern to the Saudi monarchy as well as to the Hashemite Kingdom of Jordan. The Saudis had the presence of some US air force units on Saudi soil to compensate them for this diplomatic move whereas Hussein had to be satisfied with movements of the Sixth Fleet, which obviously was a far cry from what he had hoped for.

Israel's Security Concerns

One of the ground rules that molded Arab–Israeli relations between the 1948 and 1967 wars was Israel's declared *casus belli*,[25] namely its determination to defend itself against any Arab attempt to liquidate the Jewish state. In light of its numerical inferiority, Israel favored preventive action to avoid being forced into a military move. The only strong pro-Hashemite military power in the region was Israel, whose military prowess in the early 1960s, based mainly on French-made fighter planes, was a consideration to be reckoned with.[26] Three moves directly or indirectly related to Jordan were seen by Israel as *casi belli*: the introduction of non-Jordanian forces into Jordan, the diversion of the headwaters of the Jordan River, and the closure of the Tiran Straits leading to the southern Israeli port of Eilat (and to the only Jordanian outlet to open sea in Aqaba). These conditions were no secret. On the contrary, Israel believed that by making them public, it would encourage its neighbors to refrain from taking such hostile action.

Still, Israel never articulated its stand should Israeli security be threatened from Jordan without the introduction of non-Jordanian armies. Jordan thus had to formulate its policies regarding the West Bank without knowing what Israel's real intentions were. However, Israel demonstrated considerable flexibility towards Jordan when informing[27] the US during the crisis (obviously under the assumption that Jordan would be made privy to this information) that only if the Hashemite regime were to remain in place would Israel overlook a series of ongoing violations of the armistice agreement between the two countries. Such Israeli concessions would include refraining from raising the issue of access to the Jewish holy places and to the main road to Jerusalem via Latrun, which had been in Jordanian hands since 1948. In this way Israel wished to convey to Hussein that it would concede what it considered to be major interests for the sake of the most vital interest: maintaining a non-hostile regime to the east. Israel conveyed this position to the US as part of its preparations for a possible invasion of the West Bank, explaining that Israeli restraint would be abolished should any other regime be formed in Jordan.

A major pillar of Israeli security policy between 1955 and 1967 was the conviction that the long 1949 armistice line with Jordan was almost impossible to defend, but that as long as the Hashemite monarchy, with its distrust of the West Bank Arabs, was in power, Israel had had no reason to fear a military attack, although it had to contend with ongoing terrorist activity by Palestinian *fidayin*.[28] Any change in regime in Jordan, however, would instantly endanger Israel's security. Even during the long span of non-negotiations between the two countries in 1950–60, Israel considered the Hashemite regime to be non-hostile.[29] At the time of the April 1963 crisis Israel, along with a large body of international opinion, believed that the demise of the Hashemite monarchy was inevitable, although not imminent,[30] and that any change of rule in Jordan would be tantamount to a threat to Israel. Nevertheless, Israel prioritized this threat: the assassination of the king as part of a pro-Nasserite takeover was considered the most dangerous possibility, while other eventualities were viewed as problematic but somewhat less dangerous.[31] No matter what the degree of risk, Israeli policy makers were generally of the opinion that any danger should be removed as rapidly as possible, in all probability by an Israeli takeover of the West Bank.[32]

The speed and nature of any Israeli reaction to possible developments in Jordan would depend on a series of considerations besides the actual nature of the crisis,[33] namely the likely degree of risk to Israeli security, and the speed of the crisis. A sudden change in the Jordanian regime would preclude an immediate Israeli military reaction, since Israel's defense forces would require at least 48 hours to call up its reserve units,[34] a necessary preliminary step before any Israeli strike. By contrast, a gradual process of political change in Jordan, with or without the king, would not provide Israel with the necessary trigger for rapid intervention and would ultimately force Israel into the role of aggressor once it decided that it could no longer tolerate the changes to the east. Yet another Israeli consideration would be the avoidance of adding more Arabs to its population or creating a new refugee problem.[35] The latter problem would complicate the military situation and create another reason for the superpowers to intervene.

With the emergence of potential danger in Jordan in the Israeli view, following the Iraqi and Syrian revolutions of early 1963, Western diplomats began to consider possible Israeli contingents, including an invasion of the West Bank.[36] The Canadian ambassador in Tel Aviv, probably reflecting the views of other diplomats stationed there as well, thought it could take Israel as little as 12 hours from the moment of change to an invasion of the West Bank.[37] The evidence shows that the Western powers were clearly aware of the potential threat to Israel signified by any change of regime in Jordan.

Two factors elicited Israeli concern: the April 17 unity declaration, and, approximately a week later, mounting intelligence indicating a possible revolution in Jordan. On both accounts Israel viewed its security interests as firmly bound up with the survival of the Hashemite regime. The heightened possibility of the fall of the regime prompted Israel to act both on the diplomatic level and in developing military contingency plans.

In the diplomatic arena Israel sent messages[38] in late April to all the superpowers, including the USSR, drawing their attention to the declared aim of the new Arab union to destroy the Jewish state. This was followed on May 12 by an additional letter from Ben-Gurion to President Kennedy and on June 9, one week before Ben-Gurion's last and final resignation, by another series of letters from him to the leaders of the superpowers in which he detailed Israel's peace and security concerns. Israel also filed an official complaint with the UN Security Council in late April regarding the threats embodied in the unity declaration of April 17.

The points that Israeli spokesmen reiterated were that the establishment of the new union threatened both regional security and Israeli national security, and that the best way to avoid the escalation of tension in the region would be by issuing a joint US–Soviet guarantee of the territorial integrity and security of the region. Short of this, Israel indicated, it would be satisfied with a US guarantee, but failing American assurances, the implication of the messages was that Israel would be left with no alternative but to invade the West Bank[39] should dramatic changes take place in Jordan. Additionally, Israeli representatives made plain, the new regional realities were the result not only of subversive Egyptian activity but of the massive Soviet support for Egypt and the confused US policy response, all of which could lead to an unnecessary war in the Middle East.

Legally, the Israelis argued,[40] should a change in the Jordanian regime transpire, the entire basis of Israeli–Jordanian relations – the 1949 Armistice Agreement – would no longer be valid. This agreement, they pointed out, had been signed by two independent countries, and if one of the parties were to be taken over by an outside force the agreement would be regarded as null and void. Moreover, Israel would be virtually forced to occupy the West Bank in order to fill the political vacuum that would be created. In the same vein the Israeli military advocated[41] the imminent mobilization of whole reserve units, but were satisfied in late April with a state of alert and the bringing in of army reinforcements, in many cases quite visible to the Jordanian side. With this, military sources voiced[42] their conviction to foreign attachés that a change of regime in Jordan would necessitate Israeli military action. The impression they gave was that an

Israeli move on the West Bank would be swift and therefore would not spur an all-out Middle Eastern war.

Although the public Israeli reaction to the revolutions in Iraq and Syria in early 1963 reflected self-confidence, these developments undoubtedly prompted fresh thinking. Until 1963 Israeli policy makers had believed that any change in the Jordanian regime would be the product of Egyptian subversion aimed at installing a pro-Nasserite ruler. The new circumstances, however, raised the prospect of a new Ba'th regime east of Israel, which, while not resulting in the encirclement of Israel by a single Nasserite entity would be nevertheless as hostile as the Syrian regime.[43] One of the implications of such a scenario was that an Israeli invasion of Jordan, considered almost inevitable in the event of a pro-Nasserite takeover, was only one of several options in the event of the formation of a Ba'th-type regime. An alternative option – one that could preclude an Israeli invasion of the West Bank with the establishment of a non-Nasserite regime – would be an explicit US guarantee of Israel's borders. This prospect was raised by Ben-Gurion in his June 9 letter to Kennedy but was not given serious consideration, being opposed by the State Department under Secretary of State Rusk,[44] as too pro-Israel. Israel, in the State Department view, would have to provide a *quid pro quo* that would undoubtedly be unacceptable to it: movement towards the "solution of the refugee problem, support for UNTSO [United Nations Truce Supervision Organization], avoidance of the use of force, and the exclusion of nuclear weapons from the area."[45] Moreover, a Western guidance might elicit a parallel Soviet move for the Arab side, thereby escalating superpower rivalry in the region even further.[46] This response, and particularly the inclusion of the nuclear factor in the formulation of the US position, was viewed with disappointment by Israel. In essence, Israel's request for a security guarantee that would replace, or at least significantly delay, the military option, was turned down, reinforcing the perception in Israel that it was being left to its own fate and must rely entirely on its own armed forces for its security.

Another major lesson for Israel in the wake of the crisis was that a change of regime in Jordan involving the deposing of Hussein was an imminent possibility. Three separate scenarios were considered by Israel in that event.[47] The first contingency involved the forceful removal of the king not necessarily by an organized conspiracy but through an assassination by a single gunman (the "one bullet" theory). Such a development need not automatically involve an Israeli military move. Rather, if the monarch were to be replaced by another member of the royal family, Israel would monitor the measure of control the new monarch had over the West Bank. An Iraqi revolution of the 1958 type, removing the monarchy and declaring a republic, was not anticipated in this scenario. The second contingency involved the removal of the king by local elements under the influence of non-indigenous political forces – Nasserite or Ba'th. While a Nasserite change of regime would almost automatically provoke an Israeli military move, a Ba'th-inspired change could evoke a wait-and-see reaction, albeit with the anticipation of an eventual Nasserite takeover. The third contingency involved a takeover of Jordan by nonpartisan West Bank elements. In this case, too, Israel made it clear that it would adopt a wait-and-see posture, although such a change so close to the main Israeli population centers would obviously evoke extreme concern.[48]

Significantly, the concern conveyed by Israel to the foreign powers revealed a distinction made between the West and East Banks. A degree of hostility displayed by a regime on the East Bank might perhaps be tolerated, but not if displayed by the rulers of the West Bank. Additionally, the West Bank population was perceived as more susceptible to foreign propaganda than the more loyal population of the East Bank. These perceptions were not far removed from the views of Jordanian policy makers themselves. On one occasion during the crisis, the Jordanian prime minister suggested that Nasser would be satisfied with the inclusion of the East Bank in the Egyptian–Syrian–Iraqi federation, while Israel would be allowed to annex the West Bank.[49]

The Western Players in the 1963 Crisis

While the West's overall view of the regional balance of power was unaffected by the unfolding crisis, and the pro-Western regimes – especially Saudi Arabia and Jordan – were favored, the Western powers distanced themselves from the crisis in comparison with the past. They left the regional players to take care of their own security needs, while the US in particular did not rule out cooperation with the revolutionary regimes, first and foremost Nasserite Egypt. This, in spite of the lesson for the Western forces that the Hashemite regime could not survive for long without some significant Anglo-American support.[50] This approach reflected a new foreign policy shift by President Kennedy. Nasser was no longer regarded as the villain of the Middle East, but rather as a regional leader to negotiate with. Even the fall of the monarchy in Yemen in 1962 and Nasser's involvement in that country did not bring about a change in US policies.

In the same vein, the Western powers were unconvinced,[51] at least initially, of the Israeli claim that the newly declared Arab union in any way constituted a threat to Israel or to regional stability. Their reaction was merely to consult with the local governments and to monitor developments. Even the prospect of an Israeli invasion of the West Bank was initially viewed by the US as merely a threat to induce the West to protect Jordan actively, and not seen as a real eventuality.[52] Only with the rise of domestic unrest in Jordan did the Western powers realize that the crisis was more than the passing storm so familiar in Middle Eastern politics. About ten days into the crisis the US identified[53] cumulative signs of an imminent revolution, and several days later both the US and the UK initiated contingency planning for the possibility of the collapse of the Jordanian regime.[54]

In reality, the crisis was magnified by the unspoken agreement of the Western forces not to intervene militarily on behalf of the king. While there is no positive evidence of this decision, clearly it underlay all Western diplomatic activity at that time. The maximal involvement that the US would consider[55] was the possible dispatch of a military mission to Jordan for arms negotiations, and a certain amount of US paratroop participation in Jordanian maneuvers, both at some future date. The Joint Chiefs-of-Staff also suggested[56] the deployment of part of the Sixth Fleet in the eastern Mediterranean. The explanation[57] provided to Israel by the Americans was that the US could not block an indigenous movement for change. In reality, the West was concerned by two possibilities: a Soviet military move in the event of a Western military presence in the region, and a conviction[58] that Israel would occupy the West Bank if the crisis worsened, prompting caution to avoid the appearance of Israeli–Western collusion in responsibility for the crisis, such as an Israeli occupation of the West Bank, while the West protected the Hashemite regime on the East Bank. Above all, the Western powers wanted to maintain an appearance of impartiality in their relations with the Middle Eastern states. Their main concern diplomatically[59] was how to articulate sufficient support for the king so as to prevent a hostile development, yet avoid creating the impression that he owed his survival to the hated Western colonialist regimes.

Discussion of these issues by the Western powers, while not reflected in public statements, involved a large number of participants from several countries and were probably not a secret to the Jordanian monarch. The scenarios and contingencies developed by the Western policy planners[60] followed two main avenues: how to halt the danger to the Jordanian regime in the event of a continued deterioration in the domestic situation, and how to minimize the risk of an Israeli invasion and occupation of the West Bank in the event of the collapse of the Hashemite Kingdom under West Bank Palestinian pressure domestically and Ba'th–Nasserite intervention from outside. Conceivably, the 1963 crisis convinced them that the days of the Hashemites in Jordan were numbered and that they should disassociate themselves from a losing player.[61]

Assuming the imminent collapse of the regime the US tried its best to prevent the development of a new US–USSR confrontation in the Middle East. Its main concern was that any change in Jordan would bring about an Israeli invasion, which had to be thwarted at all costs. The US policy regarding an Israeli military move under any pretext was that it was pure aggression and could not be tolerated,[62] for it might provoke the Soviets to intensify their political intervention in the region, thus turning the local crisis into a major international incident. The Soviet Union unequivocally made the point to the Western powers that Israel had no right to intervene in Jordan simply on the basis of a change in its regime,[63] while the Soviet leader at the time, Nikita Khrushchev, did not even bother to respond to the Israeli prime minister's letter concerning the crisis.[64]

Even more serious was the possibility envisaged[65] by US analysts, that a pro-Nasserite revolution in Jordan might trigger an Israeli invasion of Egypt with the aim of trying to weaken Nasserite hegemony over the Middle East. Indeed, the US believed that an Israeli invasion, which was seen as a closer possibility than a direct Egyptian involvement, might cause a new round of Middle Eastern hostilities and harm Western interests.[66] Thus, the most tangible American reaction to the looming crisis was to issue a warning[67] both to Israel and Egypt against their involvement in it. The US also considered[68] involving the UN in its attempts to dissuade the two countries from any involvement in the Jordanian crisis, but the majority of the UN members, mainly non-aligned countries, saw the American position as an additional indication of the way the US took the Israeli, not the Egyptian, side.

Israeli security concerns therefore had to be satisfied some other way in order to avoid a process of escalation. The underlying assumption by the US and Great Britain during their contingency discussions was that even a change of the Jordanian regime could be tolerated by Israel under a given set of circumstances. This approach softened to some extent at the stage of the crisis when the regime was perceived as doomed,[69] prompting the Western powers to consider the delivery of security guarantees to Israel.

One regional security umbrella discussed throughout the crisis and there-after was the dispatch of more UN troops to the West Bank under one name or another, organized along lines similar to the UNEF (United Nations Emergency Force) on the Israeli–Egyptian border.[70] These forces would be stationed on Jordanian territory and would provide Jordan with a guarantee against both Israeli and Egyptian aggression.[71] Nasser would also be deterred by the fact that his agents' activities would become trans-parent to the international community. The status quo in the West Bank would thus be maintained and reinforced. The down side of such a step was voiced[72] by the UN Secretary-General U Thant, in talks with the Canadian representative to the UN, namely the fear that strengthening UNTSO might weaken the position of the king, since it would be interpreted by the Arabs as a green light to further Western intervention in the region, and, moreover, it might not deter Israel from a military move. The only possible arrangement he could envision was increasing the number of UNTSO personnel slightly and making them more mobile so as to enable them to detect any changes in military conditions.[73]

One way or another, however, an Israeli invasion of the West Bank was anticipated, either as a result of continued anarchy on the West Bank, or once the regime collapsed. Such invasion might, in the minds of Western policy makers, lead to an Arab–Israeli war.[74] According to the assessment of the British Foreign Office,[75] which followed developments closely, even the real possibility of Egyptian air raids on Tel Aviv in the wake of an Israeli move on the West Bank would not deter Israel from invading. This assessment, based on contacts with Israeli air force officers, held that Israel could intercept any daylight Egyptian raid, while any lack of confidence regarding night-time dogfights was counterbalanced by Egypt's lack of training in this respect. Moreover, the common belief of the West, as reflected in a message from the Canadian ambassador in Cairo,[76] was that an all-out war would end in an Israeli victory. With detailed discussions of various contingencies being held by such non-intelligence parties as the Canadian ambassador to the UN and the Secretary-General,[77] clearly the demise of the kingdom was no longer merely the topic of press speculation, but was viewed by policy makers as an eventuality that might be imminent given the widespread subversive activity against the pro-Western Middle Eastern regimes.

Still, an Israeli action upon the disappearance of the Hashemite dynasty was not inevitable, Western thinking held. An idea promoted by the West was that a showdown could be avoided by granting Israel certain security guarantees; for example, a pledge by the West to demilitarize the West Bank.[78] They believed that at the very least, Israel might be satisfied with that demilitarization.[79] This step was strongly advocated[80] by Israel but was not agreeable to Jordan. The idea of demilitarization of the West Bank was no compensation for the king. Rather, it illustrated Hussein's dilemma: if he agreed to it, Israeli apprehension would be largely allayed, Jordan's western border would be secure, but this would enable the Palestinian inhabitants of the West Bank, along with the Egyptian Nasserite regime, to claim that the king had relinquished the Arab goal of liberating Palestine.

In spite of this Jordanian perception the idea of demilitarization became the topic of high-level top-secret negotiations between Israel and the US in May and June 1963. The US planning people developed this idea in 1962 at the height of the risk posed by the UAR to the existence of Jordan, probably with a potential for the West Bankers to try and subvert the Hashemite regime from within. However, the idea became ripe and was first discussed with Israel in the wake of the April 1963 crisis, suggesting that if Israel were to occupy the West Bank in the event of the Hashemite regime collapsing, the US would press for its withdrawal in exchange for the demilitarization of this territory. The timing had probably also to do with the US pressure on Israel regarding its nuclear capabilities. The US administration probably felt that it had to counterbalance its pressure on Israel by improving security on the Israeli eastern border. US diplomats went as far as to indicate to the Israelis that their Jordanian partners would accept the idea provided it came as an imposed foreign solution. This approach characterized Jordanian foreign policy regarding both Israel and the West for many years. Even though Israeli diplomats were under strict orders not to raise the issue of demilitarization with their US counterparts, the latter found ways to communicate their message to Israel. In essence, it said:[81] demilitarization might become a real possibility only against the background of a severe crisis along the Israeli–Jordanian border, or upon a change in the regime east of Israel. Even under these circumstances any agreement must be only tacit, and it might reach as far as the deployment of UN troops or even a change of sovereignty over the West Bank from the Jordanian to that of the UN. The Israeli *quid pro quo* would be a commitment to refrain from attacking the West Bank, and Israeli acceptance of only a *de facto* demilitarization, though this last phrase is not clear from the context.

The British ambassador went so far as to suggest that the US would not intervene in an efficient manner to prevent an Israeli occupation of the West Bank. Moreover, the US advised Israel that given the "right circumstances"[82] the US would recognize the need for an Israeli action on the West Bank, and that Israel would not be asked for full withdrawal from territories occupied in the West Bank. Undoubtedly, all the observers saw Israel as the second player to be affected by developments in the West Bank, after the Hashemite regime itself. Moreover, they also distinguished between the West Bank, with its Palestinian population and its potential threat to stability, and the East Bank, which never became an issue on either the international or Israeli–Arab agenda.[83]

Another line of thinking was that if the new regime to the east of Israel were acceptable to the Israeli leaders, an invasion could be avoided.[84] Plans projected by the US and the UK thus called, first of all, for a meeting of the UN Security Council[85] in the event of a takeover in Jordan in order to study the nature of the new regime and the position taken by the members should the Middle East slip into a new crisis.

Oddly, France was conspicuously absent from the US–UK–Canada consultations. The reason stated off the record was the possibility of a leak from the French government to Israel, given the intimate relations between the two governments.[86] However, a close scrutiny of the French position in the 1963 crisis points to a more significant reason: France advocated that the three original signatories of the 1950 Tripartite Declaration[87] on security in the Middle East – the US, Great Britain, and France – jointly implement the declaration, including the possibility of the dispatch of forces. The declaration, issued shortly after the annexation of the West Bank by King Abdullah in 1950, had for years served as a source of confidence for the Hashemite dynasty. It meant, first and foremost, that Israel and Jordan, two countries closely associated with the West, would be constrained from attacking each other. Although the declaration failed to deter Israel, Britain, and France from their October 1956 military operation, even that major breach did not lead to its abolition. The opposition by the other powers to including the French in the discussions may have also pointed to their belief that the Hashemite dynasty was doomed, and that the wiser course would be to adapt to the inevitable. However, so reluctant were the US and Britain to create the impression that they had any commitment to Jordan in the face of the danger it faced in 1963,[88] that they came to a secret understanding nullifying the declaration.[89] The ostensibly supporting speeches by the US president on May 8 and the British prime minister on May 14 were aimed at signaling the phasing out of the declaration although without explicitly referring to it.

The diffusion of the immediate danger to the Jordanian regime in late May did not relieve the Western powers of their concern. In the minds of many policy makers the post-crisis era was only an intermission before the next crisis. The operative conclusion was that preparations should be made and contingencies developed for the almost inevitable outcome – the fall of the extant Jordanian regime.[90]

Egypt's Growing Hostility

The April 1963 crisis entrenched Egypt's growing hostility towards both Jordan and Israel. Deeply divergent politically republican Egypt and the monarchy of Jordan viewed each other as arch-enemies by 1963. Egypt had mounted a major propaganda assault against the Hashemite dynasty, culminating in the April declaration of union with Syria and Iraq. Simultaneously, it had conducted a long subversion campaign in Jordan, justified publicly by Jordan's immediate recognition of the secessionist Syrian regime (1961) and its support of the forces loyal to the ousted *imam* in Yemen, the enemies of Egypt and the Egyptian-sponsored republican rebels (1962).[91] In Nasser's view, "Israel and Hussein [were] in fact allies."[92] Considering the longstanding Egyptian–Israeli hostility, such a statement could only mean that the Egyptian president believed that any means were legitimate in Egypt's efforts to topple the Hashemite regime.

The short-lived Egyptian–Syrian rapprochement in the wake of the unity declaration enabled Nasser, for a short while, to pursue his efforts to topple the Hashemite regime while pinning the blame on Syria.[93] According to

Samir al-Rifa'i,[94] the Jordanian ex-prime minister whose ousting was mainly to be blamed on subversive Nasserite tactics, Nasser's ultimate agenda in Jordan was to eradicate the king along with the Hashemite regime, although he would be satisfied meanwhile with a pro-Nasserite prime minister, who would pave the way for a full Nasserite takeover.[95] Rifa'i, who conveyed this analysis to a British diplomat, clearly had a British parallel in mind, namely the similar scenario in 1956 that led to the final removal of British involvement in Jordanian rule.

In the Israeli context, the crisis gave the Egyptian president a welcome opportunity to assert his status both militarily and diplomatically. In a conversation with the US ambassador in Cairo, he revealed that he had recalled some of his troops from Yemen and had redeployed them in southern Sinai, for the first time since the Israeli–Egyptian military crisis of February–March 1960. At that time Egypt had deployed large forces in the Sinai, creating a strategic threat to Israel which bordered on open hostilities.[96] The deployment of forces in both 1960 and 1963 apparently gave Egypt the false impression that Israel was indifferent to such moves. Combined with other misreadings of the military picture, Egypt had developed an inflated sense of self-confidence by 1967. In retrospect, the two major players in the 1967 war had begun preparing for that encounter during the 1960 crisis, continuing the process in 1963.

More than any crisis in the past, the events of April 1963 showed King Hussein that his reign was not secure. This was a combined crisis bringing together the domestic threat now posed by the West Bankers, with the external danger already posed in the past. This combination led Hussein not only to reassess his policies, but to take brave steps reminiscent of his grandfather's. Moreover, for the first time, Jordan was entirely surrounded by hostile forces while lacking the tangible Western guarantees that it had had in the past. Not only did its traditional Western supporters, the US and Great Britain, refrain from a clear demonstration of military and diplomatic support, but the US in particular seemed unfazed by the prospect of a Nasserite takeover of Jordan.

In fact, the King had lost even the formal intention by the West to support Jordan, as documented in the 1950 Tripartite Declaration, although whether Jordan was quite aware of the withdrawal of the powers from the declaration is unclear. Western deliberations in the spring and summer of 1963, however, made one thing absolutely clear to the king: military support along the 1958 lines was no longer an option. Western paratroops would no longer support the regime even in the presence of a clear and immediate danger.

The regional picture was not too promising either. Nasser was openly attempting to topple the Hashemite regime, while Iraq and Syria, with their newly established radical regimes, were dedicated to stamping out conservative regimes, especially Jordan's. Internally, too, the king was not secure. The West Bank Palestinian population, long identified with anti-Hashemite foreign elements, took to the streets, believing that the time had come to get rid of Hashemite rule. Under these darkening skies, Hussein had to make up his mind regarding the best course to take in order to guarantee his political and personal survival. His analysis of the April 1963 circumstances led him to the conclusion that the basic confluence of interests between the Hashemites and Israel might once again prove useful. In making his decision to resume negotiations with Israel he was well aware of Israeli designs on the West Bank, yet he was convinced that the possible loss of the West Bank presented less of a danger to his kingdom than being left without any strategic partners.

As of 1960, top Jordanian military people had engaged in a direct dialogue with Israel on military issues. Later, between 1961 and 1964 the two countries developed an indirect dialogue using the good services of the US to discuss the Yarmuk River water issue, and in the wake of the April 1963 Jordanian–Palestinian–Israeli crisis Hussein set up a top-secret open channel of negotiations between himself and the Israeli leaders. Hussein's decision in September 1963 to open that channel of communication was the result of a painful trade-off. Faced with a choice between his Palestinian citizens – hostile, subversive and exposed to foreign agitation – and Israel, with its own interest in the West Bank, seeking ways to correct the military failures of 1948 yet with a strong interest in the continued existence of the kingdom, the king opted for the lesser of the two evils.

2

The Israeli–Jordanian Military Confrontation of November 1966: A Prelude to the 1967 War

From the time King Hussein assumed power in Jordan in 1953, he consistently tried to forge a coalition with at least one of his immediate neighbors in order to prevent the possibility of full encirclement of his kingdom by other Arab countries, which he regarded as an ongoing threat. Most, if not all of his neighbors, at one point or another were enemies of the Hashemite Kingdom. With the rising danger to his kingdom with the 1963 crisis he decided to supplement his country's direct negotiations with Israel, aiming at making at least one front secure in the event of regional or domestic crisis. Still, in spite of growing mutual recognition between Israel and Jordan of their shared interests, and the opening of additional channels of communication, Israel launched several strikes against Jordan between 1965 and 1967 as a result of unabated terrorist infiltration. Jordan's perceptions of Israel were incomplete and thus left ample space for mistakes.[1] The most distressing of these attacks for Jordan was the Samu' operation of November 13, 1966, when Israel launched a raid on the Palestinian village of Samu' which, by its large scale, demonstrated Jordanian inferiority *vis-à-vis* Israel's military ability and prompted a reassessment by Hussein of his policies regarding both Israel and the Palestinians. The Samu' crisis was the last major Jordanian–Palestinian–Israeli political and military confrontation before the 1967 Middle East war, a war that did not come as a real surprise to Hussein. His Samu' experience, together with the accumulative experience of previous Jordanian–Palestinian–Israeli confrontations, had given him a rather clear perception of his antagonists' intentions.

The April 1963 Hashemite–Palestinian crisis added to Hussein's deep suspicion of his Palestinian citizens. These feelings were reinforced by further disillusionment with the hostile Palestinian reaction towards him in the wake of the Israeli raid in November 1966. All this happened against the background of widespread feelings on the East and West Banks that the 1950 union of the two Banks was unworkable, in spite of the economic prosperity of the West Bank under Hussein. The king first acknowledged these feelings as early as 1960 when he admitted[2] that he was thinking of holding a referendum to let the Palestinians voice their opinion regarding the future of the union. As well, both crises followed closely on the subsequent riots, unrest and abortive coups d'état against the king, and in the mid-1960s shaped a reassessment of the challenge presented by the subversive role of West Bank Palestinians.

Western assessment[3] was that these Jordanian concerns and policies were met by a clear-cut Israeli policy calling for the occupation of the West Bank at the slightest indication of change in the kingdom. This was already taken for granted by the Western powers in the mid-1960s in their own planning for any Middle Eastern contingency.

Several questions emanated from the post-Samu' crisis: How did Hussein perceive the encirclement of the East Bank, and thus the threat from the Palestinian West Bank and from the immediate neighboring countries? In this framework, how did the Israeli raid, in spite of his continued dialogue with Israel, add to his notion of encirclement? What lessons would result from his developed perception of the threat to his kingdom, that could be used in the next major test – the June 1967 war? The main thesis of this chapter is that after analyzing the crisis, Hussein and the Hashemite Kingdom made a frank assessment of the Palestinian and inter-Arab-induced risks involved with the activities of the Palestinian organizations from the West Bank. This reassessment paved the way for a loose coalition and closer cooperation with Israel in spite of the military confrontation between the two countries, on account of the West Bank Palestinians backed by foreign Arab countries.

Launching a raid on the Palestinian village of Samu' on November 13, 1966, Israel initiated a chain reaction between three interrelated arenas: Israeli–Jordanian relations, the domestic Jordan scene, and the Arab countries interested in destabilizing the Hashemite regime. Events were exacerbated by the hostile domestic atmosphere in Jordan[4] and an open-field approach taken by various foreign players, namely: an increase in subversive Soviet activities, and a variety of vicious moves by Egypt, Syria, and the PLO already at odds with the regime, not to mention *al-Fatah (al-Fath)*, and other radical Palestinian organizations.[5]

The initial spark that incited this chain of events was supplied by Syria. Repeating Egypt's methods of the 1950s, Syria tried to use Jordanian territory as a launching ground for terrorism, and thus, to provoke a clash between Israel and Jordan, both of which were targets of the Syrian revolutionary regime. With the inauguration by Israel of its national water supply in 1964, Syria devoted major efforts to sabotaging it and disrupting life in Israel generally. To do so, Syria adopted the Palestinian *al-Fatah* organization and backed its operations against Israeli targets. One of these operations was carried out on the night of November 11–12, 1966, leading to the killing of three Israeli soldiers. In the early hours of November 13, Israeli troops crossed the armistice line with Jordan near the southern Hebron mountain village of Samu'. The raid and the military battle which ensued, caused extensive damage in the southern Hebron mountain area.

Officials in Jordan as well as the US sensed[6] right away that the incident was a provocation intended to trigger an Israeli attack on Jordan, probably by one of the Palestinian organizations working hand in hand with one of the two partners to the newly signed defense treaty: the UAR (Egypt) and Syria. Fearing a major escalation and a possible Soviet reaction, Israel preferred a major military operation against Jordan, and not against the main instigator, Syria. General Yitzhak Rabin, the then army chief-of-staff, suggested[7] to Prime Minister Levi Eshkol that they should carry out a massive attack on Jordan. The recommendation, and the cabinet decision that followed, presented at the time a strange and problematic move on the part of Israel.[8] Even the official Israeli description of the operation, 12 years and two wars later, admits to being unable to provide an acceptable explanation. The raid turned out to be the largest, and the first integrated tank and paratroop assault in broad daylight, since the 1956 Israeli–Egyptian war. Only years later, in 1988, did Israel release documents attesting to the contents of a Soviet message on November 9 in which Israel was asked not to involve itself in imperialistic conspiracies against Syria.[9] This missing detail explains the decision not to attack Syria; it still does not explain the assault on Jordan, a partner in negotiations. Whether Hussein was aware of the contents of the message or not, it is obvious that he, like other observers of Middle Eastern politics, realized that Israel preferred the easy route of striking the West Bank instead of taking care of the main enemy of both countries, Syria.

Three factors played a role on the domestic level: Hussein's policies and reactions along with those of his court and the inner circle of politicians; the political behavior of his Palestinian citizens, most West Bankers; and finally the Jordanian Arab Army (JAA).

Personal considerations and a one-man decision-making process have characterized Hussein's political behavior throughout his reign. His 1963 decision to try and rebuild the old Zionist–Hashemite alliance was the result of his own determination to take all necessary means in order to maintain his rule and dynasty by breaking the encirclement of the kingdom by enemies. For three years, between 1963 and 1966, he was led by Israeli leaders to believe that the danger of encirclement had been eliminated by this new bond. However, in the months following Samu', Hussein could not escape the thought that only a major turn around could save his kingdom, which faced grave dangers. Under the circumstances that developed after the creation of the PLO (1964) and the beginning of *al-Fatah* activities (1965), with no break in Nasserite subversion, the king opted for the only way he knew: fight for your principles and risk getting killed in battle.[10] This militant, but courageous, view would characterize his military and political actions and decisions until the June 1967 war. The Israeli attack in November 1966 served to refine his perception of Israel: a limited ally, probably subject to the Israeli desire to rectify the outcome of 1948. In other words, in spite of Israel's implied guarantee of the continued existence of the kingdom, there was probably a price to be paid. This personal realization, and brutal disillusionment, were expressed not only in his public appearances immediately after the attack, but also in a series of conversations with foreign diplomats.[11] In these conversations the king elaborated on the raid as a preface to a major war in the Middle East, during which Israel would occupy the West Bank permanently, or at least demand security guarantees in exchange for its withdrawal.[12]

The harsh awareness of this new dimension in Israeli–Jordanian relations was only worsened by a gross Israeli insult towards Hussein: not only did the raid coincide with a visit of the King of Pakistan, but the timing matched the 31st birthday of the king, who had single-handedly taken a courageous decision like the one for which his beloved grandfather had paid with his life. Even though the raid took place nine days after the signing of the Egyptian–Syrian mutual defense treaty, from an Israeli point of view it still did not justify such a personal and military affront. The seriousness of the new circumstances was expressed by the message sent to the US government, a little over 24 hours after the raid, in which the king indicated to the US ambassador that the Israeli action amounted to a betrayal of trust and mutual agreement, and that the time had come when he had to deploy his tanks in the Hebron area – on the face of it, an obvious defensive step after a brutal attack. In reality, it was a clear indication that Israel had begun the process of abrogating the 1965 Israeli–Jordanian–US understanding[14] prohibiting Jordan from stationing tanks in the West Bank in exchange for a border free from Israeli attacks, and the supply of US-made tanks for Jordan. Even the message from President Johnson[15] that Israel had no intention of occupying the West Bank did not serve to calm the king's concerns.

The raid served to expose differences of opinion among the king's advisors. The incumbent prime minister, Wasfi al-Tall, who began his second term in February 1965 (lasting until March 1967), did not see eye to eye with other personalities close to the king, including some past and future Jordanian prime ministers. Unlike them, he saw[16] future relations with West Bank Palestinians in gloomier terms; they advocated a softer touch with the Palestinians, whereas he believed that autonomy would be granted in the West Bank, guaranteed by foreign Arab forces, in order to meet Palestinian opposition to the regime. Since these ideas were conveyed to the US ambassador, who was known to be a confidant of the king, it is highly likely that these ideas were not alien to the king. Strangely enough, a very similar approach can be identified in a proposal made by the king to the United Kingdom in 1972.[18]

Palestinians all over the West Bank reacted violently and almost uncontrollably to the Israeli raid. Only on November 29, after a wave of violent demonstrations which engulfed all West Bank cities and inflicted casualties on the demonstrators, and rumors of an imminent coup against the king, did the kingdom calm down. The suppressive measures taken by the regime during this period re-emphasized the difference in treatment accorded to the West Bank, and caused further weakening of relations between the two banks.[19] Once again, as in 1956, 1957, 1958 and 1963, Hussein was faced with an impossible dilemma: how to suppress the Palestinians, eliminate the clear danger to his kingdom, and still maintain some degree of legitimacy for his rule. In his mind, owing to the accumulated constraints, the crisis in 1966 was the worst the kingdom ever had to face, even when compared with the 1956–8 period.[20] The Palestinian reaction in November faced Hussein with an impossible choice:[21] to fight the Palestinians, disloyal, but still his citizens, or divorce himself from a misleading ally that had managed to deceive him for three years, namely: Israel.

Shock and despair were also felt in the Jordanian army, resulting in the regime's doubting their ability to resist a foreign enemy in the event of a military confrontation.[22] The army's morale was not boosted either by suggestions by leading Jordanian figures that given the impotence of the army, Egyptian and Syrian forces should be deployed on Jordanian soil. Hussein was warned by the US[23] regarding such presence, but the only proposed response – enlarging the army by general conscription – was not an option, considering the larger Palestinian representation in the army that this would produce. Furthermore, it is unclear if the army was made aware of the Israeli–Jordanian–US agreement of 1965, mentioned above, calling for a limited demilitarization of the West Bank, and hence practically forbidding substantial reinforcements, let alone a military retaliation. In any case, in the king's eyes, their post-Samu' pressure signaled a rupture in the traditional backing of the Hashemites. This had to be reckoned with and led to the redeployment of significant forces in the West Bank, lest Jordan and its army should be blamed for direct or indirect collaboration with Israel.

A Jordanian general, Muhammad Salim, produced a report that was captured by the Israeli forces during the June war.[24] The basic thesis of his account was that Israel enjoyed clear military superiority over the JAA, which he attributed in the first place to the combination of a successful intelligence-gathering system and air superiority. Furthermore, he identified a lack of Arab cooperation in the face of the Israeli aggression, in spite of the creation of the Unified Arab Command. In his concluding words he spoke of the imminent battle expected on the West Bank.

In order to suppress any criticism of the behavior of the Jordanian army, attention had to be focused elsewhere. In a press conference eight days after the Israeli raid Jordan's prime minister Wasfi al-Tall strongly criticized[25] Egypt and the United Arab Command for not supporting the kingdom militarily during the raid. No doubt Jordan did not desire any Egyptian involvement in its defenses, considering past and present relations between the two countries, but raising this issue under these particular circumstances had another aim: to serve notice to Egypt that Jordan had no interest in participating in any united Arab, or Egyptian-led, military effort against Israel. Jordan's main concern with Egypt was the continued Nasserite subversion against the monarchy and the intensive use of the Egyptian media in a propaganda war against Jordan.[26] However, even though Egyptian intelligence officers were active in Jordan all through the 1960s, aiming at organizing a popular movement to unseat the monarch, the spontaneous Palestinian reaction caught them by surprise.[27] The PLO was the first to react,[28] attempting to coordinate activities and present itself as an alternative government. Egypt followed it ten days into the crisis when it made semi-public its intention to use the raid as an excuse for a new Middle Eastern war.[29] Obviously, in the Egyptian mind Jordan had to bear the major military burden, and give away a degree of sovereignty over the West Bank in favor of other forces which would fight Israel, namely the PLO, and indirectly, Egypt. Officially, Egypt continued to support the right of the PLO to use Jordanian territory against Israel, claiming Egypt had no control over PLO activities.[30]

Encirclement from Within and Outside: the Palestinian threat

All through the 1960s Jordanian–Palestinian relations presented a sharp dichotomy. Jordan was in the most precarious position: constantly exposed to new risks to the regime, and to the king personally, from within and from outside. Palestinian political confidence and resentment of the Hashemites expressed themselves in demonstrations and occasional speeches in the mosques. These feelings increased in the wake of several political and military moves strengthening the position of the traditional adversaries of the Hashemites; among them, the Iraqi idea of a Palestinian entity (1959), the April 1963 riots following the Egyptian–Syrian–Iraqi declaration of unity, and the Arab summit resolution leading to the emergence of the PLO (1964).

Relations between Jordan and Palestine in the mid-1960s were marked by growing mutual feelings that a separation of the two banks could no longer be ruled out. Although there is only one known expression[31] of the king's belief that the West Bank would eventually secede, the brutal behavior of his General Security people (police) in suppressing the 1963 and 1966 riots strongly attested to a different treatment than that accorded to East Bankers. Among many of them, even assimilated Palestinians, a growing feeling emerged in the mid-1960s that the kingdom would be better of without the West Bank. They believed[32] that without the West Bank Palestinian population and with continued US economic support and subsidies the kingdom would flourish and be free of internal subversion.

Two new elements were added between the 1963 Jordanian–Palestinian crisis and the 1966 Israeli–Jordanian–Palestinian crisis: the establishment in 1964 of the PLO and the beginning of Palestinian *al-Fatah* armed struggle from the West Bank in 1965. These activities were aimed not only at fighting Israel, but also at taking over parts of the West Bank from the Hashemites to the Palestinian organization.

The establishment of the Palestine Liberation Organization added the dimension of struggle for legitimacy and representation. The main contention of the PLO was that it was speaking on behalf of all Palestinians, and thus representing the Palestinian citizens of Jordan in place of their incumbent government. Already in the first year of its activity the PLO began acting[33] in ways that would characterize it in the years to come: struggling for a foothold in the West Bank, and signing agreements with the central government it had no intention of honoring aside from the clauses giving the organization partial extra-territorial rights on Jordanian territory. By 1965 the presence of its offices in Jordan was described by Jordanian and foreign officials as a "Trojan Horse."[34] Shortly after it began its activity in Jordan the PLO managed to deepen doubts regarding the unity of the two banks. In his speech on January 5, 1966 the king outlined the main bones of contention between his regime and the PLO.[35] Mainly, he resisted the idea of forming inside Jordan a military power not under Jordanian law. Further, if other Arab forces were to engineer such activity, this would violate inter-Arab agreements. In fairly diplomatic language he criticized Egypt and Syria and resisted the attempts of *al-Fatah* to begin forming a nucleus of Palestinian military forces on the West Bank. Clearly, even in the wake of the raid, the king was not concerned with the actual (weak) organization of the PLO in the West Bank, he was much more worried about the PLO serving as a magnet for his disenchanted Palestinian citizens.[36]

The very nature of relations was also shaped by the accumulated alienation of West Bank Palestinians from the central government, and the mutual feelings that there was a clear failure of unity of the two banks.

Evidently, a majority of the Palestinians aligned themselves with the enemies of the monarch and monarchy, either ideologically or by actually joining subversive groups or actions. Indeed, perhaps the most ominous sign for the regime in the mid-1960s was this growing alienation of the Palestinians on the West Bank. Even Palestinians serving in senior and sensitive positions did not hesitate to voice their resentment in front of foreign diplomats.[37] As problematic as it was, this was not the only threatening development in Jordanian–Palestinian relations. Unlike at any time since the 1950 unification, the Palestinian organization tried to establish its main centers of activity and guidance from the heart of the West Bank. In the past, all Palestinian activity had been directed from Egypt and Syria and no headquarters were established in Jordan. Now, in the mid-1960s the Palestinian approach was different. A few days before the Israeli raid on Samu', the government's lack of full control over this area was dramatically demonstrated.[38] And this, in spite of the nomination[39] of an East Banker to the position of governor of the Hebron region. Opposition leaflets calling for a change in the regime were scattered all over Hebron and neighboring villages, with the Jordanian police unable to apprehend the responsible parties. This event, along with the continued infiltration into Israeli territory from this area, strongly suggests that the Palestinian organizations were gaining effective control on account of Arab resentment of the Hashemite authorities.

On the more legalistic level, the PLO was emerging in the year before the 1967 war as a major contender for the right to represent the Palestinian component of the Hashemite Kingdom. In spite of sporadic closing down of PLO offices on the West Bank and strong and public protestations by the king,[40] the PLO gained more military and diplomatic ground and won popular support among the Arab countries and the Jordanian Palestinians. Even the US, which publicly was strongly committed to the well-being of Jordan, advocated finding some common denominator between Jordan and the PLO,[41] thus circumventing the need to discuss issues of representation and legitimacy.

The Israeli raid on Samu' did not surprise the king. The failure of his continued and persistent efforts to control Palestinian infiltration into Israel[42] caused it to initiate a policy of active retaliation shortly after the first *al-Fatah* action inside Israel in early 1965. Obviously, in the military activities of *al-Fatah* and the political drive for legitimacy by the PLO, Hussein saw major contenders for the right of representing the Palestinians inside the West Bank; the activities of *al-Fatah* only added the military dimension to the king's more serious political troubles; yet it made Israel equally aware of the new danger to its citizens' daily security.

In the aftermath of the raid, Jordan defined[43] the organized Palestinian activity from its territory, be it the PLO or *al-Fatah*, as the factor most dangerous to the existence of the kingdom. At that time the regime was under the impression[44] that all West Bank Palestinians were united on three issues: the need to let other Arab forces be stationed on Jordanian soil since Jordan was not able to protect the Palestinians; giving a "green light" to the activities of Palestinian organizations from Jordan against Israel; and finally, arming West Bankers so that they would be able to defend themselves. Thus Jordan's main concerns included the establishment of Palestinian military bases on Jordanian soil, the assassination of leading Jordanian figures, including the king, and above all, the involvement of Nasserite Egypt, or other hostile Arab forces. Already during the couple of weeks immediately following the raid, a succession of demonstrations and violent actions took place; many of them carried out by the PLO using Egyptian finance.[45]

About a fortnight after the raid a royal decree announced a new law of conscription that would include West Bank Palestinians.[46] It was immediately met by hostile Palestinian reaction, mass refusal to serve, and a wave of arrests of Palestinians. The publication of the law was only the culmination of a long process of deliberations since the beginning of PLO presence in Jordan. However, in spite of those discussions, the military had not prepared training bases, indicating that implementing the decision was an improvised step taken to encounter present challenges, and probably to take young aggressive Palestinians off the streets. The introduction of the law constituted another indication of the uneasy predicament of the king. Clearly, he needed to display his sincere efforts to his Palestinian citizens, who violently protested over the impotence of the Jordanian Arab Army (JAA). Additionally, enlisting young Palestinians to the army would prevent them from being recruited by Palestinian organizations, an effort which began in earnest in the wake of the raid.[49] Equally, the new law risked creating subversive Palestinian cells within the army. Moreover, the inclusion of thousands of new Palestinian recruits could have brought pressures for them to be stationed on the border with Israel, thus elevating the prospects of a Palestinian provocation aimed at both Israel and Jordan. Succinctly put, inactivity on the part of the king would have brought heightened Palestinian bitterness and resentement, prolonging the current domestic crisis. Activating the law could only have contributed to the deferment of the crisis to a later time.

Encirclement from Within and Outside: Israel – a trustworthy partner or an enemy in disguise?

Direct Israeli–Jordanian negotiations on water supply and security issues between 1963 and 1966 were held between equals. No party presented any rationale for a special preference. Yet when it came to the public and international arenas, the king preferred to present his country as the underdog. The Samu' raid once again provided him with such an opportunity in order to maximize US political support. In an almost immediate reaction to the raid the king stated:[50] "in the last analysis Israel holds the critical key to our existence and is our major enemy." How did the two countries manage to build mutual trust, break the Jordanian and Israeli apprehension of being besieged, and apparently lose it subsequently to the Samu' raid?

Between the two crises of 1963 and 1966, Israel and Jordan developed three ways to monitor and reduce, or even eliminate, the security risk involved in the taking over of the West Bank by hostile foreign forces. One channel was the conduct of secret direct negotiations with Hussein, reflecting Israel's deep belief in shared interests between the two parties. These negotiations were kept secret even from the US until after the Samu' crisis.[51] Secondly, Israel, Jordan, and the US established a forum to monitor *al-Fatah* activities from Jordanian territory against Israeli targets; within this framework, Israel and Jordan cooperated in their attempts to arrest *al-Fatah* activists, before or after they hit at Israeli targets. Thirdly, Israel used the good services of the US almost daily in conducting indirect dialogue with the Hashemite Kingdom; this channel was also used at times of tension between the two countries in order to try and defuse it.[52] For instance, it was through this channel that Israel asked[53] the US to convey an explanatory note to Hussein after the Samu' raid, which the US refused to deliver. In addition to all these direct and indirect channels of discussion with Jordan, Israel approached the superpowers, including the Soviet Union, asking for a security guarantee that would render it impossible for any enemy to endanger Jordan's control over the West Bank, and Israeli security. Militarily, Israel also developed its options on two levels: planning for a conventional war that would lead to the occupation of the West Bank, and at the same time hinting that if all other means failed it would resort to non-conventional means.

Unlike the first two forms of negotiation between Israel and Jordan, the third one was much more under the control and supervision of the US. Throughout the 1960s the US served as a go-between conveying diplomatic correspondence between the king and the prime minister. This channel was only indirect in nature and called for an active US role, unlike the first two direct channels. Thus, the US took the liberty at times to transfer only parts of messages and at times to ignore the existence of letters altogether. On one of these occasions the US ignored an Israeli request to convey an explanatory message after the November 1966 raid; the State Department believed that considering the strong reaction by the king, such a letter would only increase his negative feelings towards Israel.[54] One consideration missing from State correspondence is the possibility that Israel chose this channel only in order to try and explore how the US would really handle the matter (as opposed to the strong US condemnation voiced at the UN and other public forums) – provided high-level negotiations between Israel and Jordan were not suspended as a result of the raid. Another possibility might be that Israel would try to use US mediation in order to resume direct contacts with the king. In any case, this incident clearly serves to illuminate Israeli and Jordanian preference for direct talks rather than any other form.

Why did Israel need the American go-between services if it already had an open and direct channel of communication with the king? The US ambassador in Tel Aviv believed[55] that Israel hoped the US would add some of its advice to the king while delivering Israeli messages. Clearly, this reflects the meeting of views between the three countries regarding the need to curb Palestinian activity from the West Bank, and its potential threat to regional stability. However, the US refrained[56] from time to time, for its own reasons, from conveying Israeli messages to Jordan. This was in part due to the impression created by contemporary documents that neither the US nor Britain were[57] aware of the developing direct-negotiations track, leading the US to the mistaken conclusion[58] that Israel, in spite of its demonstrated interest in the continued existence of the Hashemite Kingdom during the 1963 crisis, was not interested anymore in the preservation of the Hashemite regime. This assumption was based on a comment to the US ambassador in Amman that Jordan believed that Israel would not agree in future crises to Western forces flying over Israel on their way to Jordan. US diplomats interpreted this observation as an indication of diminishing Israeli interest in the future of Jordan, whereas in reality it probably reflected local Israeli–Jordanian agreements on ways of protecting the kingdom in the face of the Western unwillingness to do so, as manifested since the 1963 crisis.

During the mid-1960s Israel also developed a new, revised perception of Hussein and his chances of survival.[59] He was no longer seen as a leader immune from Israeli political and military pressures. The basic strategic interest of Israel continued to be the survival of the regime, but the increasing Palestinian violence along the border with Jordan began to take its toll on the government of Israel, which lacked good answers for its citizens. Thus, the resumption of Israel's retaliatory actions across the border in Jordanian territory aimed to accomplish some weakening in the activities of *al-Fatah*, and signal to the king the Israeli dissatisfaction with his inability to curtail terrorist activities, and above all, to draw the lines of confrontation with Jordan – only on the West Bank and no further. Western diplomatic correspondence consulted for this study strongly suggests that these Israeli interests were not alien to the king. In this way, knowing very well that it was weakening the king's hold over the West

Bank, Israel believed it was contributing to his regime on the East Bank. In this delicate calculation of pros and cons Israel evidently preferred to limit the constant low-level Palestinian threat from the West Bank and thus prevent the development of a major strategic threat if it was taken over by the Palestinians. This policy was not interpreted correctly either by Jordan or by the US administration.[60] Further, the Samu' raid convinced Hussein,[61] and through him the US, that there was an additional element missing from the messages conveyed to him: Israel was testing its abilities in preparation for the inevitable next round of Middle Eastern hostilities, during which Israel was determined to occupy the West Bank.[62] Clearly, such Israeli intentions were not to the liking of the US either, which saw Israel responding to a "nuisance" from the West Bank by a strategic threat to the Hashemite regime. Even if the Israeli distinction was explained to the king during the secret negotiations, it still did not justify the poor timing of the Israeli raid, nor did it allow the king to agree, publicly or secretly, to this policy.

In the days and weeks after the raid the king became convinced that Israel was already in the process of preparing the next war in the Middle East; an official Jordanian publication years later indicated that the raid played a major role in Hussein's decision to go to war in 1967.[63] He believed that, given Israel's superiority, it would not be satisfied with occupying the West Bank, but would aim higher: to topple the Hashemite regime,[64] and to take over the entire kingdom. This new Israeli approach, so the reasoning continues,[65] was the result of US attempts to balance the Israeli and Jordanian governments; the elimination of a pro-Western Jordan would leave Israel as the only ally of the West in the region. The most desired alternative in Israeli eyes, as interpreted by the king, would be a weak Palestinian puppet regime in the West Bank. He left open the issue of the future of the East Bank after the Hashemites. Israel would try to accomplish this major change in Middle Eastern politics through a series of Samu'-type operations, culminating in a general war between the two countries. His perception[66] of the next war was rather accurate, as future developments proved: he envisaged Israel seizing the West Bank in its entirety, putting special effort into trying to capture Nablus and Jenin, using Israeli elite units and US-made equipment. This way Israel would free itself from the narrow strip between the West Bank and the Mediterranean, which had constituted a permanent threat since 1948. Since the Jordanian army was not strong enough to withhold such a major Israeli assault, Jordan would be left with no alternative but to cooperate with the lesser of two evils: to tie itself with other Arab countries, led by the Nasserite regime of Egypt.

Whether that was the Israeli concept at the time is unclear. Strangely enough, the strong language of the US Tel Aviv ambassador unequivocally rejecting[67] this approach never made its way to official State Department assessment, for reasons to be explained later. Nonetheless, it is evident that Israel at that time pursued the idea of a security guarantee as a means of securing Israeli borders and preventing what Israel saw as a defensive war. The equation of nuclear development vs. security guarantee was mentioned many times in diplomatic correspondence between Israel and the West. The Western powers were adamant in their opposition to such an instrument,[68] raising fears in Israel that come the moment of truth, Israel would have to stand alone against its neighbors. Under these conditions, the least Israel could do on the conventional level was to occupy the West Bank in order to remove the immediate danger to the main Israeli metropolitan centers. This danger could arise from a hostile Arab takeover or a move initiated by the Palestinian organizations. This Israeli thinking was only motivated by security considerations, and not by political or demographic thinking. Clearly, Israel did not want to formally annex the West Bank with its million [sic!] Palestinians but favored the exhausting of all military advantages associated with the Israeli holding of the territory.[69]

The Israeli action in Samu' was a repetition of traditional Israeli tactics of retaliation. Since the beginning of al-Fatah operations on January 1, 1965, Israel had launched a series of raids against suspected terrorist bases in the West Bank, one of them in April 1966, not far from Samu'. None achieved any significant degree of deterrence, and Palestinian activities against Israel continued in earnest. In spite of the failure of this approach, Israel continued to see the unwilling host country as responsible rather than carry out a "surgical" operation against the heads of the organizations or supporting countries only indirectly involved with the actual filtration (such as Syria). The message thus conveyed to the Arab countries and the international community[70] was that by preferring to hit at the weakest party, Israel also indirectly absolved Syria from any responsibility for the al-Fatah activities. The magnitude of the Israeli action was meant to deter the al-Fatah people (and expectedly enough it did not), but also to signal to Hussein that the very existence of his kingdom was at risk if he did not put an end to Palestinian activities against Israel.

The April 1963 crisis saw the clash of two local Jordanian forces on Jordanian soil; Israel did not intervene in any military way. Consequently, the Israeli threat to intervene in the West Bank was entirely academic and depended solely on the deterrence posture created by Israel. In November 1966, on the other hand, another dimension altogether was added to the way Jordan appraised its chances against an Israeli invasion. The Jordanian lessons, as quoted above, were clear: Jordan would not be able to face up to an Israeli attempt at taking over the West Bank. However, Jordan as much as all the other players concerned, distinguished between the West Bank, with its Palestinian population and its potential threat for stability, and the East Bank, which has never become an issue on the international and Israeli–Arab agenda.[71] Therefore, it is possible to assume that the Jordanian perception of Israel in the wake of the crisis was that of a partner of the East Bank leaders, led by the king, though preparing to take over the West Bank in the near future.

Between the two crises, Israel added an additional component[72] to its definition of the imminent danger from the east. Since the collapse of the idea of re-establishing the UAR, the main trigger for the 1963 crisis, Nasserite Egypt and Hashemite Jordan had enjoyed a short period of relatively peaceful coexistence, giving rise to speculation about possible deployment of Egyptian arms technicians on Jordanian soil. Here Israel made its disposition quite clear to the US and Britain: not only would it not agree to this presence, but even Jordanian army reinforcements in addition to the present forces would not be tolerated. Evidently, Israel was using this relaxed period in Jordanian–Israeli relations to voice its concern lest Jordanian army units should, under one pretext or another, be put under Egyptian command. The actual occupation or number of the Egyptian technicians was of no concern; but they represented Israel's traditional fear of encirclement, this time with the slant of Jordanian forces executing Egyptian orders.

Clearly, Israel was aware of the change in Hussein's perception of Israel. In order to undo the damage a meeting between the Israeli chief-of-staff, the chief of military intelligence, and the commander of UNTSO took place in Jerusalem in early March 1967.[73] Even though such meetings were not rare, this time Israel seized the opportunity to send a firm signal to Hussein. At this particular time, several months after Samu' and with heightened tensions between Israel and Syria, Israel made an extra effort to assure the king of its continued interest in his kingdom's continued existence. Israel even retreated from its traditional interest in the whole of the West Bank by praising Jordan for pursuing rather successful anti-terrorist policies, with the exception of the southern Hebron area. Evidently, by delivering this particular message under these circumstances Israel tried to limit the king's concerns to one part of the West Bank; the overall picture once again was that Israel saw Jordan as an ally.

Encirclement from Within and Outside: the Syrian and Egyptian threats

Besieged by malicious or potentially hostile forces from within and on his borders, the king was further alarmed in early 1966 by the new coup d'état in Syria. The weakness of the new regime in Syria was one of the strong incentives for increased Soviet diplomatic and propaganda intervention. Within this framework the Soviets even tried[74] to suggest that *al-Fatah* headquarters were located not in Syria, but in Jordan, and thus ensure Israeli reprisals against Jordan rather than Syria. In US and probably in Jordanian eyes,[75] the Israeli raid on Samu' only served these interests. In line with this policy of implicating Jordan and destabilizing its regime, Syria began,[76] in late 1966, dispatching saboteurs to hit civilian targets within Jordan. The evolving Soviet–Syrian alliance, which culminated in May in a military agreement, provided the Syrians during 1966, and later, with a security umbrella unprecedented in Middle Eastern affairs.[77] It protected the Syrian regime from any defensive measure on the Jordanian side, if necessary, and also provided an iron-clad defense from an Israeli attack. Syria was fighting Israel on two fronts: dispatching armed Palestinians to attack Israel, and a daily exchange of fire along the common border. Soviet deterrence also influenced Israeli thinking regarding Jordan. The Israeli action in Samu' indicated that Israel preferred to see Jordan, the easy target, being beaten, in order to appease Israeli public opinion, rather than to risk a confrontation with a Soviet satellite. This way, the Soviet Union provided Syria with a handy tool that might enable it to provoke Israel into an assault on Jordan, which would serve Syrian–Soviet interests rather than Israeli–Jordanian interests.

This gloomy view of events to come was only reinforced by a strongly worded Soviet warning to Jordan.[78] In spite of the inter-Arab context (Jordan granted political asylum in September 1966 to the organizer of an abortive coup d'état in Syria), it suspiciously resembled the language of similar public warnings issued by the Soviet Union to Israel. It cautioned Jordan against concentrating its forces along the common border with Syria, and against any plans it might have to invade Syria. Since there were no such Jordanian designs, the Soviet message was received as an additional indication of Soviet–Syrian plans to implicate Jordan in some kind of a regional military crisis. The crisis which they were promoting, in the opinion of the Jordanian prime minister, was an early war between the Arab countries and Israel. Needless to say, Jordan had tried to shy away from any significant military confrontation, let alone one led by Syria and the Soviet Union. Obviously, the Soviet message, and the following Jordanian analysis, only served to impress on Jordan the need to devise a contingency plan for a possible war.

Jordanian anxiety was bolstered by vehement attacks by Egypt and Syria in the wake of the raid. Basically, the strong anti-Hashemite Egyptian position called for the removal of the dynasty.[79] On the Jordanian front, Egypt (UAR) acted along two lines: using the United Arab Command as a tool to facilitate intervention in Jordanian–Israeli border relations, and helping the PLO gradually take charge of the Palestinians within the West Bank. On these two levels of operation Egypt could play the innocent party and disclaim any involvement in Jordanian affairs; after all, it was only following Arab summit conference decisions. As of 1965 Egypt allowed the PLO to open, and operate, on Egyptian soil, a broadcasting station which launched vehement attacks against the Hashemite regime. As expected, numerous Jordanian approaches[80] did not convince the Nasserite regime to put an end to that activity, aimed at the potential supporters of the PLO – the Palestinians of the West Bank. This course continued[81] in earnest during the days after the Samu' raid, aiming at exploiting the tense Jordanian situation to further destabilize the regime. On top of this indirect Egyptian subversion, the UAR in 1966 began preparing for the activation of the Jordanian front in the next Arab–Israeli war, hopefully pressing Jordan for its consent. In January 1966 a group of United Arab Command officers visited[82] one of the more sensitive positions along the Israeli–Jordanian border and the scene of numerous clashes: the Latrun area dominating the main Israeli Tel Aviv–Jerusalem highway. Later in the year Jordan learnt that Egypt had planned,[83] through the United Arab Command, that in the case of a full-scale Israeli–Syrian war, Jordan would be drawn into the conflict, whereas Egypt would join only in the last stages. Put differently, as long as the outcome of the fighting was not known, Jordan would expose itself to an Israeli attack in line with Israel's prior diplomatic and military behavior, whereas Egypt would step in only to get the fruits of the victory.

Realizing the inferior Hashemite position vs. Egypt, Jordan tried to stain this adversary's inter-Arab image and score on the propaganda field. Two points were made: the fact that the lack of Egyptian air cover during the raid was not in line with United Arab Command in the past;[84] and much more important, the Egyptian policy of putting Jordan in the front line while the UAR itself refrained from taking part in the confrontation with Israel. Prime Minister al-Tall emphasized this last point in a press conference on November 21. The challenge presented to Egypt was crystal clear: how could Jordan be driven into a confrontation all by itself while Egypt was hiding behind UNEF forces on the Israeli–Egyptian border? Furthermore, Jordan's conscience was clean: it already had a past record of resisting any additional UN presence on its borders (though obviously for different reasons). Thus, the point Jordan made was that it was not opposed to the idea of a full-scale war with Israel, provided it was preceded by the removal of UNEF forces, and full-fledged Egyptian agreement to lead the military move. Needless to say, so soon after Samu', Jordan was not prepared for a military confrontation with Israel, but it definitely set the rules for the next stage. Egypt did not necessarily see this assertion as a propaganda ploy and reacted publicly and diplomatically. In an unofficial message conveyed to the Jordanian government through comments to the Jordanian press, the Egyptian ambassador in Amman indicated that the matter was under consideration.[85] Further, the official and unofficial exchange of opinions by Jordan and Egypt convinced the Amman diplomatic corps that if UNEF was to be removed from Egypt, the deployment of other Arab forces on Jordanian soil might also take place. More on the diplomatic arena, Egypt leaked information regarding its ability to fight Israel with or without a UN presence on its borders.[86]

Egypt did not stop at concern over international presence and the prospects of a new war. In a series of press articles and conferences with foreign diplomats[87] it made another crucial point: the Israeli threat of occupying the West Bank if the Jordanian regime changed no longer held any credence in Egyptian eyes. In spite of the rather diplomatic and enigmatic messages in this respect, it is safe to interpret the Egyptian position[88] as welcoming a new war, and declaring the West Bank open field in the next round of hostilities whatever the fate of the Hashemite regime would be. Any Israeli move on the West Bank, let alone an Arab victory over Israel, would spark an Egyptian response on the West Bank. Repeating these ideas in the daily *al-Ahram*[89] and expressing them to foreign diplomats in Cairo were meant to guarantee their reaching Jordanian ears. Apparently, Egypt saw a possible Middle Eastern war as an opportunity to get rid of Jordan altogether, at the most, or for taking over the West Bank, at the least.[90] These ideas were not only in unison with the strong contemporary anti-Hashemite Egyptian sentiments, but also bring to mind the Egyptian attempt to take over parts of the West Bank in 1948, which was stopped on the southern outskirts of Jerusalem. This exchange of angry recriminations served as the background for the Arab League Defense Council which took place in Cairo in early December, and decided to help Jordan financially and prepare the necessary steps to enable Saudi and Iraqi expeditionary forces to be deployed on Jordanian soil. Some unconfirmed news reports claimed that the meeting decided that Egypt should demand the withdrawal of UNEF, should fill the military vacuum in Sinai and the Gaza Strip, and should reoccupy the straits of Tiran and blockade the Gulf of Aqaba.

The weeks following the Samu' raid served to generate the king's policy reassessment on two levels: whether war with Israel was inevitable, and what would be the general *modus operandi* of Israel and Jordan, along with other Middle Eastern players, in a possible regional showdown.[91]

Guilt was one of the initial reactions of the king to the raid. His understanding following Samu' was that he had neglected the defenses of the West Bank of his kingdom. Since this was the result of the *de facto* demilitarization of the West Bank in 1965, the king had to suspect all other conclusions he drew from his relations with Israel. Abrogating the 1965 *de facto* demilitarization of the West Bank, or even the threat to do so, strongly suggest that Hussein very much doubted[92] the Israeli distinction between the West and East Banks, which had been the basis for his talks with Israel. Thus, the raid signaled Israel's desire to confront the Jordanian army and the Hashemite dynasty at large. Realizing this, the US administration tried to make Israel a more active and interested partner in the future of Jordan. On the positive side, Israel was thoroughly consulted on an arms deal in the making; on the less positive side, the price Israel had to pay for the Samu' raid was a minor Jordanian–US arms deal, whose contents were mostly approved by Israel.[93] The price, for Hussein, was a commitment not to let other Arab armies cross into Jordanian territory, in exchange for an arms deal which did not significantly change the regional military balance in favor of Jordan. Thus, in Hussein's eyes the mere suggestion that he would pay a price after being attacked could be interpreted as though even the traditional Western umbrella would not serve the king as it had in past crises; the most public step the US could take[94] in November 1966, and after an urgent visit by the third in command of the JAA, was to send a presidential message and bring forward the delivery of two new F-104S airplanes from September 1967 to July 1967!

The raid marks a high point of frustration and disappointment on the part of Hussein. Being left with no single regional or international player interested, or believing, in his survival,[95] he was faced with the need to reassess his own policies and the prognosis for his kingdom. Even his new dialogue with Israel, seen by the outside world as a cornerstone in Jordan's existence, let him down.[96] In the king's mind,[97] these talks were intended to find a mutual solution to neutralize the Palestinian risk emanating from the West Bank. Instead, they did not even provide him with a shield against their provocation, as reflected in the raid. Indeed, the raid and its repercussions does not fit with the framework of cooperation, dialogue, and mutual interests with Israel which had developed between 1963 and 1966. In retrospect, this Israeli–Jordanian military confrontation led Israel and Jordan to the establishment of ground rules to be played out during the 1967 war and later. The raid, on top of the king's contacts with the Israeli leaders, enabled him to foresee the political and military moves Israel would follow only six months later during the June 1967 war. The crisis initiated a process of Jordanian reassessment of Israeli intentions regarding the kingdom.

The predominant Jordanian understanding was that Israel's action went beyond past parameters, and thus indicated a willingness to threaten the very existence of the Hashemite Kingdom, or at least launch a process that would end with the occupation of the West Bank not merely as a defensive act, but rather as a result of Israeli determination to change Israel's strategic posture. This approach, typical of the king in the days after the raid, was not shared by his prime minister, Wasfi al-Tall.[98] In his opinion Israeli intentions were purely defensive, and the enormity of the raid was only intended to call the attention of the superpowers to the need to curtail the Palestinian organizations' activities from the West Bank. The differences in opinion dictated different recommended lines of action. Being the monarch, the king proposed sending a strong message to Israel. No doubt, following the raid, he very seriously considered[99] a counter-attack on Israel, should the Palestinians rebel against him, or if the West Bank were to be occupied.[100] His later actions during the actual Israeli occupation of the territory suggest that his orders to the troops were not to launch a counter-attack, but rather to reinforce their presence and defend the West Bank at all costs, without endangering Israeli territory. On another ingredient of Jordanian foreign and domestic policies there was some apparent consensus between the king and his prime minister: the future of the West Bank would not be as envisaged in 1950, with the unity of the two banks. Put differently, equal relations between the two banks under the Hashemite crown would not continue to serve as the only framework of relations. Autonomy might be one possible eventuality.[101]

In the ensuing days and weeks the king began to see the possible moves in an upcoming war between Israel and Jordan, and probably with more of its neighbors, and possible avenues by which to guarantee the continued existence of the kingdom after the war. Evidently, about a month after the raid he reached the working premise that was to accompany him until final separation from the West Bank in 1988. After about a month of soul searching and policy calculations he made up his mind: "the growing split between East Bank and West Bank has ruined my dreams."[102] These words, spoken to the US ambassador in Amman, mark the king's moment of decision: a war was going to break out in the region – its inevitable outcome: the loss of the West Bank. As terrible as it might be, it need not be a grave loss for the Hashemite Kingdom; maybe, quite the contrary. That critical juncture was not lost on the US, which informed Israel of Hussein's words in the utmost secrecy.[103] Even though this expression by Hussein contradicted prior Israeli assessments of his intentions it probably added to the ongoing process of internal deliberations in Israel regarding future policies towards Jordan.

Several conditions may have led to the coming war, combining to produce an uncontrolled escalation. One week after the Arab Defense Council decided[104] on the deployment of Saudi and Iraqi troops on Jordanian soil, Hussein, reacting to a semi-official public warning from Israel,[105] supplemented by a firm US position, defined the deployment of any number of foreign troops on Jordanian soil as a *casus belli* in Israeli eyes.[106] Once fighting began it was expected to follow several stages. First, after only "a few days,"[107] the UN Security Council would impose a cease-fire on the warring parties; during these few days only Jordan would pay the full territorial price; secondly, during the fighting Israel would begin by seizing the Jerusalem area, the Jordanian-held part of the main Tel

Aviv–Jerusalem highway (the Latrun area), and the Israeli enclave in Mount Scopus, and later Nablus and Jenin[108] – areas overlooking the main Israeli population centers – and finally, the whole of the West Bank. Thirdly,[109] the worst scenario would include the occupation of the West and East Banks and the possible dismemberment of the East Bank. The least ominous scenario would include the continued existence of the Hashemite Kingdom on the East Bank, with the West Bank becoming a *corpus separatum* under UNEF. In the opinion of the US Amman ambassador,[110] "a short, controlled Arab–Israeli war at the expense of Jordan [would lead] further along the road towards solution, and the remainder of that road might well be a peaceful one." Considering the effect this ambassador's communications had on policy formulation in Washington it might very well be that these analyses served to some extent to influence US decisions taken in June 1967.

The crisis added a new dimension to the political thinking of Hussein. Whereas the April 1963 crisis demonstrated the impossibility of Palestinian–Jordanian coexistence (put differently: the failure of the union of the two banks), the Samu' juncture proved to the king that Israel might try and use the Palestinian West Bank excuse as a trigger to the total elimination of the Hashemite Kingdom and the launching of a full-scale war. Left with no allies, realizing the nearing moment of truth, the king had to brace himself for the inevitable.

3

Jordan in the 1967 War: A Political Victory which Guaranteed the Survival of the Kingdom

The existence of open channels of communication between Israel and Jordan almost fully excluded the possibility of a major mistake by one of the parties. That is: even if a major Israeli strike similar to 1966 could not be avoided, all parties – the US included – knew pretty well the limits beyond which a military or political move would constitute a major threat or *casus belli* for the other side. Thus, Israel could have suspected that the 1966 raid would bring about a major outburst of Palestinian militancy, whereas Jordan could have predicted the unyielding Israeli position on the introduction of foreign forces of belligerent countries to the West Bank in 1967. These general conclusions probably could have led the two sides to a peaceful coexistence in the wake of the near disaster of November 1966. It did not happen. Within a very short span of time, in June 1967 Jordan lost the West Bank and Israel found itself controlling a large body of Jordanian citizens.

None of the open direct channels could stop the movement towards war since the reasons for the confrontation were mostly not in play on the mutual level. Hussein's talks with Israeli leaders starting in 1960 were commenced on the assumption that the two countries shared a variety of interests, foremost of them the continued existence of two independent pro-Western neighboring countries, secretly in alliance against the radical Middle Eastern forces. The mere continuation of negotiations (particularly after the loss of the West Bank in 1967!) strongly suggests that Jordan was fully assured of continued peaceful coexistence. Clearly enough, that working premise related to the survival of the Hashemite Kingdom, but without specifying geographical details.

A second, semi-secret, level of negotiations had to do with security in the face of *al-Fatah* activities against Israel, launched from Jordanian territory, but instigated by forces alien to Jordan, such as Egypt or Syria. Both countries saw these activities as a major nuisance in their attempt to reach peaceful coexistence. However, coordinating ways to combat such activities were bound to become less of a secret than negotiations among leaders, considering the actual application of any agreements reached. For that purpose both needed the United States, which became the third member of an informal committee to fight Palestinian military activity. This body began operating soon after the beginning of *al-Fatah* operations against Israel in early 1965, and continued until actual fighting broke out on June 5, 1967.

Parallel with the diplomatic moves, Israel began the process of preparing for the next war, which eventually occurred in 1967. Drawing upon the results of the 1960s crises, particularly with Syria and Egypt, the Israeli starting point was the realization that these crises had exposed weaknesses that had to be corrected given Israel's "no alternative" way of thinking. Hussein for his part had been concerned with a succession of crises and their resulting conclusions. They were nourished by the rising feeling that the failure of the union of the two banks, supplemented by the early alliance with Israel in the early 1960s, was further enhanced by the 1963 riots, and reached its peak with the brutal Palestinian response at the Samu' crossroads. Between November 1966 and June 1967 it was not a question of whether to get rid of the Palestinian West Bank, it was a question of timing alone.

Thus, the events of May–June 1967 provided the king with all the necessary elements to make Israel and not Jordan the party responsible for the Palestinians, to gain legitimacy in the Arab world, and indirectly to inflict major damage on Nasser, the enemy. Yet, Hussein played the emotional card as well as the military and political one: in a series of moves, both before and after the beginning of hostilities, he made every effort possible to lead Israel into assailing the West Bank. These moves may suggest a gamble on Hussein's part, which turned out to be rather successful. His aim was to rid himself of the disloyal Palestinian population of the West Bank, and in all probability lead his arch-enemy, Nasser of Egypt, into a strategic trap. Unlike prior analyses of the war, its roots and consequences, here Hussein and the Hashemite Kingdom were the true victors of the armed conflict. The king fully realized the ground rules gradually laid down by Israel in the 1960s. Thus, he did not risk any ambiguous moves and did whatever was in his power to bring Israel into control of the West Bank while maintaining, even strengthening, his credentials as an Arab leader. His strategic decision was to sacrifice the West Bank in order to retain Hashemite rule over the East Bank. This conclusion was reached as a result of the almost pre-destined failure of the 1950 union of the two banks; a feeling shared by East and West Bankers alike. Consequently, the 1967 war was the Arab nation's disaster,[1] but not necessarily the king's loss. Years later Hussein spoke[2] of his thoughts prior to the war, regarding the future of the kingdom, in the context of a redefinition of Jordanian–Palestinian relations, strongly suggesting the approach proposed here.

In the mid-1960s the king concluded that Israel was ready to take on Egypt and defeat it. The exact timing of a future war would depend on the appropriate *casus belli*. He reached this conclusion as a result of the accumulated lessons of the following three different but complementing trains of thought.

1. His own negotiations with Israeli leaders, which began in 1963, and which gave him first-hand impressions and messages from Israel.
2. His careful study of the evolving Israeli–Egyptian military balance after the 1960 brinkmanship duel.
3. His analysis of reports conveyed to him by his close Western allies. They all indicated that in spite of the low morale in Israel it would win in the next round of hostilities.

His working assumption[3] was that Arab military power was inferior to that of Israel, and he had no illusions of a victory for the Arab side. Almost three years after the war Hussein admitted that the decision to involve Jordan was taken in spite of the Jordanian feeling that the Arabs had no long-range plan and were ill prepared, with the potential for losses and casualties. On top of this, the United Arab Command estimated that a military balance between Israel and the Arab side would be achieved only by August 1968.

The military and political behavior of Nasser in May–June 1967 might lead one to conclude that he believed that a prolonged siege of Israel, coupled with its diplomatic and military inability, would bring about its downfall followed by the submission of the Hashemite Kingdom. If this was indeed the case, then Egypt's defeat was the outcome of miscalculation on two fronts: Israel and Jordan. Nasser was probably unaware of the changes in the Israeli army, and the Jordanian dilemma emanating from the regime's growing tension with the West Bank Palestinians. The missing element from studies on the war is the centrality of the king's dilemma in making his decisions in May–June. The 1967 war can be best described as the merging of two sets of duels. On the political level, Hussein and Nasser each acted as though they believed that Israel would behave according to their plans; and on the military level, Israel and Egypt acted as two mighty military regional forces. The strategic stakes were high, and Hussein definitely outwitted Nasser at the expense of Israel. One player whose role has been overstated is Syria. This country had all the resources necessary to disrupt normal life in northern Israel, but lacked the military planning and well-maintained equipment essential for launching a major assault. Syria participated in actual land fighting unwillingly. It was satisfied with the continued bombing of Israel during June 5–8, only to find itself under a major Israeli offensive from a victorious army. Thus, unlike Jordan, which attacked Israel on June 5, 1967, and unlike Egypt, which prepared itself for a gradual fading away of Israel under Egyptian military siege, Syria was the guilty bystander.

Hussein, on the other hand, had formed his own interpretation of the true Israeli position towards himself and his kingdom. This was the result of his meetings and negotiations with Israeli leaders and the publicized Israeli positions. For a country which is not known for its methodical preparation of policy decisions, Israel outdid itself in the period between the Samu' raid in November 1966 and the June 1967 Six Day War, in relation to formulating policy towards Jordan. It is not unreasonable to assume that Hussein knew the ingredients of this policy. In early December 1966 the Israeli minister of foreign affairs, Abba Eban, in a discussion at his office, presented several questions relating to Israeli relations with Jordan and Egypt. Based on his remarks, a top-secret inter-departmental committee was formed in order to make policy recommendations on future relations with the two countries.[4] The forum was composed of the heads of research for the military intelligence, the secret services (*Mossad*), and the foreign ministry, as well as the desk officers of these bodies. The deputy director-general of the foreign ministry, M. Gazit, chaired the committee. Its mandate was clear: define the operational and foreign-policy course to be taken by Israel in the years to come. The basic definitions still hold true today.

The basic Israeli interest, at least the one publicly voiced, has been since the mid-1960s the continued existence of Hussein's regime. Israel has stated publicly many times its willingness to defend the regime if necessary.[5] This approach represents Israel's hope to have non-hostile, and preferably friendly, regimes on as many fronts as possible. From this Israeli viewpoint the Hashemite Kingdom of Jordan has always topped the list of such countries. Jordan and Israel have always shared a long border: 336 miles between 1949 and 1967, and 150 miles since 1967. Through the years this border has seen many armed clashes, often triggered by Palestinian military provocation aimed at setting Israel and Jordan against each other.

Israel made no secret of its interest in several related Jordanian processes that might produce its *casi belli*, of which three have been of vital interest since the late 1950s.[6]

1. Keeping the Hashemite dynasty intact, and if it should fall, attempting to preserve at least the territorial integrity of this entity. In other words, ensuring the actual survival of the regime in its current *modus operandi*, by not taking part in any anti-Israeli activity, and maintaining close relations with Israel, be it in secret or in public. This

element emphasizes the continuation of the current status quo. Considering the alternatives, which range from the Syrian type (the most probable scenario in the 1960s) to a radical Muslim regime (the theoretical alternative in the 1990s), Israel has always turned a blind eye to a limited amount of anti-Israeli activity in Jordan: PLO activities in the 1960s, and the HAMAS headquarters in the late 1990s. Even the failed Israeli attempt at assassinating Khalid Mash'al, one of the top HAMAS leaders, can be seen as a local action intended to be kept secret with regard to any Israeli involvement (hence the use of slow-acting poison, rather than the more traditional small-arms). A similar occurrence in Lebanon in April 1973 was given much publicity and was portrayed by Israel as a large operation against the leadership of the PLO.[7]

2. The emergence of the Jordanian nation-state; i.e. the appearance of Jordanian awareness, and unique local and national feelings limited to the territory under Hashemite regime. The more Jordanian citizens incline to define themselves in Jordanian terms the less they will tend to use pan-Arab terminology and press the regime into taking part in Arab coalitions, which might jeopardize Israel's security. In the past these coalitions might have been centered on Nasserite Egypt; today, the potential threat of such a coalition comes from Syria or Iraq.

3. The assimilation of the Palestinian population into the Jordanian political infrastructure. This may contribute to the stability of Jordan while limiting Israel's burden regarding the resolution of the Palestinian problem – especially true in regard to the Palestinian refugees within Jordan (both banks until 1967 and the East Bank since 1967).

In terms of its *casi belli*, Israel has declared its positions from time to time so as not to be involved in any miscalculation.[8]

One of the major pillars of Israeli security policy between 1955 and 1967 was the belief that the long 1949 armistice line with Jordan was almost impossible to defend, but that as long as the Hashemite monarchy with its suspicion of the West Bank Arabs was in power, Israel did not have anything to fear except some degree of nuisance. However, any change in the regime in the Hashemite Kingdom would instantly endanger Israel's security. Even during the long span without any negotiations, between 1950 and 1960, Israel considered the Hashemite regime to be non-hostile.[9] Israel, along with other forces, believed that the demise of the Hashemite monarchy was to be expected, but not imminent,[10] and certainly not called for, and that any change in Jordan would be tantamount to the emergence of clear and immediate danger to the lives of most Israeli citizens. Yet Israel developed a list of possibilities; the assassination of the king as part of a pro-Nasserite revolution was considered the most dangerous; other possibilities were also very problematic, but perhaps a little less dangerous. In spite of the varying degree of risk, generally Israeli policy makers were of the opinion that any danger should be removed in the shortest time possible, and probably with the taking over of the West Bank.[11] Clearly, Hussein believed that even a minor threat to Israeli security would lead Israel into taking over the West Bank.[12]

Thus the king's May 1967 military agreement with Egypt was only the tip of the iceberg: it was intended to expedite the process leading to war with Israel by nourishing a false hope of success among the Egyptian leadership and provoking a major war. This move counted on the king's understanding that it would convince Israel of the need for a war, without risking an invasion of the East Bank either by Israel or by Egypt. Needless to say, the strategic balance after June 1967 enabled Israel to do so, if indeed that was its intention.[13] The 1967 war was the direct result of the accumulation of events, processes, and crises that evolved between 1960 and 1967. Clearly, as reflected in contemporary diplomatic correspondence, all players in the Middle Eastern political game were fully convinced that war would break out; the only remaining question had to do with the exact timing and the immediate trigger. Any number of motivations might have constituted a good enough reason: the emerging nuclear capabilities of Israel and an Egyptian attempt to put an end to them; the Israeli success at diverting the Jordan River water for development of other parts of Israel, and the continued Syrian efforts to put an end to the project; and last, but not least, the emerging Palestinian national movement, which presented itself as the trigger for the next war while posing a major challenge to the legitimacy of Israel and Jordan, with the intermittent support of Egypt and Syria.

Hussein's reading of Israeli intentions in case of war was clear and unmistaken. About three weeks before the beginning of the war he expressed his deep belief that Israel had military and economic interests that could be satisfied only by occupying the West Bank.[14] He on the other hand, as he disclosed years later,[15] had to stretch out his forces in the West Bank because of the great distances between the villages. What he neglected to mention for obvious reasons was his need to have garrisons on several West Bank locations in order to watch out for the Palestinian population rather than the Israeli army, clearly an assignment distracting the army from its duty against Israel.

Thus, between 1964 and 1969 the JAA barely performed its duties as a guardian of domestic Jordan and its monarch. It was, for all practical purposes, a fighting army trying to confront the Israeli armed forces. Was it the result of over-confidence on Hussein's part or was he only bowing to Arab pressure?

This question can be partly answered using sub-periods: the testimony of Hussein[16] is that participation in the united Arab plans for the 1967 war was initially forced on the king directly or indirectly as a result of his participation in the Arab summit conferences. He believed that traditionally he should break ranks with the Arab fold. That policy was even more marked in 1964 after his gloomy conclusions drawn from the 1963 domestic crisis (see chapter 1). Thus, his involvement with the Arab framework was initially forced on him. Later it changed in nature with the signing of the military agreement with Egypt on May 30, 1967, which the king willingly did. However, during the years following the war he could not bail out from the united battle against Israel when the war of attrition was raging on. Thus, for two years the JAA fought wars it did not need to fight, mainly confronting Israel, while ignoring the developing presence of the PLO which, on the basis of its Charter, claimed all of Jordan for itself.

Each of the three crises since 1958 involving Jordan produced a different Western reaction. In 1958 British paratroops were rushed to protect the dynasty, and in 1963 a major diplomatic campaign was launched in order to avert an Israeli invasion of the West Bank. In 1966 the American working assumption was strongly influenced by the close relations between the US Amman ambassador and Hussein.[17] This connection not only gave the US a rare view of the inner workings of Jordanian policy-making processes and the king's thinking, but it also left no room for other input into US thinking, such as from the US ambassador in Tel Aviv. Thus, reflecting Hussein's pessimistic mood following the raid, the US truly believed[18] that the regime in Jordan had become weaker in the previous decade (1956–66), and that an additional Samu'-type raid would bring it down. Therefore, the US should examine all contingencies, including the total downfall of the Hashemite regime. But taking account of US strategic considerations, in the first place the war in Vietnam, it is highly unlikely that any American force would have been used to salvage the regime; the same was also true for Great Britain, which followed suit, abandoning years of support for Jordan. Put in American words: the US commitment to Jordan was "approaching a moral commitment to Hussein."[19] Since Egypt, Syria, and Israel were not truly concerned[20] with the likelihood of a new war, and the elimination of Jordan as an almost inevitable outcome of the war, the most probable eventuality was either that sovereignty over the West Bank would change, or that Israel would occupy the territory. Preparing itself for that contingency the US began considering its immediate moves after the war was over.[21] First priority was given to sending more UN troops to the area, once a change had occurred. Being aware of this planning, the king strongly resisted the dispatch of UNEF forces in the wake of Samu', fearing it might expose his personal thinking and contribute to further weakening of his dynasty.[22]

Even the urgency of the crisis following Samu' and the dramatic flavor added by the king's pessimism did not necessitate a major change in the West's thinking regarding Jordan. Basically, with some minor modifications, two Western approaches were shaped before the raid, and were not essentially changed following it: one, that one day the West Bank would no longer be an integral part of the Hashemite Kingdom,[23] and secondly, that Israel would attempt a takeover of the West Bank. The latter assumption was developed following the April 1963 crisis.[24] It stemmed from Western evaluation that Israel was truly concerned about the possibility of a foreign takeover of the West Bank. This would transfer the West Bank into non-Hashemite hands, which would not see Israel as a strategic asset. The rule of such forces would threaten the dismembering of Israel in the metropolitan area north of Tel Aviv, considering the short distance between the Jordanian-held West Bank and the Mediterranean Sea. Western analysts were so confident of the Israeli desire to capture the West Bank that they believed[25] that even a pre-emptive war against Syria in connection with the diversion of the Jordan River would involve such an Israeli move.

The traditional Western allies of Israel realized that the 1963 crisis manifested the explosive potential for Israel of change in Jordan. However, without giving away any of their interests in the Arab world, they believed that the minimum requirement to satisfy Israel would be the demilitarization of the West Bank.[26] With the failure of the demilitarization concept, and upon Israeli requests, a new idea was introduced: issuing some sort of security guarantee for the current borders of Israel. Since Jordan would stand to benefit from such a declaration as well, some of the consultations were carried out with some Jordanian participation.

In the course of the deliberations, the ingredients of the Israeli concept of security as interpreted by the West and Jordan were discussed. They reflected not only Israel's self-declared security interests, but also its likely actions if such an instrument failed. The military reprisal operations and the diplomatic behavior of Israel in the 1960s along with its close contacts with Jordan and the West produced a rather accurate picture of its concerns and intentions. The main premise of this analysis[27] was that Israel was strong enough militarily to defeat any Arab military coalition. However, expectation was that once Israeli superiority was likely to disappear, Israel would strike. The contemporary assessment spoke of such an eventuality around 1966, giving rise to speculation of an Israeli pre-emptive war or a major military operation aimed at deterring potential enemies. In case of war, Israel would seize the opportunity and rectify some of the mistakes committed during the 1948 war. The document specifically mentions the Jerusalem area, the Jordanian-held part of the main Tel Aviv–Jerusalem highway (the Latrun area), and the Israeli enclave in Mount Scopus. Even though British diplomats reporting from (Jordan-held) Jerusalem could picture the next war vividly, they were not good advocates of the security-guarantee idea, basically for fear of hostile Arab reaction.[28] Indeed, such a guarantee was never issued. The lack of a Western pledge made an Israeli invasion of the West Bank the only course open to Israel, given the military and political constellation. Under these circumstances, the West had to devise the necessary contingencies and planning for the post-occupation era.

No wonder that against this background, all parties concerned saw the Samu' operation as a litmus test for the major showdown to follow. In spite of very strong US public condemnation of the Israeli raid, the US ambassador in Amman was asked[29] to point out to the Jordanian government that the continued use of Jordanian territory for raids against Israel might jeopardize regional stability. The US refrained from using any meaningful leverage it had against Israel, such as suspending arms shipments.[30] Accordingly, the subsequent UN Security Council condemnation of Israel could only be seen by Israel and Jordan as a minor slap on the wrist, and therefore, indirectly, as accepting the proposal of a possible future Israeli raid.

Even the message from President Lyndon B. Johnson[31] to the king did not supply the necessary assurances. It did speak of grave consequences for Israel, should it occupy the West Bank, but it did not detail the means available to the US in stopping any such Israeli move. Further, the message was limited to the territory of the West Bank; it said nothing about guarantees to the Hashemite regime, nor did it say a word regarding the Egyptian threat to the regime. In other words, the US could not avert the next crisis; it could only try and soften the blow, once Israel attacked the West Bank, or the Hashemite Kingdom in its entirety.

What Led the King to his Moves in May–June 1967?

The decision not to shy away from war even if the price, the West Bank, was known, was the result of a gradual process begun in 1963, enhanced in the aftermath of the November 1966 unrest, and which came to fruition between Samu' and June 1967. Perhaps the most threatening scenario to the kingdom would have been a spillover of Palestinian unrest from the West Bank to the East Bank. Early signs of this were noticed in late 1966:[32] several "Syrian saboteurs" were arrested and several explosions occurred at the studios of the Hashemite Broadcasting Service (HBS) in Amman. Since the HBS had studios in Ramallah in the West Bank, and since the targets within the Amman studios were anti-PLO material, it was believed that it was a Palestinian "inside job." It was probably intended to send a message to the Hashemite authorities that pro-PLO Palestinians could reach any target within the kingdom be it on the West or East Bank. In the coming weeks a number of incidents accumulated to indicate an aggravated source of worry for the regime (although not an immediate danger), mainly concentrated in the West Bank; actually, in spite of several Jordanian successes, it was evident that there was an ongoing effort by the regime and the pro-PLO elements assisted by Syria to win on the tactical level, preparing for a possible future showdown. An intelligence briefing gave some examples of incidents in early 1967:[33]

1. The Syrian government were using Palestinian organizations to create as much trouble as possible within Jordan.
2. *Al-Fatah* was also trying to embarrass Jordan, and its members were continuing to enter the country. A man belonging to *al-Fatah* had recently been arrested in Jerusalem.
3. Anti-regime pamphlets were still circulating in Nablus and Jenin. They were being prepared by students but the authorities had yet to discover the real organizers.
4. Reports had reached Jordanian intelligence at the end of January that the PLO were intending to smuggle ammunition from Gaza into Hebron, with a view to creating disorder there.
5. A number of anonymous letters had been received by the villagers of Halhul (near Hebron) threatening them with reprisals if they continued to cooperate with the Jordanian security authorities.

All of the above only served as a reminder of an already existing situation developed over time. In a nutshell, as already indicated, Jordan's decision to use an opportunity, if it occurred between Israel and Egypt, to improve its standing *vis-à-vis* the West Bank Palestinians, was the result of the accumulated lessons of the three previous crises analyzed in previous chapters:

1. The Israeli–Egyptian military tension in February–March 1960, which convinced Egypt of Israel's indecisiveness and probable inability to go to war against Egypt. Jordan interpreted this crisis in retrospect as a turning point in Israeli thinking.
2. The Israeli–Jordanian crisis of April–May 1963 convinced Jordan of the need to open serious negotiations with Israel.
3. The repercussions of the Israeli raid on the West Bank village of Samu' in November 1966, which convinced Jordan of the definite Israeli intention to occupy the West Bank. Hussein's 1963 lessons were re-inforced during this crisis by further disillusionment with the hostile Palestinian reaction towards him in the wake of this Israeli raid on an *al-Fatah* base in the West Bank. This raid convinced him that should he not sacrifice his West Bank, getting rid of the rebellious Palestinians

in the process, he and the kingdom might not survive Egyptian subversion coupled with Israeli territorial designs.

Sensitivity in the West Bank ran high in the months immediately preceding the war. At times it reached grotesque proportions. For instance,[34] simple blood tests for children in a Jericho Palestinian refugee camp were said to be preparations to obtain blood donations for Vietnam or Yemen, and forced a closure of schools for a few days.

On the inter-Arab level the king had two main problems: Egypt and Syria. Egypt distinguished between the two banks, and regarded subversion against the regime as going on in both, but recruiting efforts as usually being made only on the West Bank. Egyptian agents made their areas into an open field for recruiting young Palestinians, reminiscent of similar attempts at enlisting West Bankers for the *fidayin* in the 1950s. In his anti-Hashemite efforts Nasser was greatly assisted by Palestinians living on the West Bank. This population was anti-Western, pro-Nasserite and eager to encounter Israel, and was only too happy to employ terrorist tactics against Israel and Jordan.[35] The degree of attention given by the Jordanian security forces to the East Bank, generally loyal to the regime, was remarkably different from that given to the problematic West Bank. Palestinian resentment of the Hashemites expressed itself by demonstrations and occasional preaching in the mosques. These feelings were strengthened in the wake of the proclamation of the Iraqi idea of a Palestinian entity (1959) and the Arab summit resolution establishing the PLO (1964) in spite of the king's objection. All these, along with the resumption of Palestinian guerrilla activity from Jordanian territory in 1965, served to compound the vulnerability of the regime.

Egypt had been engaged in a fierce propaganda war against Jordan since the late 1950s. It intensified with the establishment of the PLO in 1964. In the months prior to the June war the countries were entangled in a propaganda duel: for Nasser, Hussein was "the whore of Jordan."[36] On the Jordanian side, throughout 1966–7, one of the main elements of its counter-propaganda[37] was that Egypt was hiding behind the UNEF and thus avoiding the duty of fighting Israel.

Reaching a Decision: the king's reading of his own relations with the West Bank Palestinians

The overall picture of relations with Egypt, Syria, and the Palestinians only added to previous developments emanating from the crises of 1963 and 1966. These served as major triggers leading Hussein to a reassessment of his overall strategic position, bringing about the resumption of secret talks with Israel and his desire to create a set of conditions that would relieve him of the Palestinian burden.

Familiar with the military balance of power, and fully comprehending the Israeli sensitivities emanating from the 1948 war, Hussein reached his decisions on his own, leading his army to brave, but futile, fighting against Israel. The army for its part probably had to discredit the low assessments of its performance emanating from the Samu' raid about six months beforehand.[38] A Jordanian participant at a Washington symposium commemorating the 25th anniversary of the 1967 war commented: "King Hussein and the Jordanian authorities interpreted Israel's actions, especially after the November 1966 raid on Samu', as designed to manipulate Syria in order to provoke Egypt to action that would provide Israel with a pretext for occupying the West Bank."[39] The way the Jordanian involvement in the war is to be interpreted is very similar, but with one major change: the manipulating power was Jordan, not Israel.

The intricate network of Jordanian interests and political–military behavior suggests very strongly that Hussein planned his participation in the 1967 war so that he would benefit from his participation in the all-Arab effort against Israel and yet would come away without his disloyal Palestinian population. Wasn't he taking a big risk? From secret and candid talks he had with several figures, it became clear in late 1966–early 1967 that the king felt that the very existence of his kingdom was at risk. Thus, only a gigantic operation would cure the major problem of Jordan, and hopefully would ensure its continued existence. Did Hussein believe this to be a safe gamble? It is difficult to believe it. However, under the circumstances that developed from within and outside, and analyzed earlier, the danger to the existence of the kingdom only increased. In any case, if the kingdom was to disappear there was no point in the king going into exile after witnessing the demise of the last of the Hashemite monarchies.

The critical deployment of two Egyptian commando battalions, one of them in the strategic area of Latrun not far from the main Israeli highway linking Jerusalem to Tel Aviv, on the eve of the war, and the careful choice of the exact point at which Jordan began its fighting, strongly suggest the emotional factor referred to earlier. The king knew from his own past experience (long and bitter skirmishes with Israeli forces in the Latrun area in the 1960s), and the experience of his grandfather whom he adored and tried to follow, that Israel could not tolerate Egyptian forces in this area. This was in addition to the Israeli insistence on eliminating any further danger to Jerusalem. In order to further enforce his point Hussein attacked Jerusalem itself – the one and only place along the long armistice line in which Israel could not tolerate an attack, mainly for emotional, historical, and political reasons. Yet, in spite of all efforts to ensure an Israeli occupation of the West Bank, the king limited the number of Egyptian troops on his soil to the minimum necessary to provoke an Israeli reaction. Again, memories of Egyptian forces in Western Palestine in 1948 – in Jerusalem and in Hebron – along with his very deep suspicion of Nasser's intentions in 1967, led Hussein to allow only the number of Egyptian troops needed to convince the Arab side that he was living up to his inter-Arab commitments and to convince Israel the road to Jerusalem was under a serious threat.

During the months preceding the war many signs accumulated indicating the growing danger to the king and his kingdom. The inherent hatred felt by the Palestinians for the West, and consequently for the Hashemite dynasty, was evident. Syria, in spite of fast escalation in the military war of attrition with Israel, including the loss of six fighter planes on April 7, 1967, usually did not carry out independent terrorist activities against Jordan. Syria made every effort possible to use the Palestinian card against both Israel[40] and Jordan, so that Hussein felt that these moves could eventually implicate Jordan, and perhaps Egypt, in a war with Israel. The Samu' incident only served to heighten the king's conviction. On May 2 he warned Egypt of such a possible escalation. But apparently, his warning was held back by Field Marshal 'Amir until May 14. On May 14, against the background of Soviet preparations to encounter an imminent Israeli attack on Syria, the Syrian press predicted an Israeli and Jordanian attack. Sixteen Jordanians were killed on May 21 by a car bomb at the Syrian–Jordanian crossing at Ramtha. This led to the breaking of diplomatic relations between the two countries on May 23.[41]

On May 18, the day UNEF concluded its mission, Hussein met the US Amman ambassador, Burns, and as usual had a candid discussion of recent developments.[42] The position he presented was quite simple: Jordan would not intervene if Israel attacked Syria. If Egypt joined in hostilities Jordan would not be in a position to refuse to fight but even so would not see itself in direct conflict with Israel. Obviously, this position raises many questions. In the first place, did the king not realize that this was no longer the right issue? However, considering his accurate reading up to that point, and the fact that he did know with all probability that Israel was not preparing an attack on Syria, the lesson is different. It is to be found in the next point he made to the ambassador: if Egypt was involved in fighting, Jordan would be drawn into hostilities, but the king "did not contemplate direct armed clash with Israel."[43] Perhaps the only way Jordan could pay its dues to the "Arab cause" could be if fighting were limited to the West Bank. The other alternative, the one attempted in 1973, the dispatch of Jordanian forces to Syrian territory, was not a viable one back in 1967 considering the deep animosity between the two countries.

On May 20 the king called a session of parliament and later his cabinet.[44]

The cabinet decided to coordinate Jordanian policies with the United Arab Military Command, and to send Liwa' (General) 'Amir Khamash to Cairo to discuss the coordinated moves. Once there he found out[45] that Syria and Egypt were planning their own military moves, ignoring altogether the United Arab Command. His trip took place in spite of, or perhaps in line with, a continued Jordanian propaganda war against Egypt.[46] The main theme coming out of Amman and Jedda, two centers of monarchies at odds with Nasser, was that the time had come for Egypt to act. Indeed, with UNEF shielding Egypt from Israel, Egypt was once again, for the first time since 1957, in direct confrontation with Israel. In the opinion of Nasser's enemies that was a cause for attacking Egyptian inaction.

A British diplomat report from (the Jordanian sector of) Jerusalem described the developing situation in rather ominous terms.[47] The removal of UNEF on orders from Nasser removed all foundation for the king's allegations against Egypt. Furthermore, this move could only encourage Syria to carry on activities against Jordan and probably against Israel from Jordanian territory, thus exposing Jordan to Israeli reprisal. Yet, there was a more immediate risk in the new situation: the Palestinians who had demonstrated their attitude time and again in the months since Samu' were almost exuberant. Jordan, and obviously its conservative ally Saudi Arabia, were again on the losing end of the Middle Eastern equation. With the change in the military balance, without UNEF, and with rising support for Nasser, that could mean deep trouble ahead for Hussein.

Tuesday, May 23, was probably a Day of Judgment for Hussein; with the rising prestige of Nasser, Hussein felt[48] he could not escape decisions anymore. If indeed he already had reached a strategic decision to sacrifice the West Bank, then this day may have signaled the tactical decision to set the wheels in motion. The picture the US diplomatic dispatch from Amman painted was that in order to avoid isolation in the Arab world, Jordan would have to let Iraqi and Saudi forces be deployed on its soil. A public announcement to that effect was made, even though Jordan did not intend to carry it out and in spite of the United Arab Command's secret clarification to Jordan, under Egyptian instructions, that such deployment was not necessary. Still, a few days later Jordan asked Saudi Arabia, and Saudi Arabia agreed,[49] to deploy troops inside Jordanian territory, and Jordan asked Iraq to send warplanes, which eventually would also include ground troops. The Saudi infantry brigade in question had to be deployed in southern Jordan north of the port city of Aqaba, a location not usually guarded too well by Jordanian forces, but at the same time an area significant to Jordan and Saudi Arabia, two monarchies threatened by Egypt, a power that could not only attack Israel in its southern flank but also do the same to the two monarchies at the one and only Jordanian outlet to the open sea. Concurrent with that move Jordan also put an end to its propaganda war against Nasser. For all practical purposes Jordan began making its way back into the united Arab fold. Without anyone's knowledge, this time Jordan had a hidden agenda: to promote the national Jordanian interest by losing the West Bank in a heroic and united Arab battle against Israel.

A few days before traveling to Cairo in order to sign his agreement with Nasser the king provided a rare insight into his state of mind, actually revealing the circumstances leading to his surprising move. He professed[50] to be in the worst strategic position in the Middle East, being expected to participate in the coming war on the side of his powerful enemy, Nasser. However, he was about to lose his kingdom if Nasser won the imminent war, and about to lose the West Bank if Israel won. He put forward precisely this dilemma to his close friend and ally the Shah of Iran, when he paid him a visit in early May. It was a time to consider options since war winds were blowing; only the timing was yet unclear. The Shah's advice to the king, clouded in diplomatic expressions, was that Jordan should fight Israel since the world would not let him be destroyed by the Israelis. The Shah, acting as an "honest broker" between Israel and Jordan, even went as far as possible in conveying his advice to Israel, indicating once more his reading of the evolving circumstances, and perhaps even in concert with Hussein. From that advice a reasonable conclusion could be drawn that a possible loss of the West Bank would not lead to the total destruction of the kingdom and might be acceptable to Jordan. Examining these pieces of evidence after the conclusion of hostilities it is not impossible to continue this train of thought: an Israeli victory would have cost less in Jordanian terms, and would not have jeopardized the very existence of the kingdom.

Obviously, the king was grim and solemn in voicing his thoughts; after all, it was not easy to approach the moment of truth and give up a region that had been part of the kingdom for nineteen years. Why, in this case, did he find it necessary to confide in a British diplomat with whom he did not have very close personal relations, unlike the US ambassador. And was he aware of the Shah's intention of conveying the contents of the conversation to Israel? One possible answer is that he used every channel to make Israel aware of his least damaging scenario. He would participate in the war, attack Israel, expected to lose the West Bank, but needed some guarantee that the price for catering to the Israeli interest of rectifying the outcome of the 1948 war would not be the destruction of his East Bank kingdom. These maneuverings could not be done with Nasser under any circumstances, and therefore he spared no channel in an attempt to get his message across to Israel and the West.

During the week preceding hostilities Hussein met the US ambassador two or three times a day. During all this time he maintained his clear-cut position that Israel was about to occupy the West Bank.[51] His intensive meetings with the ambassador did not calm his fears that this might not be the end of hostilities. His immediate neighbor, Syria, was another concern to reckon with. During these days of waiting for dramatic moves Jordan kept an eye on its frontier with Syria, where unconfirmed and probably untrue rumors spoke of Syrian concentrations along the border.[52] Actually, by repeating time and again that the US was not willing to give hypothetical answers to hypothetical questions such as its possible position in the event of an Israeli attack, the US only reinforced the king's lessons from previous crises. In a nutshell, the US would not stand by Jordan if its integrity was put in question. The mood among the US personnel in Amman at the time of the signing of the agreement with Egypt was that hostilities were inevitable. If a word of that mood got to the king, considering his very close relations with the US, it could serve only to reinforce his already existing concerns.

Preparations for a possible confrontation began on May 29 with the announcement[53] that the army would welcome volunteers born after 1940. The next day, Hussein left for Egypt on a secret mission with the aim of reaching a military agreement with Nasser, which was signed on the same day. In eleven clauses,[54] Jordan for all practical purposes joined the Egypt–Syrian defense treaty of November 1966, putting its forces, in the case of war, under Egyptian command. This trip came as a surprise to all observers of Jordan, including the US ambassador,[55] and even Nasser himself was taken by surprise. The US ambassador believed that it was the unwillingness of the US to offer Hussein a security guarantee in spite of his conviction that he was going to be attacked by Israel, that led him to this dramatic trip to his arch-enemy, Nasser. The king's intention in the opinion of the ambassador was to gain an Egyptian umbrella against Israel in case of an attack, but as it turned out it would lead to Jordan joining in on the Egyptian side rather than the other way around. In explaining his move Hussein told the US ambassador that he had gained two insights as a result of his talks with Nasser: that the Egyptian president had no designs against Saudi Arabia or Jordan, and that an Israeli attack on Syria was imminent.

This explanation only gives rise to some more questions: first, what is the connection between the sincerity, if any, of Nasser and the Israeli attack on Syria? After all, Syria during those fateful days was clearly an enemy of Jordan, and why then would Jordan publicly stand by an enemy that had not bothered to refrain from hostile acts against it? Moreover, Shuqayri, the PLO chairman, was still at least a potential enemy of the regime, if not more than that; why then should Hussein take him to the kingdom from Cairo aboard his plane after signing the agreement? Secondly, what exactly was the connection between the Egyptian commitment not to undermine the monarchies and the well-being of Syria, which was very much in a campaign against Jordan? A contemporary diplomatic dispatch voiced puzzlement at the agreement the king signed with his enemies.[56] A possible reason for any such an agreement could have been a "grand design" the king might have had in order to encounter his enemies.

Moreover, the signing of the treaty led to pro-Nasserite demonstrations in the streets of Amman, and certainly added to Jordanian worries at this tense time. On top of that, the king's trip led to the signing of an agreement with Egypt putting his army under Egyptian command, clearly in sharp contrast to the Israeli *casus belli* undoubtedly known to the king for several years. The only explanation Hussein would provide for his move came in the wake of the war, when he said[57] that he had had information that Israel had already decided to attack, and that convinced him to hurry to Cairo in order to build up Arab deterrence. His efforts to secure a US declaration that would satisfy the Arab side and avert a war failed,[58] probably as the king expected given the necessary deviation in such a document from its traditional policies of avoiding taking sides between Israel and its neighbors. On the ground, the treaty allowed Egyptian forces to be deployed at one of the most sensitive locations for Israel: in Latrun. This location was totally unacceptable to Israel on two counts: first, it was a critical location endangering uninterrupted Israeli movement between Tel Aviv and its capital city of Jerusalem. Secondly, this very issue, the siege of Jerusalem in 1948, had led Israel to a long succession of abortive attacks on Latrun in 1948 resulting in a very large number of casualties and the need to circumvent Latrun in the following years. Thus, after 1948, Latrun remained as a daily reminder of the 1948 failure on this front. Allowing Egyptian commandos to be positioned at Latrun could justify, in the king's eyes, a strong Israeli military reaction but was not enough to risk a takeover of the West Bank by Egypt.

His signing leaves much room for interpretation in investigating the true reasons behind Hussein's move. After all, this treaty and its subsequent implementation might have put Jordan in grave danger, which it really did less than one week later. The simple explanation is that without tangible US support Hussein had to look for regional help; but still, why would Nasser, dedicated to the idea of dismantling the Hashemite Kingdom, provide Hussein with any kind of support? And why would Hussein with his sharp reading of Middle Eastern realities seek an Egyptian guarantee that might never work? On the other hand, if, in spite of the messages from the United Arab Command, Hussein were to accept Egyptian forces into his kingdom, how could he be assured that they would not turn against him in support of the Palestinians? Moreover, if the rumors concerning Egyptian encouragement to the PLO to declare a Palestinian state in the West Bank and the Gaza Strip were true, how would the deployment of Egyptian forces stop such a move, as the US reading of the newly signed treaty went?[59]

Assuming that Hussein was not a willing participant in the survival efforts of the Syrian regime; that the agreement was not helpful in maintaining domestic law and order; and that he professed, to the US, to sign it as a means of purchasing an insurance policy; what was he protecting himself from? The answer might be found on two levels: first, during his conversation with the US ambassador on the afternoon after signing the treaty, Hussein emphasized[60] Nasser's determination to keep the Gulf of Aqaba straits closed. Jordan obviously paid its dues to the Arab cause and on May 24 Prime Minister Sa'd Jum'ah issued a communiqué supporting the closure of the straits.[61] However, this being the only Jordanian outlet to the open sea, the UAR's move put Jordan at the mercy of President Nasser. The diversion of a US ship full of ammunition destined for Jordan, after the closure of the straits, only amplified Hussein's anxiety.[62] Given past rocky relations between the two leaders, even a short intermission in hostility could not dispel Hussein's concerns over that move, especially since he was in no position to challenge the UAR's move in the straits, politically as well as militarily. The significance of this consideration will become even more evident later in the book, in chapter 5, when discussing the issue of access to the Mediterranean, which Hussein raised time and again during his peace quest after the war. Secondly, if all explanations of the signing were unconvincing, and even the straits issue might have provided only a temporary relief considering their strategic importance, then knowing very well the Israeli sensitivities, Hussein may have assessed that the closure of the straits indeed constituted a *casus belli* for Israel, that war was inevitable and that the support manifested for Nasser in Jordan in the wake of the agreement was only the last straw leading to Hussein's possible decision to exploit the evolving situation in order to guarantee the well-being and survival of his kingdom for a long time, for a price.

Hussein's relations with his fellow Arab leaders were not the only issue to be affected by the treaty. A pre-emptive Israeli strike may have been contemplated and thus, on June 1, the very day Egyptian General Riad arrived in Amman to assume command of the Jordanian army, the Jordanian officer representing his country at the Mixed Armistice Committee assured Israel of Jordan's peaceful intentions in spite of the treaty.[63] No less important was the question of relations with the US.[64] After all, concluding an agreement with the client of the Soviet Union supposedly in order to bail out another client from its troubles with a client of the US certainly put Hussein on the wrong side from a Western point of view. As a traditional ally of the West who wished to signal a break with the past, but with the benefit of hindsight, by the resumption of cordial relations in the summer of 1967 after the war, and in the context of a similar move during the 1990–1 Gulf crisis, a possible explanation of Hussein's moves might be that aligning himself temporarily with his main enemy was a recurrent model of political behavior. This policy could only be implemented working on the premise, which proved right time and again, that the US along with Israel would not let Jordan disintegrate, since the alternative would mean regional chaos. Thus, Hussein enjoyed a leverage larger than that usually ascribed to him.

That kind of leverage was not to be found in Hussein's relations with his Arab neighbors. On June 2, although the king's interest was nothing more than Iraqi air cover, the first Iraqi ground forces began their movement into the Hashemite Kingdom. Eventually, an Iraqi brigade was deployed not far from Jerusalem, to the east.[65] On June 4, Iraq signed a defense pact with the UAR, making the presence of its forces on Jordanian soil a fulfillment of an inter-Arab commitment rather than the result of a bilateral agreement with Jordan. This move obviously made any Jordanian objection to the Iraqi presence in the future a question to be dealt with by more bodies than these two parties. That meant that as of June 4, Jordan gave up two elements of its sovereignty: the army was under an Egyptian general, and the presence of a foreign expeditionary force was no longer subject to the good will of the Amman government.

War

Hussein's prewar policies and considerations did not change on June 5, 1967. Probably, the most important of them was the internal threat from the Palestinian West Bank as a result of a mistaken decision by the king.[66]

During the war the Arab [Jordanian] Legion [Army] operated according to its defense plan, which had been devised long before the war by Jordanian officers and exercised time and again. The plan, code-named "al-Hussein" after Hussein's late great-grandfather, divided the West Bank into two fronts: the Western front, including the West Bank and the Jordan Valley, and the Eastern front, which included the whole of the East Bank. Obviously, the Western battleground was allocated much more military force: seven infantry brigades, two M-47 and Patton tank battalions, and most of the Jordanian artillery. The East Bank got one infantry brigade, two tank brigades (nos 40 and 60), two artillery battalions and one brigade of the Royal Guard assigned the sensitive duty of protecting the king. These forces barely made it to the end of the war: only two out of nine brigades fully survived the war. One tank brigade was completely destroyed and most of the artillery and air force were destroyed.

The activities of the Jordanian army during the first stages of the war suggest very strongly that they were intended to draw Israel into the war. They were not those of a party attempting to avert war. Still, the semi-official Jordanian version puts the blame[67] retroactively on the Egyptian commander of the Jordanian forces, who in effect drew Jordan into a war it did not want to fight. Moreover, the Jordanian intention was obviously not to inflict casualties on themselves, but only to draw Israel into a short war that would not be very expensive in terms of human lives. After all, the Jordanian Arab Army had never been trained as an offensive force,[68] but was intended rather as a defensive tool. That tool was much more necessary on the East Bank than on the West Bank. A careful study of the war's stages also indicates that with the exception of the attack on the UN headquarters in Jerusalem, intended to draw Israel into fighting, Jordan did not use ground forces in any other moves; again, an indication of the Jordanian tactic to limit casualties and frontal confrontation with the Israeli forces.

In a succession of provocative moves, Hussein played all Israeli weak spots – strategic as well as emotional. With the commencement of hostilities he announced that his army was operating under an Egyptian general, Abd al-Mun'im Riad, against all his knowledge of the public Israeli *casus belli*. That general took his orders from Field Marshal Abd al-Hakim 'Amir in Cairo.[69] Years later Hussein claimed[70] that the United Arab Command had launched the military moves; in reality his responsibility was at least the free hand he gave the Egyptian general. Indeed, for years Israel repeated its strong opposition to the presence of any foreign troops on Jordanian territory. Even though it never specified whether this presence would be treated differently if it was limited to the East or the West Bank, it was widely believed that the closer the foreign forces get to Israel the higher was the risk of an Israeli pre-emptive strike. In this respect Jordan made two fairly safe moves, to ensure an Israeli assault on the West Bank, yet, not put at risk the existence of the East Bank as an independent Hashemite-ruled territory. Those moves were the position granted to an Egyptian general as the top commanding officer of the Jordanian forces, and the deployment of an Egyptian commando unit on the Israeli border at Latrun.[71]

Hussein did not wait for news from the Egyptian front to summon foreign ambassadors, at around 8:30 a.m. local time on June 5, before even a single shot was fired across his line with Israel. At that meeting he told them that "war had broken out between Israel and Jordan,"[72] and that the Jordanian forces were under the command of General Riad. One cannot escape the thought that the message prior to any actual military showdown with Israel was intended to reach the ears of its leaders and convince them to go to war along that front. While this meeting with the ambassadors was taking place, General Riad at 8:50 a.m. issued orders to the Jordanian forces to commence firing along the line with Israel and prepare to open artillery fire;[73] another order had it that the Jordanian forces would occupy United Nations Truce Supervision Organization (UNTSO) headquarters in Jerusalem. At 9:00 a.m., with the commencement of hostilities between

Israel and the Egyptian army, the deputy director-general of the Israeli foreign ministry summoned General Odd Bull, chief-of-staff of the UNTSO. The Israeli official informed the UN general on behalf of the foreign minister that Israel would like him to convey an urgent message to Hussein to the effect that Israel would not attack Jordan if Jordan kept aloof from the fighting.[74] However, if Jordan joined in hostilities Israel would "hit back hard."[75] This message was indeed delivered to the king, according to General Bull's testimony, but officials in Jordan denied its existence long after the war. It was not the first message of its kind during the three weeks preceding the war. The Jordanian response to the Israeli message came when the Jordanian Army opened small-arms fire and later used all guns at its disposal against the new City of Jerusalem and Mount Scopus.

At 9:45 a.m. the Jordanian Arab Army (JAA) in Jerusalem opened small-arms fire on Jerusalem, and around 11:00 a.m. it was supplemented by artillery fire.[76] Later the Jordanian forces opened artillery fire all over the long armistice line with Israel. Israel could still interpret this as a token participation in the all-Arab effort against Israel,[77] or in other words, as a Jordanian move which did not justify any Israeli military action beyond firing back with Israeli artillery. However, the occupation of the UNTSO headquarters in Jerusalem, in the area between the lines, was a more aggressive move and led Israel to put into action its plans for the occupation of (the Jordanian-held part of) Jerusalem. The artillery shelling of Tel Aviv from the West Bank during the evening hours of June 5 probably intended a similar effect in drawing Israel into a wider conflict. That barrage was not heavy enough to inflict any significant casualties on Israel but such a bombing of the main Israeli populated area along with the Jerusalem fighting had to press Israel into further confrontation with Jordan.

A second attempt at reaching an end to violence came at 10:40 a.m. when General Bull asked the two sides for a full cease-fire by 12:00.[78] The Jordanian shelling continued "in default of reply by the Israelis for an hour"[79] and covered wider areas including some which were not far from the main population centers of Israel. The first Jordanian communiqué announcing the beginning of the war was issued around noontime on June 5. It simply stated that the enemy had opened fire in the Jerusalem area at 11:30 a.m. and that the Jordanian forces responded by opening artillery fire all along the Jordanian–Israeli front.[80] Shortly afterwards the king delivered a radio speech to the nation. He said, *inter alia*: "The enemy has launched its attack against our land."[81]

General Bull repeated his call for a cease-fire for the third time at 12:20, asking for a cease-fire at 12:30. The Jordanian forces disregarded this also.[82] At that time most if not all the air forces of the Arab countries neighboring Israel were out of commission and no air cover was available for the

Jordanian forces.[83] Still the response came in a military form: by 12:43 on June 5 the United Arab Command issued a communiqué[84] saying that Arab forces had occupied the headquarters of the United Nations Truce Supervision Organization at the former High Commissioner's palace. That attack was actually concluded around 1 p.m. with the Jordanian occupation of the site. The JAA attack on a neutral location belonging to the UN was meant to convey the message that Jordan was participating in the war in a very significant way and that it would not be deterred by any foreign intervention – be it the UN or the US. Indeed, the king refused an Israeli communication conveyed through the US channel, asking him to withdraw from UNTSO headquarters in return for an Israeli guarantee to refrain from attacking Jordan.

Hussein's version[85] of the events of June 5 is, in a way, a response to Bull's intervention. Hussein denied that Israel had delivered three messages to him on June 5. Actually, he said, only two messages had been delivered: the first through General Bull, after hostilities commenced, and the second through the US embassy during the evening hours. He said that he was convinced then, and remained so after the war as well, that Israel had looked for ways to occupy Jerusalem and the West Bank.

Hussein's political and military behavior during the first 24 hours of fighting strongly suggests that he was fully aware of the contents of all Israeli messages throughout the crisis but that he chose to ignore them. This way, the semi-official Jordanian position[86] that Israeli warnings on June 5 were insincere cannot be accepted at face value. Further, this approach also speaks of a possible Israeli fabrication of messages from Egyptian military headquarters to (Egyptian) General Riad, who was in command of the Jordanian forces on behalf of the Joint Arab Command, claiming spectacular Egyptian successes. Whether these Egyptian reports were, or were not, Israeli fabrications, they were not limited to secret messages.[87] Radio Cairo began speaking of Egyptian victory shortly after the beginning of hostilities between Israel and Egypt around 8 a.m. on June 5.

During June 6 the magnitude of the defeat began to unfold, since the forces on the West Bank not only lost air cover as of the first day of the war, but they also lost for all practical purposes the tank units which were supposed to carry most of the fighting.[88] Indeed, it was clear from Hussein's second appearance on TV[89] since the beginning of the war, shortly after midnight on the night of June 5/6, that he was gravely upset and shocked at the very quick pace of Israeli advance and the widespread Jordanian and Arab losses. Early postwar estimates tended to bring down the number of Jordanian casualties and describe these losses in a less scaring way than the impression given by the king's appearance.[90] Even though in territorial terms Israel had not yet gained any major areas on the West Bank, its forces had already crossed the 1949 armistice line, seized strategic locations overlooking the Old City of Jerusalem, occupied the Latrun area and totally destroyed the Jordanian air force.[91] At this point the cost for Jordan seemed terrible. It was only reasonable to guess that contrary to all past analyses Israel would not stop at the Jordan River, and while exploiting its emerging success would altogether destroy the Hashemite Kingdom. The mood of Hussein was reflected in two desperate moves: the forging of a new conspiracy with Nasser, and a plea for a cease-fire. In the latter, the US was supposed to bail Hussein out, the former move targeted the US as the enemy of the Arabs. In the early hours of June 6 Hussein and Nasser had a telephone conversation in which they decided to blame the US and Great Britain for helping Israel.[92] Two more parties were fully aware of the contents of that dramatic conversation: Israel, which intercepted it, and made propaganda capital out of it, and the US, which was told of the conversation right away by Hussein,[93] undoubtedly in order to demonstrate his desperate condition and in order to deflect any possible penalty by the US against him once the false allegations were made public. His need of the US as a mediator for a cease-fire had never been so great.

Since a cease-fire at this time, while Israeli forces were advancing in the Sinai Peninsula, would be tantamount to publicly betraying the united Arab front which Hussein had just fortified, and cause him at least some public embarrassment, he asked the US that Israel be approached in order to put an end to the violent attacks:[94] in effect, an undeclared cease-fire, supposedly not on any Jordanian initiative. That position was not in reality against Egyptian interests since Nasser himself asked Hussein[95] to intervene with the US to apply pressure on Israel so that it would unilaterally cease its fighting in the Sinai. Failing to secure an Israeli acceptance of the cease-fire, Hussein desired "a decrease in punitive destructive actions,"[96] or that the superpowers impose a cease-fire. Before any significant American response was formed Hussein summoned the ambassadors from the four powers to his office, begging them[97] to arrange a cease-fire. The king presented his plea, indicating that the Egyptian general, Riad, was backing it and that he had already notified Cairo of his position.[98] Israel received the Jordanian request, made around noontime through the US channel, in the evening of June 6 and rejected it. The US ambassador in Tel Aviv met the Israeli prime minister and interpreted the Israeli response as though it was "too late to arouse any interest in Israel for preservation of Hussein and his regime."[99] Moreover, the Israeli position detailed almost one by one the Israeli *casi belli* in action, reciting them as the reason for continuing the war: accepting a UAR commander, initiating hostilities in Jerusalem, shelling some 30 settlements in areas north of Tel Aviv, and an attack on the main street of the coastal town of Netanya.

A short while after the king's meeting with the ambassadors, at 2:30 p.m., Field Marshal 'Amir cabled Hussein:[100] "We invest all our efforts in securing cease-fire and we agree to the withdrawal of the regular army, try to arm the local people for popular resistance." The JAA did not function any more as a military organization and Hussein debated whether to order evacuation or let as many soldiers as possible stay on the West Bank. He answered[101] Field Marshal 'Amir that he was attempting to let the Jordanian forces stay on so that the cease-fire would find them in the West Bank. This, supposedly, was no longer for purposes of fighting, but his reading was probably that Israel was determined to totally destroy his army and he would be keen to save as many lives as possible, so a withdrawal would have cost many more lives. Additionally, even without any military formations, the mere existence of Jordanian troops on the ground would grant Hussein a standing in any future diplomatic process especially since the Security Council was already considering a cease-fire. Late that evening Nasser advised Hussein to withdraw from the West Bank while seeking a cease-fire.[102] That message, if made public, would have made any such Jordanian move legitimate in the eyes of the Arab people at large.

With the Israeli refusal delivered to Hussein, the US ambassador received from him,[103] around 11 p.m. on June 6, a realistic assessment of the current conditions. At that point he was considering ordering an immediate evacuation of his forces from the West Bank. He also mentioned the Egyptian commander of these forces, so as to indicate that his moves were not against any consensus with the UAR. In the context of this conversation Hussein gave an indication of the way he had expected the war to unfold: "no one had anticipated conflict would escalate so far and so fast." Clearly, a rare insight into the scenario he had created for himself before June 5 – the military inferiority of the JAA would indeed have led to the loss of the West Bank but through a less costly war to the Hashemite Kingdom in terms of human and material resources.

The UN Security Council passed a cease-fire resolution on the evening of June 6, which the advancing Israeli forces did not obey. Consequently, the US begged Israel to comply,[104] indicating its belief that the continued disregard of that resolution might bring down the Hashemite regime. Jordan did not share that assessment. Its prime minister believed that Israel was trying to complete the total occupation of the West Bank.[105] Still, the lingering doubts regarding Israel's true intentions made Jordan invest any effort possible to convince Israel of its sincerity in search of a cease-fire. Shortly after the passage of the resolution the Jordanian government asked the Iraqi air force to stop flying in Jordanian airspace. Interestingly enough, just a day earlier on June 5, Jordan could not order its own forces to stop their activities since they had been put under an Egyptian commanding officer. A possible explanation can perhaps be found in the changing circumstances: on June 5 Jordan had to participate in the Arab effort and perhaps follow its national interest and lose the West Bank. A day later the picture was different and the very existence of the kingdom was at stake.

In spite of the negative Israeli response to the cease-fire proposal quiet began to fall on growing areas of the West Bank during the night between June 6 and June 7. Jordan still made efforts[106] to convince Israel through foreign ambassadors to halt its fire but Israel tried to consolidate its holdings in the West Bank and wrap up operations, leading to the complete occupation of the territory. Arising from the new circumstances, a unique opportunity for Israel to consolidate its newly acquired position as the winning regional party led to an Israeli agreement that its commando units would participate in the evacuation of US personnel from Amman if necessary.[107] That consent, in response to an American approach to Israel, only served to indicate the slim chances the US gave to the survival of the Hashemite regime, compounded with the realization that the only regional power to be counted on to contribute to that survival would be Israel. Alternatively, Israel might cooperate with the US in shaping the future face of the East Bank without the Hashemites, in a way acceptable to Israel and the US. Had the US believed that Israeli units in Amman would serve as a bridgehead to further Israeli advancements on the East Bank it would probably have not asked Israel for that intervention, which never materialized.

Meanwhile, though Israeli forces were advancing along the battle lines, Jordan for its part was intent on continuing its presence on the West Bank whatever the price, and orders to that effect were issued to its army in the early hours of June 7.[108] Israel could not take the Jordanian pleas too seriously since the Jordanian forces, or what was left of them, continued to fire on Israeli positions especially around Jerusalem. At this point the US advice was that Hussein should accept the cease-fire, something he had still not done by around midday on June 7. Conditions on the ground, that is the feeling in Amman that the JAA was on the verge of total collapse and the realization that the West Bank was lost, along with the American pressure, finally led Jordan to publicly announce its acceptance of the cease-fire[109] in the early afternoon of June 7. Following the full occupation of the West Bank by Israel, and the US appeals to Israel, directly or through General Bull,[110] Jordan finally accepted the cease-fire. At 11:59 GMT on June 7 the war came to an end.

One last episode relating to the military confrontation had to do with the crossing of some 30 Israeli tanks into the East Bank on June 8.[111] Israel explained that their mission was the demolition of bridges over the Jordan River and nothing more. After US intervention they were all ordered back, bringing to an end that stage in the Israeli–Jordanian dimension of the Israeli–Arab war. The excuse given years later by the local commanding officer was also that the mission of the unit had to do with the blowing up of the Jordan valley bridges – an unacceptable explanation which served as an indication of the gravity with which official Israel looked upon any Israeli activity east of the river in the context of the war.

Certainly, when the Genie is out of the bottle there are sometimes unexpected dangers; in this case the imminent conflict in late May/early June had the potential to develop into an all-out Israeli attack on Jordan, as indeed did happen, leading either to the elimination of the kingdom altogether or parts of it, or to a major Egyptian victory over Israel that would lead to the same outcome. Hussein was prepared for at least the Israeli contingency since as a close follower of Israeli politics he knew very well that the very existence of his regime was one of the pillars of Israeli security. This impression was strongly enhanced during the talks he conducted with Israel. Still, participating in the new war between Israel and its Arab neighbors was a losing proposition from the start. At least this is how Hussein referred to it[112] a short while before the 1973 war. Two major points revealed by the king at that opportunity add to the theory that he knew what he was doing: first, even though the JAA was put under Egyptian command the ultimate decisions rested with the king, who chose to continue the fighting in spite of Israeli warnings; secondly, and perhaps even more important, Israel was in a position to occupy the West Bank at any moment before the war, which again reinforces the idea that Hussein entered the war in order to lose the West Bank.

This scheme worked so efficiently that Israel, so well prepared for any military contingency, did not have a coherent policy for the postwar era. Rather, the June 1967 war moves, along with the subsequent political moves in the Arab world, proved the king right. In the first place Egypt ceased to pose a threat to the Hashemite Kingdom, thus ensuring its continued existence. Israel, which had no high-level contacts with any other Arab country, had to rely on Jordan to find a way to resolve the Palestinian issue. In this respect, Israeli strategic thinking prior to the war proved problematic at best: there was no long-range planning regarding the implementation of the contingencies so well rehearsed on the military level since the 1960 crisis. This deficiency of Israeli policy making manifested itself for the most part in the variety of unanswered questions on the Palestinian–West Bank levels. Unlike Israel, which won militarily but had no clear idea of the policy goals, Hussein was the clear winner. Through participation in the Arab war effort he got rid of the West Bank, passed the responsibility for the Palestinians over to Israel, which was unable to operate without his involvement, and secured his throne for many more years. The UAR was the clear loser.

4

Jordanian Composite Nationalism

Hussein had a very strong sense of history, and many of his political expressions should not be analyzed only against current events, but should be appreciated in the light of his own sentiment, voiced so many times, that he was only a link in a chain begun by the Prophet Muhammad himself. It is impossible to determine an exact date when Hussein began putting together his vision of Jordanian nationalism. However, this vision is publicly evident after the war, even though its roots pre-empt the June 1967 crisis.[1] These ideas have not basically changed throughout the years but have been refined in response to national crises presented by Israel and the Palestinians. It is for this reason that often even the pillars of Jordanian ideology are presented by way of explaining what is not Palestinian or Israeli.[2]

The concept of Jordanian nationalism is the result of three interwoven processes:

1. The evolution of mutual alienation between the Hashemite central government and the West Bankers as the result of the 1963 and 1966 crises.
2. The need to put together a coherent national ideology as the basis for the East Bankers to be united for further challenges. With the loss of the West Bank it became imperative to manifest the identity between Jordan and the East Bank.
3. The 1974 Rabat formula making the PLO the sole and legitimate representative of the Palestinian people raised once again the question of affiliation and loyalty of the Palestinians living on the East Bank.

A Model of Composite Nationalism

The term "composite" used in the current context indicates the amalgamation of ideas and elements of nationalism, which are to be found in other national movements and political entities in addition to many unique

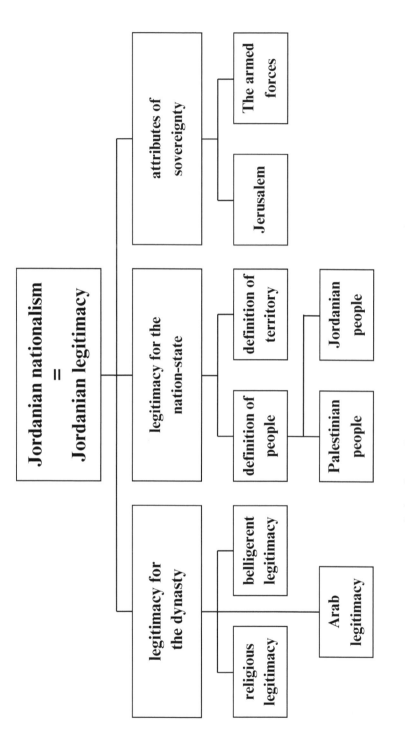

Model of Jordanian composite nationalism

ingredients aimed at producing a new ideological approach. Additionally, it means the artificial creation of a national identity and ideology, which in most cases would evolve on its own without any elaborate human touch. This almost laboratory approach enabled Hussein to create throughout his reign a model intended to respond to changing circumstances. Jordanian nationalism is not the result of a philosopher's effort to provide his countrymen with some talking points. This is the product of the accumulated effect of bringing forth answers to the daily challenges facing Jordan in the years since 1967.

The main motive behind Jordanian nationalism has been the acute need to define relations between the East Bank and its citizens, and the West Bank lost to Israel in the armed conflict of 1967, including its Palestinian population. However, the war occurred only three years after the creation of the Palestine Liberation Organization, a body overtly devoted to the liberation of Palestine, namely the 1948 territories (Israel), and covertly not denying the ultimate wish to take control of all the territory of the former Mandatory Palestine, namely the two banks of the Jordan River. The Palestinian challenge has not been the only constraint on the kingdom's political behavior, and thus on the king's expressions. Since its very inception the kingdom has been sandwiched between stronger Arab actors, always vying for control over Jordan and the rest of the Middle East. These forces have in effect caused the creation of a political terminology, or a set of rhetoric rules, using the element of Arab unity as its centerpiece. Hussein, in responding to these Palestinian and Arab challenges, had at the same time to emphasize the unique nature of his kingdom, that is, to provide the ideological basis for its existence outside of Palestinian political ambitions, and yet to pay lip service to the more general Arab cause in order not to find himself and his kingdom totally out of the Arab consensus. By analyzing a select body of the king's public appearances a model of composite nationalism can be reconstructed. The latter are the result of changing political circumstances necessitating a change of political course. However, the only field in which the king had to introduce major political changes was in relations with the Palestinians. Thus, he devoted much effort to detailing his policies and ideology *vis-à-vis* the Palestinians, always very careful to distinguish between Palestinians and Jordanians.

The first layer has to do with the most crucial political challenge: legitimacy for the Hashemite dynasty. This broad term includes several elements: *Muslim religious legitimacy*, *Arab historical legitimacy*, and *current belligerent legitimacy in opposition to the Zionist movement*. All three are obviously interwoven, but it is not very difficult to identify all elements and define them, as will be done in the following pages.

The second layer is more specific to the Jordanian entity and deals with issues of the *legitimacy for the nation-state*, namely: *territory and national identity of the indigenous people.* A most crucial component in this respect is the definition of the *people* in general and the *Jordanian people* in particular, and the relations between them and the *Palestinian people* – past, present, and possible future contenders for the same territory.

The third layer has to do with *attributes of sovereignty.* Loyalty to these elements means full acceptance of the kingdom and its nationalism. This layer combines the first two in the meaning that it connects the (legitimate) Hashemite Kingdom to the (legitimate) Jordanian national and geographical entity. Two major symbols of sovereignty are analyzed in this chapter: *Jerusalem,* and the *armed forces.*

Being a grandson of King Abdullah could not be easily reconciled with the need to develop an ideology for only one part of the Arab homeland. After all, the father of Abdullah had rebelled against the Ottomans back in 1916, raising the banner of one single Arab kingdom. Abdullah himself established the Jordanian kingdom but raised from time to time the flag of Arab unity. What is more, Hussein saw in his grandfather a role model, and often mentioned him as laying the groundwork for the Hashemite entity. To follow in the political and ideological footsteps of King Abdullah was an important ingredient in Hussein's ideology. Undoubtedly, the founding monarch could not see in the establishment of a small emirate the fulfilling of the Hashemite family's political vision after World War I. Thus, before any particular ideology could be developed, that contradiction had to be grappled with.

One of the early theaters to hear the message that Abdullah was really a Jordanian monarch was no less than the forum of Arab rulers in its entirety. Already in November 1970 while the civil war was raging, and the most obvious question among Arab leaders could be regarding the true Arab spirit of Hussein, he found the right time to address that issue. True, with the passing away of President Nasser in September 1970, the last symbol of Arab nationalism was gone. Still it took a courageous decision by the king to send all of the Arab leaders a message in November 1970[3] in which he presented the creation of the kingdom as the only way in which the Arab national movement could evade the outcome of the Balfour Declaration. Put differently, the establishment of a separate political unit in eastern Jordan, as much as it was against the interests and beliefs of Arabs at that time, did fulfill a necessary function. The continued existence of the kingdom also meant that it had full legitimacy to follow its own national interests, which at times were not identical with Arab interests at large. Saying all that a couple of months after the abortive Syrian invasion and the peak of the bloody civil war was in effect one of the occasions on which the king made clear his position. He was the leader of a unique nation, far away from the one single Arab nation his grandfather had envisioned.

Legitimacy for the Hashemite Dynasty: Muslim, Arab, and defender of the Arab nation against Zionism (*belligerent legitimacy*)

Within the larger context of Islam, and many generations after the collapse of the concept of *ummah* (one Muslim political and religious community over all Muslim territories), the king tried to place his kingdom, his dynasty and himself in the focal point of Islam, the Hashemite family and himself as the leader, continuing this magnificent tradition. Over the years, Hussein built the religious dimension of his legitimacy on several elements: the fact that his legitimacy lay in his direct descent from the Prophet Muhammad, hence his repeated references to his own lineage, and to the Prophet's son-in-law and the "guided" Caliph 'Ali ibn Abi Talib (ruled 656–61) as the personal, ideological, and historical starting point of the Hashemite dynasty; his quotation of verses from the Qur'an and other religious expressions; and finally, the usage of early Muslim terminology.

In spite of the division between religion and politics that has developed over centuries, Hussein tried to create some degree of association between them in the minds of his audiences. Many times he used the sentence: "For it was Almighty God who honored me with my Jordanian, Arab and Hashemite affiliation,"[4] or he referred to the Prophet's tradition (*hadith*). The religious dimension was deeply rooted in the king's mind and it is obvious from his speeches that Hussein saw Islam as the backbone of his support, and the cohesion of his country. Even his political moves were presented as being guided by Islam. Thus, the convening of the National Council,[5] for example, was in reality the implementation of the traditional principle of *shura* – consultation – which used to be used in classical Islam. This impression was further emphasized by his using Muslim terminology continually, in all of his speeches to the nation, and by a long succession of speeches regarding his ancestors dating back to ancient times.

By emphasizing the Hashemites' noble ancestry and the mythical founder of the family, and Hashim's relations with Gaza, Hussein alluded[6] to his lineage. Jordan was a monarchy; more than that, it was a Muslim country based on tradition and right. Time and again he described Jordan as the continuation of the great Arab kingdoms of the past. In his mind he was picking up Muslim tradition and Arab political history from two points: first, from the Prophet himself and the "guided" Caliph, 'Ali ibn Abi Talib, and secondly, from his great-grandfather, Sharif Hussein b. 'Ali (1852/3–1931), the leader of the Great Arab Revolt and a major participant in laying the ground work for modern Arab nationalism[7] by his correspondence with the British McMahon. Alluding to these two figures, the way he did, indicates the equal weight he gave to the Muslim and Arab sources of the family, and of the kingdom. Thus, it gave Hussein great pride to stress and re-stress his lineage, almost as a way of presenting time and again his credentials as an Arab and Muslim leader deserving of being the head and leader of the Jordanian family.[8]

Just as the concept of Jordanian nationalism was a political tool in the hands of an able ruler, so was the mentioning of *qur'anic* verses. Clearly, they were not only supposed to provide a general legitimacy to a Muslim ruler but also served as the basis for current politics. Several speeches between 1989 and 1994 revealed numerous inter-relations between the two. Perhaps the most pressing issue on the eve of the parliamentary elections in November 1989 was the radical Muslim threat, which was the topic of a speech on October 7. The approaching elections provided the king with an opportunity to cite[9] several verses all preaching moderation and the need to avoid using violence, in a message to his people not to abuse the newly acquired attributes of democracy and vote for the Muslim fundamentalists. Moreover, Hussein used this opportunity to cautiously promote the status of women in his kingdom, another indication of the way he desired to build modern Jordan: holding free elections and yet curtailing the more acute aspects of radical Islam by rallying one half of his nation behind his modern message of female equality. A few months after the Muslim ministers left the Jordanian cabinet Hussein once again called on his Muslim legitimacy to rally popular support behind him. In another speech rich with *qur'anic* references[10] he spoke about the renovation of the *ka'bah* in Mecca in spite of local sagging economy and and foreign dangers. The message was simple, he appealed to his people in a language clear to all, to try and overcome current difficulties. However, in case the message was lost on his listeners he reiterated his words, calling for more popular efforts in the field of economy and hinting at the gradual movement towards democracy. This was clearly a direction different from the rather simplistic "Islam is the solution" of the Muslim leaders, and yet using all the right Muslim connotations.

Time and again *qur'anic* references were used to provide religious legitimacy to current political moves which might be interpreted as not being in line with fundamentalist Islam. Such cases are two "legacy speeches" of November 1992;[11] the exact timing of these unique speeches was the return of Hussein from medical treatment in the US after being diagnosed with cancer. However, it was also a while after the approval of the new Political Parties Law. Thus, while connecting all elements of Jordanian legitimacy with issues of democracy, human rights and personal liberties, Hussein drew heavily on his family heritage, and its connection to Jerusalem and to the army. It is clear that his desired legacy was a mixture of Islam and new democratic values. In these emotional and landmark speeches he obviously quoted several *qur'anic* verses with the purpose of creating a new source of national solidarity: past religious roots with present and future democratic values.

Another element borrowed from Muslim history was the *Muhajirun* and the *Ansar*,[12] originally terms indicating the followers of the Prophet Muhammad who moved from Mecca to Medina and hid local supporters in Medina. This comparison of himself, a descendant of the Prophet, to Muhammad himself, was clearly intended to add to his long-standing religious legitimacy.

In January 1967, Hussein addressed his people in the wake of the unrest resulting from the Samu' raid. Shortly after he began, he stated: "I am honored to belong to the family of Hussein ibn 'Ali, leader of the great Arab Revolution," that is: he is a leader commemorating the Hashemite connection as his main source of legitimacy.[13] So, not only does he trace himself back to 'Ali, a heroic yet controversial figure in early Islam, but he also links himself to the Arab Revolution, a symbol of Arab glory and strength. This was a clear political move in that he presented Jordan as a distinctly Muslim state with himself as a worthy Muhammed-linked leader, and at the same time displayed his connection to the head of a great pan-Arab cause.

At a time in which the figure of 'Ali served as a sheer reminder of the glorious past, that of the great-grandfather of the king, Hussein b. 'Ali, served three additional political functions: once again, the significance of Jerusalem, the burial place of Hussein b. 'Ali; secondly, the special Hashemite responsibility of caring for the larger Arab people by struggling for Arab unity; and finally, a contemporary Arab legacy of confronting foreign enemies. Thus, being the first Arab leader in modern times to combat colonialism, and operating within the larger Arab homeland, his message was loud and clear: the Arab people should struggle for Arab unity, full liberation, and independence.[14]

Discussing this dimension of legitimacy leads to an undeniable conclusion: the Hashemite dynasty is very well anchored in early Islam, religiously and politically. Thus, any attempt to harm the dynasty, and the king as the incumbent leader, means a violation of sacred traditions of adhering to the legitimate head of the Muslim *ummah*.

The issue of Arab legitimacy is usually presented in the context of the Arab–Israeli confrontation. This association is obviously a little easier to make while there are hostilities along the border, yet Hussein spoke of this legitimacy with the war of attrition over and with the urgent need to base Arab legitimacy on the crushing of the PLO. While addressing both his houses in Amman he spoke[15] of the special place of Jordan, serving as a buffer in front of Israel. The collapse of Jordan would open the way for an Arab catastrophe. Saying this in the wake of the Syrian invasion, with the proof of the might of the Jordanian army, sends a clear message to that country and other fellow Arab leaders: Jordan must continue to exist as it is with the blessing of all other Arab countries.

A blunt expression of this came in January 1978 in an interview with the BBC's London correspondent. Hussein forcefully put down any ideas of establishing a Palestinian state on Jordanian soil. He said, "We are part of the Arab past, its present, its future, maybe. But this East Bank is not a void. It has its people and they have their rights. And it is not a vacant lot for others to come and solve their problems at the expense of the East Jordanians."[16] It is also interesting to point out Hussein's use of the term "East Bank" and "East Jordanians." This is a continuation of the pre-1967 terminology of the United Hashemite Kingdom of Jordan.

The connections between Israel, Palestinian rights and Palestinian territory, and Jordanian unity are repeated many more times. The king's motive for employing the "Arab" card becomes clear when, after affirming the rights and responsibility of Arabs, he claims the existence of divisions, which were the cause of the collapse of Arab solidarity and which will enable Israel to implement its own designs.[17] These comments, made in the wake of the 1982 Israeli invasion of Lebanon, also serve to indicate an uncompromising effort by King Hussein to use his special position between Israel and the Palestinians in order to gain once more, by way of representing the Palestinians.

This approach was repeated almost right up to the signing of peace with Israel. One of the most outstanding expressions to this effect declared that the Hashemite family "shall continue to bear the nation's standard, generation after generation, true to the honor and spirit of their descent."[18]

The signing of the 1994 Jordanian–Israeli peace treaty marks the disappearance of an element so often found in most Arab national ideologies: the foreign enemy embodied in Israel.[19] The new vocabulary regarding Israel signaled a dramatic change in the king's public expressions. This positive language was not the one used over the very long period of secret contacts accompanying what appeared at times to the naked eye to be tense relations between two hostile nations. This public view of Israel had been marked by a long succession of expressions used to present a composite sketch of Israel as a hostile entity in the Middle East. The approach was hardly ever broken prior to the treaty.

Losing the West Bank in the context of a brave, all-Arab military effort catapulted Hussein into a new phase in his political endeavor to build his Hashemite Kingdom as a Jordanian nation-state. He had to formulate an ideology that would be anti-Israeli so as to unite his people, but at the same time would release him from any more moves against the enemy and for the Palestinians. Clearly, any national ideology, at least during its initial stages, benefits from the awareness of an external enemy. Israel, the aggressor of 1967, could very well fit this pattern and ideologically bring back the Palestinians, who comprised more than half of the East Bank residents. The development of the Israeli image along such lines had another purpose as well: with his continued clandestine diplomacy with Israel, and the ongoing competition with the PLO, the king had to present himself, in line with King Abdullah's political behavior, as the champion of Arab nationalism against Israel. Indeed, the terminology applied for so long was not addressed towards Israel. The primary audience was his citizens, the Jordanian people, including East Bank Palestinians, and the Arab world at large; whereas the secondary audience, especially at foreign press interviews, was made up of Western decision makers. Indeed, Israel's leaders did not need the king's speeches to realize the nature of relations. This way the king provided his main audience with a ready enemy to move their attention from the Hashemite crown, and created for his own people a source of national pride by confronting the enemy. It served Hussein's purpose of promoting the notion of one united Jordanian people as part of a united Arab people, to heighten Israel's position as the ultimate enemy. This also explains why the available speeches and interviews shed almost no light on the true nature of relations between the two countries until the actual signing of the peace treaty.

Obviously, the bitter relations between Jordanians and Palestinians, or the two banks of the river, before the war only highlighted the need to form a basis for any national ideological approach. Even the presentation of Israel as the enemy was risky to the king, forcing him to formulate a more offensive posture versus the enemy. It is in this light that the consequences of the 1967 war should be studied. Whereas the earlier crises could not be translated into a new public national ideology, the circumstances dramatically changed in 1967.

The close acquaintance between Hussein and successive Israeli prime ministers did not rid the king of some, albeit sporadic, expressions which were reminiscent of the difficult Jewish history. On a more emotional level, such expressions, rare as they were, represent a major slip of the tongue on the king's part. In reference to the situation in Lebanon, under Israeli occupation, the king portrays himself as a humanitarian, concerned for the "half a million citizens who are besieged" and "liable to extermination," which "brings to mind the worst images of the Nazi atrocities recorded in books and historical documents."[20]

From an historical perspective, the King tended[21] to highlight the initial contact between the Arab national movement under the Hashemites and Zionism, local and international. The contact and the personality of his great-grandfather Hussein b. 'Ali, who announced the Great Arab Revolt against the Ottomans in 1916, provided the king with an opportunity to strengthen his legitimacy on two levels: being the descendant of the *sharif*, and continuing his historical struggle against Zionist schemes in Palestine. This connection was extremely important in uniting all Jordanians and providing them with an historical legitimacy, since Zionist aims were identical to those of Israel, namely, unlimited aspirations on the Arab homeland.[22] However, Israel added to that a distinction between short-range aspirations and long-range ones: first, Israel was working to separate Jordanians from Palestinians so that the transition to the next stage would be smooth. This stage consisted of territorial expansion, which began in 1947 and continued later. This policy had been the historical basis for Israel's refusal to recognize others' rights in the region. That characteristic of Israel, namely its intransigence and policy of *fait accompli*, is also notable after the 1967 war, considering Israeli policies in the territories. Hussein presented[23] this factor as indicating another source of solidarity between Jordan and its fellow Arab countries. Hence, a recurrent element is the confrontation with these elements, whatever the results.

During the initial period after the 1967 war and even until after the suppression of the civil war in Jordan, the harsh language is evident. Israel is portrayed in very radical terms and undoubtedly serves as a common enemy of all Jordanians. During that time the king continually demonstrates[24] throughout his speeches and interviews that Israel was to blame for all acts of aggression and violation of UN resolutions in the region, and that he is bitter about the fact that Israel gets more media attention and United States arms support. This way, other Arab players, led by Egypt, which launched a war of attrition against Israel, or by the armed Palestinian organizations within the kingdom, claiming to replace the monarchy by a more national regime, could not blame King Hussein. Likewise, by joining ranks with other belligerent regimes Jordan boosted its legitimacy and added to its own acceptance by the people living on the East Bank. The violent confrontation with Israel until 1970 provided the king with an opportunity to point to the more emotional elements of his national ideology. In 1968, as the *fidayin* were persistently attacking Israel from within Jordan and Israel was striking back, killing civilians, Hussein spoke to his people, making martyrdom for Jordan a sublime value,[25] but still careful enough not to incite his listeners by using the loaded term *jihad*.

In this context Israel is presented, at least until 1977, the year of political change in Israel, as a monolithic entity comprised of left and right, supported by international Zionism and all aspiring to the same goals.[26] However, it is not Israel itself that constitutes a problem, it is its actions, positions and complexes.[27] With the Palestinian uprising the different shades in the Israeli public become more noticeable.[28] The Israeli people at large, not necessarily in line with their government, support peace. The government is basically a colonizing one, imperialist, land grabbing, and aggressive in nature and has been since 1967. The Likud government in particular is a questionable partner for peace as long as it maintains its ideology that all of Palestine belongs to the Jewish people.[29] On the eve of the 1984 and 1988 Israeli national parliamentary elections Hussein even went as far as he could in pointing to the kind of government he would like to see in Israel.[30] However, it did not deter him from his portrayal of the Israeli people as peace-loving. This multilayered presentation portrays official Israel as an antithesis to the Hashemite Kingdom, which is careful in keeping its international commitments, and therefore should be rewarded by the traditional supporters of Israel. Still, it does not exclude the right of the Israeli people to live in peace. Indeed, since the world recognizes Israel against the wishes of the Arab countries in the Middle East, the local leaders should not confront world opinion by over-emphasizing any differences with the Israeli people at large.

Still unacceptable to the Israeli state of mind, but very much in line with the king's national interests, is the description of Israel as a manipulative country trying to stir unrest and friction both on the Arab side and among the superpowers, and inside Jordan as well, meaning that Israel presented a real threat to Jordanian nationalism and international standing. This element ties also with the attempt to win over Western support for the kingdom, on account of Israel. The response to these threats was not to be found in diplomacy, but rather in the armed forces, another symbol of Jordanian nationalism. Only the determination and courage of the Jordanian forces eventually prevailed[31] – an allusion to the Karameh incident. This feeling of competing with Israel over US support permeated from time to time in the king's speeches. On many occasions he voiced his extreme dissatisfaction[32] and was critical of the manipulative power that Israel had gained over the US Congress. The conclusion was crystal clear: Israel was not only an abstract enemy but capable of manipulating the US, and therefore this superpower should not give Israel the right to act this way. A quotation from 1981 probably best reflects this attitude: "unlimited US aid and absolute support for Israel, as well as US approval of all that is done by Israel, make me feel frankly that the United States no longer possesses the freedom to maneuver."[33]

These statements and others like them cannot conceal for long the true interest of Hussein: a peace process that would enable Israel and Jordan to promote their secret agreements into an international instrument acceptable regionally and internationally. However, even this long journey has to begin at home. It is thus rather reflective of such a thought that at the time of the final implementation of the Israeli–Egyptian peace treaty Hussein introduced a new term to his political vocabulary: total withdrawal for total peace.[34] However, with the emerging change in relations with the PLO, alongside continued secret contacts with Israel, such expressions could not contribute to the accomplishment of Hussein's interests. Picking up on the uprising in 1987 Hussein had to divorce himself from any connection with Israel.

Thus, the period following the outbreak of violence in the territories is marked by yet another wave of harsh language towards Zionism and Israel. Zionism is described[35] as an antithesis to the universal values of freedom and self-determination, and thus as an enemy of the Arab nation at large. Hussein's reading[36] of the unfolding situation as presented by the new realities is that Israel is trying to reverse the tide of history and that indeed this neighbor of Jordan is in dire straits. This analysis of the Israeli situation is added to his past condemnation of the Israeli occupation and settlement policy.[37] Clearly, the spontaneous uprising of the Palestinians and the prospects for a local leadership made this expression of dissatisfaction with Israel an acceptable text in the international and inter-Arab arena at that time. No one would interpret his words in the current situation as a call for the return of the West Bank into Israeli hands.

In spite of the very harsh language used at times with regard to Israel, one major seed of recognition of Israel in the pre-1967 borders was not missing from the king's ideology. Whenever he referred to the 1948 war he explained that Jordanian involvement was intended "to rescue the West Bank" and aimed at "the redemption of the lion's share of Palestine which remained Arab."[38] These expressions are exceptionally important since they define the conflict with the neighbor to the west simply as a territorial one. In this approach Hussein became the first Arab leader to trace the roots of the conflict back to what he saw as the usurping of Palestinian rights. This way Jordan had no quarrel with the existence of a Jewish–Zionist political entity in the Middle East. However, for a variety of reasons, all having to do with the lack of legitimacy of the king on the inter-Arab arena, he could not translate his acceptance of the pre-1967 Israel into an internationally binding instrument. Yet, even before the beginning of the Israeli–Egyptian peace process in 1977, Hussein had already crossed the psychological barrier of an indirect recognition of Israel. Obviously, one of the reasons for his rather pragmatic approach was the 1946–50 process of negotiations between his grandfather, Abdullah, and representatives of the Zionist leadership. Years later, in 1986, Hussein would mention[39] the UN Partition Resolution 181 as the basis for the creation of Israel and indirectly as the source of its legitimacy. This resolution, besides affirming the rights of an Arab state as well as a Jewish state in Western Palestine, was also the only document which recognized the borders of these two states. Put differently, even though Israel had the right to exist as an independent country it also had its own internationally recognized borders, those specified by the General Assembly Resolution 181.

Strangely enough, however, Hussein never traced back the beginnings of the Arab–Israeli conflict to the early times of the "secret agreements" of World War I. At least one possible explanation has to do with the fact that those instruments, so much attacked by Arab speakers, provided the legal basis in international law for the creation of the Hashemite Kingdom of Jordan. As much as the king was concerned with popular and national legitimacy for his kingdom, he was far from ignoring the diplomatic and historical roots of his national entity. The early encounters merely signaled the prelude to the conflict, which began in earnest only in 1948.[40] In his speeches Hussein divides the Israeli–Jordanian conflict into three distinct chapters: 1948–67, 1967–74, and 1974–94. During the former two, Jordan (with, and later without, the West Bank) was in the forefront of powers dedicated to the rights of the Palestinians. After the 1974 Rabat formula, Jordan had to relinquish this responsibility to the PLO.

In the king's public expressions the concept of the "enemy" is strongly connected with issues of territory and Palestinian rights. Thus, even in the worst days of Palestinian–Jordanian relations in the late 1960s and 1970 he made an effort to portray himself and his kingdom as working hand in hand with the Palestinian organizations against Israel, ignoring the fact that the exact reverse may have been true at least in the eyes of members of these organizations. Moreover, on another occasion he presented himself as cooperating with the better part of the Palestinian people against Israel, implying that the PLO was really helping the enemy by weakening Jordan. Nevertheless, "Jordan never received the West Bank from the PLO."[41] Hussein continually puts forward the idea of a united Jordan to his people, using Israel as a means. In Hussein's opinion the main problem in the Middle East is "Israel's seizure of the entire territory of Palestine, expulsion of its people and occupation of other parts of our Arab land adjoining Palestine."[42]

With the changing times, after the explusion in 1970 of the PLO from Jordan, the 1974 Rabat formula and the 1976 Israeli "Jordanian option," the challenge facing the king was somewhat different: how could he avoid public negotiations with Israel without any diplomatic damage to the kingdom? Nevertheless, in spite of the changing diplomatic and military environment in the aftermath of the 1973 war, the rhetoric almost never changed, since the audience remained the same. His basic premise was that Israel had to make the critical decision between peace and land. Indeed, Israel had not made clear whether it chose security or continued occupation by Arabs, "because it's impossible to have both."[43] Hussein believed that Israel had to make up its mind, not only because this was the Arab position, but also since the continued settlement policy of Israel was an example of the remains of colonialism, which was no longer accepted by the civilized world.[44] The king made it clear to Israel that it could not have peace and land together. Likewise, Israel must recognize the rights of the

Palestinian people and withdraw completely from the West Bank. Indeed, in Hussein's mind there was a clear distinction between Israel and Palestine. He believed[45] that Israel had occupied all of Palestine, indicating that he had no quarrel with Israel in its pre-1967 borders; the conflict was over the 1967 occupied territories alone.

Again and again the king alludes to the sources of Israeli strength.[46] On the one hand, it is a ready explanation for the formidability of this great rival. On the other hand, the lesson for Jordan and Jordanians is clear: the kingdom should try to follow suit and adopt some of the Israeli tactics. Indeed, it is significant to shed light on the least used expressions, which found their way from time to time into the king's public speeches. In essence, Israel owes its robust existence to the international Jewish community, especially in the United States, and to the strong and almost unlimited support of successive American administrations.

With the completion of putting together the Jordanian national ideology and the signing of the 1994 peace treaty with Israel, much changed. One of the elements changing after the Israeli–Jordanian peace treaty had to do with the way the king depicted Israel. As portrayed by Hussein prior to the treaty, Jordan saw Israel as the eternal, ideological, and military enemy. During the era of public confrontation, references to Israel were made on two levels: first, the long-range, including analysis of the role played by Jordan against Zionist and Israeli aggression throughout history; and secondly, sporadic comments made on current affairs. These expressions constitute a composite sketch of the enemy and its main negative qualities. On these two levels, the picture is bleak and uncompromising: Israel has been the aggressor in this part of the world, while Jordan stood guard over Arab interests.

A Jordanian Entity

In terms of territory Jordan is definitely a legitimate country on the East Bank only, since this area was not made part of the Jewish national home.[47] In this respect Jordan is the Arab shield against Israeli expansionist designs and its aim to gain hegemony over all the Middle East. Hussein is consistent here in criticizing the concept of the Balfour Declaration, which indirectly also contributed to the establishment of the Hashemite Kingdom.

One week before the municipal elections in the Israeli-held Palestinian territories, and at a time in which Israeli Arabs began to demand their national rights, Hussein provided his people with a key to their national identity. Simply put, people living on the East Bank are Jordanians while those living on the West Bank are Palestinians.[48] The East Bank, in the mind of the king,[49] was that part of Palestine which the Hashemite family managed to snatch from the Jewish national home promised during World War I. In many of his speeches before and after, the king repeated this approach. However, the timing here is significant: with rising national tensions among the Palestinians of Jordan, Israel and the territories, he made his position in an open and clear way.

On another occasion, again at a time of great national tension in the territories, Hussein repeated his position. In November 1980, alluding to the possibility of establishing a Jordanian–Palestinian confederation, he announced that "this will not take place until after the restoration of the land to its kinfolk and owners and until after the sons of Palestine choose such a relationship in total freedom."[50]

Regional politics in the Middle East today are very different from the conditions a generation or two ago. At the time the Great Arab Revolt was declared by the Hashemites and their leader Sharif Hussein ibn 'Ali, the great-grandfather of Hussein, against the Ottomans in 1916, the order of the day was the creation of one united Arab kingdom under the Hashemites. This struggle for one united Arab entity continued even after the Hashemites became irrelevant in terms of Arab unity. However, it is widely accepted that the political entities of the region have crossed a threshold: from working for or paying lip service to Arab unity, all leaders admit today, in one way or another, that they lead nation-states. In most cases this is the result of a national liberation struggle against a Western power. The Hashemite Kingdom is an exception: its citizens had never fought a foreign oppressor and they lacked a center of national solidarity. This was the result of the absence of a spontaneous national movement leading to a national definition of their particular Arab political entity. Still, even under these favorable conditions the king was rather successful in creating a sense of solidarity among his subjects. Over fifty years after independence (in 1946), Jordan is a nation-state among others in the Middle East with a very well established national ideology. All elements of this ideology are the result of a tedious effort by the king – put together brick by brick until the wall of unique identity was complete.

Hussein includes many encouragements of unity throughout his speeches. He refers to "true nationalists, tolerant believers, and strong fighters," "Jordan's immortal Journey,"[51] and says that Jordan "is a cohesive and strong country by virtue of an inherited mission." These expressions are in reality the core of the overall message of Jordanian nationalism. They intend to present in a nutshell the message of unity between Islam, Arabism, history, and the fate of the Jordanian nation-state.

Being the product of a Western education, the king linked terms like "people" and "representation" in his political thinking. Thus, the process leading to the international recognition of the Palestinian people was rather problematical for him. Until 1967 his citizens on the West Bank were part and parcel of his own kingdom, serving in parliament and paying taxes to the monarchy. Yet, the consecutive crises outlined in previous chapters, the establishment of the PLO in 1964, and later on, in a much more significant way, the outcome of the 1967 war, underlined the need to define relations between the two banks. Furthermore, even the loss of the West Bank in the context of the 1967 war did not mean a full Jordanian agreement to these people being represented by another body, let alone, a political competitor.

Hussein saw himself as king of the Jordanian people, a people that had two wings until 1967, but then split into two distinct peoples, still keeping their special family ties. They all belong to the larger Arab people. Thus, the dilemma facing the king after 1967 was clear. Had he recognized the people living on the West Bank as belonging to his own nation, that would have constituted a deviation from his own interest in seeing them as not a part of his kingdom, and after the 1974 Rabat resolutions it would also have constituted a violation of the Arab consensus. Yet, giving away all rights of representation would mean giving away a potential springboard for at least a diplomatic campaign involving the kingdom. Obviously, the main obstacle in relating to the West Bank Palestinians as belonging in one way or another to the Jordanian people stemmed from the rise of the PLO. After the civil war, the king alluded several times to his dilemma. On one occasion he even tried[52] to date the Palestinian people back hundreds of years, so that the special relationship between them and the Jordanians would indicate deep historical roots for both peoples. In a word: legitimacy by proxy, or an attempt to use growing Palestinian acceptance for his own purposes. Between the final stages of the civil war in 1971 and the 1985 agreement with Arafat, Hussein tried publicly to define his people – a people inhabiting the two banks – and consequently to work out mutual relations with the Hashemite authority.

Indeed, the 1967 war, as much as it put an end to the unity of the two banks (declared in 1950), legitimized the term "Palestinian nationalism" as a means of mobilizing Arab and international support for the self-determination of a people under occupation. This development forced the king to define the national identity of his entity since the original Palestine included his territory as well, and accordingly he had to emphasize the unique nature of his country to deny the PLO any claims on it. Moreover, putting together the elements of a "Jordan people" had also to justify the very deep Jordanian involvement in Palestinian affairs in the West Bank even after 1967 – this, while refraining from open interference in the international activities of the PLO. However, the urgent and immediate need to define these relations stemmed from the 1970 civil war and the military–political domestic processes. Before that war he still expressed his belief that he had inherited the responsibility of protecting the Palestinian people, its land and rights, even though they enjoyed a separate identity.[53] That did not necessarily mean returning to the old regime of relations between the two banks of the Jordan River, but it clearly indicted his wish to speak for the Palestinians. In the aftermath of that war the king began a political and diplomatic process separating him and his kingdom from the Palestinian people, but never forgetting his traditional fear and concerns stemming from the very rocky past outlined elsewhere in this book. But the above-mentioned considerations along with further emergence of the term "Palestinian nationalism" did not fully separate the Jordanians from the Palestinians in terms of their mutual interest in each other's affairs. That was also an element Hussein had to take into account.[54]

The outcome of those considerations and processes was a series of references, all introducing the concept of a Jordanian people. The main pillar defining the Jordanian people was its existence in its land and country. Therefore, between 1950 and 1967 the concept in retrospect was that of one country, one nation.[55] In this context Hussein spoke of the interdependence between state and nation. In other words, living together under one leader inside the same borders made them all belong to the same people and the same family. The logical result of this concept was that *after* the 1967 war there was no longer one country, and consequently two nations began to exist. In an attempt to refrain from post-1967 definitions and still explain to his various audiences what he really meant he referred to the relations that existed from 1950 to 1967, the time of unity and the two banks. Even though the need to define people, Jordanian people and Palestinian people, was a direct result of the 1967 war, Hussein resorted to historical examples to illustrate his point. In his worldview the inhabitants of the West and East Banks belonged to the same people and family until 1967.

In spite of the frequent use of the term "people," he never defined the full contents of this term. In lieu of that, he used a language that defined their duties,[56] and the necessary nature of relations between the citizens of the two banks of the river. Indeed, the exact nature of relations with the Palestinians was not that clear. After the war they continued to belong to the same family and to share the same destiny,[57] but ceased their common affiliation with the same people. Thus, one cannot belong to the Jordanian nation and the Palestinian nation simultaneously. This does not exclude emotional unity, but only political unity between the two. These ingredients did not change in the wake of the 1967 war; only their wider interpretation changed with the different borders, and hence West Bank Palestinians who used to belong to the same people could not claim this affiliation any more.

Through the king's eyes the main ideological issue facing him was how to include East Bank Palestinians in his concept of Jordanian nationalism. With the ideological groundwork he had laid it was not too complicated since all East Bankers were Jordanians.[58] In one of his interviews after the civil war, for instance, the king spoke[59] of the Jordanian people, making it clear that it was composed of Palestinians and Jordanians together. Although he was not clear where exactly that people lived, the context strongly suggests that it was the East Bank. The elements of this definition become much more noticeable following the Rabat Conference, when the king continually mentioned his support for the united Arab decision to make the PLO the sole representatives of the Palestinian people. It is during this period that he makes the terms "PLO" and "the Palestinian people" synonymous. Yet in his mind Palestinians live on the West Bank and are represented by their organization. This genuine acceptance of the Rabat resolutions is reflected in a variety of terms used:[60] "we are the closer to the Palestinian people," "Palestinian and Jordanian entities strongly tied together," and "one family with unique identities." Clearly, the way Hussein defined these people had a lot to do with contemporary challenges to his regime and policies.

However, one element is demonstrated time and again: the relations between the Palestinian and Jordanian peoples are not the same as the relations of these two peoples with any other Arab people. Even after the loss of the West Bank, the civil war and the Rabat resolutions, all people living in these locations continue to belong to the same family; still a certain degree of unclarity is always kept regarding the exact nature of relations between the two.[61] The term "family" is unclear in this context: what exactly are the interrelations between the three cycles: the Jordanian, the Palestinian–Jordanian, and the Arab? In spite of the lack of clarity, one element should be made crystal clear: Hussein was very careful not to define the special relations as relations between two distinct peoples. Acknowledging such existence would pull the carpet from under his diminishing demand to represent the people living on both sides of the river. Thus, only rarely did he speak[62] in clear-cut terms of Jordanian and Palestinian identities. On such occasions his main thesis was that the Palestinians lived in their own land,[63] which is another territorial definition of a nation; obviously they lived in Palestine – that is, between the Jordan River and the Mediterranean. On all other occasions his most preferred term was "family." The family that is the subject of the king's speeches was wide enough to attract all kinds of interpretations. It is composed of two distinct identities: the Jordanian and the Palestinian;[64] at times they are referred to as two wings of the same people.[65] These two "are united on a variety of issues: similar historical past and current exposure to the same danger."[66] In most cases, Hussein's references with regard to the Palestinians are ambiguous. While he was careful not to include them in his own Jordanian people, he had to emphasize his own special relationship with them. Consequently, the nature of relations between Jordanians and Palestinians is a constant subject of explanations and expressions.

Symbols of Sovereignty

Most of the elements composing Jordanian nationalism take their inspiration from the harsh, daily political realities. It is no wonder that Jerusalem, the Holy City as much as the burial place of the founder of the Arab national movement, Sharif Hussein b. 'Ali, the great-grandfather of the king, is different from other cities. Many of the references to Jerusalem are more emotional and religious than political, but this approach cannot hide the detailed use of Jerusalem as another pillar of Jordanian nationalism. The relation of the centrality of Jerusalem in the minds of his people, Hussein emphasized in line with his grandfather,[67] was not only the obvious Muslim connection, but also from time to time the Christian connection to the city and the justification for *jihad*, which under the present circumstances could not be declared. Strangely enough, this is one of the few cases in which a source of legitimacy rests outside the national territory, very strongly suggesting an element of irredentism – clearly not Jordanian policy towards the territories other than Jerusalem.

Twice or three times a year after 1967 and until his death Hussein used to mention Jerusalem in his public appearances. Those numerous references make it easy to define his legacy in terms of the Holy City. It is composed of two main interwoven ingredients: a definition of Jerusalem's natural and geographical borders for political purposes, and the definition of the political mechanism needed to get Jerusalem out of Israeli occupying hands.

"Arab Jerusalem" is the most common reference to the city. That area includes the Holy Places, the whole of the eastern city, and the Arab neighborhoods surrounding it that should be kept as such – Arab Jerusalem.[68] This general definition does not suggest any opposition to an Israeli presence in Western Jerusalem, yet an Israeli declaration of the city, or any part of it, as the capital city was not acceptable.[69]

The issue of political mechanisms is more complex. For years Hussein did not specify ways of getting back control over Jerusalem. He spoke[70] about the city as being separate from the rest of the occupied territories and therefore as not a part of the overall process; it necessitated a different approach altogether. Securing Arab sovereignty over the city was viewed as a necessary move on the road to a more comprehensive process.[71] On the other hand, with the Oslo process going on and moving further, he had to be satisfied with much less than that. In the Israeli–Jordanian Treaty of

Peace agreement, Jordan was granted a special role in Muslim Holy Shrines in Jerusalem. With that agreement Hussein also gave up his wish to liberate Jerusalem for the Muslim world and for his own family. Clearly, signing this agreement with Israel meant for him giving away the dream he had nurtured for years: to get back for the Hashemite family the third Holy Place of Islam after they had lost the first two in Mecca and Medina, to the Saudis back in the 1920s. That painful association was clearly present in Hussein's mind; it was rarely alluded to in public,[72] but it was definitely part of his drive to establish a foothold once again in Jerusalem.

His emotional connection to Jerusalem and his wish to see it reincorporated into his kingdom led the king, throughout his reign, to separate this issue from the more general question of the territories. Whereas he consistently kept the secret political process with Israel alive he never hinted to the Israeli leaders or his Western allies of any agreement to discuss Jerusalem. Hence his public position, meaning the means to recruit national support for his ideology, was crystal clear: Jerusalem was occupied territory and should be treated in line with Resolution 242,[73] which calls for the return of occupied territories. Obviously, Resolution 181, which calls *inter alia* for a *corpus separatum* for Jerusalem, is problematic in this context. After all, one cannot choose to respect some resolutions and ignore others. In a rare reference to this dilemma he spoke[74] of the need to implement Resolution 181 in its entirety, including the re-partition of Palestine, knowing very well that it was totally impossible, but on another occasion he rejected the idea of Jerusalem as an international city.[75] The practical and diplomatic dimension of these expressions regarding Jerusalem and Resolution 181 will be further discussed in chapter 5.

References to the Jordanian army were made time and again in Hussein's public appearances. They are not made as frequently as the references to Jerusalem but both serve the same purpose: they provide two pillars of sovereignty in the form of national symbols, one spiritual, one materialistic.

If Jerusalem is a source of inspiration and a reason for *jihad*,[76] then the armed forces are the Jordanian connection with the past, the carrier of *jihad* and the unchanging, solid foundation Jordan is built on. Moreover, they connect all other elements of Jordanian nationalism – among them, the whole Arab nation – since their prime directive is the defense of Arab sovereignty, Arab pride, and Arab civilization.[77] Throughout the king's speeches, these expressions tied in very clearly with the concept of Israel as an enemy, since it is the Jordanian army that protects for the Arab nation the longest border with Israel.

The armed forces are in a sense Jordan itself, for the kingdom began with the great Arab Revolt and so did the armed forces.[78] Identifying the armed forces with Jordan, Arabism, and Islam was a recurrent motif in the king's speeches. On many occasions he spoke of the army being the spearhead of Jordan and its defenses. In fact, there is full identification between the 70,000 troops, their families and people, and Jordan itself.

In addition to occupying a clear ideological place, the army is also a weapon to head off any domestic criticism regarding economic conditions. This dimension was evident during the deep economic crisis in 1989, which was explained by the king[79] as being the result of military procurement. The connection he made rendered impertinent any criticism regarding corruption and mismanagement.

In this attempt to put together Hussein's national ideology, the obvious question to be asked is: How successful was he in putting this unique nationalism into action? With advancing time, after the 1967 war and the gradual disengagement from the Palestinian issue, that undertaking became more and more successful. Many of the national challenges to face Jordan in the years leading to the end of Hussein's rule did not reflect a Palestinian–Jordanian dichotomy. Moreover, many Palestinians living in the kingdom, while not giving up their Palestinian identity, present themselves as Jordanians. This definition may in the future affect many Palestinian issues and future relations between East Bank Palestinians and West Bank Palestinians, in that in spite of belonging to the same family, their national allegiances already lie in different political fields.

5

Is Peace Without the Territories Possible? Hussein's Reading of the Palestinian Issue between the Six Day War and UN Resolution 242

A new dawn rose over the Hashemite Kingdom on June 9, 1967. The day before, Hussein spoke to his people in the wake of the cease-fire,[1] which concluded a short but fateful war. On that day he calmly verified with the US whether there was any danger of getting back the West Bank; that is, whether he had to devise any response to a situation similar to 1957 when Israel had had to withdraw from occupied Egyptian territories without an agreement. The US response was reassuring: "I can promise you nothing specific,"[2] the US ambassador in Amman told the Hashemite monarch. Without knowing it Jordan had just entered four years of internal unrest. However, at the cease-fire the king's mood also changed: from the despair reflected in his public appearances during the war, he now exhibited a rather relaxed posture.[3] Was this due to the new realities and the fact that the strategic gamble of the king had paid off, with responsibility for the Palestinian issue resting now with Israel, and the mainland of Jordan, the East Bank, left almost intact? Yet, the price for Jordan was very high in terms of human casualties and loss of war material. Would the gamble be as successful in the years to come? Would the king be able to build a Hashemite Kingdom in the new "Smaller Jordan," which would be able to absorb all East Bank Palestinians and make them into full-fledged Jordanian Hashemite citizens? Indeed, with the guns falling silent, Hussein had to devise a policy that would at the same time present the king as a loyal member of the Arab coalition, thus assuring him and his nation a safe place among Arab states. Concurrent with that he had to build bridges of cooperation and peace with Israel, thus ensuring a security shield for the kingdom.

This double-edged view is best reflected in the public position taken by

Hussein until the summer of 1988: offering full peace in exchange for a full Israeli withdrawal. At the time the Israeli withdrawal in Hussein's speeches is qualified by speaking about small, insignificant changes in the border. This position is indicative since Hussein was well aware of the Israeli stand regarding the *quid pro quo* for peace. Whatever approach was adopted by Israel at different times, it always insisted on giving up much less than 100 percent of the territories, including Jerusalem. Thus, Hussein's demand for such a withdrawal represented his insurance policy that an agreement which would bring him back the West Bank along with its population would never be feasible, and therefore, anything agreed would be less than that: no return at all since 100 percent was not an option, and therefore any agreement would be less than full public peace. Put differently, by taking this track the king pursued true Jordanian national interests: not only did he act to secure his own rule, but considering the dangers to the kingdom, the decisions taken were definitely those of a ruler concerned with the well-being of his nation-state. In a nutshell, the final settlement approach of the king from now on would be twofold: publicly he would claim the West Bank (carefully avoiding most of the time any reference to the Gaza Strip); whereas behind the scenes he would claim only the right of representation of the Palestinians, so that whatever solution might develop on the West Bank it would not endanger the Hashemite regime.

In the months immediately following the war, Hussein built a three-layer approach to the regional issues of Israel and its Arab neighbors. He truly needed and desired peace. His goal and that of his kingdom could in his mind be accomplished through the good services of the United States. Failing that, he preferred[4] a UN intervention that would bring about some internationally agreed-upon formula to pursue a peace process. Meanwhile, he believed in keeping open channels of communication with Israel and thus securing his tactical and military position in the context of the uncertainties involving future Israeli positions and military posture.

Thus, analyzing Hussein's positions in this period involves three elements:

1. The kingdom's circumstances and its contemporary national needs and interests.
2. The positions of pertinent foreign and domestic players – the super-powers, Arab players, among them the Palestinians, and Israel – and the way they affected the formulation of Jordanian national interests.
3. Finally, the synthesis of both of the above and their reflection on the actual positions pursued by Hussein.

The Kingdom's Circumstances and its National Needs: immediate postwar circumstances

Assessing the policy to be taken, Hussein had a mixed bag to reckon with. On the one hand, a series of improved conditions without the West Bank Palestinians, and on the other hand, new challenges to the regime, this time on the East Bank. Already with the cessation of hostilities and in spite of Hussein's sacrificing the West Bank and thus saving the East Bank as a Hashemite Kingdom, the latter itself became a battleground in the struggle with the PLO over sovereignty in the aftermath of the war. The first months after the war and until the November UN Security Council Resolution 242 witnessed a dramatic improvement in the stability of the regime.[5] Surprisingly enough and without any public indication from the throne, most East Bankers were glad to finally be rid of the West Bank.[6] These months were also marked by the spontaneous rise of Jordan to the status of other confrontation states that had stood against the Zionist enemy, and lost the battle. One indication of Hussein's new self-confidence is to be found[7] in his attempt, as early as the cease-fire, to call an urgent Arab summit and agree on one unified Arab stand. The kingdom had waited years to enjoy such a status on the inter-Arab arena. This period also saw the king's efforts to secure the outcome of the war by making a *de facto* peace with Israel without getting back the West Bank. Such an agreement was almost a must for Jordan considering the belief among Western diplomats (which probably made its way to Hussein) that Israel wanted a peace settlement with its neighbor to the east, whatever the price.[8] A peace move had to be accomplished without going through the Israeli–Jordanian channel, which had lost its significance during the period between the war and the November 1967 Security Council resolution, although still in existence. It was replaced in importance by the US–Jordanian link, which saw the introduction of new thinking in Washington. That process of American deliberations and study of the new Middle East realities, codenamed Sandstorm, served as the basis for the US proposal that Israel and Jordan should reach a working agreement under US sponsorship. The Sandstorm ideas were mainly based on ideas expressed by Hussein himself during the weeks following the war.

In the aftermath of the war several difficulties emerged, most of them to do with the Palestinian issue. One of the ill effects of the 1967 war was the influx of some 300,000 refugees from the West Bank to the East Bank,[9] which Jordan had tried to limit through its appeal to the Great Powers to convince Israel "not to send the West Bank population out to be refugees."[10] The Israeli policy of "open bridges," which opened the door for further Jordanian involvement in the life of the West Bankers, allowed Jordan to try and influence developments without being formally responsible for the territory. Unlike the prewar conditions, the king had no more territorial assets to sacrifice, and the upcoming battle was over the very existence of Jordan as a unique Hashemite nation-state distinct from a Palestinian republic. In his struggle the king expressed the public position he held as a result of his need to respond to moves by Israel and the Palestinians in his immediate circle, and the superpowers on the outer circle. Throughout his intricate network of contacts – some public, some secret – the king was able to build a secret framework that would bring about the political realities he was interested in. In a nutshell Hussein acted during these months and later years to ensure that the West Bank would never again serve as a base for activity against his kingdom. He preferred his interests to be accomplished through a concerted effort with Israel, and without getting back any territory. This policy, if implemented, would have to present the king as a champion of peace in the Middle East and a full member of the family of Arab states. It was also aimed at simultaneously getting political support from the US and financial support from the oil-rich Arab countries.

Indeed, another major Hashemite concern had to do with the Jordanian national economy. Even though the immediate picture was not too encouraging, the outlook for the future was much more optimistic. Prior to the war, estimates put the domestic income of the government for 1967 around 32 million Jordanian dinars, whereas it was adjusted to 21 million JD after the war.[11] This compared with prewar estimated expenditure of 49 million JD. Moreover, the West Bank contributed 35–40 percent of the Jordanian Gross National Product. However, this gloomy picture should be somewhat modified to reflect the fact that most Jordanian investments in infrastructure were not lost during the war. After all, in 1966 about 90 percent of all public-sector investments were in the East Bank. This is a clear indication of the preference given to the East Bank and also an illustration of the point that the June defeat was much more than the loss of the West Bank, and a significant military defeat. But it was not a strategic blow to the very existence of the kingdom. Moreover, based on 1966 figures any swift return of the West Bank would have meant continued movement of about 10,000 workers each year from the West Bank to the East Bank, making unemployment a little more problematic. With the June 1967 war over, that annual supplement had to be absorbed by Israel, relieving the kingdom from any concern for their employment.

Thus, in the wake of the war the most pressing issue was the need to rehabilitate the army, which obviously was given first priority. The rehabilitation of the army along with a new reorganization plan (see chapter 6), all implemented within three months after the war, put another burden on the Jordanian economy. Even though the term "rehabilitation" referred to morale and war material, and in spite of the blow to the prestige of the army, most of the officers, being East Bankers, could not have been too sad to lose the domestic threat from the Palestinians, who were under-represented in the army. After all, most Palestinians did not fight for the West Bank.

All these considerations, along with rising unemployment,[12] combined to produce a major economic crisis in the months immediately after the war. Under these circumstances any hasty return of the West Bank to Jordan, which was only theoretical at this point, would have meant deepening the crisis and exposing the Hashemite regime to even more critical confrontation with its dissatisfied and hungry citizens. All this while the recent dramatic events were still too close to allow for arrangements with any economic power to try and cover some of the unexpected Jordanian expenses. Thus, in every political and diplomatic move, Jordan had to take into account the interests of prospective powers that might bail the kingdom out. These powers, the regional oil-rich countries and the United States, were obviously known for their moderate policies. However, they all believed in one way or another that the West Bank should return to Jordan, a position Hussein accepted publicly while having grave doubts about its applicability to his kingdom.

With the war over, Hussein had to finally find a way out of his foreign and domestic difficulties prior to the war and secure the continued existence of his kingdom. Succinctly put they were divided into three main groups:

1. The in-house Palestinian threat had now to be transformed from a Hashemite attempt to curtail their hostile activity on the West Bank into a positive effort to make the remaining Palestinians on the East Bank full and equal Jordanian citizens. This policy had begun in the early 1960s, but owing to the developing circumstances described and analyzed in this book, it underwent significant changes after 1963. Such policy after the war had to take into account the interrelations between the Palestinians of the two banks, including family ties, and to try and work out with Israel a way to eliminate the West Bank as a hotbed of subversive activities against the two countries. In this Hussein was supported by the surprising degree of sympathy for him shown by West Bank Palestinians,[13] and the Israeli policy of "open bridges," which allowed Jordan to financially support the West Bank and gain access through the king's actions. Naturally, a hostile attitude in the West Bank might have spilled over to the East Bank.

Success on this level would have brought about the elimination of any PLO attempt to use East Bank Palestinians as a subversive force. On this level the new, more convenient atmosphere regarding Jordan in the Arab world helped the king. Past precedents taught[14] that domestic opposition flourished only as far as it was assisted by foreign powers. Thus, in the immediate aftermath of the war the potential for meaningful subversive opposition was remarkably low compared with the prewar months and years. However, there was no way of telling, in light of the traumatic military and political shock of June 1967, if this precedent was not going to change.

2. The inter-Arab siege, which had affected Jordanian policies and political behavior prior to the June war, had to be broken. The lynchpin holding all hostile forces together was Nasserite Egypt. Thus, any Jordanian policy line to be followed had to use the weakening position of Egypt and yet not alienate President Nasser in a way that would lead him, in spite of his troubles, to renew subversive activity against Jordan. Indeed, the first indications after the war were positive from Hussein's point of view. His defeat made Nasser more amenable than ever to a diplomatic process, though not necessarily similar to the one led by Hussein. But clearly in the post-June period he did not see the military option as the one and only way to deal with Israel.[15]

3. With the almost indifferent reaction of the United States to the 1963 and 1966 crises, during which the very existence of the Hashemite dynasty was at stake, the king had to reconvince this superpower of the need for a strong Jordan.

This short list of cardinal priorities explains why Hussein's main concern was not a formal treaty,[16] which was anyway dependent on the unrealistic expectation that Israel would withdraw from the West Bank and Jerusalem in their entirety, but rather a way to avoid Jordan being flooded by a million Palestinian refugees and allow it to keep its identity as the Jordanian, not Palestinian, nation-state he envisioned. Any agreement had to be a means for cohesion and survival rather than an end in itself. The king's reading of possible regional diplomatic and political contingencies led him to believe that the refugee issue was as pivotal to the security of Jordan as it was to the well-being of Israel, whose traditional policy since 1948 was one of resisting the Palestinian refugees' "right of return." His consideration was not limited to the East Bank: his true interest in the West Bank was the curtailing of any potential threat from the emergence of a leadership hostile to the Hashemites. Accordingly, the first priority in the king's mind was to resume his relations with the notables of the West Bank. The best scenario would see a Palestinian leadership capable of working hand in hand with Jordan, especially in Jerusalem. A less favorable scenario would only avert a possible collapse of the local leadership, be it friendly or hostile to Jordan, which might have resulted in a wave of refugees leaving for the East Bank.

Only one more element within the larger framework of the desired solution equaled this in significance and it had to do with the sense of isolation developed in the years of President Nasser. Jordan needed an outlet to the Mediterranean, free of any potential for Egypt to tamper with Jordanian interests. Thus, an effective working solution had to include a settlement of the refugee issue at their current locations, using the Gaza Strip as the natural environment, under Jordanian auspices. The corridor allowed to Jordan for that area would at the same time be used to grant it the long-desired access to the Mediterranean.[17]

No Arab leader, as can be judged from the material available today, was made privy to the true Jordanian position. Western and Israeli leaders, on the other hand, were made more aware of the nature of his needs and constraints, but not of his wish to accomplish the elements mentioned above as part of a peace plan. Not long after the war was over the king left for a lengthy tour overseas. The first postwar trip, between June 24 and July 7, 1976, took him to Italy, France, the US, Britain, Greece and Egypt. During this trip he underlined[18] Jordan's need for physical rehabilitation of the East Bank and the army in exchange for peace. While initial thoughts regarding the future of the Middle East were exchanged, the king was careful enough not to suggest any concrete formula for peace under which he would be given back the West Bank. Still, even at that early stage he distinguished between Jerusalem and the rest of the West Bank.[19]

The Positions of Pertinent Players as seen from Jordan

One tangible accomplishment emanating from the outcome of the war was the dramatic change in Jordan's position in the Middle East. This improvement was only enhanced as a result of the Khartoum summit conference in August. This change gave the king that extra self-confidence necessary for presenting his ideas regarding future peaceful relations in the region. The change manifested itself in several ways:[20]

1. Jordan no longer served as a target of attacks by other Arab countries.
2. Egypt, the most vehement of enemies, voiced public support for the king.
3. The two superpowers agreed on the need to prevent a new war in the Middle East. That meant an extra bolstering of Jordan's position, being the only country of the confrontation states which stood to lose its very existence in the event of a new war.

Under these conditions, the main uncertainty facing the king was how to legitimize his intended peace negotiations with Israel, since his apprehension of breaking Arab ranks was the main stumbling block keeping him from publicizing his peaceful intentions – this became phase one in his plan. In his negotiations with the US he urged an early move leading to some progress: a joint US–USSR decision imposing on the Arab countries an end to the state of belligerency with Israel. The reasoning behind such a move is obvious: the Arab countries, in the immediate aftermath of the war, could not resist any such pressure, whereas Israel did not oppose such an action. The US for its part believed[21] that the United Nations should appoint a special peace emissary to the region, and that the Israeli–Jordanian peace negotiations would be held behind his back, using him as a camouflage for the real peace process. Hussein himself, on the eve of the approval of UN Security Council Resolution 242, saw[22] such a mechanism as being the right channel for direct negotiations, and consequently he was actively involved in its formulation.

One of Hussein's major assets in the months following the war was the defeated Egypt and its leader, President Nasser, who still enjoyed the popular prestige associated with his reputation as the "leader of the Arab," though it was rapidly disappearing. In those months Nasser symbolized disillusion with past concepts and beliefs. Still, Hussein was at his side at the worst of times, namely the June defeat (misled by Nasser according to most Jordanians[23]), connived with him against the Western superpowers, and shared the same lot. At this juncture no one in the Arab world could accuse the king, as had been done previously, of being a Western stooge. Once and for all the king could rid himself of the old Hashemite reputation of preferring Western interests over Arab interests. However, lest President Nasser forget these lessons, Hussein repeated time and again that he had been in effect almost an innocent victim of his reliance on the Egyptian military umbrella.[24] Many Jordanians shared this belief and resented Egypt. Egypt had erred and consequently many other Arab countries paid a price. The logical result of this line was that Egypt had now to lead the way in finding a solution; failing that, all other countries, Jordan included, would be free to pursue their own independent path.

Jordan's position regarding Israel between June and November was basically composed of two considerations: the tactical, namely to eliminate any immediate danger of resumed hostilities; and the strategic, to find the right avenue to bring full and comprehensive peace between the two countries without getting back the occupied Jordanian territories.

On the tactical level Jordan had a major problem with the expeditionary forces deployed on its territory and PLO elements moving their center of activity from the West Bank to the East Bank. Those units, from Iraq and Saudi Arabia, had their own agendas, obviously emanating from Baghdad and Riyadh respectively. If the latter was at least potentially of the same persuasion as the monarchy of Jordan, that was not true of Iraq. This country, the only major power fighting Israel in 1948 not to have signed an armistice agreement, had been a republic since 1958 after a bloody anti-Hashemite revolution. At least potentially the Iraqi units in Jordan had an interest in keeping up a steady war of attrition against Israel. This would serve the PLO, which in turn would contribute to the destabilization of the Hashemite regime and might lead to a regime more agreeable to that of Iraq. This presence and its consequences were not to the liking of most Jordanians, who did not like the foreigners.[25] These concerns were on the mind of the king immediately after the end of hostilities and he looked for ways to limit the Iraqi–Israeli confrontation on account of Jordan.

It is hard to determine who initiated Hussein's first meeting with a leading Israeli figure after the war. The United States needed more time to discuss with the king the necessary elements for a new diplomatic approach to the conflict; Israel, as Pedatzur puts it,[26] favored a Palestinian option, and even the king's approach was rather strange. An Israeli source suggests that during this first meeting with a leading Israeli figure Hussein was rather vague in terms of future borders and relations with Israel. The same source, quoting the minutes of the Hussein–Jacob Herzog meeting, on July 2, 1967, describes a general conversation on the outcome of the war, with some evasive references by Hussein to the issue of peace. The king even neglected to speak on the need to see Israel withdrawing from the West Bank. This conversation with the then director-general of the Israeli prime minister's office was puzzling to Israeli observers. They believed President Nasser of Egypt had authorized the king to get the West Bank back from Israel in exchange for Jordan discontinuing the state of belligerency that had existed between the two countries since 1948. Years later it would be revealed[27] that that was indeed the position of the Egyptian president.

Israel's failure to comprehend the true meaning of the king's evasive language led to another mistake:[28] on July 4, 1967, the prime minister of Israel nominated an inter-departmental committee to suggest a negotiating strategy, which on July 18 proposed ways of making peace between the two countries. The main fault of this initiative was not the issue of the West Bank, since it did not say a word on the future of the territory, in line with an Israeli cabinet resolution of June 19 regarding future peace moves that said nothing regarding this territory. The only reference to the West Bank was the call for its demilitarization. The possibility of an Israeli withdrawal from the West Bank was not precluded but was not a part of the plan. Thus, even though the king was prepared for a far-reaching agreement he was waiting for the US response to his ideas and refrained from giving a clear message to Herzog on July 2 in London. Since the US–Jordanian negotiations at that point were already rather detailed it is probably a strong indication that an agreement on Sandstorm was indeed being shaped between these two players. However, none of the parties immediately passed on to Israel the detailed peace blueprint Jordan presented to the US. This, in spite of the degree of risk the king was willing to take upon himself, which was incompatible with any diplomatic move he had made in the past.

Indeed the king's position presented an enigma to the US as well. Only three months later President Johnson's security advisor Walt W. Rostow suspected[29] that Hussein was interested in reaching a peace deal through direct negotiations with Israel that would not involve the return of the West Bank to Jordan. However, in July the working assumption of the US, later confirmed by Hussein himself,[30] was that President Nasser of Egypt gave his blessing to Hussein, in the wake of the war, to reach an agreement with Israel. The strings attached were that there should be no peace treaty and no direct negotiations. With the sound of gunfire still in the air he was determined to make a full and comprehensive peace with Israel as long as his definition of the Jordanian national interest would be met. Getting back the West Bank was definitely not one of these interests. Against this background the emerging Israeli position could not have come at a better time. On 8 July 1967, Prime Minister Eshkol said, in an interview with *Le Monde*,[31] that it was possible to consider the establishment of an autonomous Palestinian regime to include all the large population centers on the West Bank. That state would establish ties of various kinds with Israel. The next day, Hussein said: "We have rejected every idea of dealing with our problem as a Jordanian problem and we shall continue to do so as there is a ray of hope for . . . a Summit Conference."[32] Whether that was a direct response or a reconfirmation of a traditional stance, such a Jordanian approach does not rule out the possibility of agreement to a solution that would not restore Jordanian sovereignty over the West Bank. Actually, implementing such an approach would have advanced Jordanian national interests, as long as Jordan enjoyed some degree of influence over the formation of that entity and as long as the rest of the Arab leaders agreed upon it at a summit conference.

June to November 1967 marked for Hussein a break with the past of being presented as a pawn state taking its orders from the West. It was not only Jordan's fighting shoulder to shoulder with Egypt, and sharing the disastrous outcome of the war. It was also Hussein's very significant role in putting together with President Nasser the story of the American and British involvement in the fighting on Israel's side. This approach, so annoying to the two Western players, along with the decline in Nasser's standing, helped the king to pursue his pre-planned policy of holding substantial talks with the US regarding a peaceful future in the Middle East.

If during the crises of 1963 and 1966 the US had refrained from any military intervention on behalf of Jordan, this time it suggested a new approach. A mutual Israeli–Jordanian working agreement that would lead not to a full public peace, but to the elimination of exposure to the explosive potential of the Palestinians. The exact date of this approach, referred to as Sandstorm, is not clear from contemporary documents, but it did not yet exist during the visit of the Jordanian foreign minister, Ahamd Tuqan, to Washington in mid-July 1967 shortly after the royal visit,[33] or it was not revealed to him. Another indication of the new US approach to Israeli–Jordanian relations was to be found in the *quid pro quo* for the king's acceptance of the Sandstorm ideas. It had to be the resumption of arms shipments to Jordan, but only after receiving Israeli consent for them. The price Israel had to pay was that it would not develop its own independent channels to Jordan. Even before the beginning of Sandstorm the US was apparently behind the British refusal to serve as a channel to the king.[34] However, as realistic as the American plan was, it failed to realize one major element in Hussein's thinking: it indeed distinguished between Jerusalem and the West Bank, as the king did, but its starting point was that the king desired the return of both.[35] On the issue of Jerusalem the US indicated to its ambassador in Tel Aviv, probably with the government of Israel in mind as the final destination, that it was ready to deviate from its traditional public policy of internationalizing Jerusalem. In the words of Secretary Rusk,[36] in line with the position already voiced to the partners in the past and in secret: "We could probably accept any solution on which GOI [Government of Israel] and Hussein could agree." Again, here was a major US contribution to one of Jordan's main national symbols – its share in sovereignty over Jerusalem. Interestingly enough, Jordan followed the US example and while resisting the internationalizing plan prescribed by UN General Assembly Resolution 181 of November 29, 1947, Hussein publicly supported the partition plan.[37]

Sandstorm might indicate a new concept in protecting the existence of Jordan, consisting mainly of adopting the Jordanian approach and presenting it to Israel as a US proposal[38] after some minor modifications. The US adopted an asymmetrical approach to the two major players, based mainly on the survival interests of Jordan: Israel had to be pressured into the Sandstorm process whereas Jordan had only to be advised of the positive outcome of this process.[39] The American approach was that any agreement had in the first place to solve two major issues: the refugees, and Jerusalem, that is, the two most disturbing questions for Jordan. Moreover, any agreement had to eliminate any possibility of any Palestinian entity in the territories, under whatever name; again, a translation of an Israeli–Jordanian common interest into American policy. The US analysis weighed the possible consequences of the lack of a peaceful settlement between the two countries – in the first place, the distintegration of Jordan one way or another.

However, the United States and Great Britain did not read into the king's words what it was he was really saying. They insisted on defining the nature of the issue of future relations with Israel in territorial terms, an obvious mistake while listening to the king's public appearances[40] and not distinguishing between his public-consumption rhetoric and his behind-the-scenes expressions of true Jordanian national interests. In mid-September, for instance, this inner Western discussion centered on the need to urge the king, albeit in a very careful way, to hurry up the peace process in order "to get back most of the West Bank . . . and being able to negotiate a satisfactory agreement about Jerusalem."[41] In November, the US ambassador to the UN, Arthur Goldberg, reaffirmed US commitment to "Israeli withdrawal from all Arab territories,"[42] but with some modifications on the Israeli–Jordanian line. The Western misreading of Hussein's true intentions led him to reconsider his position. During November 1967, with his failure to secure an acceptable agreement through the US, Hussein took a different line and considered other ways to try and bring about the solution he desired. In early November he was looking into ways to distance himself from the Western approach of trying to convince him to negotiate an agreement over the West Bank. His attitude at that point,[43] at least the one publicly expressed, was that such an agreement should be part and parcel of a more comprehensive process, or in other words, that the issue of the territories should not be discussed separately between Israel and Jordan. Rather, it was now much more of an Arab issue to be discussed as one with the United States. Lest the message be lost on his audience he repeated it in late November in a *Le Monde* interview,[44] expressing his hope that the appointment of a mediator by a UN Security Council resolution would open the way to discussions. Obviously, he did not repeat in public his past observation that such a figure would enable the two countries' true negotiations to be held behind his back, an idea borrowed from the US in earlier contacts.[45]

Re-shaping the Term "Peace" in the Face of Domestic and External Pressures

The overt processes led mainly to the formulation of uncompromising public positions, whereas the true Jordanian position was much more complex. Thus, its partners in negotiations, Israel and the United States, and partly Britain, gradually discovered the secret and innovative Jordanian disposition. The public Jordanian position towards the Palestinian issue and Israel was initially molded by a succession of military and diplomatic challenges stemming from the realities after June 1967, and later the deliberations leading to Resolution 242. Simultaneously, Israel and the US pressed the king for some open demonstration of goodwill towards Israel leading to some public agreement. Hussein for his part confided[46] in his allies that he could not afford himself such a gesture lest he be blamed for making a diplomatic move before even setting foot on occupied Arab land. The delicate maneuvering of the king between the PLO, the West and East Bank Palestinians, Israel and the US led him to devise a response to the new challenges: a secret non-belligerency agreement with Israel, leading to full normalization, without getting back the West Bank. This policy had to be the outcome of a two-phase diplomatic process: first, Jordanian–US agreement on the ingredients of the settlement, then, a secret process with Israel behind the back of a UN-nominated emissary, to be appointed by a Security Council resolution.

This approach guided Hussein throughout the deliberations leading up to Resolution 242 and eventually to his acceptance of the resolution, based on his own interpretation.[47] This policy was also in line with the UAR, which also accepted the resolution and agreed to the nomination of the Jarring mission. The emissary had already visited the two countries in late December 1967. However, a few years later he would explain[48] that his agreement to Resolution 242 was in line with the Khartoum summit conference resolutions and the Arab agreement to leave Egypt and Jordan free to choose their policies regarding the territories. Furthermore, his understanding[49] was that Israel would withdraw from the occupied territories within six months of the acceptance of Resolution 242. Did he really mean to resume a political presence on the West Bank six months after 242? Was that a reasonable position or only an excuse to accept a resolution he had helped to inspire? Knowing the depths of relations with Israeli leaders it is doubtful whether he believed the resolution would still be applicable in six months.

Anyway, accepting 242 did not deter Hussein from keeping the secret track with Israel open while, behind the scenes, very carefully designing his renouncement of the 1950 Jordanian claim to sovereignty over the West Bank. During these formative months the Hashemite policy was the result of interplay between innovation and reaction on three levels. Militarily, combating the PLO; diplomatically, towards the West Bank, an attempt to stay close to local centers of power; while towards the international community, building the necessary tools to eventually separate the West Bank from the East Bank with minimal risk to the Hashemites. All of these brought the king closer to the realization of his vision of a "Smaller Jordan" on the East Bank.

When assessing Hussein's position regarding peace in the Middle East the question should be rephrased. It was no longer whether he was willing to make some unclear agreement, but rather how he would lead the US to put a peace plan in place in a way that would enable him to accept it. In spite of his traditional uncertainty over a possible reaction by President

Nasser, the king notified[50] the US and Great Britain on July 12, 1967, of his reading of the new Arab–Israeli realities. This secret approach came in the wake of his public announcement that he had no interest in an independent Jordanian channel to the postwar discussions.[51] As he disclosed[52] years later, at about that time he agreed with President Nasser that each of the Arab parties would refrain from separate deals, since Nasser had already agreed that Hussein would get the West Bank from the US as long as it was not "a separate peace treaty." Secretly, his assessment was that "Jordan could not wait indefinitely for return [of the] West Bank," and therefore must pursue a discrete path leading to a separate Israeli–Jordanian agreement. Consequently, on July 18, 1967, the State Department Control Group dealing with the Middle East situation notified[53] the special National Security Council committee of the king's willingness "to make a unilateral settlement with Israel." This obviously depended on the not yet secured Israeli agreement to withdraw from 100 percent of the territory. A few days later the king elaborated on his previous message and placed his vision of peace and settlement with Israel in the global and regional context.[54]

The Arab summit conference in Khartoum, Sudan (August 29–September 1, 1967), was successful in getting an Arab consensus to its resolutions and making Egypt and Jordan recognized as worthy of receiving subsidies from the oil-rich countries to help them recover from the consequences of the war.[55] Indeed, in spite of the three "no"s (no peace, no negotiations, and no recognition of Israel), there was no longer the traditional call for non-diplomatic moves against Israel. However, even these mild resolutions, compared with past summit meetings, could not convince Hussein that he could publicly talk to Israel and get away with it. On the other hand, the resolution rejecting any negotiations with Israel did not specifically mention negotiations through third parties like the US or the UN. Furthermore, an agreement without getting back the West Bank would undoubtedly have been seen by other Arab leaders as a sell-out of the Arab cause, being contradictory to one of the resolutions calling for the return of the occupied land. Concurrent with the summit, anti-Hussein sentiment became widespread in the territories,[56] reminding the king once again of his past lessons not to try to speak for the Palestinians and that any agreement might revive the risk to his kingdom from this population. With all this happening, the king could only watch hopelessly,[57] and with alarm, as Palestinian refugees, even from the Gaza Strip, crossed to his kingdom, threatening to upset once more the internal balance of power. His insistence on continuing his political and economic ties with the West Bank obviously could not have even the same partial effect he had enjoyed over this territory during prewar times.

Fast recovering from the outcome of the war, the king was clear in the message he conveyed to world leaders. In a nutshell he wanted peace, but without using this term as long as he was the only Arab leader to reach it. In line with his habit in public appearances he did not deliver his message in one piece, but rather, built it slowly so that his counterparts would be made gradually aware of his true intentions. The main tenor of the above-mentioned first postwar trip, in private meetings and public appearances, was that Jordan was willing to work for a peace settlement in the Middle East.[58]

Using the term "peace" under the contemporary circumstances was in itself a landmark. Indeed, removing the major initial psychological impediment in the way of negotiations with Israel, Hussein was willing to move further. Clearly, once the barrier was broken, and the political debate centered on the contents of peaceful relations with Israel rather than the mere concept, the individual players could fill in the details. At that stage, six weeks after the war and about three weeks after the resumption of negotiations,[59] the king was willing to make full peace with Israel. However, he was careful enough to indicate that publicly it would be referred to as "non-belligerency." The format he preferred for reaching peace was a two-stage approach: first, secret Jordanian–US negotiations on the mechanism and contents, and later, secret Israeli–Jordanian negotiations with full US participation. The participation of Jordanians would be introduced only at the second stage. Clearly, no Jordanians could take part until it was clear that there was a chance for peace. In this way the king tried to avoid the embarrassment his grandfather had experienced, who had found it impossible to get his cabinet to approve an agreement with Israel back in 1950. This approach, unknown to the ministers, led them to some paradoxical political behavior resulting from their ignorance. Even his foreign minister, Ahamd Tuqan, warned[60] the US against pushing Jordan into a separate peace at a time when the king was putting together the details of his version of a political settlement.

As well as continuing the lifelong wish of Abdullah for coexistence, Hussein added a term that would become, years later, a key word in Israel–Arab peace negotiations: "normalization." For him, any peace treaty had to include at least the following three ingredients: a solution to the refugee problem, a Mediterranean outlet, and overflight rights. This modest list incorporates the major guarantees for the survival of the Hashemite Kingdom. First, and perhaps the most important element: any solution to the refugee issue would have to guarantee that Jordan would not be flooded by Palestinians, would keep its Jordanian nature and thus would continue to exist as an independent entity. Secondly, it was necessary to bypass the Egyptian ability to close the Red Sea straits at any time in the future (in July 1967 that was only a remote possibility since Israel controlled the straits).

The impression gathered from contemporary evidence is that repeating the expression "the return of the occupied lands" was merely lip service, but never something to be accomplished. The picture is different when dealing with the term "normalization," supposedly much more significant to Hussein. Indeed, he was very modest in explaining the Jordanian interpretation of this term. Although there are no details of the way he saw the Israeli definition of it, he had at least two reliable sources to bring him in on it. First, his continued negotiations with Israeli leaders prior to the war; and secondly, his very close relations with the Iranian Shah. The latter for years enjoyed *de facto* diplomatic relations with Israel, which were kept half-secret.

The accumulated body of documents, minutes and public speeches all attest to Hussein's wish to live in peace with Israel, without making it public, and without using this term, which was barred from the Arab political vocabulary at the Khartoum summit. The best alternative for this unattainable objective was declaring the need to achieve peace in stages,[61] and in the meantime putting an end to the state of belligerency between Israel and Jordan, and replacing this with full normalization.

During his conference with the prime minister of Great Britain, Harold Wilson, Hussein made two points[62] which would characterize his attitude in relation to the final status of the Middle East for years to come. First, the Arab–Israeli conflict had begun in 1948, and the armed confrontation in 1967 was in fact the final phase of that war. Therefore, with the main bones of contention between Israel and Jordan removed, the time had come for peace. Obviously, he spoke about peace between the Arab side and Israel, but the way he presented his views left nothing to be guessed. The king was searching for a way to conclude any agreement with Israel. Clearly with his insistence,[63] right after the end of the war, on a unified Arab position, he ruled out the possibility of an early return of the West Bank. After all, Hussein could envision the differences of opinion among the Arab leaders, and the disagreement over possible ways to regain the territories lost. Under these circumstances it is possible to assume that the king began an attempt to initiate a second track: while talking of a secret agreement with Israel through the US services, he tried to secure his newly acquired acceptance by the Arab leaders led by President Nasser.

After detailing the necessary elements of a full peace settlement, including full and public mutual recognition, Hussein turned to other issues. Only in this part of his initiative did he speak of the need to change the old armistice lines. Moreover, as he declared elsewhere,[64] Jordan and Israel had not had any formal borders before the 1967 war. Those were simply the lines of the positions at which battles came to an end back in 1948. Still, at the end of hostilities in 1967,[65] he believed that this question, which obviously had to be reflected on the ground, would have to wait until final peace, including *de jure* recognition, could be agreed upon. He expressed his understanding that only then would an agreement on final borders be arrived at. However, in contrast to the minor reference made to the question of borders (not even the issue of the territories, or the West Bank, or the Palestinians), he did not refrain from speaking on the issue of Jerusalem. In his mind, this was the only issue that would serve as a precondition for negotiations.

Even though Hussein never stopped using the phrase: "the return of the occupied lands," he was never too specific about it. It is impossible to find a call for the return of the territories to Jordanian hands; it is almost always "Arab" hands.

His true concern had to do with Jerusalem and his hope[66] of eliminating the emergence of any hostile leadership. Indeed, not the least significant was the central place he devoted in his presentations to the issue of Jerusalem.[67] He accentuated, as he did time and again in his public appearances, the Islamic significance of Jerusalem, and appealed for its restoration to the Hashemite family. The distinction between Jerusalem and the West Bank is striking: Jerusalem must be returned to Hashemite hands. Both Israel and Jordan on the other hand, leave the West Bank, which unlike Jerusalem was not annexed to Israel, open for future negotiations. Thus, the West Bank is not mentioned[68] in the clear and unequivocal way Jerusalem is treated. Furthermore, instead of bringing up the Palestinian issue of the West Bank the king usually alludes to the question of Jordanian access to the Mediterranean through Israeli territory, a distinct Jordanian national interest. However, even on this most sensitive issue and less than a month after Israel annexed[69] East Jerusalem, Hussein was careful enough to leave a wide space for negotiations with Israel. His message in this context[70] was that: "Israeli sovereignty over all Jerusalem would bring out the worst . . ." – a possible indication of some compromise on the final status of Jerusalem. Perhaps re-dividing the city, with full access rights to the Jewish Holy Places, might have been a basis for a settlement, as indicated[71] by the Jordanian foreign minister.

The Khartoum Arab Summit Conference and the Change in Hussein's Position

The culmination of Hussein's disappointment with the US position caused a change in his own positions between Khartoum and Resolution 242. Uncertainty regarding his next moves replaced the feeling among the Western powers that he was about to make some sort of a coexistence agreement with Israel.[72] Even though the US had already established[73] a secret communication channel between the two countries, and Foreign

Minister Eban of Israel had already communicated with the king, no agreement was in sight. Moreover, the US totally missed the points Hussein was trying to make: he needed a framework for some strategic alliance with Israel, thereby removing the Palestinian risk to his East Bank rule. He did not wish any return to the pre-1967 conditions, which had threatened his Hashemite Kingdom in the past. Time and again he said precisely this to Western audiences, but to no avail. On one of these occasions, in a TV interview in Britain, later reported by diplomatic channels to Washington,[74] he could not have been more open and clear: "the map of Israel's borders had to 'basically go back to what it was'." He did not specify under whose sovereignty it should be. In fact, throughout his references to the final status of the territories he refrained from a clear-cut call for a return to Hashemite sovereignty.

In historical retrospect, the next turning point came in the form of UN Security Council Resolution 242 of November 22, 1967, a resolution that matched the early American idea of establishing a red herring to enable secret and open negotiations between the parties. However, by that time the king was probably fully aware of his inability to convince the US to move towards peace his way. Therefore, the November milestone really represents the loss of a historical opportunity to make an early peace between Israel and Jordan. Had the US not insisted on the return of the West Bank to Jordan, perhaps history would have been different. Moreover, in spite of the resumption of direct Israeli–Jordanian negotiations at that period, the messages exchanged were not too substantial or sufficient for Israel to ascertain the true Jordanian intentions.

The missed peace had five elements: secret non-belligerency; no return of the West Bank to Jordan; a Hashemite presence in Jerusalem; a lasting US guarantee of the survival of Jordan; and the encouragement of moderate Palestinians on the West Bank while totally ignoring the PLO.

6

The Israeli and Palestinian Challenge

A double-pronged challenge is probably the best description of the period between Resolution 242 and the final crushing of the civil war in the summer of 1971. On the one hand, there were the two aspects of the Palestinian challenge: the military effort to take over sovereignty over parts of the East Bank, and the diplomatic effort in every international and regional arena to claim the right to represent all Palestinians. The other arm was Israel, with which Hussein conducted a dangerous game: military confrontation along the common border supplemented by a secret diplomatic process aiming at reaching a diplomatic solution to the conflict that would not stain the king as a collaborator in the eyes of his fellow Arab leaders. During this period of about four years the king once again was plunged into the depths of despair, only to prevail once again.

Perhaps the main test of Jordanian nationalism came in this period since the accumulation of challenges was unmatched by the 1967 ordeal. After all, the loss of the West Bank was a blessed consequence of a short, albeit disastrous, war. Now, there were times when it looked as though the very existence of Jordan was about to be lost. The above-mentioned challenges were supplemented by a score of domestic and external issues: the loyalty of the East Bank citizens, Palestinian as well as Trans-Jordanian, was called into question, and even the allegiance of his prime minister for most of the period, Bahjat Talhuni, could not be taken for granted. On the inter-Arab scene, there was no success in bringing Nasser, with whom Hussein had reasonable working relations, closer to the Hashemite point of view in regard to the developing internal Palestinian threat. The failure in achieving peace with Israel, the growing domestic Palestinian challenge, and later the civil war brought to mind once again the old feeling of being besieged; from both within and without.[1] Moreover, the sense of one national Jordanian nation-state had not been reached yet and loyalty to the Hashemite Kingdom was limited at times to the king and his devoted assistants. Each crisis confronted the king with another factor in the kingdom's security and survival. Analyzing the development of Jordanian national interests, and their pursuit in relation to the two continuous crises and processes with Israel and the Palestinians, leads to a better understanding of the constraints and impediments on the way to King Hussein's attaining his defined and declared national goals. In March 1968 the Israeli attack on Karameh led to a PLO–Hashemite coalition and the preservation of Hashemite sovereignty, but with a major boost to PLO prestige. In 1970 it was the Israeli–Hashemite coalition which won the civil war over sovereignty in the East Bank. Meanwhile, efforts continued within the kingdom to secure domestic loyalty, while out of the kingdom most of the period saw the continuation of direct Israeli–Jordanian secret negotiations. Basically, they were aimed at defining common ground in a mutual agreement to work towards the maintenance of the status quo and the continued existence of the kingdom.

On the far horizon, but still with enormous effect on Jordan's future, the US continued its Sandstorm policy of attempting to make peace in the Middle East. In the immediate region, Egypt (the UAR), Syria and Israel were entangled in a bitter, static war of attrition. Within the kingdom the PLO was trying to re-establish itself after being forced by the Israeli army to flee the West Bank. All these issues, and mainly the combined pressure of the Israeli and Palestinian dimensions, built up to a major crisis in the summer of 1970, after boiling down to a series of turning points which helped in shaping a new term in the king's efforts to redefine Jordanian national identity as different from that of the West Bank – the United Kingdom plan of March 1972. The crises on the way are no less revealing when studying the stages leading to this first public indication of the plan to abandon the West Bank – the secret policy gradually turning into an official one in a cautious process ending only in 1988.

Eventually, the Israeli–Egyptian cease-fire of August 1970, and the passing away of Nasser in September, turned the page on that picture of despair and hopelessness. Moreover, dissatisfaction with the US gave way to open cooperation with America and Israel in putting down the civil war, a war that threatened to place one element of the Jordanian people against another. And yet, with this period over and the United Kingdom plan issued, it became evident that most Jordanians still kept their loyalty to the Hashemite Kingdom. Additionally, the war of attrition between Israel, the UAR and Syria came to an end at about the time the Jordanian civil war reached its peak, thus easing somewhat the Arab pressure on Jordan to let the PLO fight Israel from Jordanian territory. On the foreign front, the US once again returned to its position as the protector of the kingdom, whereas Israel and Jordan, mostly under US auspices, resumed substantial high-level negotiations. In a word, a period that began with a series of blows to Jordan ended up with the first indications that Jordanian nationalism, ideologically and structurally, was working. This chapter deals with the challenges facing Hussein until the beginning of the civil war with the clashes in the outskirts of Amman in February 1970. However, as political processes, the events following February are in reality only the continuation of those analyzed before that time.

Mounting Domestic Pressures

No unrest was recorded anywhere in the kingdom during the war, or until about the end of 1967.[2] Early 1968 already saw a clear change for the worse in terms of domestic security and loyalty. During the war, public expressions had almost become violent, but even in spite of the alleged US and British involvement, their representatives were not attacked. Even though the absence of violence is a testimony to the determination of the Jordanian authorities to stop any violence, it is also a demonstration of loyalty. After all, such cases did take place in Jordan at other times in spite of the Hashemite efforts to prevent them. Clearly, the scenes on the streets in Amman and elsewhere in the kingdom on June 5, 1967, attested to a degree of national solidarity with Jordan and the regime. Strangely enough, this degree of loyalty surprised at times even the higher echelons of the Jordanian government.

At the end of the war, many Jordanians believed[3] their king to have been misled by Nasser. They voiced support for their monarch and did not blame him for the loss of the West Bank. Quite the contrary, they believed that the time had come for Jordan to rebuild itself as an East Bank entity combining Palestinians who had immigrated to Jordan in 1948 and old Trans-Jordanians. Even in the wake of the war the king and his advisors were not too concerned with the loyalty of the army even though they believed that the war losses had to be rectified as soon as possible.[4] One token indication of their apprehension was that in spite of the heavy defeat, the army took no action against deserters and other undisciplined elements. General Khammash, the chief-of-staff, explained that this was in order "not to upset the Army."[5] Thus, the first item on Hussein's agenda, equal in importance to his peace initiative, was the rehabilitation of the army using possible contacts with the Soviet Union as a leverage against the US and Great Britain. The only alternative to that had to be a return of the occupied West Bank to Jordanian hands so that it would not serve as a constant reminder of the JAA's defeat. Obviously, that was even more problematic than adding the Soviet Union to the list of countries supplying armaments to Jordan. Indeed, the postwar years witnessed continued tests of the army's loyalty.

Within a few months after the conclusion of hostilities the army returned to its usual functioning, which seemed insufficient in the face of the new challenges. Arms shipments from traditional sources along with the use of emergency stocks enabled the regime to put together two infantry divisions and a tank brigade to be deployed on the East Bank. Even though during the fighting the army had lost seven infantry brigades, one tank brigade, most of the artillery and the air force, in the fall of 1967 it managed to project the impression of getting back to normal. After all, the army was one of the pillars of the Jordanian regime and nationalism, as Hussein saw it, and he could not afford an unsatisfied rank and file. Moreover, the make-up of the Jordanian armed forces reflected the heavy dependence of the Hashemite regime on the Bedouin, giving them strong representation in contrast to the under-representation of the Palestinians. Any significant sign of a loosening of military loyalty to the king might have indicated a rupture in the very foundations of the regime since not only were the Palestinians barely represented but the PLO was fighting for their support. Whereas King Hussein had no way of replacing a rebellious army, the PLO was up and coming with its own alternative army. Indeed, between 1967 and 1971 the army was put to the test time and again to prove its full loyalty to king and dynasty in spite of the king's apprehension[6] and his giving in occasionally to militant views within the armed forces. In this respect the army proved that whatever the origin of officers and troops, for the most part they saw Jordan as their national affiliation, and only some abstract affiliation with Arab nationalism.

The almost peaceful course of domestic events post-June did not last long.[7] Not long after the war the PLO and other organizations began to form a major threat to the existence of the Hashemite Kingdom while anti-American sentiment began to spread in the armed forces. With the Israeli efforts to get the PLO out of the occupied West Bank, the organization found refuge in Jordan. Very much against Hussein's interest its members began crossing the river to operate against Israeli targets, thus reviving the pre-June conditions of attempting to create a new dimension to the Jordanian–Israeli dispute. In early September 1967, upon his return from the Arab summit, Hussein still felt self-confident enough to voice his guarded disapproval of these activities.[8] However, not long after the war the PLO began to turn the tide of popular support for the king and the dynasty. As early as January 1968, contemporaneous with an ongoing secret diplomatic process, Hussein began to feel that he was losing the support of his army while his own citizens voiced support for the fighting party, the Palestinian organizations, which saw Israel and the Hashemites in the same light. What was even more worrisome was the attraction that the PLO presented to young, educated East Bankers, the kind of people Hussein saw as the backbone of his Jordan. Additionally, growing areas of the kingdom, especially in the eastern Jordan valley but in the major cities as well, began to be controlled by members of the Palestinian organizations. The king's efforts were to no avail: even his troops, under orders to shoot members of the PLO in and out of action in Israel, refused to carry out their orders. Also, the strikes at Israel and the Israeli counter-strikes produced a steady stream of refugees moving to the outskirts of Amman, which gradually became a menace to the regime.

Strangely enough, under these difficult conditions almost the one and only piece of good news was the continued service of Bahjat Talhuni as the prime minister.[9] He was probably the only person in the court who could claim truly cordial relations with the UAR, whose support at this critical juncture was essential, and undoubtedly he was against any frontal attack against the Palestinian organizations. For the time being, at least until March 1969, he was able to buy time for the king. In the Western corridors of power as well as with Jarring the prevailing mood was one of despair, as though the demise of Hashemite Jordan was rapidly approaching. The only way possible of relieving pressure on the king, in the American and British view, would be to convince Israel to allow the people displaced in 1967 to return to the territories so that they would not serve as a pressure group and as potential recruits within Jordan. At this particular moment in early 1968 the Western powers concluded, as they had done in the past, that: "In recent months Israel has come to regard King Hussein as expendable."[10]

Unfortunately for Jordan the unrest and the domestic troubles were much more deep rooted. The East Bank was not exempt from the lessons of 1963 and 1966 in the West Bank: no Jordanian or Palestinian would give up his or her affiliation with the Arab people at large when threatened by Israel. Thus, the regime in early 1968 went back to where it was at the peak of Nasser's subversion: blamed by its own people for not full-heartedly confronting Israel. Only this time around, the challenge was much more complicated: it was mainly of local origin and with almost no significant outside incitement. Under these circumstances easing the pressure of the 1967 displaced persons could bring some relief, but the main change had to be the result of a diplomatic move that would retroactively change the outcome of the June war, which in turn would have brought back under Jordanian sovereignty the very same elements that were fighting against it. Indeed, neither Israel nor Jordan could contribute at this critical juncture to a lasting solution to the Jordanian predicament. Perhaps the only avenue open to these countries, finding themselves once again in the same boat against the Palestinian threat, was to resume secret negotiations with the hope of finding tactical solutions to emerging military situations while keeping the open border conflict at a level sufficient to convince other parties that Jordan was participating in the anti-Israeli fighting. The trick was to choose very carefully the level of conflict and the choice of targets so as not to add insult to the injuries of the regime.

While the Jordanian monarch was running out of possible courses of action the Western powers were contemplating possible scenarios – all involving the disappearance of the king. The most intriguing of them[11] was that being faced with a choice between civil war and making peace with Israel, Hussein would abdicate. This approach ignored the pattern of behavior the king had adopted in the early 1960s: public support for Arab causes and solidarity with the Palestinian issue while building an Israeli security guarantee of the existence of the kingdom. This approach did not exclude the retreat to arms if and when necessary: with the Palestinian organizations as a major policy tool until July 1971 and with Israel as a forced participant in the war of attrition.

The Two Faces of Relations with Israel

Soon after the end of hostilities Israel initiated a policy of "open bridges," namely: allowing residents of the West Bank to conduct their economic exchanges with the East Bank as though nothing had happened in June. It did not take long for the West Bank economy to integrate into the Israeli economy. Even the implementation of the Oslo Accords in the 1990s, years later, would not significantly alter this picture. The immediate effects of this integration, to be fully understood only years later, were two: the availability of jobs for the Palestinians in Israel, and a gradual rise in their economic quality of life. Thus, whatever the motives behind Jordan's military and political behavior in June 1967, in all probability it did not need the West Bank to be reintegrated into the East Bank, lest it bring about high unemployment and a sharp decline in the economic quality of life in Jordan proper. In other words, Jordan could only benefit from the new conditions. It served as the only true Palestinian outlet to the Arab world, while leaving Israel with the burden of the population, which had never been too sympathetic to the Hashemites. That meant that the daily concerns of security and financing rested with Israel while the Jordanian influence over political figures and decisions relating to Palestinian affairs could be strengthened through a shrewd stick-and-carrot Jordanian policy. Obviously, such a policy could not have existed without at least some tacit Israeli consent, which was willingly expressed both in public and in secret.

As much as Jordan was concerned with assessing possible Israeli calculations, so was Israel engaged in a continuous effort to formulate a policy towards the West Bank, and consequently towards Jordan. Strangely enough, neither the failure of the king's peace efforts in the summer of 1967 nor the military escalation along the border, between 1967 and 1970, caused a lasting break in the ongoing negotiations and the reaching of practical agreements. The period from 1967 to 1972 was characterized at first by parallel policy negotiations between the two countries and continuous exchange of fire along the border. Later, after the Israeli assistance to the very existence of the kingdom in 1970, negotiations continued, but still there was no possibility of any agreement since the envisioned settlements, in the eyes of the two partners, were so far apart. Jordan wanted Israel to bear the responsibility of finding a way out of the Palestinian predicament while taking Hashemite interests into consideration. The Israeli position was much more simplistic: to find the right formula for returning the territories to Jordan while keeping intact the few Israeli settlements in that area.

This conflict of interests explains why although negotiations went on – with each side trying to score points with the US and UN – no major agreements were reached. However, both sides were able to agree on several well-defined, but less important issues. A comparison of the timeframe of the negotiations and the border clashes tells a story of two neighboring countries at open war while working out a secret peace – very much in line with the pre-1967 conditions. Thus, the period 1968–70 did not see any significant change in the nature of relations between Jordan and Israel.

After the passing of Resolution 242 Hussein adopted a line that was to be part and parcel of Jordanian foreign policy in years to come, which is that Resolution 242 is based on the principle of the inadmissibility of the acquisition of territory by war, and on the exchange of land for peace; however, independently of any other application of 242, its basic interpretation was that Israel, like all other Middle Eastern nations, was recognized and that the process of Israeli withdrawal would not be automatic but should be the result of negotiations.[12] However, while accepting Resolution 242, that policy has never included the return of any territories to Jordanian hands; territories had to be returned to Arab hands, not necessarily Jordanian. Formally, it followed the line of Arab League resolutions after the 1948 war, which recognized the Jordanian presence in the West Bank as a trusteeship. Still, if indeed Hussein wanted the territory back he could at least secretly tell that to the US, which obviously was not bound by any Arab League resolution. Furthermore, Hussein also made it a pillar of his policy that Resolutions 242 and 338 (to be passed in 1973), while confirming the principle of territory for peace, must be further elaborated to provide for Israel's security and recognition, and not necessarily for the return of Jordanian sovereignty over the lost territories.[13] After the war the American support for Jordan, so eagerly looked for before the June war, became clear and unmistaken. Once again, the US took upon itself to protect Jordan against regional threats, whether from Israel or any Arab country.

Some of the reservations regarding Resolution 242 were expressed in an interview with NBC in January 1981. There, King Hussein took a strong and unequivocally clear position against 242. His interpretation was that it "really dealt with the aftermath of the war of 1967. . . . It did not deal with the most important element in the equation. It did not deal with the Palestinian problem adequately . . . [he does] not believe that . . . 242 is the answer for efforts to achieve a comprehensive peace both now and in the future."[14] He goes on to say that there is "No Jordanian option" for a peace plan and that the PLO is the "only representative" of the Palestinians.

The first meeting between an Israeli official and the king after the United Nations Security Council (UNSC) adopted Resolution 242, took place in London in December 1967. About the same time, Rasul al-Kaylani, the head of Jordanian military intelligence, visited London, ostensibly in order to arrange for a Jordanian officer to specialize in a British intelligence department. However, there was a more serious reason for his visit: briefing the British on the current Jordanian position. It cannot be ruled out that a similar position, perhaps more detailed, was presented to Israel. That thinking included the following elements.[15] There were two issues to be addressed – Jerusalem and the West Bank. The latter could be given up as long as Jerusalem was returned to Jordanian hands. Jerusalem in this context means its pre-June 1967 borders including the Wailing Wall, for which the Jews would be given special rights of access. In other words, a return to the 1949 armistice agreement as far as Jerusalem was concerned, in exchange for an Israeli and Jordanian agreement that the West Bank would not be returned to the Hashemite Kingdom. For reasons of legitimacy in the Arab world any Israeli–Jordanian agreement could not bear the title "peace," and should be presented as a non-belligerency pact rather than a peace treaty. However, reaching such an agreement would pave the way for Nasser to follow suit and present his moves as if being dragged into such an agreement.

Kaylani's words represent a clear deviation from past Jordanian tactics: any diplomatic move was no longer the sole initiative of the king. Such an approach was one of the reasons for the failure of King Abdullah in pursuing his peace policy after 1948. Now, with Resolution 242 in place there was an accepted basis to try and broaden the infrastructure for Hussein's initiatives. For King Hussein, Resolution 242 signaled as usual a mixed blessing:[16] finally, it was an international recognition of the need to talk peace, something he had been doing already, and a departure from Sandstorm, which had impeded his peace campaign; and yet it put the return of occupied territories as a pre-condition for peace, obviously a prerequisite in the Jordanian popular view for every Jordanian move or concession. However, in his continued and more rigorous attempts to build a stable and secure nation-state Hussein had to face a series of challenges, once again confronting Israel and the Palestinians on his account.

On the Israeli side, the Israeli foreign minister, Abba Eban, proposed a blueprint for peace that would include the return of most territories to

Jordan while recognizing united Jerusalem as the capital city of Israel.[17] That approach resulted in a slight change in the semi-official Jordanian position regarding future agreements with Israel. Zayd al-Rifa'i, a close confidant of Hussein, indicated[18] a cautious acceptance of an interim agreement approach that would bring the kingdom once again in touch with its former citizens on the West Bank. Interestingly enough, while speaking of the need to "communicate" he never mentioned the term "sovereignty" in any context – another minor indication of the need to form a new relationship between the banks once Israel withdrew. These remarks were echoed, and in fact elaborated on,[19] by the king himself, who made it clear that a final settlement should include full Israeli withdrawal and that "not one Jordanian soldier" would be allowed on the West Bank. Once again, the issue of future relations between the two banks was left untouched. This sequence of behind-the-scenes exchanges may suggest that Hussein was the first to raise the idea of an interim agreement in the region; an agreement that would include elements of a comprehensive settlement but would still be far from it. However, even after one more Jordanian–Israeli meeting in late January 1968, once again in London, no movement was recorded.[20] This meeting, with the participation of Israeli minister Yigal Allon, was the one during which the famous Israeli Allon plan was presented to the king and rejected.

However, Israel did not take too much into consideration the mounting domestic Hashemite challenges even though it was made aware of them by the Western powers. Once again, in a series of political and military episodes reminiscent of the 1966 Samu' crisis, Jordan and its king came to a "to be or not to be" moment of truth. With between 10,000 and 12,000 Iraqi troops on Jordanian soil, not necessarily loyal to the Hashemite regime since the 1967 war, and terrorists infiltrating from Syria into Israel through Jordanian sovereign territory, not much of Jordan was controlled by Hashemite hands. Moreover, Palestinian organizations were taking over more and more areas of Jordan, making them off limits for Jordanian authorities, the king included. On top of that extremely dangerous situation, developed to a large degree by foreign Arab powers, Jordan itself was no longer a safe home for the Hashemites. The ordinary Jordanian, influenced by the Palestinians' fight for their occupied territories, suspecting the king of collaborating with Israel and wishing to imitate the Viet Cong fighting the US, felt the urgent need for change – a change that could not come from the monarch.

Those circumstances resulted in further military actions against Israel by the Palestinian organizations and the Iraqi forces, directly or indirectly; all felt immune from Israeli punishment. The Iraqi forces were not putting any of their fellow countrymen at risk by attacking Israel and the Palestinians could only benefit from continued Israeli strikes: more refugees from the border areas would flood Amman bringing pressure on the king and his entourage and causing a refugee explosion from which only they would gain. The Israeli side for its part could not tolerate any attacks on its territory, making a retaliatory action contingent on the number and seriousness of casualties. In reality the king had no viable course of action: moving against the organizations would alienate sections of his armed forces at home, externally contradict UAR policy and create an open confrontation with Syria, and lead to a possible civil war, whereas attacking Israel, a partner in negotiations, would amount to public suicide.

The ongoing Israeli–Jordanian dialogue was under pressure of two kinds: the political, namely the scores of meetings Eshkol held with Palestinian leaders,[21] thus indicating that a settlement with Hussein was not necessarily the most preferred option in Israeli eyes, and military pressures, rather violent at times, applied by both sides. Consequently, between the January meeting and the March moves, and simultaneous with the deteriorating position of Hussein within his own kingdom, neither side refrained from major military strikes, contributing to a serious border escalation.[22] Israel struck fiercely whereas Jordanian units not only retaliated against Israeli military moves but also initiated some of their own, with the tacit agreement of the king. Still, the most significant of these was the Israeli attack on February 15 that contributed to talk of the possible disappearance of the dynasty. During eight or nine hours of fighting across the Israeli–Jordanian cease-fire line, Israel used its air force, Jordan attacked Israeli villages, and at the end of the day 53 Jordanians were dead, 46 civilians and seven soldiers; heavy damage was inflicted on the Israeli settlements. The Israeli reaction caused the flight of about 70,000 Jordanians from the Jordan valley to the outskirts of Amman and also caused some dissent in the Jordanian army, especially the lower echelons that wanted to see more cooperation with the *fidayin*. The combined pressure of the fleeing Jordanians, and the unrest of the army and other organizations, contributed to economic uncertainties and, all in all, added to the already tense and uncertain future of relations within the kingdom. All of which once again directly destabilized the position of King Hussein and obviously diminished his ability to conclude any agreement with Israel.

And yet, all this did not deter both players from continuing their strange diplomatic tango. In a rather unexpected move Hussein let the Western diplomats know that he was about to confront the *fidayin*.[23] That message suggests that the clash with Israel on February 15 had the effect the Israeli side was hoping for: to induce Hussein into a showdown with the terror organizations in spite of their widespread popular support among Jordanian citizens. However, the delay in the king's moves until 1970–1 obviously raises the question of the reasons for the king's not acting in 1968. The most probable answer has to do with the make-up of Hussein's cabinet: his prime minister Bahjat Talhuni, as well as some ministers, would not participate in any moves against the PLO, seeing a grave danger to the regime, thus removing them at that critical hour was out of the question. Furthermore, in spite of the ongoing dialogue with Israel there was no shred of evidence to support the possibility that Israel would come to the rescue if necessary, since Hussein was not sure of Israel's interest in the continued existence of his kingdom. Thus, in mid-February Hussein probably reached the conclusion that a major confrontation was coming but that he would take the initiative once conditions in the kingdom were improved. It is unclear whether Israel was made aware by the Western powers of Hussein's state of mind, but there is no doubt that they urged Israel to take steps to encourage Hussein in his moves.

In late February Israel indicated its willingness to resume contacts with Jordan and stop work in Jerusalem so as not to prejudice the future outcome of possible negotiations.[24] Considering the centrality of Jerusalem for Israel and the existence of an Israeli national unity government, this may indicate that leading Israeli decision makers believed that concessions with regard to Jerusalem were an appropriate *quid pro quo* for the continued existence of the Hashemite dynasty.

The Western impression that a scenario involving the king's disappearance should be elaborated on[25] was further reinforced as a result of the aforementioned Israeli attack of February 15, 1968. The two powers once again concluded that in the event of the king's disappearance he would be replaced by elements not interested in peace negotiations with Israel, but most probably with ties to the PLO. In spite of Hussein's belief to the contrary throughout most of 1968, and in spite of Israel's diplomatic assurance and actual actions indicating its continued interest in Jordan's existence, it is unclear whether Israel wanted to see the disappearance of the kingdom, let alone have a radical regime replace the more sympathetic one of Hussein.[26] Actually, Israel helped Jordan in getting the approval of Capitol Hill for a US–Jordanian arms deal, indicated a willingness to discuss tactical military issues *tête-à-tête* with Jordanian officers, and stepped up efforts to resume direct negotiations through the mediation services of West Bank notables. All that and more: without publicly committing itself to the Western approach to the 1967 displaced persons, Israel sped up the process of family reunification, catering by that to the root source of the king's troubles as the West saw it.

Early March 1968 saw the repetition of negotiating tactics, so familiar by now, with the king:[27] in public, using the Jarring mission to reflect Jordanian willingness to discuss peace with Israel, while claiming the right to represent the West Bank Palestinians, and in secret, working behind the scenes, either with the US as mediators or independently of any third-party involvement.

The former tactic concentrated on two issues: how to put together a Jordanian delegation to talks with Israel headed by Jarring in Cyprus with Egyptian participation, so that it would at the same time reflect Jordanian national interests and yet receive West Bank Palestinian legitimacy; and secondly, how to legitimize and publicize any functioning agreements between Israel and Jordan and yet leave the Jerusalem issue to the personal discretion of the leaders. In mid-March Jordan scored a diplomatic success by accepting the draft document proposed by Jarring as a basis for the Cyprus meeting, against Egyptian and Israeli reservations, and withdrawing from its initial intention to resort to the Security Council in order to request an agreed-upon interpretation of Resolution 242.[28] Such a request would not help US peace efforts since it would once again bring the UN to center stage and diminish the success prospects of the US-sponsored secret track. It is possible that this Jordanian move in spite of the complicated domestic circumstances further convinced the US of the need to bolster Hussein's position, and thus had some impact on the US decision to side with the king regarding the Israeli raid in Karahmeh (see below).

The secret track was marked during March by US efforts to resume secret peace negotiations between Israel and Jordan aimed at reaching a bilateral (meaning separate) peace agreement within the Sandstorm approach, which was still in operation. One of the reasons for the US urgency was their apprehension that Hussein would engage in secret contacts with Israel without their knowledge, thus pursuing national Jordanian interests, not necessarily in line with those of the US. Until then no bilateral negotiations had produced any tangible results. Quite the contrary, they were limited to a general exchange of views. In sharp contrast with past approaches, in mid-March 1968 the US ambassador in Amman suggested a new American approach, unquestionably influenced by ideas he had heard in his post. He saw an Israeli statement regarding Jerusalem as a starter for such negotiations. This distinction between Jerusalem and the rest of the West Bank was definitely a move in the right direction, separating the Jerusalem issue from the rest of the territorial element. Furthermore, in his proposals to the State Department the ambassador did not take it for granted that an Israeli withdrawal from the West Bank would be complete – he still saw an Israeli evacuation in favor of Jordan but did not envision full Israeli withdrawal as a prerequisite for an Israeli–Jordanian agreement.

In this effort to bolster Jordan's position Hussein was greatly helped by the US, which, considering the grave danger to the regime, began transmitting[29] and comparing intelligence reports on Israeli military preparations to launch an attack against Jordan. The American information was accurate enough to indicate possible Israeli military efforts on Jordanian sovereign territory. The proximity in time suggests that once

Jarring left Amman in the afternoon of March 20, the Israeli military machine was set in motion. On the other hand, King Hussein promised Western diplomats to make sure his forces would not provide Israel with a ready provocation that could trigger an Israeli retaliation. It was within this framework of US-sponsored diplomacy, and its fear of the Hashemite collapse on top of a successful arms deal which went through in early 1968,[30] that the US caused Jordan once again to act against its own national interests: a source well acquainted with Israeli–Jordanian relations during these years very strongly suggests[31] that a prior American warning of an imminent Israeli attack caused a local Israeli defeat. Whether that was the case or not is not absolutely clear, but the UAR also claimed[32] responsibility for an early warning to Jordan.

On March 21, 1968, King Hussein was handed a golden opportunity to make a military and diplomatic point *vis-à-vis* all other players in the Middle Eastern political game. The Israeli strike in Karameh on the Jordanian side of the Jordan valley, and at another location south of the Dead Sea, provided him with an opportunity to openly confront Israel militarily along with the PLO[33] and demonstrate his unique ability of forming *ad hoc* short-lived coalitions even with the most unlikely partners once pushed to it by the need to protect his throne. Obviously, this act was also very much in line with his ideas of the special Hashemite responsibility for the Palestinians. It is not conceivable with the political and military picture now uncovered that there was a tacit Israeli–Jordanian understanding about the raid, or at least an Israeli expectation that the regular Jordanian army would not intervene in strength in the fighting between the Israeli Defense Forces and the *fidayin*. A Swiss paper[34] stated that Hussein had earlier hinted to West Bank notables who had visited him that he would not object to Israel's destroying *al-Fatah* bases in Jordan. The paper noted that there was a secret agreement to this effect and that it was broken either by Hussein or as a result of the initiative of local army commanders. Judging from past secret understandings of the king with Israel it would be highly unlikely that local commanders would be made privy to such agreements; however, at that particular moment, with his own future hanging in the balance, there was no reason for him not to join forces with his Palestinian enemies against Israel in order to buy time and prestige.

For Israel the raid produced results symmetrically opposed to those hoped for.[35] On top of the heavy Israeli casualties and the internal debate stemming from it, the first such outcome since Israel's astounding victory in June 1967, the raid galvanized for a short while the rocky, *ad hoc* and temporary coalition between Hussein and the Palestinian organizations. Fighting side by side against Israel and each suffering scores of casualties made *al-Fatah* as much as the Jordanian army brothers in arms against a common enemy, thus applying more pressure on the king to make concessions to the Palestinian organizations, in terms of sovereignty, necessary for confronting the enemy, and obviously making any agreement with Israel a remote possibility. Moreover, in the aftermath of the fighting Israel emerged as less of a threat than prior, which once again diminished the Jordanian need for any military understanding with Israel. All that, in the US view,[36] might have led the Middle East into another round of hostilities, with the king this time paying the full price.

In retrospect, that Jordanian victory served as a Pyrrhic victory: Jordan had no interest in publicizing too much its success over a partner in secret negotiations, whereas the *al-Fatah* people had every reason both to present the Karameh incident as their own success on the ground, since in the aftermath of the battle they managed to gain control over the road to the Allenby bridge, and to use the whole incident as a springboard for increased popular support in Jordan and further massive recruiting.[37] That battle caused much enthusiasm among the Palestinians of the East Bank and curtailed the regime's ability to confront the ever-increasing areas controlled by the organizations. This led to greater success for the organizations in enlisting new recruits, and later, a major military clash between the Palestinian military organizations and the central Jordanian government, in May 1968. This ever-escalating turn of events between the central government and the Palestinian organizations had a negative effect on Jordan's ability to make good the promise made by General Khammash to Israel in May[38] to quieten down the border with Israel. This inability was probably one of the reasons for Israel's disappointment with Hussein and his regime. These developments would eventually lead, along with other factors, to the major test of the king and his government: the 1970 civil war.

One of the unmistakable results of the Israeli Karameh operation and the continued Israeli–Jordanian border tension was the feeling among Western diplomats in Amman that a possible "coup de grâce to the present regime"[39] might come soon from the Israeli side. Another adverse outcome of the raid was a temporary disruption of the Israeli–Jordanian negotiations following the clash, because the raid was a firm indication that Israel had, to some extent, given up on the chances of Hussein surviving on his throne, and perhaps was willing to consider occupying the eastern side of the Jordan valley.[40] Put differently, the decision to strike indicated a profound distrust in Hussein's ability to carry on any action against the Palestinian organizations; quite the contrary, during the period before the raid Jordanian units provided cover to terrorists crossing the border into Israeli-held territory, and also shelled Israeli settlements. This, in the Israeli mind, indicated Hussein's inability to make any public agreement with Israel. Moreover, with the Palestinian organizations taking root in Jordan it looked as though they were about to take over the kingdom and replace the king. Western diplomatic reports emanating from Amman carried the strange feeling that, without admitting it, Israel and the Palestinian organizations shared a common interest in changing the regime and finding a solution to the Palestinian issue. It is small wonder that under these circumstances neither Israel nor Jordan could carry on a diplomatic process.

However, in line with the public relations dimension of the apparently dying diplomatic process, both sides tried to give the impression of their own positive attitude in spite of the unfavorable circumstances. Not a week after the Israeli raid, the king confidentially indicated his willingness to resume talks with Israel, with which his army was after all too weak to fight.[41] Israel, for its part, spoke in two voices. Secretly, a fortnight after the military operation it conveyed a message[42] to the king and to Nasser through the good services of Hikmat al-Masri, a leading Nablus figure and a partner in talks on behalf of Israel, who had been summoned to the Israeli Foreign Ministry to be given the message alongside a comprehensive briefing. Publicly, in a meeting of the Labor Party Center on April 21, minister Allon referred to a solution to the Palestinian problem, he said that the matter was "one of self-determination, in which Israel would not interfere," but added that he did not discount the possibility that, in order to solve the complex demographic problem, Israel might look for a solution by helping the Palestinians to solve it through self-administration. Only one day earlier in another forum of the Labor Party, the party's secretary, Golda Meir, spoke of the Israeli desire to return the local population to their Monarch.[43] If this confusion was not enough, then the Israeli messages were not dissimilar: the secret one indicated a willingness to negotiate with the king, whereas the public one underlined a pro-Palestinian tendency, at least on the part of Allon, a leading decision-maker at the time.

Indeed, the message which was handed over to al-Masri at the Foreign Ministry was carefully worded to reflect a power struggle within Israel between the Israeli military hardliners and the more moderate foreign-policy personnel. It was in essence a call to King Hussein to join forces in fighting the more militant elements and start a process of discussing the main issues. The Israeli condition was the commencement of direct negotiations. On all other issues Israel was not too specific but tried to project a rather conciliatory and compromising stand. The message had to be read in light of past direct, but secret, talks between the two countries, which may indicate an Israeli intention to upgrade such contacts into a public forum, perhaps under the auspices of the Jarring mission. The use of al-Masri in this context, in spite of the veiling secrecy, may well suggest an intention by Israel to make the contents of this call for a renewed political process at least semi-public to third parties. The timing of the message, on the eve of a royal visit to the UAR, clearly represented an Israeli understanding that no significant Jordanian move could be made by the king without Nasser's approval, which was not forthcoming at least on the public level against the background of the Israeli–UAR military situation. All that leads to the inevitable conclusion that Jordan could not take this Israeli move seriously, as did the US, which was made aware of it through Jordan.

The message episode serves to illustrate the point that most, if not all, players at the time did not realize the multi-track approach the king adopted before and in the aftermath of Karameh. His efforts were intended to realize three main interests: first, to try to negotiate as little as possible with the Palestinian organizations and use the other players to create conditions that would curb the Palestinian military presence and activity from his territory against Israel, so that the dangers of further clashes with Israel would be diminished and the movement of the organizations to the inner centers of population in Jordan would be limited; secondly, to reach *de facto* peace conditions with Israel without making it public; and thirdly, to secure support for these moves from Egypt, which still had the potential of subversion against the Hashemite regime, and from the US, which held the key to the well-being of the kingdom, diplomatically as well militarily.

In order to pursue his interests Hussein acted simultaneously on three tracks, presenting parts of his position on each one so that eventually he would be able to tie in the loose ends and realize his goals. All players obviously knew of all the tracks but it is not certain if all were made privy to all the contents of other tracks. It is quite possible that only parts of those deliberations made their way to other players. Perhaps the most open track in relation to the others was that of the Jarring mission and the Western powers, which tried to help the UN-appointed mediator to provide the formal basis for any possible agreement that would be reached elsewhere. Here negotiations concentrated on the formal basis for the open negotiations and a possible agreement, and its ingredients.[44] Hussein's opening argument in this context was that Israel was refusing to move ahead with a political process based on the implementation of Resolution 242. Obviously, Jordan had adopted that resolution, which made it the party living up to international standards, unlike Israel.

Jordan's position in this regard was different from the common Arab reading that Israel had to withdraw from all the territories occupied in the 1967 conflict. The king read into it "to reach agreement on boundaries (including Jerusalem), the refugees and the Canal."[45] Thus, about six months after the passing of Resolution 242 he demonstrated a stand very much in line with his position right after the war (see chapter 5) – he did not find it necessary to speak about Israeli withdrawal from (at least) the West Bank, but rather, wished to define ways of making peace between the two countries; moreover, he did not like the idea of a solution imposed by the superpowers. After all, such an approach would force him to agree to the most common interpretation of 242 – the one he did not like since it might have reintroduced the West Bank Palestinians to his kingdom. As for the forum for discussing possible solutions, Hussein's position based on his agreement with Nasser, as expressed to the Western negotiators, was that he agreed to engage in indirect negotiations in New York, in which Jordan would be more forthcoming than the UAR – including a Jordanian recognition of Israel. Jordan's position was greatly helped by the Western acceptance of its position that the Jarring track should not be based on direct negotiations with Israel.[46]

On the Israeli side the feeling that Hussein gave the Israeli negotiators in May was that the UAR, in giving limited consent to more forthcoming Jordanian moves, would be interpreted by the king as being "ready for a peace treaty through secret, direct negotiations under cover of the Jarring mission."[47] However, the US believed that any process leading to a public agreement should not be the outcome of direct negotiations. Israel partially shared this view and preferred combining direct and indirect negotiations between Israel and Jordan through the US.[48] That position served Hussein's interest in reaching a working understanding with Israel, which for its part insisted on a more public and comprehensive agreement. The king's reaction, in the wake of a meeting in May 1968 with Israeli representatives, was conveyed to the Western powers by his complaining that Israel had refrained from defining its secure borders and thus a formal agreement was not possible because of Israel. That position, so often repeated during 1968, very strongly suggests that a leader who sought total withdrawal would not insist on the issue of the concrete border that his adversaries would like to have. In reply, Israel explained in mid-July that the way they saw it, the final outcome of the negotiations was that Jordan would get back sovereignty over most of the West Bank, get an outlet to the Mediterranean Sea, and that a formula based on one unified Jerusalem under Israeli sovereignty would be found that would accommodate Jordan's interests in the Muslim Holy Sites as a representative of the Muslim world. The Jordanian reaction to that was understandable: no separate deal but no return to the UN Security Council, meaning that talks would continue but only for the purpose of limited agreements not involving any return of territories.

With exchanges of fire continuing along the border with Israel there was no change in the difficult position of the king between the rock and a hard place. Publicly, he had to voice support for *al-Fatah* activities inside the territories, though obviously, not from the East Bank; whereas secretly, in spite of powerful Israeli strikes, he found a way to persuade the US to resume any channel available with Israel.[49] The message was clear: the technique was separate and secret talks, and peace was much more about practical arrangements that would satisfy both countries' strategic interests. Indeed, in two meetings between the king and Israeli representatives in May and September 1968 the idea of exchange of territories was discussed. After the May meeting, Eban reported[50] to his cabinet colleagues that the king had asked for a clear-cut Israeli proposal, which was to be presented and rejected during the September meeting, and yet the Israeli position, the Allon plan, continued to serve for a while as the basis of negotiations between the two parties. All this probably leads to the conclusion that in spite of successive failures in reaching any kind of peace the king did not retreat from the basic elements of peace as defined by him in the aftermath of the June war.

The deteriorating situation along the Israeli–Jordanian border throughout 1968 threatened the king with the loss of one of the main pillars of the Jordanian security concept since 1960: his alliance with Israel. Preoccupied with tactical considerations rather than long-range planning, Israel concluded[51] that the Hashemite regime could no longer serve as a strategic partner of Israel due to its failure in curbing *al-Fatah*, and therefore, Israel could do better without the king and the Jordanian monarchy; General Dayan in a public message even proposed the establishment of a Palestinian state on the West Bank, that is, that no territory would be returned to Jordan. This revolutionary change in the Israeli position caused concern in Jordan and even found its way to the lower echelons of the Israeli government; it was not the result of any cabinet decision but it definitely affected negatively the nature of contacts between the two countries throughout 1968 since it was at least suspected by the king.

The Egyptian track[52] was intended in the first place to placate Nasser and keep up his impression that Jordan would not move without his knowledge and preferably his consent, even though the basic intention of Hussein was to get Egyptian consent for talks and then move much further with Israel without any further UAR agreement. However, in spite of his interest in continued talks with Israel, Hussein was not prepared to conclude a peace agreement, as he claimed the US had asked him to do. He needed an Egyptian position to support negotiations, which would not lead to peace. In the background of his negotiations with Nasser were Nasser's connections with *al-Fatah* and his potential to use the organization against the king if the policy to be taken ran against Nasser's policy. During the April meeting between the two leaders Nasser expressed his view that no political solution was possible at that time (meaning before a full Israeli withdrawal from occupied Arab territories), and that direct negotiations with Israel or even indirect discussions in the region (Nicosia being the venue proposed by Jarring) were out of the question. Given the differences in their goals it is no wonder that no joint formula could be worked out. Thus, the most the two leaders could agree on was a formula not ruling out talks in New York. Hence the public line adopted by Hussein was that the two leaders saw eye to eye on the dangers to the kingdom arising from the Israeli refusal to move ahead with a political process based on the implementation of 242. Against that refusal it was much easier for these two parties to agree to engage in indirect negotiations in New York, in which Jordan would be more flexible than the UAR.

Whereas the talks with Nasser were supposed to produce a rather firm front very much in line with the Egyptian position, the US track was different. Here Jordan could state its real position, counting on a sympathetic American ear. Whatever his true position was, Hussein could not bow to US pressures "to force Jordan into making a unilateral agreement."[53] After all, the term "peace" had very different meanings for these two parties: the return of all territories, in the US reading; a functional, secret arrangement not necessarily putting an end to border clashes, in the Hashemite perception. Jordan could still send a high-level delegation to engage in direct negotiations with Israel, unlike the UAR's preferred method. The main premise of such a delegation would be to take upon itself the burden of representing the Palestinians in the West Bank and the Gaza Strip. The king's approach was that all those issues were Jordanian whereas Jerusalem was an Arab problem. While in London in early May, during which time he met with Israeli representatives, Hussein revealed[54] his tactics: with the UN Security Council resolution in place there was no need to revert to the UN; the best track would be to use Jarring's services. However, this public track very much depended on Nasser's consent, but did not exclude the possibility of continuing into more substantial bilateral talks with Israel.

Perhaps the most important potential deterrent to this approach might have come from the UAR wing, based on Nasser's apprehension lest the two countries should reach an agreement more far-reaching than one the UAR could agree to. Such a turn of events might have received its airing through a UAR call for a meeting of the Security Council. This call could have found any justification that had to do with any Israeli military move, and was supported by the Soviet Union. Thus, Jordanian diplomatic activity was concentrated in June–July on efforts intended to prevent such a meeting of the UN Security Council.[55]

With the specter of a disaster to US regional interests it not only intervened on the eve of the Karameh raid on behalf of Jordan, but also took upon itself to bring about the resumption of Israeli–Jordanian talks, eliminating the direct line between the two countries, which had bothered the US so much in the past. Thus, in the wake of Karameh, Hussein managed to once again use his desperate situation to convince the US to pressure Israel to resume negotiations. Additionally, in the American reading, the minor differences between Jordan and the UAR notwithstanding, the apparent meeting of interests between their two leaders and the possibility of losing Israel as a tacit ally in maintaining Hussein's kingdom, triggered a US presidential message rather in the style of an ultimatum urging Israel to renew negotiations.[56] The main underlying premise of the message was that Israel had to confirm its support for Hussein's regime owing to the numerous indications to the contrary. The Israeli ambassador's meeting at the State Department in early June was probably the response to that, with the Israeli assurances that "there was no more talk of overthrowing Hussein."[57] With the violent exchange of fire and the Washington meeting on June 4 over, once again, admitted or not, Israel and Jordan reached a secret agreement under US auspices to return to the old set of rules: total separation, as much as it was possible between the tense border situation and the strikes and counter-strikes, concurrent with continued secret negotiations, albeit under American auspices and not necessarily direct.

By summer 1968, US diplomacy could mark success in their initial objective:[58] getting the partners talking again. Furthermore, probably as a result of that US intervention, the Israeli inner cabinet, the prime minister, Allon and Dayan, decided in October 1968 to ignore the objections of their right-wing main coalition partner, and to hold negotiations with the king on the basic understanding that no public agreements could be reached. Three US decision makers who were behind this diplomatic process – the president, the secretary of state and Mr Katzenbach, the under-secretary of state – served as the steering committee behind the scenes, perhaps without Israel's knowledge. Thus, in spite of the flare-up in March and the following military and political developments, by August 1968 the Israeli cabinet voted in favor of the so-called Jordanian Option,[59] namely: recognizing Jordan and not the PLO as the partner for negotiations on a lasting settlement of the Palestinian issue. The intensive American efforts necessitated a smoke screen to disguise the ongoing process. Thus, in mid-September in a major policy statement the king strongly attacked Israel and criticized the US role in the process,[60] explaining that the US was backing Israeli positions; but simultaneously preparing an alibi for a possible acceptance of positions far from the original Jordanian views. Meanwhile, on the ground the impression among many Jordanians was that Jordan had refrained from action against aggressive Israel.[61] If this was indeed true it was probably the result not of a lack of resources as the king's critics indicated, but of his wish to prepare a better background for secretly carrying on talking with Israel.

In a series of meetings in September and October 1968 between King Hussein, ministers Allon and Eban of Israel and American top-level personalities, the Hashemite monarch while rejecting the Allon plan presented a clear-cut picture: he wanted to move along two interwoven tracks. Publicly, he desired the Jarring mission to be kept alive since he needed a cover behind which to conduct his peace moves. He had also prepared his alibi specifically *vis-à-vis* Egypt using Nasser's agreement that Jordan would discuss Resolution 242 with Israel in order to broaden the scope of negotiations. The US for its part tried to broaden Egyptian backing for Jordan's moves. On that level, Hussein insisted on an Israeli declaration accepting 242 through Jarring in order for the negotiations to move on. This position was the one to be later presented to the world: the UN-sponsored talks would serve as the clearinghouse for a secretly reached understanding – the same role as that of the Rhodes talks in 1949. Secretly, Jarring engaged in detailed negotiations with the aforementioned Israeli representatives. The king's response to the Allon plan presented to him in September in London was negative, but that did not deter the two partners from continuing their dialogue. In September the foreign minister of Israel, Abba Eban, detailed six elements of an agreement. The king was not satisfied yet, he believed the Israeli proposals to be too general, but that was not of major importance to the US. The main benefit of their move was that Israel and Jordan were talking to each other again.

Still, in late October, while carefully taking steps to prepare his people for a possible move, Hussein received and responded[62] to a more detailed Israeli message outlining the ingredients of the Israeli position. Basically, he opposed any Israeli presence, military or civilian, on the West Bank; however, he did not speak of the return of these territories to Jordanian hands. His main point was that any agreement should be made under the implementation of Resolution 242. The only area on which Jordanian sovereignty was a possibility was in Jerusalem and only in the form of a corridor to the Muslim Holy Places, and that would be in exchange for Jordanian access to Israeli Mediterranean ports. The rest of Jerusalem should be returned to Arab hands. The distinction made here by the king regarding the corridor and the rest of Jerusalem, let alone the West Bank, lends credence to the view that Hussein never wanted a Jordanian return to the territories; with the exception of a small area in Jerusalem, the Holy Places and their access, even East Jerusalem had to go to Arab control, not necessarily Hashemite hands. On the issue of refugees, a major issue in Jordanian domestic politics, the king suggested a larger forum to discuss it since neither Jordan nor Israel could resolve it on their own. The serious dialogue between the two leaderships, since none confided in his ministers, produced at least one tangible outcome. One of the accomplishments of this renewed process was that in October 1968 the Israeli chief-of-staff, General Bar Lev, presented to the king the main ingredients of Israeli security concepts. In late October the Jordanian and Israeli chiefs-of-staff, under the auspices of King Hussein, concluded a tactical military agreement[63] aimed at responding to the serious escalation along their common border.

With the advancing contacts between the two countries Hussein was ready to move to more strategic negotiations,[64] engaging in detailed talks regarding the new border with Israel as part of a comprehensive peace discussion. For that the king was even willing to try and get UAR support in spite of the escalating conditions along the Suez Canal. Egypt for its part responded by direct messages from its president to the king inquiring about the deteriorating domestic situation in the kingdom, thus indicating dissatisfaction with Hussein's courageous yet uncoordinated peace moves.[65]

On January 14, 1969, the foreign minister of Israel and the king met once again and discussed the possibility of attending negotiations under Jarring's auspices, but once again without any tangible results – it seems that both believed that the only benefit of the meeting was that it indicated some continuity in the negotiating process.[66] However, shortly afterwards the two countries were upset by the new Nixon administration's initiative aimed at returning the territories to Jordan without any direct negotiations, whereas the Jordanian position voiced time and again to the Western powers was that the kingdom was interested in the implementation of UNSC Resolution 242.[67] The distinction between this terminology and the "return of the territories" or "Israeli withdrawal" so often used by all players but Jordan is striking. Moreover, Hussein indicated clearly that a public Israeli consent to implement Resolution 242 would pave the way to direct negotiations under the auspices of Jarring. That meant that in accordance with 242 Israel had to take upon itself to withdraw from territories occupied in 1967 on all fronts, thus clearing the way to remove any UAR opposition to such negotiations, which, as the king had indicated since November 1967, he was prepared to take further than Egypt. Meantime, he was ready to continue the secret track with Israel and reach understandings, but to decide the contents of any peace accord on the basis of the overall body of agreements reached, and only on condition that there would be no Egyptian opposition. Otherwise, all had to be kept secret.

Probably unaware of the nuances in Jordan's position, the new administration continued the traditional US Middle East policy and declared its goals as reaching "a binding contractual agreement, though not necessarily a peace treaty"[68] based on minimal border changes. Such an agreement would be the outcome of negotiations, which at least during the first stages would not be conducted through direct contacts. Shortly after these developments the prime minister of Israel, Levi Eshkol, died. As is customary between two countries in cordial relations Hussein conveyed a condolence message[69] to the acting prime minister, Allon, using US services. The Israeli leader reciprocated the gesture by thanking the king, once again through the secret US channel. That unprecedented correspondence not only manifested the developing warm relations between these two apparent enemies, but also triggered an exchange of messages between US diplomats in Amman, Tel Aviv, and Washington debating and discarding the possibility of a US presidential message to the Israeli and Jordanian leaders using this exchange as a springboard for further negotiations. Eventually the State

Department's apprehension of an apparent pressure on the two sides, especially that of the king, prevailed and no further action was taken. Still, the ongoing dialogue was advancing to the degree that Israel considered[70] moving one step ahead, and letting the behind-the-scenes talks with Jordan take place under the auspices of Jarring – that is, holding the direct negotiations in public and striving for international recognition of their legitimacy, thus bypassing potential Egyptian opposition, which in spite of the outbreak of the acute stage of the war of attrition had not emerged yet. Such a move had obviously to be agreed upon by both parties, and in concert with the US, and therefore had to wait until the Jordanian monarch's visit to Washington and meeting with President Nixon in April. Later, with that visit over, the Jordanian position was crystal clear:[71] Jordan needed an agreement in six months in order to be able to curb Palestinian armed activities from its territory. That agreement could include the following elements:

1. The end of all belligerency.
2. Respect for and acknowledgment of the sovereignty, territorial integrity and political independence of all states in the area.
3. Recognition of the right of all to live in peace within secure and recognized boundaries free from threats or acts of war.
4. Guaranteeing for all, freedom of navigation through the Gulf of Aqaba and the Suez Canal.
5. Guaranteeing the territorial inviolability of all states in the area through whatever measures are necessary including the establishment of demilitarized zones on both sides of the new border.
6. Accepting a just settlement of the refugee problem.

These six points, which present Hussein's interpretation of Resolution 242, indicated that Israel's right to exist was no longer an issue and that Jordan, in line with Egypt, would sign any agreement with Israel short of a peace agreement. On the territorial dimension, Jordan insisted on re-establishing the 1967 borders, but if Israel could reveal some flexibility on Gaza, Jordan was willing to make substantial concessions on the West Bank. This expression of Jordanian views is fascinating: Jerusalem is not mentioned, but during public appearances throughout the April 1969 tour the king indicated his willingness to reach a solution on Jerusalem that would separate its new eastern part and should return to Jordanian hands its Holy Shrines, over which the rights of all three monotheistic religions should be respected. Further, Hussein and his entourage indicated that they were willing to consider demilitarizing the West Bank as part of a settlement, and were adamant on access to Gaza – meaning, an outlet to the Mediterranean – but they said nothing regarding sovereignty over the territories. On that, "his main aim was to ensure that Arab Palestine came under one umbrella; while its ties with East Jordan must remain, there should be more emphasis in the future on 'retaining the characteristics of both sides within the Jordan family'."[72]

In the wake of the visit and for the first time since the war the American administration, this time the new cabinet of President Nixon, did not insist on direct Jordanian–Israeli negotiations, sparking public and angry Israeli reactions by the Israeli prime minister Meir and her foreign minister, Eban.[73] Furthermore, US preparations for issuing a new diplomatic initiative, later to be known as the Rogers Plan, contributed to Israeli nervousness and an easier hand on the trigger in response to PLO infiltration and actions against Israel from Jordanian territory.

As was the case with many failing superpower plans to bring peace, or at least stability, to the region – the last of them the four-power discussions in 1969 – the Rogers Plan was no exception. Its main benefit at least in Jordanian eyes was that it allowed for the US to be a mediator between the regional actors without exposing the other powers to the sensitive contents of that communication channel. While the Americans prepared to issue their proposals another attempt to bring together Jordanian and Israeli representatives was launched.[74] In June and July 1969 Hussein met Eban and they had a fairly detailed discussion of the Israeli position – perhaps the most forthcoming on the Israeli side ever. Eban hinted at the possibility that an agreement in principle be achieved before the Israeli parliamentary elections scheduled for 1969. Only then, picking up on previous precedents, would formal negotiations commence. As for substance, Israel proposed that the Allon plan, which had been presented to the king and rejected, be modified, and that most of the territory and people of the West Bank be returned to Jordan in exchange for declaring the West Bank a demilitarized region. Jordan could be given an outlet to the Mediterranean Sea through one of the Israeli sea-ports, and perhaps even Gaza, as long as Jordan and Egypt would not share a border in the Gaza Strip, lest it be used by Egypt for subverting the Hashemite regime. Hussein, for his part, in line with the new Israeli flexibility, in early July introduced a reshuffle within the army ranks, bringing in personalities known for their strong opposition to the Palestinian organizations,[75] thereby signaling to Israel his determination to lessen the weight of the Palestinian organizations; he was instantly rewarded by an end to Israeli attacks on the East Ghor canal.

Still, the huge shadow of Nasser hovered over these contacts even though Hussein presented a line to Israel saying that he had Nasser's approval, probably in order to encourage Israel to go into a more detailed presentation. Clearly, with his apprehension of the Egyptian president, entangled at that time in an escalating war of attrition with Israel, and no progress on the issue of Jerusalem, Hussein could not proceed any further with this move. In July he resumed his multi-track approach and once again aimed for the international umbrella, which had the potential of relieving him of the Nasserite pressure, since one of the four powers prepared to take part in the process was the Soviet Union, the patron of the UAR. However, his hopes of gaining some multinational backing were upset in late July, forcing him once again to resort to the beaten track of secret negotiations with Israel,[76] which had produced no tangible results to that point.

Thus, with an ever-escalating war of attrition between Israel and the UAR, internal pressures from within by the *fidayin*, and diminishing chances of gaining anything from talks with Israel either under cover of the four powers, or through Jarring, or any other secret track, the only avenue open to Hussein was to publicly close ranks with Nasser and the Palestinian organizations. In mid-August 1969 he reappointed Bahjat Talhuni instead of Abd al-Mun'im al-Rifa'i in the hope of playing for time and preparing for the inevitable showdown with the organizations behind the back of this pro-UAR, pro-organizations cabinet. Now, in line with the intricate web Hussein had previously put together he had newly appointed army commanders, eager to prove themselves against the Palestinian organizations, serving alongside a prime minister and a cabinet more sympathetic to Egypt and the organizations while at the same time contributing to the formation of an opposition group, probably under the quiet and careful guidance of Wasfi al-Tall.[77] Meanwhile the king himself began a tour of Arab capitals calling for the convening of a new Arab summit conference that one way or another would sanction the legitimacy of Hussein as comrade-in-arms of all Arab countries fighting Israel. If all this was not enough, Hussein found a way to communicate to the US his determination to hold secret and direct negotiations with Jordan on a final settlement focusing on the Jerusalem issue. Perhaps the only precondition Jordan presented was its demand for US assurances that Jerusalem was negotiable.[78]

With the region once again in turmoil the US was not sure if the two local actors were not engaged in talks that were being kept secret from the US; in fact, all three parties suspected each other of having secret negotiations with the other partner.[79] This suspicion served as the background for two meetings between Zayd al-Rifa'i and the US under-secretary of state Joseph Sisco in October and December 1969. The Jordanian position at that point advocated a document agreed upon by the four powers along the lines of the US–Jordanian negotiations. Such a document would have provided the basis for a solution imposed on the Middle East. On the other hand, the great detail with which Rifa'i explained the Jordanian position and responded to prior Israeli proposals, and Eban's insistence that the two countries did not need US help in arranging their negotiations, could have created the impression that it was the outcome of talks with the Israeli side that indeed reflected prior secret understandings. As had been the case since the mid-1960s the UN wanted peace and a settlement in the Middle East but definitely one that would include this superpower as a leading actor; any direct and secret channel could not serve that goal. However, by November 1969 Hussein declared publicly[80] that there was no ongoing dialogue with Israel.

Still, the growing domestic military pressure of the Palestinians and their becoming another strong local actor to be reckoned with brought Israel and Jordan again to the secret bilateral track. Thus, in March 1970, only a few weeks after the beginning of sporadic Palestinian–Jordanian clashes, the king met General Dayan, the Israeli minister of defense. The two leaders worked out a series of steps to be taken in order to bolster the position of the king; among them, the return of Israeli-occupied territory south of the Dead Sea. The Israeli withdrawal was presented in the Jordanian press[81] as the result of a battle between Jordanian and Israeli forces in early April 1970. But perhaps the most significant accomplishment of this period was not a peace treaty, for none was realized, but rather the continued Israeli guarantee to the existence of Jordan. Even the non-conclusive negotiations were a preferred option compared with the peril of the PLO. This understanding would constitute the foundation on which both sides, in concert with the US, would coordinate their action during the acute stages of the Jordanian civil war.

7

The 1970s: From a Survival Struggle to the Consolidation of Political Success

A little over ten years after Syrian tank units invaded Jordan the two countries once again were on the verge of another military clash. But the period between September 1970 and November 1980 is an indication of another layer of the legacy that Hussein would leave behind, which is that even though the basic ingredients of his challenges never altered, their implications for Jordan did. Hussein's survival struggle underwent a major change in the 1970s: it was no longer a question of basic survival, it was about the quality of political life in a usually unfriendly Middle East.

Tension and stability along the Israeli–Jordanian border in the wake of the war began to spill over to the East Bank at the end of 1967. However, it only reached its peak in September 1970 – the watershed in the civil war between the Hashemites and the Palestinian organizations, which raged between February 1970 and July 1971. With the final crushing of the Palestinian activists engaged in civil war, Jordan entered a period characterized mainly by diplomatic moves.

On the domestic arena, after 1967 new opposition alliances began to emerge positioning local elements along with Palestinian activists against the regime. However, many Palestinians had a stake in the incumbent Jordanian regime and economy, in contrast to the Palestinian organizations. The slow but undeniable deteriorating domestic situation was mainly the result of the growing friction between the central government and the Palestinian organizations. Opposition elements joined in the expressions of overall public dissatisfaction with the regime by organizing the National Grouping in mid-1968 with the former prime minister Sulayman al-Nabulsi (who had become a symbol of opposition to the Hashemite regime in the mid-1950s) as chairman.[1] In November 1968, amid demonstrations organized by the Grouping against the Balfour Declaration, the US embassy in Amman was attacked,[2] bringing the tense Jordanian situation closer to the West. Intensive fighting in Amman between Jordanian and Palestinian forces followed that attack. Like all other confrontations between these forces it served notice of the growing support for the organizations within Jordan. Still, in retrospect, the loyal forces had the upper hand, giving a first glimpse of the tactics to be used later, in 1970, by a determined army, counting on the support of the Bedouin.

This developing confrontation with the PLO finally brought about the expected change in the *modus operandi* of the JAA. Indeed, 1969 saw the JAA returning to its old function: protecting the regime and transferring troops to the internal security forces.[3] In spite of the continued war of attrition with Israel the JAA began putting together a commando battalion and a General Security (i.e. police) brigade – not necessarily the kind of forces to confront Israel but no doubt capable of encountering any internal danger to the regime. The gradual change in the centrality of Israel as the enemy, along with the growing risk posed by the Palestinian organizations and Syria, found its mirror image in depicting Syria in the central role as enemy. There is a direct line connecting the apprehension voiced[4] by the king in January and February 1968 regarding Syria, its increasing encouragement of the *Sa'iqa* people to infiltrate into Jordan in late 1969, and its subsequent invasion in September 1970. Thereafter Jordanian security doctrine concentrated on domestic operations, as had been the case until 1964, and picked Syria and Israel as the main enemies of the kingdom.

The worsening situation was also demonstrated by the uncovering in early October 1969 of an alleged coup attempt by the small, insignificant *Hizb al-Tahrir* (Liberation Party), namely, the Muslim Brotherhood.[5] The announcement to that effect by the minister of the interior only served to further heighten the tension and apprehension of the rapidly growing local opposition. Indeed, before the incidents of September 1970 there were about 60,000 armed *fidayin* in Amman, who deprived the government of its authority; *fidayin* bases surrounded even Hussein's palace.[6] Moreover, Hussein had to accommodate the organizations within Jordan until there was no alternative but a confrontation.

Thus, only a few weeks before the Arab summit conference in Rabat, Morocco, in December 1969, which granted Yasir Arafat a status equal to all other Arab heads of state, Hussein declared Jordanian national objectives as follows:[7] (1) restoring Arab occupied territories in full, and (2) recognition that the Palestinian people have a lawful right to their usurped homeland. The message to both Houses of the Jordanian Parliament was crystal clear: namely that Israel should withdraw from all territories, but as far as the West Bank was concerned this should be in favor of the Palestinians, not necessarily of Jordan. Obviously, a distinction should be made here between the PLO, an arch-enemy at the time of the speech, and Hussein's interest in having a friendly Palestinian regime in the West Bank.

Several key developments characterized the civil war: the prohibition on personal arms in the Jordanian towns, in February, intensified the already existing tension between the Jordanian government and the Palestinian organizations and probably led to the outbreak of violence on a large scale. In August, apprehensive lest the Iraqi units would join in the fighting, Hussein asked Israel, through the US[8] – which refrained from conveying his message to Israel – for its position on possible Iraqi provocations. Actually, until the last stages of the civil war Hussein was more concerned[9] with the possibility that other Arab powers would see the existing circumstances as a pretext for the creation of a PLO state on both banks of the river. Perhaps one of the turning points leading to the final confrontation was public expression of contempt and disregard for the Jordanian regime by top PLO leaders in the context of the May 1970 Palestinian National Council. Later in the summer the Egyptians assessed that the US was widening the gap between Jordan and the PLO for its own purposes; this position was not in the king's favor since it meant calling for more agreements between Hussein and his enemies, that is to say, Hussein could be clear that Egypt at best would not take sides in the looming domestic crisis, and at worst would adopt an anti-Hashemite line.[10]

The domestic confrontation changed from an intensive series of Palestinian attacks on Jordanian targets into a full-fledged civil war on September 17.[11] The main burden of fighting fell on the Jordanian army, which mercilessly attacked the rebelling Palestinians. On September 20 the conflict changed from a domestic affair into an inter-state conflict with about 300 Syrian tanks crossing into Jordanian territory and capturing the northern town of Irbid; of these tanks about 130 would eventually be lost. That invasion prompted a state of alert among US troops. Only about six weeks after the UAR, in defiance of their cease-fire with Israel, had redeployed their ground-to-air missiles, the US badly needed to remedy its credibility after having done nothing in response to the Egyptian move. Iraq was no longer involved in the conflict, since on September 21, a 12,000-strong Iraqi expeditionary force left Jordan. Meanwhile, Israeli forces upon prior coordination with the US took positions and overflew the invading Syrian forces, indicating Israeli preparations to intervene on behalf of Hussein. The Jordanian moves along with the Israeli ones forced a Syrian retreat. This, along with the sudden passing of President Nasser, granted Hussein the time he needed to crush the Palestinian fighting until the final Hashemite victory in July 1971.

The events of 1970–1 serve as a clear indication of the newly acquired position of Hussein: in spite of the superficial similarity with the crises of 1963 and 1966, this one developed in a very different way in terms of its outcome. It is not only that Jordan was no longer besieged, but that it was able to rally the support of both Israel and the US behind its regime without any further negative regional repercussions. Another conclusion of the war was that the Palestinians as a coherent group living in Jordan did not on the whole take to arms against the regime, and after the war did not voice any national aspirations.[12] In this sense, the crisis in 1970–1 was remarkably different from those of the 1960s. Accounts emanating from US sources[13] suggest that Hussein was aware of the US military movements and the deliberations in Washington regarding the crisis at its peak during September 1970. Furthermore, other American moves involving the movement of troops and naval vessels were deliberately done in a way that would be picked up by the Soviets, so that their Syrian client would be deterred from any further action against Jordan. Thus, in spite of his stringent conditions, Hussein could draw a large degree of encouragement from the way the US acted. Indeed, in spite of the ongoing war in Vietnam the US saw this crisis as the most important since President Nixon came to office, and deemed it necessary to intervene and save the Hashemite rule. Actually, American policy makers were astonished to see Hussein wait until so late in September before reacting to the Palestinian activities. In hindsight this may indicate a tendency of Hussein to refrain from any drastic measures but to act, and decisively so, only when there was no other alternative – a pattern of political behavior that can be observed in many a crisis.

Hussein's moves during September 1970 were taken in concert with the US, which also served as the go-between with Israel. This public picture of American support for Jordan, let alone with the active participation of Israel, a public-enemy figure of the Arabs, could perhaps be drawn only as a result of the August developments. In early August 1970 Egypt, a leader in the war of attrition against Israel and a Soviet client, accepted a US-mediated cease-fire with Israel thus clearing the way to accepting the US as a broker. Hussein obviously took that precedent one step further – a move that would later produce the continued substantial, though fruitless, negotiations after 1970, especially in June 1972 with the Israeli offer of a mutual defense treaty.[14] This American approach not only brought about the Israeli intervention which eventually supplied the last element necessary to the survival of the kingdom, but also compelled Israel to finally make up its mind in favor of the continued existence of the Hashemite Kingdom.

However, even after the peak of hostilities in September 1970, but before the final conclusion of the civil war in July 1971, the king drew his own conclusions. Military means were not the only way to encounter the Palestinian threat. The new approach combined the king's public acknowledgments[15] of the need to create some sort of a Palestinian entity based at least publicly on a referendum among the Palestinians, with the reinforcing of notions of Jordanian nationalism as opposed to Palestinian nationalism. This is probably the first indication of the would-be "United Kingdom" plan. The best way of promoting this approach was obviously through diplomatic means. It is therefore important to examine an interview by Prime Minister Wasfi al-Tall (1965–7; 1970–1, until his assassination), broadcast[16] by Jordanian television in early 1971. The interview is not only a testimony to the success of the king in his efforts to disseminate Jordanian nationalism. It is also the political legacy of a leading Jordanian figure, destined to be assassinated less than a year after expressing these views. In a carefully worded answer during the interview al-Tall indicated clearly that Jordan had its own interests and that they could be accomplished only through diplomatic means. All through his response to questions and comments he was very careful to speak in Jordanian terminology: criticizing the Palestinian organizations, and indirectly rejecting the call of the late UAR president, Nasser, for a return of the territories by military means. This interview, as well as public expressions from other leading figures, suggested a new line, to be announced by the king in March 1972: a new, brave and definitely independent approach to the Palestinian issue.

After the civil war, military cooperation with the US expanded. It included the establishment of a joint committee of the two chiefs-of-staff to meet twice a year either in the US or in Jordan. In addition to the routine exchange of intelligence, a permanent representative of the CIA was assigned to Amman, his mission being to see the king on a regular basis.

The main burden of preparing his people for the new initiative was, after all, the task of King Hussein. Clearly, in his mind the civil war was only one of the scenarios used by the Palestinians to try and subvert the Hashemite monarchy. Even before the final stage of the fighting he was quick enough to lay the groundwork for a diplomatic effort on the Palestinian track to accomplish whatever was not possible through military confrontation. Once again, and at a fast pace, Hussein was moving against the Arab consensus of siding with the PLO, and he spoke for Jordan. Undoubtedly, this was a sign of self-confidence on the eve of the final crushing of the PLO, but also a desperate sign that he had no alternative policy. Already the new approach had been heralded by a message sent from Hussein to other Arab leaders shortly after the civil war reached its peak: it was sent on November 25, 1970, but was only made public by the Jordanian media four months later.[17] Between 1967 and 1972 the line presented by the king spoke of the relations between the peoples living on the two banks of the river and hinted at his political commitment to the two peoples. However, that commitment did not necessarily mean giving away the right of representation to the PLO. Nor did it mean Jordanian agreement to any independent Palestinian political entity. The domestic pressure reached its peak with the civil war, but its suppression did not solve much in terms of the ongoing diplomatic duel with the PLO. A solution became necessary; it had to reconcile Palestinian wishes on the West Bank with containment of the risk they posed to the Hashemite dynasty, and yet not get them back as full citizens.

The option most preferred by the king[18] until after the civil war was for West Bank local leaders to work hand in hand with Jordan. However, the outcome of the confrontation was the declaration of a new approach to Jordanian–Palestinian relations. On March 15, 1972, he declared his new policy:[19] the creation of a "United Kingdom" modeled on the British example. The plan spoke of two distinct provinces (*qutr*), Palestinian and Jordanian – clearly neither two separate countries nor full integration prior to 1967. In his mind the Palestinian province would constitute the Palestinian homeland but would be subject to Jordanian sovereignty. If accepted by the Palestinians and the Arab consensus, this could mean less Jordanian responsibility for them, whereas overall sovereignty and, obviously, security matters would be left in Amman's hands. Had he had it his way it would have meant an end to the PLO's claim of representing the Palestinian people, and made the king the rightful leader of all Palestinians, within the East and the West Banks. Later that year, in November 1972, against the context of possible interim agreements between Israel and Egypt, Hussein declared that all talk about partial agreements and individual enterprises was meaningless.[20] Using the Egyptian context he rejected the right of the PLO to move ahead with any agreement, leaving that right to Jordan itself. A few years later in a 1977 interview, he explained his approach:

> a couple [*sic*!] of years ago we presented a proposal to the world for creating a Jordanian–Palestinian federation which would go into effect the moment these territories became liberated from Israeli occupation. It caused much disgust and criticism of us at that time. Close relations exist and must exist between the two people if the West Bank should be able to exist as a state entity. It seems simply impossible that there should be no legal, constitutional connection between these two parts. I think that developments lead towards confederation from which later on a Jordanian–Palestinian federation will emerge, a unity with cantons.[21]

The idea of a "united kingdom" between two national entities became irrelevant with the resolutions of the Arab summit conference held in Rabat, Morocco, in late October 1974. Another approach, which also became obsolete, was Security Council Resolution 242. In retrospect, adopting the Rabat resolutions released Hussein, in his opinion,[22] from implementing 242. Put differently, with the Rabat resolutions in place, Hussein could find a legal, international basis not to claim any part of the West Bank, a move that clearly matched his strategy.

As of the Rabat conference, Hussein's language pertaining to the Palestinians changed drastically. Under pressure from the Arab world, he reluctantly let go of the claim to represent the Palestinian people. This conference was the stage for a united Arab resolution in favor of the prominence of the PLO in the Palestinian question. First and foremost, the conference resolution recognized the PLO as the sole and legitimate representative of the Palestinian people; in this way, depriving King Hussein of any future claim to represent the people of the West Bank. The resolution also confirmed the right of the Palestinian people to return to their country and determine their own future. The resolution spoke of the return of any liberated Palestinian territory to the Palestinian people under the leadership of the PLO. Moreover, it called for the establishment of a Palestinian state in the West Bank and the Gaza Strip once Israel withdrew its troops from all or part of the territories.

What is more, the resolution did not specify future relations between the Palestinian organizations and the Palestinian people of the East Bank. Hence, in one way or another the resolution even challenged the rule of the Hashemite king over his kingdom, which was inhabited predominantly by Palestinian subjects. The Rabat formula, later accepted as a cornerstone of any future settlement of the issue, shattered the hope of the king to represent the Palestinian people in the West Bank and indirectly induced him to seek further clarification of his position regarding relations among his own people on the East Bank. The need to bolster national cohesion became more urgent than ever. Succumbing to Arab pressure, King Hussein, who originally opposed the resolution, had to subordinate his own interests and comply with those of his fellow Arab leaders. In the wake of the conference he stopped referring to "this people which is composed of a Jordanian wing and a Palestinian wing."[23] From then on he refers time and again to the issue of the two peoples, Jordanian and Palestinian, clearly trying to distinguish between his own Jordanian citizens and the West Bank Palestinians. Still, on one element of the issue he did not change his opinion: the fact that the organization, as its name indicates, was representative of the Palestinian people for the purpose of liberating its territories from occupation, did not necessarily mean that once liberation had been accomplished all dimensions of Palestinian life would be the responsibility of the PLO. If that were the case, undoubtedly the very existence of the kingdom would be jeopardized. This premise led to the conclusion that the PLO's *raison d'être* would be lost and that it should be dissolved with the end of the occupation.

This position was obviously symmetrically opposed to that of the rest of the Arab countries, and obviously to that of the PLO. Still, Hussein's position was taken in order to give Jordan some standing or some leverage towards other Arab countries once a solution was being considered. This way Jordan would have some input into this critical process even though it might be only a token one. In order to secure it Jordan insisted throughout the years it was negotiating with Israel that whatever the final status of the West Bank, Jordan as the sovereign of land which was subject to hostile occupation, had the right to speak on behalf of its territory since any giving up of that right would open the way to an Israeli annexation, claiming that there was no other legal sovereign over this territory. Clearly, these views put Jordan and the PLO on a collision course that the Rabat resolution could not remove. However, in spite of those resolutions Jordan did not give up on its inclusion among the confrontation states aiming to remove the PLO from the political picture. While this was not possible considering the inter-Arab constellation, Jordan's persistence along these lines gave it the necessary Arab legitimacy in its dealings, public or secret, with Israel. Indeed, in spite of the spreading rumors since the mid-1970s of Israeli–Jordanian negotiations, and although Jordan received Arab subsidies as a confrontation state, it did not take long to legitimize its connections with Israel after the Oslo Accords were agreed, and to make public peace with Israel.

The main result of the Rabat formula was the beginning of a confrontation between Jordan on the one hand and the rest of the Arab world on the other. After all, the resolution took away from Jordan any right of representation or of speaking on behalf of the West Bankers. That formula forced Jordan to adopt more indirect ways to try and resolve the Palestinian issue its way. Indeed, seven years after the 1967 armed conflict with Israel, and the king's attempt to work out a secret *de facto* peace, he was put once more at square one by his fellow Arab leaders.

There followed a series of unofficial visits in Amman by PLO figures and a decision by the PLO Central Committee to open negotiations with Jordan. Officially, negotiations began in February 1977 with the visit of Khalid al-Fahum, which in turn paved the way for the historic March 1977 Hussein–Arafat summit in Cairo. The topic on the agenda was almost dictated by Jordan: to define ways to implement the March 1972 United Kingdom plan. Arafat's total refusal to discuss the plan led to the failure of the meeting. However, in retrospect it was convenient for Hussein to blame the failure of his negotiations in 1976–7 on President Sadat's visit to Jerusalem in November 1977, which in his words "caused the failure of action and coordination with Egypt, Syria, and the PLO aiming at the resumption of the international conference with the PLO's participation."[24]

Almost no contacts are recorded between Jordan and the PLO between 1971 and the Rabat summit conference in 1974. The process of "Jordanization" initiated by Hussein in the wake of the conference was interpreted by the PLO as a call to establish new channels of communication between the two players, in spite of their mutual hatred. Clearly, in the period post-Rabat the PLO held the key to negotiating on behalf of the Palestinians whereas Jordan held the key to Jerusalem and Washington.

Avoiding one of these two players would have brought any attempt to negotiate on the Palestinian issue to a dead end. Yet, there is nowhere any indication of any significant dialogue between the two until late 1976, although some low-level contacts were recorded on the eve of the convening of the Jordanian Lower House in 1976.

By the end of 1976 and after a period of almost no contact between Jordan and the PLO since the last military confrontation of July 1971, limited negotiations were resumed. With their continued interest in influencing the diplomatic processes relating to the West Bank and the PLO, damaged by the outbreak of the civil war in Lebanon and its subsequent stages, both sides had a renewed interest in talking to each other. After a series of informal contacts Hussein and Arafat met in Cairo in March 1977. However, with the continued insistence of Hussein on his United Kingdom plan there was almost no room for any common formula leading to a breakthrough in the negotiations.

Official contacts between Jordan and the PLO were resumed in late 1976. Apparently, this had nothing to do with interim agreements between Israel and its other neighbors. At that time there were no significant Israeli–Jordanian negotiations on any ingredient of a possible agreement.[25] This obviously leads to the issue of timing: what led these two enemies, not long ago engaged in a bloody military confrontation, to sit together and discuss political cooperation? The answer to that question lies with two sources: first, three countries pressed Jordan and the PLO to close ranks at a time in which Israel was seen as a weak link in the Middle East, and therefore as bound to make major concessions to a united Arab front. Considering the make-up of this front, the king could not ignore it: Saudi Arabia, the regional Arab banker; Egypt, the leading power in times of war (1973) and diplomacy (1974, 1975); and Syria, the mighty neighbor with which Jordan had followed a careful process of rapprochement since 1975 (until 1980). From a Jordanian point of view the time was ripe: with the Lebanese civil war going on since April 1975 the PLO was no longer the powerful player that had threatened the existence of the kingdom only five or six years earlier.

Jordan and its king entered a new phase of relations with the PLO during 1977. This stage, continuing until the abortive agreement between Hussein and Arafat in 1985, was drastically influenced by the new axis emerging between Jerusalem and Cairo, which eventually led to the 1979 Israeli–Egyptian peace treaty. The process, the first of its kind, brought Jordan and the PLO closer together in their opposition to these moves. This rapprochement was also the result of the 1975 US–Israeli memorandum of understanding in which, as part of the Israeli–Egyptian disengagement agreement, the US took upon herself not to open a dialogue with the PLO for as long as it failed to meet two specified conditions: to recognize Israel's right to exist; and to accept Security Council Resolutions 242 and 338. These developments coming on top of the Rabat resolutions deprived Jordan of any right of representation of the Palestinians, but left the kingdom as the only player in the Palestinian context capable of talking to Israel and the US. Thus, the PLO and Jordan began to operate as the Siamese twins of the conflict.

This change in the Jordanian position and the long-range effects of Rabat on the political thinking and behavior of the king are reflected in an interview held in 1977. On this occasion King Hussein voiced his reflections on the conference, stating:

> everything stems from the fact that we never at any time succeeded in obtaining the support necessary to recover the least part of the territories lost in June 1967. We did not participate in the 1973 conflict . . . to this we must add the feeling in the Arab world that the Palestinians must participate in any solution. . . . (It was) a decision that we had to accept. The only other option open to us was to fight not only Israel, but the entire Arab world and the Palestinian people . . . we had to yield.[26]

Emerging mutual interests and common political needs did not rid Jordan of its fears of the PLO. The king intended neither to improve his relations with the PLO, nor to reach a full understanding with them. Under the leadership of Hussein, Jordan was committed to work diligently to enable the Palestinian people to regain their rights and live in peace; however, the King also stressed that the PLO must work hard to represent the people of Palestine and must not be forced upon them, as might have happened. To ensure the security of Jordan from PLO aggression, Hussein warned that "Palestinian fighting and *fedayeen* organizations will never get a foothold or basis in Jordan, but we are always willing to partake in an open political dialogue and to cooperate constructively with the PLO."[27] The king also remarked that Jordan must be able to demand that the PLO meet Jordan's expectations as well as the desires of the Palestinian people.

The Developing 1973 Arab–Israeli War and the Period of Interim Agreements

With the aims of the June war fully realized Jordan did not need any more military confrontations with Israel. An Arab victory would undoubtedly have brought it once again into the focus of confrontation with the Palestinians, while an Arab defeat would jeopardize its East Bank, and indeed the very existence of the kingdom. Furthermore, the years since the 1967 war, and the failed peace attempts, brought Israel and Jordan closer together, and the king had no interest in sacrificing these ties for an unclear future among his Arab neighbors. On the eve of a new round of hostilities between Israel and some of its neighbors, Jordan and the king personally found themselves in dire straits. While agonizing to reach the right decision the king rushed to Tel Aviv to see the prime minister of Israel and warn her of the imminent danger. Failing in his efforts to get Israel to avert a war, either by military or by diplomatic means, he ordered that two armored brigades and one commando battalion be sent to the Syrian–Israeli front at the Golan Heights. Of these forces, only one brigade actually participated in the war. Even with this participation, the exact motives behind the king's moves both before and during the fighting are open to question, not because of his meeting with the prime minister of Israel, which is understandable considering past relations between the two countries, but rather, the choice of tank brigade no. 40 as the only force to engage in battle. After all, only three years beforehand, in September 1970, this very brigade had bravely fought the Syrian forces invading Jordan. It is therefore doubtful whether the king had in mind any really effective cooperation and coordination between his forces on Syrian territory, knowing the role Israel had played in saving their country, and between the local Syrian forces.

In May 1973, after Israel declared a state of alert, fearing another round of fighting with its Arab neighbors, the king made sure Israel knew he had no part in it. Moreover, in a message to his officers leaked to the Lebanese French-language daily *L'Orient le Jour* he elaborated[28] on the possibility of Jordanian participation in a new war. In short it would mean the destruction of the East Bank, in effect the disappearance of the Hashemite Kingdom. It is possible that this particular document, probably along with other expressions of reluctance, led Presidents Sadat and Asad not to invite King Hussein to participate in the 1973 war. Since he himself mentioned that he had not been privy to the preparations, in a speech at the October 1974 Arab summit conference in the presence of the two presidents, there is no reason to doubt this.

The military endeavors of Egypt and Syria in October 1973 could no longer be justified as part of a concerted inter-Arab effort, led by Egypt, to defeat Israel, as was the case in 1967. The 1973 war was, more than anything else, the outcome of joint Egyptian and Syrian national interests aimed at gaining diplomatic benefits and emanating from six years of frustration and fatalism. Obviously, Jordan did not share these feelings. One reason being that with its diplomatic relations with Egypt severed since the Jordanian announcement of the United Kingdom plan, Jordan was no longer considered a partner of Egypt in diplomacy and war. The most the two countries managed to accomplish on the eve of the October war was to resume diplomatic relations. Moreover, as already indicated, the kingdom was not too sorry about losing a large Palestinian population to Israel in 1967. Jordan's worst fear in 1973 was a war that would bring the

West Bank back into Hashemite hands. Furthermore, the movement of these two countries away from general Arab causes reduced the risk of Jordan being punished for not participating in an Arab move. The first indication of this emerging pattern was seen in Syria's failed attempts to interfere in the 1970 civil war in Jordan for its own interests and not for the Palestinians. These factors encouraged King Hussein to take an unprecedented risk[29] for himself and the Hashemite Kingdom by meeting Prime Minister Golda Meir in late September 1973 on the eve of the October war, and giving her an early warning of the impending Arab attack on Israel. Undoubtedly, King Hussein was putting his political future and legitimacy at risk in order to rescue his closest ally and, in line with noble Bedouin tradition, pay Israel back the debt of honor he owed from 1970 when Israel had come to his rescue. Publicly, Jordan refrained from participation in the 1973 war and was content to dispatch some military forces to the Golan Heights front. Clearly, the 1970 and 1973 episodes should be seen as two sides of the same coin: the mutual Jordanian–Israeli security guarantee was not put to the test in a major crisis where it was relevant. In 1981 Israeli airplanes on a mission to bomb the Iraqi nuclear reactor were spotted by the king himself, but no Arab action was taken against them. This strongly suggests that once the king thought the planes were not on their way to bomb targets in his kingdom, the level of Jordanian readiness to involve itself in another military confrontation was very low.

The king's decision to take a symbolic part in the October 1973 war the way he did reflected simultaneously his acquired status among his fellow Arab leaders, which enabled him to refrain from direct involvement from his own sovereign territory, and his concern lest the Arab side should win the war. His concerns and attempt to keep in touch with what was happening came to be reflected in his participation in the December 1973 Geneva Conference and, later on, the shuttle diplomacy conducted between Israel and the confrontation countries, including Jordan, by the US Secretary of State, Henry Kissinger. Publicly, Jordan tried to reach its own disengagement agreement with Israel.[30]

Actually, the political and military lessons of 1973 were very carefully studied by the JAA. The main assumption behind the Jordanian analysis was that Iraq and Syria constituted much more of a danger than Israel, but that any overt defensive effort in their direction would be impertinent considering the possible inter-Arab political fall-out. Thus, the new army reorganization plan implemented in early 1977 can be interpreted as a step in that direction and away from confrontation with Israel. The main change in conceptual terms had to do with the longer range of activity now available to the Jordanian forces – ranges which could be seen as overkill as far as Israel was concerned, but were necessary if Syria and Iraq were the undeclared enemy. Basically, the infantry units were mostly transformed into mechanized units, the armored and mechanized units were supplied with longer-range diesel engines, and above all, the commando units, one of which had already demonstrated their combat readiness in 1975 in Oman, were now re-equipped with more sophisticated war material. In sum, the JAA was reduced from five divisions to four, but they all enjoyed more capability than ever before, especially if the unthinkable should happen and Jordan was once more attacked by any of its neighbors, from whatever direction.

In a nutshell, the reorganization plan should be seen as preparing for new enemies but in a way that would not alarm Hussein's Arab neighbors.

During the October war the JAA did not operate from Jordanian sovereign territory, but through an expeditionary force which participated in the fighting on the Israeli–Syrian front. This force advanced in the direction of the Israeli forces in the newly occupied Syrian enclave and was deployed for a short while opposite the Israeli forces. However, only a minor exchange of fire was ever recorded between these two armies. Moreover, even though the Jordanian order of battle on Syrian soil reached, as of October 19, two armored brigades and one commando battalion, only one tank brigade was actually involved in fighting (no. 40). The Jordanian expeditionary force was evacuated from Syrian territory on January 1, 1974.

In spite of Israeli help in encountering the Syrian invasion and the clear Israeli policy against the PLO and in favor of the survival of Jordan during the civil war, the king was not convinced at least publicly of the purity of Israel's intentions. In a message to Arab leaders in November 1970 he spoke[31] of the possibility that Israel would concentrate its efforts in turning Jordan and the territories into an alternative homeland for the Palestinians instead of the Hashemite Kingdom.

The October war paved the way for a series of talks and indirect negotiations between Israel and its neighbors – a process alien to the king's policy of trying to keep the Israeli track open and coming to secret understandings without setting foot on the West Bank. In this respect the token participation of Jordan in the October war contributed to its exclusion from the interim talks between Egypt, Syria and Israel. Throughout 1974 King Hussein tried to be included in similar talks, and he met an Israeli delegation in the summer of 1974 in this context,[32] but to no avail; after all he had not gained or lost any territory to Israel during October 1973. However, an obvious question in this regard should be his true interest in the interim agreement with Israel. Would it give a new boost to his emerging Jordanian nation-state, or would it only put him on a collision course with the PLO, which at that time was working on a way to become recognized as the representative of all Palestinians? The backbone of the interim agreements reached in 1974 and 1975 was a degree of Israeli withdrawal in exchange for a degree of normalization. For Jordan, that was not too attractive: it did not need even the smallest piece of land from the West Bank, and it already had a degree of normalization with Israel unprecedented compared with all other Arab countries. This does not mean that Jordan liked the idea of the PLO gaining international legitimacy; obviously, its main interest was to secure continued influence over the West Bank, whereas the PLO offered a whole new set of rules. Indeed, four years after Black September, King Hussein did not want the West Bank back, but preferred a friendly leadership rather than the enemy, the PLO. Perhaps one part of the answer is to be found in Riad's memoirs. While discussing the maneuvers regarding the possible convening of the Geneva Conference, he states:[33] "Jordan demanded that a disengagement agreement on the Jordanian front be reached first, with Israel withdrawing some eight to ten kilometres from the River Jordan. Israel refused the Jordanian proposal, adhering to Allon's project which advocated the continued occupation of positions along the River Jordan in any future settlement." Since Hussein had already known for several years that Israel insisted on the implementation of the Allon plan, how could he genuinely propose a settlement based on any other blueprint?

Hussein's public stand in favor of an interim agreement, which probably did not reflect his true interests and was voiced in order for his kingdom to continue being included among the peace-loving nations of the Middle East, did not mean that he did not want to continue his efforts at reaching a secret working agreement with Israel. At Israeli insistence on conducting negotiations with Jordan ("the Jordanian option"), Hussein reaffirmed publicly in 1976 that he had no alternative but to accept the Rabat resolution. In an attempt to clarify his stand on the Palestinian issue, he explained, "up to the Rabat Conference we strove to regain the territory and place it under international control to enable the population to exert the right of self-determination on its future. Rabat changed all that. PLO has assumed responsibility. It was a uniform Arab decision and we support it."[34] His modified approach to relations between the Palestinians and Jordanians was clearly displayed in speeches made to delegations from the occupied territories. Addressing his guests he stressed that historic, geographic, and pan-Arab factors meant that his relationship with the Palestinians remained solid, firm, and lasting. However, from this period on he used cordial but not political terms, describing the nature of relations between two distinct peoples living on both banks of the river. In his words: "there are no barriers between us. I am one of you and you are one of us. I am a brother to you and you are family to me in all conditions and circumstances."[35]

Even though publicly he denied all accusations of trying to represent the Palestinian people, often his old political ambitions would still surface, indicating his basic concerns regarding the Palestinians. On one occasion in early 1976, he invited 30 members from the former House of Representatives (which had been dissolved following the Rabat Conference) who represented the West Bank. The Arab world saw this as an initiative aimed at gaining influence over the West Bank Palestinians and as a revocation of the king's acceptance of the Rabat summit resolutions. It was during this period that Hussein tried to distinguish between the violent PLO and the Palestinian people. He created an equation in which the PLO equaled violence and terror. When questioned about his relations with the PLO, he stated, "there are no problems between Jordan and the PLO and previous acts of violence by the Palestinian people were only caused by despair."[36] In other words, the king still envisaged a small role for himself, representing those Palestinians who did not see eye to eye with the PLO.

Also between June and October 1974 the US invested some diplomatic effort in an attempt to secure an Israeli–Jordanian disengagement agreement to fit into the Nixon administration's policy after the 1973 war, to use that agreement as a springboard for furthering the regional peace process. That policy in its Jordanian dimension came to an end in October 1974 with the Rabat summit resolutions.

During the financial year 1974/5 the East Bank enjoyed many economic advantages from Israeli control over the West Bank. During that year Jordan had a real profit of 6.5 million Jordanian dinars (mJD) in its balance of payments with the West Bank. Additionally, the West Bank had at its disposal financial resources emanating from Israel to the amount of 4.5 mJD. Thus, Jordan stood to lose 11 mJD if Israel withdrew from the West Bank. These resources amounted to about 2.5 percent of total Jordanian resources: not a figure to influence political and strategic decisions, but still it had to be taken into account in a country with a shaky economy like Jordan's. Moreover, the continued exposure of the West Bank to Israel and the Western way of life increased the import of goods to the West Bank enormously. In 1974/5 the West Bank's imports exceeded its exports by 22 mJD. If added to the Jordanian export/import balance, that would have meant a 20 percent increase in the Jordanian national export/import deficit. This of course might have added to Jordan's political vulnerability and made it even more of a captive in the hands of the countries financing it. The advantages of Jordan's position only added to an already flourishing economy: between 1972 and 1982 the Jordanian gross domestic product increased by 8 percent annually, and if transfers from ex-patriots were added the increase would be 10 percent. This economic picture is probably primarily the result of the flow of petro-dollars from the oil-rich Arab countries.[37]

During the presidency of Jimmy Carter, relations between Israel and Jordan did not go well, as a result of the king's decision not to join the

Camp David process. The annual US financial support for Jordan dropped as a result from $40 million in 1978 to $20 million in 1980.[38]

A Pillar of Legacy: *ad hoc* coalitions with one of the neighbors

Perhaps one of the main strategic assets of the Hashemite Kingdom is its location at the heart of the Arab world. Thus, removing this national entity might cause a diplomatic tremor leading to unexpected results. Accordingly, even during the ordeal of the 1960s Hussein was not sure whether he or his regime would survive Nasser but he was confident that the Jordanian entity, under whatever name or regime, would outlast its leaders. With the gradual yet clear improvement in Hussein's prestige after the 1967 war and his active participation in most consensual processes, including summit conferences of confrontation states, he ceased to be a pariah leader. This change helped him to launch another pillar of his regional policy, one that would characterize the Hashemite Kingdom after the 1967 war, but was clearly evident in the 1970s and the 1980s.

The gist of this policy was that Jordan should at all times align itself with one of its immediate Arab neighbors while keeping open channels to Israel and the US, realizing that the joint Israeli–US interest was to prefer Hussein, whatever his regional policy, to any other alternative. Thus, even coalitions with declared enemies of the US could be forgiven. Moreover, considering the similarity in interests between the Hashemite and the Saudi kingdoms even a policy contrary to that of the latter would not have set off any irreversible processes. Given these premises the real choice facing Jordan for a long period, at least since the 1967 war, was: should the closer ally be Syria or Iraq, neither of which was an ally of the West? Indeed, for most of the time since 1973 the choice was Iraq and not Syria. This policy was successfully tested regarding Syria during the era of interim accords in the middle and late 1970s and in the 1990–1 Gulf crisis and war involving Iraq. However, in Hussein's inter-Arab relations he definitely preferred Iraq to Syria, leading him at times to critical moments in his security considerations. Syria served as the closest ally between 1975 and 1980 whereas Iraq basically served in this capacity from the time of the outbreak of the Iraq–Iran war in 1980. What led to these coalitions and why was the alliance with Syria abandoned in favor of Iraq? Answering these questions attests to the basic strategic interests of Jordan, which did not dramatically change during the life of Hussein.

Syrian–Jordanian rapprochement during the 1970s is probably an indication of Jordanian strategic interests in action. This process began to unfold in the wake of the 1973 war only a few weeks after the resumption of diplomatic relations, which had been cut off in July 1971 in the context of the Jordanian civil war. Jordan participated on Syria's side but did not open fire from its own territory. In all probability if his aim was to re-occupy the West Bank then the coordinated Syrian–Egyptian attack might have given Hussein a golden opportunity. Even if he was not a party to the planning, his meeting with the Israeli prime minister proved that he was aware of at least some of the plans and could put his forces on alert for an eventuality leading him to an attack on the West Bank. His token partici-pation in the war indicates a possible determination on his part not to be drawn into a war in which he might find himself holding parts of the 1967 occupied territories. On that account he found himself, at the end of the 1973 war, in a situation not very different from that of Syria: he could not seek an agreement with Israel since it could not be reached in a way that would guarantee Jordanian security, with the West Bank turning into a PLO enclave, reviving fresh memories of 1970. That consideration became more acute in the wake of the Rabat resolution, which given the right circumstances could be interpreted as the preamble for such a PLO entity without giving Jordan any way of resisting it. Syria, along similar lines, had no immediate interest in reclaiming the Golan Heights. However, it certainly needed the removal of the threat to Damascus in the form of Israeli forces deployed several dozen miles from its capital. Thus, with Jordan paying its dues through its participation in the war but without any interest whatsoever in an open settlement with Israel, and Syria for its part not interested in a series of disengagement agreements along the Egyptian track, the meeting of interests was evident.

However, in retrospect it is safe to assume that aside from that tactical meeting of interests Syria had much less to offer Jordan compared with Iraq. After all, the latter had oil, much larger foreign currency reserves, and in times of potential or real threat to the Iraqi ports, Aqaba could serve that function for Iraq. Syria did not possess any of the above, though it did have its own open outlet to the Mediterranean. Jordanian–Iraqi relations have been less hostile and aggressive than those with Syria. In spite of the 1958 republican revolution and the bloody end to the Iraqi Hashemite dynasty, relations between the two countries were restored in 1960. Even though these relations have mirrored relations with Syria they have differed in nature, quality, and duration. If any Arab country during Hussein's reign was a true ally it was Iraq, not Saudi Arabia, and definitely not Syria.

Actually, the warm relations between Syria and Jordan in the mid-1970s came to an abrupt end later in 1980 after about seven years of multi-track processes demonstrating their then shared interests. That period can be divided into two: the period immediate after the 1973 war, and the time between 1975 and 1980. The first stage, coming right after the 1973 cease-fire, saw continued preparations for the possibility of resuming the war against Israel. Jordan had a clear interest in preventing any further military moves, since both Israel and Syria were rather anxious that the area of Irbid and the Umm Qays ridge in Jordan might serve the other party as an attack route. For Jordan that possibility, if used by any of the parties, would undoubtedly have jeopardized either Jordanian standing among the Arab nations, if it would not allow the Syrian army to try and foil such an attack as it was developing on Jordanian territory, or its secret but warm relations with Israel, if Syria *was* allowed to attack Israel. Furthermore, as recently as September 1970 Syria had used these routes or others close to them to invade Jordan, so how could Jordan trust Syria so soon afterwards not to use the inter-Arab anti-Israeli context to try and take over parts of northern Jordan, harming in the process the one party which had stood by Israel back in 1970.

Obviously, these strategic considerations caused by the unclear political and military conditions, and the mutual suspicion caused by them, were supplemented by many more Jordanian considerations shared with Syria. The Palestinian dimension was one of them. During 1974 Egypt had sided more and more with the PLO until the Rabat resolution was adopted. Jordan, worried about its status in any upcoming political process, found an ally in Syria, which did not have any interest in an Egyptian-led or Egyptian-inspired process either. During 1975 and 1976 that *ad hoc* coalition of interests saw a succession of steps, taken by both sides, indicating the emergence of very close relations: from the Hussein–Asad meeting in Damascus in April 1975 and the agreement on joint military procedures, which never took place, to a higher coordination committee made up of the two prime ministers, and a higher leadership committee composed of President Asad and King Hussein. The initial Jordanian support for Sadat's November 1977 initiative in coming to Jerusalem did not change the nature of relations on the surface. Rather, this last episode was probably the move which caused Hussein once again to try and bolster his connections with Syria. However, the period between Sadat's visit and the Camp David accords was not an easy one for either country. Syria used its media to voice dissatisfaction with Jordanian positions, which were interpreted as supporting Sadat's views. Armed groups began infiltrating from Syria with the aim of hitting Jordanian targets.

The Syrian opposition to Sadat's peace moves was met by Jordanian uncertainty regarding the place allocated for Jordan in the proposed framework for peace in the Middle East worked out by Egypt and Israel. The Camp David accords agreed upon by Israel and Egypt in September 1978 were not the result of any significant consultations with Jordan and were actually a dictate by both parties – something Jordan could not agree to. Still, this Jordanian opposition did not serve as a basis for rebuilding Syrian–Jordanian relations. Jordan's moves bringing it closer to Iraq served to highlight fears and concerns regarding Syria, throwing the two countries further apart. The Israeli–Egyptian peace treaty of March 1979, which followed the Camp David accords, only added to the insult. For Syria however, this diplomatic constellation presented an opportunity to align itself with Jordan, a country enjoying warm relations with the US, a cornerstone of any diplomatic process in the Middle East, and thus keep an eye in developing processes, a country also that had open channels to Saudi Arabia, whose importance as the main Arab banker was incomparable at this time of the energy crisis. With these foundations of relations laid down gradually in the 1970s it was only natural that Hussein would add his own personal touch and develop the political association into a personal friendship with President Asad, reflected in a large number of meetings between the two leaders.

With the outbreak of the Iraq–Iran war in September 1980 both countries reassessed their respective policies. Syria sided with Iran whereas Jordan sided with Iraq. That watershed in the course of the war also marked a change in the nature of relations between Jordan and Syria. From a Syrian viewpoint the new coalitions threatened its basic premises: the diplomatic process in the region, or to be more accurate the opposition to the process, was no longer the focus of attention for the regional powers and for international players. The Persian Gulf area and the security of the oil pipelines became much more acute for most of the parties. Furthermore, the new Iraq–Jordan coalition marked a point of potential threat for Syria – with these two countries aligned together, probably with potential help from the US, Syria as a client of the Soviet Union might have found itself in a defensive position. This led *inter alia* to the conclusion of a Treaty of Friendship and Cooperation between the two countries in October 1980, further contributing to the rapid deterioration of relations between Jordan and Syria.

Concurrent with the processes involving Syria, Jordan improved its relations with Egypt in addition to the creation of the new axis with Baghdad. These moves highlighted a change in the inter-Arab standing of Jordan: from a marginal country forced to forge a coalition with Syria, it found itself at center stage, a position which could have exposed Jordan to some subversive activity on the part of Syria. After all, Jordan in Syrian eyes was the secondary partner in their coalition, but would be an essential part of any coalition which might turn against Syria. Thus, the two countries made their moves in anticipation of possible future moves. Jordan, in line with past precedents, called for the convening of an Arab summit, which eventually met in Amman in late November 1980. Syria not only boycotted the conference but also, in addition to incitement in the form of broadcasts from Damascus depicting Hussein as a traitor, began to build up its forces along the Syrian–Jordanian common border. During the last week of November 1980 and concurrent with the summit, Syria deployed two armored divisions along the border, creating a major threat not only for Jordan but also for Israel, which interpreted this build-up as a two-pronged risk. For Israel it was a *déjà vu* of 1970. The reaction was similar: as in 1970, Israel stood guard and deterred Syria from taking aggressive measures against the kingdom by calling in some reserve units and deploying them along the Israeli–Jordanian border with Syria. Once again, with US involvement and Saudi mediation efforts, the danger was removed. This did not deter Syria from voicing its resentment at Jordanian policies, but did not lead to any further military showdown. The final outcome of the crisis underlined the evident meeting of interests between Israel, Jordan, and the US with the involvement of Saudi Arabia. Clearly, the 1970 and 1980 understandings and precedents further improved the mutual appreciation of the roles of Israel and Jordan in the region.

The Rabat formula and the processes leading to its acceptance proved to Hussein, and not for the first time, the fragility of his standing among the Arab nations. Thus, the Arab summit conference served as the beginning of a new process of improving the inter-Arab standing of the kingdom. It was a policy which resulted in the warming up of relations with Syria, and the Jordanization process somewhat improved Jordan's position *vis-à-vis* other Arab countries so that by 1976, with new discussions regarding the reconvening of the Geneva Conference, it could take a position calling for Jordanian participation in the conference under the 1972 banner of a "United Kingdom." Throughout 1977 Jordan became bolder and bolder in expressing its views in public. It advocated signing a peace treaty with Israel in exchange for a full Israeli withdrawal, including from Jerusalem, and Israeli recognition of the Palestinian right to self-determination. In terms where Jordan really stood as opposed to public opinion, it signaled a further closing of the gap between the two: Jordan was not calling for an Israeli withdrawal in favor of the kingdom, but for an unspecified form of Palestinian self-determination, namely one that would be influenced by Jordanian interests. That approach was expressed in the Jordanian reading of the Geneva Conference issue: Jordan believed that the conference should be as binding as possible on the participants, that is, any Israeli–Jordanian agreement could be presented as the result of giving in to international pressures, whereas in terms of representation Jordan believed that the Palestinians should be included in a unified Arab delegation, that is to say, in spite of the Rabat resolutions the PLO would not gain an independent right of representation.

There is no indication to suggest that Hussein knew ahead of time of the upcoming visit of Egyptian President Sadat to Jerusalem. In spite of his surprise Hussein reacted positively to the visit and the diplomatic process that followed. Clearly, his hope was that by sanctioning Sadat's moves the road would be opened for him to make his contacts with Israel not only public but also acceptable if and when he could reach a workable comprehensive agreement with Israel. However, in spite of his hopes and discreet efforts to be admitted to the negotiations he could not join the process for two reasons. In September 1978 Israel and Egypt concluded their Camp David accords calling for autonomy for the Palestinians in the territories, which were not too specific regarding the role that Jordan should play in determining the future of the Palestinian question. Later that year, the Arab summit in Baghdad did not allow Hussein to evade a decision any longer. After all, all Arab countries with the exception of Egypt were united in their opposition to Sadat's policies and Hussein, in line with past models of political behavior, could not be left alone as the only party to break up the Arab consensus opposing any agreement with Israel. Thus, Hussein adopted a line calling for the conclusion of a wider agreement on the Palestinian issue that would address all the issues not tackled by the Camp David accords.

The Israeli–Egyptian diplomatic process, begun in 1977 without the participation of Hussein, confronted him once again with an almost impossible dilemma: how to get into public negotiations with Israel, thus legitimizing all prior contacts and understandings, and yet not act in a way contrary to the Rabat formula, namely leaving the right of representation in the hands of the PLO. The king's efforts to demonstrate his repudiation of any representation of the Palestinian people still left a small crack for his own political ambitions in the period 1977–85, and clearly he made an effort to demonstrate his national interest in peace. After the historic visit of Egyptian President Sadat to Jerusalem, but before the agreements reached in Camp David, Hussein prepared the groundwork for not participating in the process due to his lack of legitimacy in representing the Palestinians. In an interview with the BBC in January 1978 Hussein, when asked why he had not given Sadat his wholehearted support, stated: "But I have. I tried my best to help with the rest of the Arab world, to try to bring it together. But I have made it very clear from the beginning that President Sadat's initiative was a very brave, courageous one." He later went on to applaud the Arab effort at peace and included himself in that effort by saying: "I don't think that anyone could have done more for the cause of peace, and if it fails it is not on *our* heads, on *our* shoulders, in terms of the blame, but on Israel." Hussein also said that Sadat had "represented the world and the Arab view and the Arab aspiration and feeling before the world."[39]

In a September 1978 press conference in Amman, Hussein once again demonstrated to the public that the interests of Jordanian sovereignty superseded its efforts to liberate the occupied territories. Hussein remarked, "Jordan will not close any doors that may lead to the termination of the occupation and the salvation of our people under occupation. We will, however, not sacrifice our principles or national rights."[40] He refers to the Palestinian people under occupation as "our people" in the context of making a connection between them and his kingdom. In Hussein's approach, distinguishing between them and the PLO attests to the bond between Jordanians and Palestinians, which is strong but rather emotional and does not provide any tangible results for the Palestinians. Yet, according to this line of thinking the lands would end up in Palestinian possession (with some sort of Jordanian influence), which does not equal PLO presence or possession. This approach is probably one of the indications of the still unchanged interest of Hussein to exert influence over the West Bank through a friendly, yet local Palestinian leadership.

Perhaps the most important lesson of the 1970s is that the embattled country of Jordan is in the Middle East to stay, along with its Hashemite ruling dynasty, at least for the foreseeable future. Moreover, that decade marked a sharp improvement in the status of Hussein and his kingdom: most of the traditional secret or semi-public supporters expressed their support for the continued existence of the Hashemite Kingdom, siding with Jordan against foreign threats. It was a decade that helped Hussein to acquire enough self-confidence to let him take public positions contrary to those of his main supporters, Israel and the US, knowing very well that their positions would harm Jordanian interests in the long run. That process of gradually uncovering the real nature of the political behavior of Hussein, as a regional leader and not someone led by others, was revealed through a chain of events which made him demonstrate his mastery of political tricks and maneuvers. The accumulation of challenges, most of them regional with the major exception of the 1970/1 civil war, poised Hussein and Jordan in positions forcing it to make up its mind in regard to the Palestinian issue after the civil war and the Rabat resolutions; respond to the developing 1973 Arab–Israeli war and consequently the interim-agreements policy of the US, and eventually the Israeli–Egyptian peace process of the late 1970s; and in 1980 once again face another Syrian challenge.

8

The Palestinian Decade and the
Final Closing of the West Bank Issue

In retrospect, the years of Hussein's reign since 1980, with what was almost a showdown with Syria and the outbreak of the Iraq–Iran war, were perhaps one of the most successful periods of Jordan under its king. This was an era of solidifying the most significant accomplishment of Hussein's reign, which had already become evident in the 1970s: Jordan along with its Hashemite dynasty was a fact of life in a volatile region. Moreover, since the existence of the Hashemite entity was in no more danger, Hussein could cautiously try some more active domestic and foreign policy moves on behalf of his Jordanian nation-state. This rather optimistic picture is the combined outcome of the Israeli–Egyptian peace process, which while legitimizing such a process with Israel, gave Hussein the opportunity to publicly side with the opponents of the process and be given a clean slate from his fellow Arab leaders in spite of his own ongoing talks with Israeli leaders. Even the tension with Syria bordering on an open military confrontation was less threatening, with the lack of an actual Syrian invasion, but it helped explore once again the powers that would protect Jordan in time of need – conditions which were hard to reach in the 1960s. The Israeli war in Lebanon along with the weakening of the PLO and the continued process of gradual disengagement from the West Bank allowed Hussein, albeit in a limited way, to resume parliamentary life in Jordan in early 1984. The PLO's exclusive right of representation along with the Jordanian dialogue with Israel and the United States brought Hussein and Arafat to another round of touch and go politics in 1985 and 1986 which led, after no tangible outcome was accomplished, to the Palestinian uprising in the territories. It seems that while officially disconnecting his ties with the West Bank, a move which he had envisaged many years back, Hussein could uninterruptedly devote his full attention to the closing of loose ends and to Jordanian domestic challenges. Thus, he put in place some of the last bricks of his political legacy: the conclusion of the public disengagement process from the West Bank, and the resumption of parliamentary life; all that on top of making Jordan a country acceptable both regionally and internationally.

The Palestinian uprising which broke out in 1987 gave Hussein one of the very few opportunities to speak frankly about his true interests. In a speech at the June 1988 Arab summit in Algiers he denied altogether that Jordan had ever annexed the West Bank.[1] The relationship was a union based on the popular demand of the Palestinians, answering the issues of the time, which were no longer valid at the time of Hussein's speech. In many ways this was not only an admission of the strategy of Hussein not to get back the territories, but was actually based on the current reading of the 1950 experience, a preamble to the public renouncing of the West Bank several months later. Undoubtedly, there is a direct line connecting the suspension of talks between Jordan and the PLO in February 1986 and the Jordanian cabinet decision in February 1999, saying that the king was incapable of ruling Jordan, and declaring Prince Abdullah as regent. On these two occasions the reins were apparently not in the hands of King Hussein, and yet on both, everything moved according to his pre-planned blueprint. The result was the same: a small step for the kingdom but one manifesting its robust political system.

An Alternative Homeland for the Palestinians (*watan badil*)[2]

Perhaps the main concern of King Hussein during the succession of challenges during the 1980s was that Israel and the PLO would simultaneously adopt the concept that Jordan should serve as an alternative homeland for the Palestinians (*watan badil*), and take steps towards that aim. This idea was first raised as a response to Israeli concerns on the Palestinian front in the late 1960s. The first Israeli figure to speak against the Hashemite presence on the East Bank was a leading Israeli academic close to the Israeli Labor Party, Professor Shlomo Avineri, who less than 24 hours after the Karameh clash called for the elimination of the king.[3] The idea that the East Bank should serve as the homeland of the Palestinians was further reinforced in the context of the civil war, during which the PLO as well as certain policy makers in Israel, especially from the right-wing parties, toyed[4] with the idea that instead of an Israeli withdrawal from the territories, two independent countries – Palestinian on the East Bank and Israeli on part of the former western Mandatory Palestine – would jointly discuss the future of the West Bank. The Israeli intervention on behalf of the king in 1970, in spite of some dissident ideas, suspended that talk but not for long.

On each significant Palestinian–Hashemite juncture until the signing of the peace treaty, this idea came back to life, even if for only a short time, to the vocal and public dismay of Jordan.

These concerns caused Hussein to somewhat change his rhetoric. In the past, "Jordan is Palestine and Palestine is Jordan" had seemed the right phrase to resist independent decisions by the PLO.[5] In later years this could have been interpreted as Jordanian acquiescence to the idea that the East Bank should serve as a Palestinian state. Still, the passing of the Rabat formula in late 1974 caused another round of public Israeli expressions regarding the future of the Hashemite dynasty and its nation. One of the most significant Israeli responses to the Rabat summit conference, though from an opposition spokesman in 1974, came in the form of a renewed call by General (Res.) Ariel Sharon[6] for talks with the Palestinians aimed at the removal of the Hashemites from Jordan.

The Israeli parliamentary elections of 1977 brought to power for the first time the center-right-wing party, the Likud. The predecessor of this party had not recognized for years the 1922 British White Paper which in effect created the East Bank entity of Trans-Jordan. Since that party believed that Jordan had no right to exist and that its very existence reflected a violation of the promises made to the Jews in 1917, in the Balfour Declaration, so this logic goes, Israel after June 1967 had to accept the new realities and acknowledge the kingdom while embracing the annexation of the West Bank. Upon coming to power and negotiating peace with Egypt the two countries approved the Camp David accords which, *inter alia*, called for autonomy for the Palestinians in the West Bank, to the dismay of Jordan, which had not even been consulted on the issue.[7] Still, the coming to power of the Likud meant basically that Jordan would not have to be worried about any Israeli withdrawal that might bring it back to this undesired position. Moreover, the 1978 autonomy plan recognized certain links between Jordan and the West Bank, which also meant that very much in line with its basic interests, Jordan would be a partner with Israel in eliminating any risk to regional security stemming from any PLO activity in this particular area.

With the mounting pressures on Israel from the PLO in the summer of 1981 and the almost imposed indirect Israeli recognition of the PLO, which eventually was one of the reasons for Israel's launching the 1982 war in Lebanon, the "alternative homeland" idea came to life again. This time Sharon in his capacity as minister of defense was not the only Israeli to support the idea. Perhaps the more significant advocate for it was the foreign minister of Israel, Yitzhak Shamir, who became the most vocal supporter of these ideas during that summer, and who was supported by the Israeli ambassador to Washington, Moshe Arens.[8] Thus most of the inner circle of Israel's administration during the Lebanon war shared the opinion that Jordan should be turned into a Palestinian state without the

Hashemites. The Lebanon affair supplied ample opportunities for Israeli politicians to discuss the alternative homeland idea, causing concern and worries among the Hashemite policy makers. The Israeli siege on Beirut and the repetition of these ideas from Israel caused grave concerns in Jordan, with Crown Prince Hassan assuming the role of spokesman for Jordan and against the Israeli designs.[9] Obviously Hussein, who less than a year beforehand had once again used Israeli help in deterring Syria (see pp. 155–6), preferred that his brother should speak to the world on that issue.

As mentioned, certain Israeli leaders saw the war in Lebanon as a golden opportunity to promote the idea of Jordan as a Palestinian state. That ominous vision sent the commander of the armed forces, Zayd bin Shaker, in August on a visit to Washington in order to rally US support behind Jordan.[10] This was in order that Syria would not try to use Jordan once again as a transition station en route to Israel, thus exposing Jordan to Israeli reprisals while Syria enjoyed the clash between Israel and Jordan. With the PLO withdrawal from Lebanon there was also the possibility that Jordan would be pressured to allow the organization to operate from Hashemite territory. Even after finding other locations for the PLO, and its actual expulsion in late August, Israel did not give up the idea of an alternative homeland.[11]

King Hussein had high hopes, with the election of President Reagan in late 1980. However, with the lack of progress in relations between the US and Jordan, the king soon began orally attacking the new administration. These expressions of disappointment came to an end with the publishing of the Reagan initiative in August 1982, putting an end to the first stage of the Israeli war in Lebanon. When Secretary Shultz replaced Secretary Haig in late 1982 the focus of US policy in the region changed for the better from a Jordanian point of view. Jordan, for years a minor player in regional politics, became a focus of attention as a result of the initiative and the personal changes in the American administration. In reality, the initiative aimed at practically removing the obstacle of the Rabat formula. The Israeli government at the time, along with Israeli public opinion, believed for a while that perhaps the time had come to discuss options for a Jordanian–Palestinian solution and the "Jordan to Palestine" debate resumed, but not for long. Basically, all writers emphasized[12] historical and strategic advantages or disadvantages only to find out that this was, as always, a mere academic exercise and nothing more; all this was obviously to the liking of the Hashemite court, which as usual was a devout reader of the Israeli press.

In his speech suspending negotiations with the PLO in early 1986 Hussein once again mentioned[13] that Israel had a plan aimed at pressing the Palestinian people to leave their areas. In clear terms he alluded to the strong connections between Jordan and the Palestinians as indicating that

Jordan had paid enough for the solution of the Palestine issue and it should not be subject to more Palestinian immigration into its own territory.

The most vocal supporter in Israel for the alternative homeland idea, Ariel Sharon, admitted[14] in 1989 that it had been a mistake, and he withdrew from that idea. Senior officials in Hussein's entourage finally agreed to see him as a partner during Sharon's visit to Jordan in August 1997 to discuss water issues.[15] Perhaps the last advocate of this approach, Israeli Prime Minister Shamir, retreated from his position in 1991 after the Gulf War proved the importance of Jordan as a buffer state. Had Jordan become a Palestinian state with aspirations over the West Bank, Israel might have found itself facing the Iraqi army right on its borders.[16] During a meeting in December 1994 between the then leader of the Israeli opposition Benjamin Netanyahu, a member of the Likud bloc, and King Hussein, with Crown Prince Hassan present, Netanyahu renounced the idea that "Jordan is Palestine."[17]

The Palestinian Issue

The ongoing Israeli–Egyptian negotiations and the subsequent agreements apparently threw Jordan and the PLO into a similar position: uniting their resistance to agreements which did not take their interests into account. However, this presentation is somewhat misleading since it only highlights the current meeting of interest while ignoring past and present strategic differences. All the above served as the basis for a 1979 rapprochement with the PLO[18] resulting from a series of meetings between Hussein and Arafat (September and December 1978, June 1980), which failed in translating the apparent reading of the political map into a more tangible alliance and caused further tension and friction between Jordan and the PLO in 1980–1.[19] In essence, Hussein preferred the "united kingdom" solution whereas Arafat insisted on the already recognized rights of the PLO. Still, this series of contacts, which also included lower-level officials, induced the two parties to voice their opinions in public; the PLO agreed to the principle of Jordan's sovereignty over its lands and citizens, meaning that the PLO practically gave up any claim on the East Bank, but continued to demand the right to act militarily against Israel from Jordanian territory. Jordan, on its part, was satisfied in recognizing all rights of the PLO with the exception of political rights, that is it demanded a united kingdom along the lines of the 1972 plan.[20] Obviously, the PLO was not too satisfied with the Jordanian position since the feeling of the Palestinian leaders was that Jordan was evading the substantial issues to be discussed between the two parties and was not abiding by the Rabat resolutions. The Palestine National Council, which met in Damascus in April 1981, devoted much time to deploring Jordan's policy *vis-à-vis* the PLO, a stand repeated before and after the meeting.[21]

The escalating confrontation between Israel and the PLO led to a ten-day artillery duel across the Israeli–Lebanese border in the summer of 1981, and to the Israeli invasion of June 1982. The Israeli operation presented a dual challenge to Hussein: on the one hand, any defeat of the PLO was welcome and might have heralded less of a Palestinian threat to the Hashemite regime; on the other hand, the evacuation of the PLO from Lebanon might have caused a focusing of Arab pressures to let the organization return to Jordan. At this point the US-mediated evacuation of the PLO leadership from Lebanon to Tunis in late August 1982, concurrent with the publication of the US plan known as the Reagan plan, were intended *inter alia* to resolve the Jordanian dilemma.[22] Not only did the PLO find a refuge away from Jordan, but the kingdom was slated as well for becoming the main diplomatic beneficiary from the PLO's defeat.

The Reagan plan saw Jordan as the principal actor in relation to the Palestinian issue as a result of the PLO's weak position in the immediate postwar period. The main US premise at this point was that in the wake of the war the weakening of the PLO would allow Hussein to negotiate an agreement with Israel without the traditional hovering shadow of the PLO. In the Israeli reading[23] of the emerging political map the US was trying to open a new path leading to Hussein's participation in negotiations on the future of the West Bank under a different set of terms of reference from the Camp David accords. Even prior to the US plan Jordan believed that any taking part in a diplomatic process had to be based not only on a US plan, the US being a player foreign to the region, but also on all pertinent Arab resolutions, including the resolutions of the summit conferences in Rabat and Fez (1982), which did not oppose the Reagan plan but did not adopt it in any way either. Jordan's reading was that since it had open channels to Israel and the US – which, under a 1975 memorandum of understanding with Israel, refrained from talking to the PLO – it had to bring aboard the legitimate representative, namely the PLO, in order to promote an agreement satisfying its needs. Such a move had to be backed by the US rather than letting the indigenous parties work out their agreement without any foreign involvement, obviously a position asking for some public US encouragement to the Jordanian side.[24] That involvement never came, leaving Jordan and the PLO to try and find by themselves some common ground. Subsequently, this first serious attempt by Jordan to work out a formula for joint action with the PLO and later with the rest of the Arab countries, which lasted between October 1982 and April 1983, did not produce the necessary results in spite of Arafat's apparent acceptance of the Jordanian initiative. That probably led Hussein to announce that the Palestinians could be represented by others than the PLO but only in concert with the organization.[25] Actually, the weakened standing of the PLO after the first stage of the war in Lebanon only served to emphasize that Jordan needed the PLO only to provide it with a fig leaf. In reality Jordan very strongly coveted the *de facto* right of representation both before, and certainly after, the war in Lebanon.[26]

Hussein's response to the Reagan plan is very revealing of the way he reacted to plans that he had to resist but to which he had to respond positively for reasons which had to do with the international standing of Jordan. From the outset Hussein was not a great believer in the initiative; he preferred an international conference, which would obviously satisfy all parties in terms of international and inter-Arab legitimacy. He voiced his reservations in several letters to the US president, albeit[27] with no success; the plan became US official policy, and so he gave it the chance it deserved. However, even though only giving the plan a slim chance, he negotiated with the US the conditions for its acceptance in the hope that if it failed, as he anticipated, he would be seen as the innocent party while Israel would be blamed for its falling apart.[28] With his conditions not met, namely no US guarantee for an Israeli withdrawal from the West Bank and Lebanon, his disillusionment grew and in early 1984 he announced[29] his withdrawal from the plan.

It was natural that the PLO would respond positively to Jordan's moves, without giving up its long-range interests, as the PLO was eager for some tactical cooperation with Jordan – aiming to replace its lost base in Lebanon. Upon the PLO initiative the Palestinian National Council met in Amman in November 1984 to listen to a rather unusual speech by Hussein to the convened members in which he called for joint Palestinian–Jordanian action on the basis of trading territory for peace.[30] This gathering opened the way to the resumption of negotiations between the two parties. The next round of talks, laden with disputes and disagreements between the two leaders, produced in February 1985 the Hussein–Arafat formula for future cooperation. The formula consisted of five pillars according to Hussein:[31] peace in exchange for territory in line with UN resolutions; then the right of self-determination for the Palestinian people in the framework of a confederation between two countries, Jordan and Palestine; a solution to the refugee issue in line with UN resolutions; a solution to the Palestinian issue in all its aspects; and all the preceding elements would serve as the basis for peace negotiations under an international conference. The PLO would be represented at the conference within a joint Jordanian–Palestinian delegation. What is unclear is the extent of the Palestinian representation accorded to the PLO, its conformity with the Rabat resolutions, and the desired outcome of the process. The parties reached that formula mainly through the fact that at that time each of the parties had something the other needed; in effect they behaved as Siamese twins – the PLO had the right of representation granted to them in Rabat, while Hussein had open channels to the other two significant participants in any diplomatic process, Israel and the US.

From a Jordanian viewpoint the agreement answered all their concerns: even though it had to go along with the Rabat resolutions it called for the establishment of a political entity that would satisfy PLO demands for independence and yet would tie that entity to Jordan; in other words Hussein would not retain his sovereignty over the West Bank but would have a significant role in its decision-making processes so that he would not be threatened by the new entity. Moreover, this formula, if indeed adopted as the basis for future relations between the two banks, would put an end to PLO designs on the West Bank and would also release Jordan from any concerns about being flooded with more refugees or Palestinians.

The Palestinian side saw the agreement merely as a device to delay processes it could not benefit from, as a result of its weakness due to the after effects of the war in Lebanon and the realization that Jordan would stop at nothing (including, like Syria, encouraging renegade Palestinian groups) in its attempts to curb the PLO's return to a pivotal role in the region. The organization for its part was eager for a presence in Jordan of its people, who could lead some of its activities. Moreover, a continued dialogue with Jordan would probably signal to the US a movement towards some moderation within the organization. Clearly, with a zero sum game played by Jordan and the PLO since 1964, that formula could not have worked. However, the Jordanian satisfaction only attested to the vague language of the document, which led eventually to its demise. Even the US could not have been fully convinced by the good intentions of Arafat in reaching this agreement. A series of Palestinian attacks on Israeli and American targets and Israeli counter-attacks, among them Larnaca, *Achile Lauro*, and later the Israeli bombing of the PLO headquarters in Tunis, only underlined that US reluctance.[32]

In this game of two experienced players trying to outwit each other Hussein had the upper hand, but not for long. In spite of the consent of the higher echelons of the PLO and *al-Fatah*, the agreement fell through for several reasons that can be summarized as the vagueness of the document. Several key issues were addressed in a way that gave Hussein the temporary upper hand. First, the formula was based on the spirit of the Fez summit conference rather than the actual resolution. The reason being that the resolution spoke of the Palestinian right of self-determination under the leadership of the PLO. Using the term "spirit" obviously indicated a Jordanian interest in seeing something less than that, perhaps in accordance with the traditional Jordanian interest of giving the West Bank a status which would not constitute a threat to the Hashemite Kingdom. This issue is further reflected when examining the final goal of the agreement, which is rather vaguely put – in the Jordanian interpretation it is a conference between two independent entities subject to Jordanian supremacy. This is in clear contradiction to the Palestinian interest in declaring independence, and only then, if the Palestinian governing bodies wished it, declaring a confederation. The issue of Jordanian supremacy was also noted in the reference to the make-up of the Arab delegation. The PLO preferred an all-Arab delegation so that the PLO and Jordan would enjoy equal status; a Jordanian–Palestinian delegation would put pressure on the PLO to follow the Jordanian lead. These bones of contention were later addressed by a message from the PLO, which was attached to the agreement, in reality making a supposedly mutually accepted document into a dead letter.

Nonetheless, the appearance of an agreement served the interests of both sides for a year: Jordan recaptured a position of influence over the process, leading to a solution to the Palestinian issue based on an agreement with the holder of the right to represent the Palestinians; the PLO, by supposedly making an agreement with Jordan, fortified its position as a pragmatic partner in future US-led diplomatic processes. Indeed, with the following US invitation for a Jordanian–Palestinian delegation and the rejection of this idea by the PLO, Jordan once again scored a diplomatic success: while adhering to the Arab consensus it signed an agreement with the PLO but demonstrated that no solution to the Palestinian issue could be accomplished without its leading role. Jordan played a similar role in its contacts with the US between February 1985 and February 1986 – it informed the US that the PLO was prepared to recognize Resolution 242 in exchange for a US dialogue with the organization; this, in spite of Hussein's clear knowledge that the US had issued a commitment to Israel in September 1975 which in fact ruled out such a dialogue.

These Jordanian positions were not to the liking of the PLO, which could perhaps have had hopes for establishing some renewed presence in Jordan at least as a byproduct of the ongoing dialogue with the US through Jordan. With their failure in achieving that, the road to the collapse of the agreement was open. Perhaps the main reason for that failure came in the form of Arafat's refusal to accept UN Security Council Resolution 242, which shattered all hopes, and in February 1986 Hussein decided unilaterally to suspend his talks with the PLO, close down *al-Fatah* offices in Amman and expel the present *al-Fatah* personnel.[33] That by itself did not change the strategic reading of Hussein: his country continued to voice its desire to see the return of the occupied lands and, as had been customary for many years, without detailing which Arab side would get the land,[34] and at the same time Jordan desired the return of Palestinian national rights. Another element central to Hussein's thinking at that time was that any

Palestinian–Jordanian solution was their distinct issue and no third parties could intervene.

If indeed the 1985 formula with the PLO was only a ploy by both sides to try and snatch some diplomatic gains from the other partner, then the suspension of the agreement by Hussein in February 1986 only ended a period which produced no such tangible benefits at least for the PLO. Hussein's suspension opened a period of time-out, which came to an end with the outbreak of the Palestinian uprising in December 1987. With all cards out in the open Jordan had a clear list of interests it had to accomplish. The PLO leaders were in Tunis and removed from the immediate scene, and there seemed to develop a possibility that Israel might agree to a peace process with the participation of authentic leaders, which meant leaders from the West Bank. Under such conditions Jordan could in the first place have an interest in cornering the PLO into a token participation in any future negotiations, while Jordan would develop its own local pro-Hashemite representatives. Such a process, if feasible at all, carried both risks and positive prospects. It had to be in line at least publicly and formally with the Rabat resolutions and yet had to sweep local leaders under a formula recognizing Rabat and giving them the actual right of representation. As the *Intifadah* events would demonstrate, a local leadership did emerge but it preferred to align itself with the PLO and not with Jordan. However, between 1986 and the outbreak of the uprising Jordan tried to encourage such local leadership by economic means. Also, during that short period of time Jordan had an interest in winning over as many Arab partners as possible against the PLO so that the Jordanian interest of formally recognizing Rabat while shutting out the organization would not be used against the kingdom. For that purpose Jordan tried to build an Arab consensus to support it, culminating in the emergency Arab summit in Jordan in November 1987.

A cornerstone of any Jordanian initiative had to be a strong backing by the US aimed at presenting Jordan, and not the PLO, as the only player with whom both the US and Israel would talk, and thus demonstrating that only Jordan could represent the Arab parties in any future talks. Even for countries removed from the pro-US camp such an approach could perhaps appeal, and Syria was a player likely at least to consider Jordanian help in removing the results of the 1967 war. This complicated picture of at times conflicting interests was not, as it had been in the past, a device to guarantee the continued survival of the kingdom. Now, it was a complicated maneuver aimed at weakening the PLO to the extent that Jordan would be able to call the shots in the West Bank without being directly involved; but clearly with the elimination of the PLO as a significant player, the only role it could play was that of the sole representative under Jordanian auspices. Thus, its role as a participant in future negotiations could not be fully ignored, but it could probably be limited to that of almost a token representative.

In order to accomplish these interests Hussein opened a multi-track initiative aimed at convincing all interested parties, the US and Israel included, that only Jordan was capable of initiating a peace process, being the linchpin connecting all players. This campaign had several steps, to be taken separately but at times overlapping chronologically. With the Palestinian issue at the heart of the Jordanian policy, Jordan distinguished between two components: the policy and steps regarding the PLO and the formal right of representation, and the local residents of the territories under Israeli occupation.

The obvious primary target was the Palestinians in the territories. During a meeting between Hussein and the Egyptian president, Mubarak, in May 1986 they discussed[35] the possibility of setting up an Egyptian-backed autonomous area in the Gaza Strip, an idea which fell within the parameters of the Israeli–Egyptian understandings stemming from the 1978 Camp David accords and the 1979 peace treaty. The advantages for Hussein were crystal clear: with the failure of attempts to coordinate policy with the PLO, such a framework might provide him with a precedent to be followed in the West Bank. However, these consultations never developed into any tangible plan, basically because Egypt could not take upon itself to choose sides between Jordan and the PLO in promoting a track bypassing the PLO.

The Palestinians on the West Bank were offered an ambitious development plan. In October 1986 Jordan announced[36] a 1.4 billion US$ five-year development plan for the West Bank (which never materialized) mainly intended to reassert Jordan's involvement in West Bank affairs. It also aimed at ensuring that whatever the political developments, Jordan would make sure that the West Bankers were content in their current places of residence and would not look to the East Bank as a possible alternative.

In the summer of 1987 Jordan increased its activities questioning the exclusive right of the PLO to represent the Palestinians.[37] It made preparations to convene a popular meeting that would in fact serve as a counter-balance to the Palestinian National Council, and it allowed the refugee camps in Jordan to elect their own representatives to the parliament. Concurrent with these efforts Jordan continued to advocate the idea of an international conference with the participation of the five permanent members of the UN Security Council and the PLO in addition to all other interested regional parties.[38] This approach was indeed a brilliant policy line: the PLO could not resist a forum that would provide the organization with a way to bypass Israeli and US opposition to talking to the PLO, which would once again underline Jordan's pivotal role, and on the other hand there was no risk in this approach since Israel by rejecting it would underline Jordan's positive role in regional affairs and would probably deny the PLO a legitimate standing which Jordan was willing to grant.

Israel, next in line of importance, had to be convinced that Jordan was still, in spite of Rabat and the 1985 agreement with Arafat, a partner for negotiations. In the spring of 1987, concurrent with the talks on an abortive London agreement with Israel, the main avenue preferred by the king[39] in order to legitimize his policies and publicize them was an international conference. Indeed, this was once more an avenue opposed by most Israelis and consequently a sure recipe to conclude more understandings with Israel while keeping them secret. In addition to the mostly secret track with Israel, Jordan had to satisfy Arab public opinion, and that came with the alliance with Syria, another enemy of Arafat. That association, constituting a potential threat to Iraq, could alienate that country, and thus Jordan had to find a way to reconcile these two hostile countries.

Clearly Hussein was wise to use the Israeli card as long as Israel played by the traditional rules, namely rejecting any PLO participation in the process. Hussein disagreed with two elements alien to its political thinking, which were that the Soviet Union had to participate in the conference, alongside the PLO – two impediments making Israeli participation impossible. Israel insisted that the Soviet Union, which had broken off diplomatic relations with it in 1967, should resume them, and Israel strongly and unequivocally opposed the participation of the PLO. Thus, to the outside observer it was a clever Hashemite position: it emphasized Jordanian willingness to discuss peace with Israel in the framework of an international conference, a traditional position by now, which would make Israel the intransigent party – in effect, making any meaningful public peace process, including Israeli withdrawal from the territories, impossible. However, if by some miracle a settlement were to be found it would not be a unilateral one, thus providing Jordan with the international umbrella it had been looking for for a long time. Another byproduct of this position was the appeasing of local Palestinian and trade union opposition to any infringement regarding the rights of the PLO, and the elimination, at least partial and temporary, of a potential domestic threat to the regime.[40]

The outbreak of the Palestinian uprising in the territories in December 1987 caught Jordan as well as the PLO by surprise. As in past crises Jordan could find in the new developments a mixture of bad and good news: the initial reaction was probably a concern lest the new wave of violence would spill over to the East Bank, but with the passage of time and in spite of the traditional fear of the PLO, Jordan could finally publicly relinquish any claim on the West Bank. This cautious line was well reflected in the Jordanian media and public. On the one hand, concerned with the possibility that Jordan might be asked to open its borders to Palestinian activity against Israel, the press proposed[41] during the first stages of the uprising that Lebanon should open its borders for anti-Israeli activity. On the other hand, it voiced support for the uprising as long as it was conducted only in the territories, using harsh language against Israel in its reporting. The uprising also sparked a spontaneous reaction, which the regime did not try to halt: the collection of food, medications, and material contributions for the Palestinians along with sporadic demonstrations. Hussein himself, who publicly adopted an uncompromising stand against Israel, approved of this line. His continued recognition of the Palestinian people was not new, but from the time of the uprising his references to the Palestinians were more as an equal partner rather than to people in need of representation. In this context, Hussein also abandoned any talk of a confederation, which had been a topic of discussion in the mid-1980s. Clearly, he was no longer in sympathy with the PLO, and preferred the indigenous population to develop its own leadership, a tendency that is indirectly alluded to in a press interview[42] a few weeks after the beginning of the uprising. At that time he underscored the role of the local Palestinians and played down the possibility that they had been given instructions from outside. However, after the US recognized the organization in late 1988, as a direct outcome of the uprising, Hussein evaded the question of representation. Gradually, his public line meets the policy he had pursued all along: the West Bank and its people perhaps have traditional and emotional ties with the East Bank, but are definitely not the responsibility of the Hashemite Kingdom. This line eventually becomes official policy with the separation speech on July 31, 1988. His pragmatic yet far-sighted policy manifested itself again when he adapted himself to the changing circumstances and agreed to a joint Jordanian–Palestinian delegation to the October 1991 Madrid conference, which in effect split immediately into two distinct teams.

The uprising, a popular rebellion against Israel, gave Hussein the opportunity he had been looking for since 1967 to combine the secret track of peace with Israel while renouncing the West Bank along with any recognition of the PLO. Moreover, the PLO presence outside the territories at the outbreak of the uprising gave Hussein an opportunity to once again signal his preference for dealing with a local West Bank leadership rather than with the PLO, his traditional adversary.[43] Yet, another issue to reckon with had to do with the final political outcome of the new realities. After all, the uprising was the first opportunity since the 1967 war for the question of the final status of the territories to be addressed. Past experience of negotiations between the king and Arafat, in 1985, had produced an unworkable formula, in part because at that time it was a question of representation in negotiating forums from which the PLO was barred. This time around, the Palestinians had a winning card: they were fighting Israel and were quickly reaching a position in which they could influence decisions relevant to their future.

No doubt Jordan would have preferred to give away the West Bank, or the claim to it, to a different contender, but still, with the realization that no spill-over effect would be involved, the PLO could be accepted only eight months after the beginning of the *Intifadah*. However, the picture of violence in the territories served to indicate the most appropriate timing, with a careful start, and later, in late July, the king himself announced the end to Jordanian interest in the territories.[44]

The uprising provided him with the opportunity, after spending some time defining the right track, to adopt a new posture in his foreign and domestic affairs. At this stage all the political processes discussed in this book came to fruition. The policy pursued between the *Intifadah* and the Israeli–Jordanian peace treaty in October 1944 is clearly that of a national leader aware of his role in world politics. These two turning points along with the US–Iraq war of 1991, as significant as they were, did not constitute any more dynasty-risking crises. However, they joined to put the final touches to a national policy for the kingdom and to manifest its functioning as a nation-state. As such, Jordan now had a new, broader agenda. As had been his custom for years, King Hussein chose the opportunity of his speech before the new graduates of the General Staff College, a week after the outbreak of the *Intifadah*, to draw up a new list of priorities, to which he added later at the Arab summit conference in Algiers in June 1988.[45] Even though the future of the West Bank was very much on his mind, he added to his list the Iraq–Iran war, which at the time was drawing to an end, and a new dimension regarding Israel: its nuclear armament, and the distinction between Likud and Labor in Israeli politics. The negative references to Israel do not disappear, but they sound much more like relations between two competing countries rather than two enemies. During this period Hussein is much more precise in his reading of the Israeli political scene as he prepares, especially after the 1993 Israeli–Palestinian Declaration of Principles, for his own move. Furthermore, those years also saw Jordan embarking on the road to democracy – one of the major elements in the political legacy of the king.

Hussein saw the advantages of the unfolding situation: unloading the West Bank Palestinian issue from his shoulders also allowed him for the first time since 1967 to hold parliamentary elections, which heralded the final stage of building of his nation-state. Thus, a significant part of Hussein's political legacy is not only the identification between the kingdom and the East Bank, but also the reintroduction of representative political institutions. The new beginning of political life in Jordan was the direct outcome of the uprising, the severing of relations with the West Bank, and the final and genuine divorce from the claim to represent the Palestinians.

All that is on the bright side. On the side of possible trouble the king had the potential of having to deal with the idea of autonomy for the Palestinians, which in turn might raise the question of under whose sovereignty that entity would operate. As much as King Hussein did not want any risk to his kingdom from the future solution, he did not want to see it re-incorporated into his kingdom either, and made it clear[46] all through the uprising that autonomy was out of the question. Moreover, with the progress of the Palestinian uprising it became evident that the PLO was capturing the position Jordan had never held: as the one and only partner that could publicly discuss diplomatic agreements with Israel. That finally gave Jordan the ability to declare its previously secret policy, and on July 31, 1988 Hussein announced an end to any connections with the West Bank. In his speech he was very clear about the distinction between a Palestinian state and the Hashemite Kingdom and went so far as to deny the phrase so often used in the past; this time he said: Jordan is not Palestine. Nevertheless, he was careful enough to qualify his words by saying that his moves concerned the occupied Palestinian territory and its people and had nothing to do with the Jordanian citizens of Palestinian origin of the Hashemite Kingdom. The clarification that Jordan was in no way an alternative homeland for the Palestinians was reminiscent of past disagreements with Israeli leaders on the issue, as discussed earlier in this chapter. Even the Oslo process did not lay to rest that particular concern of the king, and even after the rise of the center-right Likud coalition in Israel he again spoke of this distinction.[47]

In his cautious way Hussein prepared world opinion and indirectly his own people for a major shift in his public policy, and in an interview with the German *Der Spiegel*, about two months after the uprising in the territories began, he released himself from responsibility for the Palestinians in the territories.[48] His expression of moral solidarity with the Palestinians, similar to that of any other Arabs, was rather strange. It was not clear yet whether any major potential risk for the kingdom was involved, yet Hussein was quick to use the opportunity to prepare the way for another phase of uncovering his true design regarding the West Bank. Moreover, on another occasion,[49] about two months later, in light of the growing power of the PLO resulting from the uprising, he is even clearer. Though he may have seen himself for years as a possible bridge between Israel and the PLO he is not willing to take that burden upon himself anymore. His new approach, the one he advocated throughout the uprising and even before his final separation policy, was that the PLO should participate as an independent player at an international conference. This policy is not only a passive consent to the newly emerging political realities. It is an attempt to divorce himself from any representation and yet carry the torch of special responsibility for the fate of the Palestinians in line with his personal commitment to his former citizens.

In late July 1988, in the wake of the Algiers Arab summit conference which further strengthened the PLO position, the Jordanian government announced that it was canceling its ambitious 1.4 billion US$ five-year development plan of 1986 for the West Bank along with the dissolution of the development, bidding, and procurement committees dealing with the West Bank.[50] Economically and practically the step taken had almost no substance since Jordan did not actually implement the plan, but politically it signaled another Jordanian recognition of the new standing of the PLO in the territories as the *de facto* and *de jure* representative for the West Bank as a result of the uprising. In the Jordanian reading[51] the upcoming decisions marked the opportunity to launch a process of reorganizing public life on the East Bank without taking the West Bank into account. Taking this domestic trend further, Hussein announced on July 30 that he was dissolving the Lower House of Parliament, which consisted of 60 members. Since this parliament had originally been elected in April 1967 and was equally divided between East and West Bankers any move to dissolve it might have been interpreted as renouncing Hussein's public demand for the return of the West Bank. Now, with all the changes in the diplomatic standing of the PLO it was finally possible to hold new parliamentary elections along with reform of the system.

Palestinian views reflected[52] Jordanian acquiescence to the price Jordan had to pay for its final relinquishing of rights on the West Bank: genuine acknowledgment of the transfer of the right of representation for the West Bank from Jordan to the PLO, thus guiding Israel and the US to begin talking to the PLO. Spokesmen for the organization reflected[53] in their reactions their apprehension lest the potential partners would not talk to the PLO. Thus, the reactions emphasized satisfaction with the Jordanian moves but still spoke of the Jordanian–Palestinian confederation as a preferred solution.

On July 31, 1988 the king brought to a climax the process he had initiated, and officially declared in a speech to the nation that he was severing all Jordanian ties to the West Bank. The explanation usually given is that he was concerned lest the uprising in the territories would spill into the East Bank. That argument was not valid anymore since the few disturbances were delicately dealt with and the East Bank Palestinians, who still remembered 1970, usually kept away from trouble.[54] However, from a national Jordanian point of view this move was only a natural outcome of a policy begun in 1966–7. For the first time, the inside track and the public track were united in denouncing formal relations between the two banks. Even the long and tedious references to the term "people" became crystal clear.

During the separation speech Hussein explained[55] that the unity of the banks back in 1950 was only the result of the interest of true Arab unity between two Arab peoples. Later on, he denounced any previous references to any future link with a Palestinian state.

Even the idea of confederation, so long discussed in the 1980s, had eventually been abandoned in favor of two distinct nations.[56] Israeli strategists saw that alternative as the most preferred by Israel provided it remained part of the arrangement – even after the king discarded this approach.[57] Obviously, even this revised version of the "Jordanian option" was far from being in Hussein's interests. Several future attempts at reviving the idea (see below) never materialized. One source suggests[58] that the confederation plan lost any chance of being realized after Arafat suggested to Hussein that they should alternate in the position of the leader of the confederation once it was established. The reaction of the Palestinian press reflected confusion and disagreement:[59] on the one hand, apprehension prevailed concerning the economic implications of this move and the possibility that the West Bank would be cut off from the rest of the Arab world; on the other hand, it reflected the success of the Palestinian uprising and the newly acquired role for the PLO. All in all, this final touch from Hussein did not raise any more aggressive or threatening moves by any party. On the surface, it was only his consent to grant the PLO its rightful standing, acquired many years earlier. Interestingly enough even in the context of these more or less conclusive moves, Hussein still kept one last political tool to influence West Bank politics, albeit on a personal and not a national level, with his decision that West Bankers would be able to continue using their Jordanian passports.[60]

Jordan's moves obviously did not indicate any interest in promoting the PLO in a way that would remove the kingdom from any influence it still mustered in the West Bank. Thus, with the events of July–August 1988, the economic situation in the territories deteriorated. The Arab countries did not live up to their commitment to grant a monthly subsidy of US$ 43 million to the residents of the territories through the PLO. Combined with an increase in unemployment of 75,000 workers in the West Bank, resulting from ending the payment of salaries by the Jordanian government, this meant that the PLO, which was now in charge of taking care of the Palestinian population, was seen in the area and outside as failing in its duty of supporting the people.[61]

Jordanian domestic developments as well as mounting US pressure to conduct a meaningful process took their toll of Hussein in late 1989. Since most of the developments strengthened the international standing of the PLO, Hussein had once again to exercise a tactical retreat from previous positions in order to evade the effect of these developments. With the emerging rapprochement Jordan allowed *al-Fatah* to reopen its offices in Amman, and invited visits by the leaders of the PFLP and the DFLP, as well as Arafat. Even though by that time Jordan had long acknowledged the rights of representation of the PLO, it still preferred at that time to negotiate separately with some of the organizations on elements of life in the West Bank. In late February it transferred to the PLO's Amman office the right to sanction the import of agricultural products from the West Bank to Jordan, and in March it agreed with the DFLP on broadcasting educational programs from Jordan to the West Bank. Rumors circulating in Jordan at that time suggested that Jordan and the PLO had agreed that any topic the PLO wished to deal with would indeed be transferred to its responsibility on two conditions: that no terrorist activities would be launched against Israel from Jordanian territory and that no PLO action would be taken against any member of the Hashemite family.

However, with the lingering doubts regarding the ability of the PLO to translate the initial success of the uprising into tangible diplomatic accomplishments, Jordan and Egypt somewhat modified their positions in late 1989. At that time Jordan was once again trying to gain a position of influence through local leaders as a result of Egyptian pressure aimed at promoting the notion of a confederation between the West Bank and Jordan. One possible explanation for this Egyptian position was that being the only Arab country to have peace relations with Israel, such a Jordanian move towards creating a confederation would enable Israel to proceed in the peace process in spite of the Israeli objections to PLO participation in the process. The PLO position at that time, demanding an independent Palestinian state as a precondition to any confederation plan, might have deterred Israel from proceeding. Moreover, a confederation plan if rejected by Israel would clearly worsen its position in regard to the US Bush administration, which was not considered to be too sympathetic to Israel anyway. It is within this context that the pro-Jordanian Jerusalem newspaper *al-Nahar* published in November 1989 a series of articles citing the demand of the Muslim Brotherhood in Jordan to reverse the renouncing of the West Bank, since only through cooperation with Jordan might a real outcome be reached.[62] Against this background and the shared feeling that both Hussein and Arafat needed each other, they resumed their dialogue with the latter's visit to Amman in December 1989. During this visit they decided[63] to resume the activities of the joint Jordan–PLO committee. They also discussed possible definitions of future relations: federation or confederation, and a leading role for the PLO in putting together the Palestinian delegation for the international conference.

The uprising once again demonstrated the danger that Israel would try to solve the Palestinian issue on account of Jordan. However, Jordan's position this time was clearly different from what it had been years ago. Hussein addressed the issue in a meeting with students in early 1989,[64] but was no longer voicing his concern. Rather, he was sending a message to Israel that such ideas were no longer possible. Israel for its part tried to discourage Hussein from hosting the tactical headquarters of the Palestinian organizations guiding the uprising, by cautiously leaking news items hinting that if Jordanian cooperation with the organizations were to continue, the idea of an alternative homeland was still a viable option.[65]

Improved Regional Standing

The war in Lebanon and the following Reagan plan did not contribute to any improvement in relations between Jordan and Syria. Quite the contrary, they only added to already strained relations not only as a result of the 1980 crisis but also due to mutual subversion activities in 1981 and 1982.[66] The Palestine National Council met in Damascus in April 1981 and adopted an anti-Hashemite line,[67] deploring Hussein's tendency to ignore the Rabat resolutions and indirectly distinguishing between the monarch and his people. Later, the Syrian authorities blamed Jordan for supporting the Muslim Brotherhood in Syria, a move that led to the bloody events in al-Hamah in March 1982. In October 1983, members of Abu Nidal, probably under direction from Syria, began to carry out terrorist attacks in Jordan.[68] If indeed Jordan sent saboteurs to operate in Syria it clearly marked a change compared with past behavior *vis-à-vis* Syria; a change that might indicate a high degree of acquired self-confidence by Hussein, probably as the accumulated result of the 1970 and 1980 crises and the new reliance on the US as a pillar of support for the kingdom. Strangely enough an indirect acquittal of Jordan of those Syrian allegations came in 1982, when Jordan began receiving Soviet-made weaponry.

In the wake of the 1980 crisis with Syria a new atmosphere prevailed in relations between Jordan and the US. During 1981 the US suggested that a Jordanian rapid-deployment force should be established that would be available for the US. In late 1983 the Congress granted its consent for financing the project.[69] The reasons given were the already high profile of Jordanian forces in the UAE, Yemen, Oman, and other Gulf countries. Even though that project never materialized it served as an indication of the self-confidence of the Hashemite regime. Exposing Jordanian officers and troops to life in the Gulf would have served at other times as a possible trigger for potential conspirators.

With the Syrian tension over and the Arab world more fragmented than ever, Jordan could adopt a more assertive posture. With the diminishing pressure over Egypt it became possible for Hussein to resume diplomatic relations, only formally severed because of the peace treaty with Israel, in September 1984. This was clearly a move intended to signal to the US Jordan's interest in a peace process – not necessarily along the lines of the 1982 US proposals, but still a move compatible with the traditional friendship between the two countries and an additional demonstration of the central and positive role of Jordan in the region. Hussein could afford this policy since most of his potential adversaries were in no position to challenge him. Syria was more than ever an ally and client of the Soviet Union at a time when the diplomatic process was led by the US; Syria also sided with Iran, an enemy of most Arab countries, in its war with Iraq. Thus, being isolated and removed from the Arab consensus, Syria was less threatening than at any time previously. Iraq, using the Aqaba port as its main marine outlet to the world during a bloody war with Iran, needed Jordan more than ever before. In addition to these conditions relating to two potential enemies, the PLO was also at bay, very much to the liking of Hussein who was eager to use this timing to extract some critical concessions from the organization. The Jordanian approach was two-pronged. First, an attempt to reach an agreement with the organization which would bring it under Jordanian auspices, while keeping the basic Jordanian interests satisfied at the same time as making a tactical concession to the PLO. A first indication of a change in Hussein's position regarding the territories can perhaps be found in a remark not widely publicized when it was made. In mid-1984 he said[70] that Jordan was not involved in the Palestinian issue to the degree that the Palestinians themselves were involved. Jordan's commitment, according to Hussein, was only due to its past responsibility on this issue. The second element of Jordan's approach was a continued interest and involvement in the life of the Palestinians in the West Bank.

The 1986 Jordanian–Syrian rapprochement was interpreted by some Palestinian observers as one of the reasons for the suspension of Jordanian–PLO relations in February.[71] The Syrian logic, so this argument goes, is that Syria was interested in creating an alternative Palestinian leadership very much in line with Jordan, which obviously had suspected Arafat for many years of designs against the Hashemite regime. During the years since the 1982 Israeli–Lebanon war both Jordan and Syria were interested in using that opportunity to curtail the power of the PLO. For Syria it would have been very much in line with the bloody confrontations it had initiated with the Palestinians in Tel al-Za'atar and Jisr al-Basha in 1976, which had inflicted heavy casualties on the Palestinians. For Jordan this was an historic opportunity to settle accounts in the context of the events of 1970–1. Thus, in spite of their long-term differences on the Palestinian issue both countries could agree.

Syria did not agree with the political process envisaged as a result of the Jordanian–PLO agreement of February 1985. If successful, such a process would have demonstrated the diplomatic independence of the PLO and the inability of Syria to veto any diplomatic move not to its liking. As long as Jordan believed that the agreement was workable, and the negotiations between the PLO and Jordan between February 1985 and February 1986 did not indicate that Hussein genuinely saw the process this way, Syria was not a necessary ingredient in the equation with the PLO. However, with the faltering efforts to reach a working formula as opposed to the statement formula of 1985, Jordan needed another regional power to back it up in its resistance to the PLO. Syrian opposition became public as soon as the agreement was signed, but it was only in late 1985 after the joint Palestinian–Jordanian delegation failed to present a united approach to the Palestinian issue during a visit to London, that all the pieces began to fall into place. Thus, without renouncing the Rabat formula, which in effect released Jordan from representing the Palestinians, Jordan once again closed ranks with Syria, signaling the February 1986 suspension decision.[72] The fact that the incumbent prime minister was Zayd al-Rifa'i, known for his pro-Syrian tendencies and a close associate of Hussein for many years, only smoothed the process of rediscovering this problematic ally. The new Damascus–Amman axis was clearly demonstrated during Hussein's talks with the Egyptian president, Mubarak, in May 1987, during which he ruled out any international conference without Syrian participation,[73] an additional indication of the need of Hussein to have an Arab, Syrian-backed consensus, before he could conclude any public accord with Israel.

The new warming relations with Syria could not hide the traditional mutual suspicion. In essence that was also the Jordanian position regarding the PLO. It was revealed to Israel in a rather strange way in April 1987 when the then foreign minister of Israel, Shimon Peres, reached what he believed to be an agreement with Hussein regarding the next step in the diplomatic process, namely the convening of an international conference.[74] What was left ambiguous in that agreement was the question of the representation of the PLO: since the Rabat resolutions had been in operation since 1974, Hussein could not participate in any public forum without the organization, and he worked out a formula calling for participation in the international conference of those who accepted UN Security Council Resolutions 242 and 338 and renounced terrorism. This formula was not included in the written text. From a Jordanian point of view the London agreement was a masterpiece of diplomacy: it clearly attested to the Jordanian willingness to participate in a forum acceptable to most Arab parties and with the participation of the PLO. However, there is a strong probability that Hussein believed that he would not have to make good on his understanding with the Israeli representative: first, any agreement with a foreign minister necessitated the approval of both the prime minister, who opposed the idea of an international conference, and probably also the entire cabinet; secondly, being bound by the Rabat resolutions the Jordanian–Palestinian delegation had to include Palestinian representatives who would at least be approved by the PLO, an impossibility for Israel and for the organization, which shortly before the agreement had announced the annulment of the 1985 agreement with Jordan. Thus, the London exercise could very well succeed since, as had happened in the past, all other parties would save Hussein the effort of trying to implement the document.

However, that was not to be. Peres went further, notifying the US of the agreement and involving the then US secretary of state in the process. Meanwhile, realizing that for once there were chances of building a significant support for this approach, Hussein renounced publicly any possibility of talks with Israel without the PLO. Under these conditions the Israeli cabinet would not approve an agreement which at the same time could have brought the PLO to the negotiating table with Israel through a back door while forcing Hussein to grant to an organization he had never trusted, a status equal to that of Jordan. With the failure of this exercise (which was perhaps one of the first indications of the tendencies of some Israeli leaders to back the PLO on account of Hussein), Israel, under Shamir, and Hussein renewed their ongoing dialogue, which was much less threatening to the king than any other approach.

Another indication that this agreement was not the major breakthrough that had been hoped for in Israel, came during the meeting between the Israeli prime minister Shamir and Hussein in July in London. During that meeting not even once was the so-called agreement discussed; this, in spite of the many other elements of a possible peace process that were raised. In retrospect, it is possible to assess Hussein's position as advocating continued secret diplomacy, hopefully with some secret understandings, but without any public agreement. Thus, the principle of territories for peace was repeated to Prime Minister Shamir, for whom this was an anathema; and Foreign Minister Peres, who accepted this formula, was asked to include the PLO in the diplomatic process. It is hard to verify if by that time Peres had already begun thinking of the inclusion of the PLO in the process, so that Hussein's position was no longer valid, or whether these negotiations convinced him of the need to include the PLO in order to add some momentum to the process. Hussein probably did not want the organization in the process and his position was based on stubborn Israeli resistance to the PLO, leading to Hussein's exclusion from the Oslo process six years later.

The negotiations with Peres as well as the attempt at reconciling Syria and Iraq, which did not produce any tangible results, all point to an effort to change the Jordanian order of priorities. Relations with the PLO, at their best from a Jordanian vantage point, would not remain so for long. After the February 1986 suspension of coordination, the PLO in Tunis lacked a channel to communicate with the US and thus its participation in any political process was doubtful at best. Jordan, on the other hand, in line with the Rabat resolutions and its own interests, did not aspire to represent the Palestinians, only to alleviate their tough conditions, rehabilitating its contacts with the West Bank leadership in the process. Still, to stand up and almost publicly intervene in West Bank affairs necessitated a wide backing, which was supposed to be provided by the April agreement with Israel. Also in April 1987, Jordan initiated[75] a summit meeting between the Syrian and Iraqi leaders in Amman – another indication of the Jordanian determination to abandon its Palestinian priority in favor of improving its own inter-Arab standing. Perhaps mediation efforts between the two countries were not only a way of enhancing Jordan's position but also a way to try to have cordial relations with both without having to choose sides – an approach which history tells is usually futile, as this one was.

Two processes stand out as the contribution of the 1980s to further advancement of Jordanian interests: the crisis with Syria was over with much less diplomatic and military activity than those used for resolving the 1970 crisis with Syria, an attestation to the acquired standing of Jordan. Secondly, the *Intifadah* did not threaten Jordan at any point; it merely helped Hussein to finally announce his separation from this problematic piece of land. It is not surprising that in spite of the continued contacts with successive Israeli cabinet ministers no concrete agreement was concluded. Hussein could not reach any agreement with the Israelis, but he could very well prepare the foundations for a possible scenario that would enable him to negotiate a public peace with them. Thus, his talks with Peres and the London agreement were only the preamble to a possible next stage. That stage was begun by the disengagement in July 1988 and was concluded by a peace treaty only after Israel and the PLO had signed their own Declaration of Principles.

9

From the Gulf War to Peace, and the Road to Democracy

Perhaps the 1990s can best be described as "closing the book": several major issues were resolved one way or another; the initial elements of a new democratic Jordan were laid and peace was signed between Jordan and Israel. One cannot escape the thought that many of the political processes analyzed in this book were accelerated to some extent by Hussein's being diagnosed with cancer in 1992 and his feeling, so well conveyed that year to his people, that it was time to conclude. However, before that turning point Hussein managed to support Iraq during its conflict with the US-led coalition; briefly alienated the US, Saudi Arabia, and Israel; only to put together the joint Palestinian–Jordanian delegation mechanism which opened the road to subsequent diplomatic moves in the region.

Regional Politics: the Gulf crisis and war, 1990–1 and later

One of the most intriguing issues regarding Hussein's policies had to do with his position during the Gulf crisis and war between August 1990 and February 1991. On the one hand, economically and politically he had every reason to continue his close relations with the US, his main backer for years, and with Saudi Arabia. Not long before the crisis erupted, in early June 1990 and in the wake of the Baghdad summit, Saudi Arabia promised[1] to Jordan a subsidy of US$ 500 million; later that month it transferred US$ 100 million to Jordan as the first installment of US$ 200 million promised earlier in April 1990. That was not enough to convince Hussein to continue his traditional policies *vis-à-vis* these countries. Moreover, by that time Iraq had become the main supplier of oil to Jordan, mainly on the basis of barter.[2]

One source suggests[3] that Hussein believed, as did the US, that Saudi Arabia was next in line to be at war with Iraq, not any other country, and definitely not Jordan. On top of that, Iraq needed Jordan as an outlet to the sea and any attempt on the regime might have undermined the urgent Iraqi need for stability in that country. Moreover, the incumbent Hashemite regime enjoyed Western backing, albeit muted to some extent during the crisis, which no Iraqi-installed regime would enjoy. Even though the prospect of an Israeli attack on the East Bank or a counter-attack on Iraq escalated as a result of the Iraqi invasion and later during actual fighting, it was still seen in Amman as a very remote scenario considering the deep-rooted relations between the Kingdom, Israel, and the US. This diplomatic shield over Jordan safeguarded the Iraqi eastern front to a large extent from an attack, as indeed was the case during the war.

The Gulf crisis, which began with the Iraqi invasion of Kuwait on August 2, 1990, made Hussein a player on three distinct scenes, with a different role on each. On the domestic scene, it was a conscious attempt to cater to the public feeling of sympathy with that new symbol of Arab solidarity, Saddam Hussein; on the foreign diplomatic and media scene, in short, the Western field, it was a clear effort to convince his audience that he did not really mean to harm Western interests or to deviate from his traditional pro-Western policies; thirdly, while allowing his people to publicly attack Israel he continued his secret dialogue with its leaders – a complicated game of global, regional and local interests which eventually, in spite of the temporary setback after the war, paid off and not only guaranteed once more the preservation of the regime, but as early as the spring of 1991 made Jordan a pivotal power in the US approach to the peace process, a position unequalled at any time before the war.

The invasion by Iraq, a neighbor and potential threat to Jordan, and later on the actual fighting between Iraq and a US-led coalition, did not constitute a military threat for Jordan, rather it meant prolonged economic and demographic problems. Even before any political decisions were taken Jordan began to witness yet another economic crisis.[4] Several reasons affected the deteriorating economy: concerns among Jordanians that Jordan might be drawn into the war on Iraq's side had a negative impact on public morale and economic behavior. As veterans of several wars Jordanians began hoarding foodstuff and preparing for a long crisis. Moreover, since about 400,000 Palestinians worked in Kuwait and normally transferred funds to about one million people among their families in Jordan and the West Bank, those beneficiaries had to withdraw money from their life savings and borrow from local banks. All this increased unemployment, worsened the balance of payments, and generally brought down the rate of the Jordanian dinar sharply. Demographically, some 350,000 Palestinian workers returned to Jordan and tens of thousands of non-Arab Asians were stranded along with them.[5]

Several reasons affected Hussein's decision to support Iraq during the conflict in spite of his early attempts to negotiate a settlement of the conflict. They ranged from the immediate history of close cooperation with that neighbor, to domestic, political and economic considerations, as well as a well-honed survival instinct.[6] The public mood was that the coalition the US was putting together was intended in the first place to defend "Israeli expansionism," and that only Saddam Hussein could bring back Arab honor and prestige.[7] However, one should realize that although King Hussein took that public stand he secretly hoped – and after early 1991 and his meeting with the prime minister of Israel on January 5 on his initiative, he knew – that Israel would do its utmost not to undermine his position or that of his kingdom.[8] This assessment of the Israeli position had one built-in deficiency: in spite of the continued interest of Israel in the regional status quo it was led at the time by leaders who had for years advocated the notion that Jordan should serve as the Palestinian alternative homeland. The small crack between these two Israeli approaches symbolized Hussein's space for maneuver. The security policy against the threatening invasion of the Israeli policy is to be found in the close relations with Iraq. Against this background it should be mentioned that by the time of the invasion Jordan and Iraq had already had a past of close relations, which *inter alia*, included permission for Iraq to overfly Hashemite territory in order to execute intelligence sorties aimed at gathering information on Israel.[9]

Perhaps one of the most significant reasons for the positions taken by King Hussein was his concern with his country's public solidarity with Saddam Hussein. The message he conveyed to Western diplomats during the weeks after the invasion was that there was a distinction to be made between his public support for Saddam Hussein for domestic reasons and his real, covert position, which basically had not changed. As much as this position appealed to old-time observers of the king it was not an accurate reflection of his wholehearted support of his neighbor to the east.[10] It was true, but far from the whole truth. On the domestic level, over a year after the food riots which had poised the Southern Bedouin against the regime, and with the Palestinians and sympathizers of radical Islam closing ranks in support of Saddam Hussein, it was not easy for King Hussein not to back Iraq. One example of the kind of domestic pressures the regime was under can be found in a leaflet distributed by the Muslim Brotherhood on August 5, calling[11] for the closing of ranks among the Arabs as well as confrontation with the Crusader US, an ally of the Jewish state. All this conveyed a clear message to Hussein, who with his parliamentary move in the Fall of 1989, opened the door to a degree of freedom of speech never before experienced in Jordan. The *quid prop quo* for such a change was obviously that such opinions should be taken into account in forming Jordanian positions.

On the Palestinian track, the support of the PLO for Saddam Hussein and the popular sentiment of the Palestinians in the East Bank made it a matter of domestic security for the king to take this position.[12]

Economically, the resumption of a critical situation in which Iraq was involved promised the hope of a revival of the port of Aqaba as a main incoming port for Iraq. With the conclusion of the Iraq–Iran war in 1988 that port city had ceased to serve Iraqi interests, causing high unemployment among the citizens of southern Jordan. With Iraq once again under outside pressure, Jordan could perhaps benefit once more from making Aqaba available to goods destined for Iraq.

The degree of risks taken by Hussein during the Gulf crisis was again reflected in an exchange of messages between him and his parliamentary Speaker on the occasion of the opening of the second session of Parliament in mid-November 1990.[13] This exchange, which had become customary and ceremonial over the years, turned this time into a political dialogue between Hussein and his Speaker of the Muslim Brotherhood, Arabiyyat. In his response, read to Parliament, the Speaker practically presented a list of political demands to be met by the king. Arabiyyat spoke of the need for domestic reforms, among them the abolition of emergency laws, a tough stand on corruption, the release of political detainees, freedom of the press, and the strengthening of the Popular Army through arming Jordanians for any eventuality. On foreign affairs he emphasized the dangers posed by the continued Jewish immigration to Israel, and called for the uprooting of the foreign entity from the region, meaning Israel. Whatever the outcome of this unusual exchange it could only indicate that with the emerging new political rules, politicians from the opposition had acquired a new right: that of adding topics to the national Jordanian agenda.

Jordanian–PLO Relations in the Wake of the Uprising

The Palestinian factor as one of the reasons affecting Hussein's decision to side with Saddam Hussein marked the beginning of a decade that can be best described as a period during which the book was closed on the issue of territories. As usual it was a threesome affair: Jordan, the Palestinians, and Israel. Since 1967 Jordan had seen itself as providing the political framework necessary to resolve the Palestinian issue. In spite of the October 1974 Rabat resolution King Hussein insisted that any solution could be arrived at only through the good services of Jordan. This position, even though accommodated at times by other Arab players, had never been to their liking. The Arab consensus reached at the Rabat summit was incumbent on all Arab countries. Furthermore, in terms of legitimacy of representation, most Arab leaders preferred Arafat's legitimacy to that of Hussein. The uprising, while underlining the newly acquired independent status of the PLO, weakened Jordan's standing. However, in spite of the US–PLO dialogue opened in 1988, its suspension by the US in 1990 still left a thin thread in Jordanian hands. The party to change that was Israel with the signing of the 1993 Oslo Accords with the PLO. Thus, the Oslo agreements marked a pressing need on the part of Jordan to change course. On the other hand, it enabled Jordan to finally get to discuss a peace treaty with Israel considering the accumulated effect of the Egyptian moves in the late 1970s and, to a greater extent, the Palestinian-granted legitimacy of such a process.

Jordan's participation in the process can be traced back to earlier days: Hussein believed that any agreement should be the result of an international conference, unless it was secret, and should not incriminate the kingdom in the eyes of other Arab countries. Indeed, after many years of ineffective efforts to gain Arab legitimacy for his moves Hussein was finally successful in the wake of the 1991 Gulf War. Since both he and Arafat supported the Iraqi cause there was no question of taking a pro-Western side. The Jordanian position, whatever the price in terms of relations with the US, gave Jordan a standing at least equal with that of the PLO regarding any political process that would emanate from the war. But even before any meaningful process could begin, Jordan once again returned to an uncomfortable situation, forced to absorb Palestinian refugees, this time from the Gulf. Since the refugees were Palestinians and since Jordan had already relinquished any connection with the West Bank it was only natural that two other players would have to take care of this increasing population: Israel and the PLO. In July 1991 Jordan put this issue on the table and blamed[14] Israel for limiting the number of Palestinians allowed into the territories, causing about 60,000 people to be delayed in Jordan. This is clearly one indication that the issue of refugees was very much on the Jordanian mind on the eve of the new phase of the negotiations. This number reflected only a small portion of the total refugee population which found its way back to Jordan in the wake of the war.[15] Their return threatened Jordan with an addition to its already large Palestinian population and further enhanced the acute economic crisis of the kingdom. In early August, Crown Prince Hassan expressed Jordan's demand that Kuwait should compensate Jordan for the return of some 300,000 Palestinians, most of them unemployed, from its territory to the kingdom. In his opinion the cost should be covered from the compensation to be paid to Kuwait by Iraq. In his interview[16] he went so far as to indicate that the continued crisis created by that exodus might impair Jordan's ability to participate in the coming peace process.

Nevertheless, in the wake of the war and in spite of the friction and tension between Jordan and the US, compared with the PLO Jordan enjoyed better standing towards other countries. One indication of the situation was Hussein's position after the war, during the Madrid conference and probably until the signing of the Oslo Accords,[17] reiterating his position that Jordan could not negotiate for the Palestinians, but that if the PLO were keen on returning to the confederation approach, Hussein would support them. His consent to the idea depended on three conditions:[18]

1. The sort of a Palestinian entity or government that was to be created on the West Bank;
2. That such a confederation should not be, in any future development, an application of the "Jordan option" (substituting Jordan for any Palestinian entity);
3. That a referendum should be held in Jordan and among the Palestinians about such a confederation.

Even the gradual improvement in Jordan's position in international politics did not make a lot of difference in the bilateral Jordan–PLO contacts. Inherently, the PLO had the upper hand and it had every intention of using it in the next stage. One of the major stumbling blocks between the two parties had to do with the make-up of a joint delegation to the conference. The PLO believed[19] it had every right to appoint all the Palestinian members with no Jordanian interference. Jordan at this point was intent on maintaining at least some influence over the deliberations of the delegation so that the PLO's positions would not be utterly opposed to those of Jordan – a move similar to the inclusion of a Jordanian representative at the 1964 Palestinian National Council in Jerusalem, establishing the PLO. But that was not to be. Whatever the source of the report that Jordan was considering retreating from the 1988 separation decision,[20] it was denied and never used as a source of pressure on the PLO. Whatever the circumstances, and despite the possible outcome that the PLO would become the sole party to decide on the future of the West Bank, Jordan did not want to find itself competing for control over that territory. Thus, as early as June 1991 all the chips were in place: Jordan would respect any position taken independently by the PLO,[21] whereas Hussein would seize any independent PLO stance if it produced the right political constellation to reach peace with Israel through direct negotiations.[22] In retrospect, this policy statement, careful as it was, signaled the route Hussein would take in the wake of the Oslo agreements a little over two years later. On the eve of the Madrid conference Hussein spoke[23] of his guidelines, foremost of which was: "Jordan, which had taken the disengagement decision in 1988, prefers Palestinian participation to take place on the basis of an Israeli–Palestinian committee, i.e. an independent Palestinian delegation to attend the conference." Differently put, Jordan was as genuine as it could be in its determination not to intervene in the Palestinian decision-making process. At this stage Hussein provided the PLO with a hosting delegation to facilitate Israeli–PLO negotiations, nothing more than that. This is clearly further evidence of the adaptable position so often taken by Hussein – he still needed some input in the political process in order to prevent any decisions contrary to his interests but once his main goal was accomplished, namely, that he was not responsible for the West Bank, he could go along with a fully independent PLO delegation.

Since the new Israeli administration, which came to power in the summer of 1992, believed that the "Jordanian option" was lost, it embarked on a Palestinian track leading to the Oslo Accords of September 1993.[24] That course was followed secretly, in spite of continuing the semi-public track resulting from the Madrid conference. Parallel to this track and without the king being made privy to its contents, he continued his contacts with the PLO, believing that with US assistance it might be possible to reach a new formula that would give Jordan a leading role in determining the future of the West Bank. These talks, which included meetings between the US and Jordan and between Arafat and Hussein during the summer of 1993, served in retrospect as a smoke-screen put up by the PLO, to cover what would become the Israeli–Palestinian Declaration of Principles. Following rumours that an agreement was about to be concluded, Hussein reacted as though he had been caught off guard. In late August he left for Damascus to confer with Hafiz al-Asad, an enemy of the PLO, as the Jordanian press attacked the emerging accord. A couple of days later the prime minister of Jordan reacted positively to the agreement, reflecting a traditional Jordanian position of not opposing a *fait accompli* that could not be changed. Later, Hussein himself announced his support on condition that the bridges that provided a passage to Jordan would not be handed over to the Palestinians, another indication of his concern lest the Palestinians took the opportunity to flood into Jordan. On the other hand, with the moment approaching when the Israeli–Palestinian accord was to be signed, Israel and Jordan agreed that this signing would lead to the signing of an agreement between the two countries on the agenda for their own talks, which took place a couple of days after the Declaration of Principles was signed at the White House. However, in regard to the PLO, the line adopted[25] was that the PLO was indeed the sole and legitimate representative of the Palestinian people, and that this people had the right to its national land. Having said that, Hussein was critical of the PLO and was far from satisfied with this people's choice of Arafat as their leader, obviously a traditional feature of Hussein's worldview.[26] This approach is probably an indication of the king's feeling of superiority towards the Palestinian leadership, along with feeling some justification for his not being able to agree with the policies adopted by the organization. Unspoken of is probably his traditional suspicion of the Palestinians, which given the right Israeli government might once again be turned from a potential threat into a clear and present danger to the Hashemite regime.

That suspicion would increase after the formal ceremony of signing the Israeli–Palestinian accord, since Hussein believed there were secret understandings between the parties, while the PLO was convinced that Jordan would try and reimpose its influence over the autonomous areas.

Until the Oslo Accords Israel saw King Hussein as the one and only partner for negotiations on the Palestinian issue. The change in the Israeli position weakened Hussein's position, making him only one of several diplomatic partners. Undoubtedly, the Oslo Accords came as a disappointing surprise to Hussein, not only because of the Israeli decision to prefer the Palestinian to the Jordanian option, but also because of Hussein's belief that Arafat was not the right person to represent the Palestinians. Already at the 1988 summit held in Algiers, Hussein had voiced his mistrust of the PLO – certainly, one of the very few expressions of this by King Hussein. The Oslo Accords dealt a blow to Hussein's aspirations regarding future relations between the West Bank and the Hashemite Kingdom.[27] Even though he had given up on the West Bank many years before, Hussein still desired that the territory should not turn into a springboard for elements hostile to his regime. He did not agree to the Palestinians taking over Jerusalem either, which would constitute a major blow to Hashemite prestige if an agreement were to be reached without Jordanian participation. Even though this issue was discussed between Jordan and the PLO within the framework of the subcommittee dedicated to the issues resulting from the Madrid conference, no progress on this question was ever reported.

Undoubtedly, Arafat and the PLO constituted a danger on all fronts. Indeed, throughout the rocky relations between the kingdom and the organization, Hussein had to give in to the Arab consensus preferring Arafat to him. Now that Israel followed suit Hussein could not have been too delighted. Hussein's moves *vis-à-vis* the West Bank were never intended to bring back his rule, however, and along the same vein, never meant to create a hostile PLO entity either. Thus, only when it was crystal clear that the PLO was about to take over the territories in the wake of the Oslo process did Hussein give up on his efforts to disrupt PLO activities regarding the territories. Thus, it is small wonder that the Oslo Accords were not given a warm welcome among the higher Jordanian echelons. In fact, the dialogue leading initially to that agreement was the result of a process begun at the Madrid peace conference with a joint Jordanian–Palestinian delegation intended to demonstrate Jordanian supremacy. The Jordanian feeling in the wake of Oslo was one of disappointment, as reflected in one of Hussein's speeches[28] during the period immediately after the agreement, speaking of the Jordanian umbrella being thrown out with the trash once the PLO did not need it anymore. These feelings did not deter the two sides from concluding, in January 1994, a so-called economic agreement, which in fact was no more than an expression of their mutual interest in reaching some sort of a temporary diplomatic cease-fire, considering the need not to interfere with each other's interests while continuing the dialogue with Israel. Thus, in spite of being called an economic agreement it was in effect a list of issues to be discussed in the future between the two parties: the main topics were of course the refugees and Jerusalem. In other words, the agreement did not produce any tangible success for any of the parties, it simply provided them with a list of issues to be discussed in the future when the time was ripe.

In early 1990, around the time of the meeting of the four leaders of the Arab Cooperation Council – the presidents of Egypt and Yemen and the kings of Saudi Arabia and Jordan – Israeli decision makers leaked to the press their concern over the processes unfolding in Jordan.[29] In their reading the democratization process as well as the rising power of the Muslim fundamentalists was endangering the continued stability of the Hashemite regime – a reading very much in line with past precedents in the 1950s and 1960s but far from the self-confidence currently projected from Amman. Perhaps the main Israeli concern had to do with the moving to Amman of the Palestinian apparatuses guiding the Palestinian uprising and the continued rapprochement with Iraq, which had the potential of bringing the Iraqi threat closer to home. With the Israeli signals not sparking any public Jordanian renouncement of its military cooperation with Iraq, and with preparations to establish joint military formations, Israel became more anxious regarding the development of a dangerous strategic situation along the common border. The public pronouncements were obviously addressed to Jordan, but the main culprit was Iraq. Even the thought that the warming Iraqi–Jordanian relations stemmed from the Jordanian economic situation, since both countries had been members of the Arab Cooperation Council since its creation in January 1989, and that the military dimension was not so threatening, could not alleviate Israeli concerns, which eventually were proved wrong during the Gulf crisis and war.

Israeli–Jordanian contacts before the 1991 Gulf War consolidated the parameters of behavior during the actual fighting, namely that Israel would try not to use Jordanian territory if it had to operate militarily.[30] Since that position made an Israeli response to the Iraqi missiles very difficult it practically eliminated any Israeli reprisal action as long as keeping Hussein in place justified the price of losing some Israeli potential for deterrence. The basis for that position was the public change in the Israeli position regarding Jordan as an alternative homeland. Right after the invasion, Israel voiced in many ways its continued interest in maintaining the status quo in Jordan, including, obviously, the continued rule of the Hashemites over the East Bank. Jordan, for its part, publicly sided with Iraq in accordance with its traditional policy of minimizing risks from its neighbors. Moreover, with the growing solidarity of its Palestinian population with Saddam Hussein, Jordan had to take sides, and naturally this was in line with the support that the PLO expressed for the Iraqi ruler. Even the Jordanian press, usually reflecting the general sympathies of the king, tried not to use the term "invasion" and called for an inter-Arab solution to the crisis rather than let outside forces intervene. However, in spite of the US anger with Hussein it is possible to determine in hindsight that his role was rather positive. In mid-August he tried in vain to broker some compromise between the US and Iraq, or at least to let Saddam continue using the port of Aqaba, also with no success. Later, as a country situated between Iraq and Israel and enjoying good relations with both, Jordan served during the war as a buffer state separating the two countries.

In the aftermath of the war Jordan needed to repair its relations with the US, but with Arab public support continuing for Saddam, King Hussein had to walk a tightrope. Thus, while conveying messages of peace and reconciliation directed at Israel and the US, indicating that he would be willing to participate at an international conference, he let some anti-Israeli elements loose along the border with Israel. With the continued activity of some of the Palestinian organization's offices in Amman, he managed to raise some concern in Israel lest he was losing control over those elements.[31] Actually, it was the traditional Hussein chess game in action once again. Hussein's response was typical: in an interview with the French *Le Point*,[32] which was quoted by all Israeli media outlets, he spoke of an early meeting between himself and the Israeli leaders. Simultaneously Hussein opened a careful process of disengagement from Saddam Hussein, with whom he never again returned to the degree of coordination and agreement he had during the weeks before and during the war. In his attempts to project a peaceful façade Hussein agreed in principle to his country participating in an international conference, responding positively to the initiative of US Secretary of State Baker. Once again, the agreement in principle to talk to Israel was there, as it had been in the past, but it was not yet a definite commitment to really meet the Israeli leaders before the eyes of the world.

In reality, Hussein's position did not change: an international conference had to serve as the source of legitimacy for any agreement to be reached in the future. His wish for an international umbrella to legitimize his contacts with Israel and if possible to let them out into the open was finally rewarded. The two powers, the US and the Soviet Union – soon to disappear from the world scene – issued a joint invitation to all concerned parties to participate at the Madrid peace conference to take place in October 1991. Jordan and the Palestinians had to be represented by a joint delegation, because of the continued insistence of Israel that it would not talk to the PLO. This conference marked the beginning of another chapter of open diplomacy between the two countries, similar to some extent to the Rhodes armistice negotiations: the accredited delegates could continue their discussions, but the real decisions were to be made within the region.

After the Madrid conference several rounds of negotiations took place between Israel and other Arab parties to the process. The attitude taken by the Jordanian delegation during those talks was symptomatic of past negotiations: Jordan insisted on a comprehensive peace, which meant that it would not sign any separate agreement with Israel as long as other Arab parties did not do so first. Jordan participated in the process, but the real work had to wait for the leaders first to reach secret agreements, and for a public agreement between Israel and the PLO as a precondition to any open and public discussions between Israel and Jordan.

In June 1992, in the framework of the diplomatic process with Israel resulting from the Madrid conference, Palestinian sources projected a Hussein–Arafat agreement, or at least coordination, leading to the implementation of the notion of a confederation in the context of a diplomatic solution. However, instead of such an agreement the Israeli government which came to power in the summer of 1992 abandoned a generations-long history of preferring the Hashemite partner to any other potential co-signatory to a peace treaty, the so-called "Jordanian option," and embarked on the track leading to the September 1993 Oslo Accords with the PLO. Moreover, Israel probably neglected the nuances of its position, as the following quote from a couple of years later reveals:[33] "'King Hussein has never really abandoned his interest in the West Bank,' I [Peres] continued. 'Even when he proclaimed he was out of the game, he didn't mean it. He expected to be called back. That didn't happen, and meanwhile we in Israel wanted to rid ourselves of the burden of occupying the Palestinians.'"

Peres claims in his autobiography[34] that while negotiating the Oslo Accords: "we were motivated not only by our own direct and obvious security interests but also by those of Jordan." True or not, Jordan was not made aware of the new track between Israel and the PLO and the Oslo agreement did not provide any solution that was to the liking of Jordan regarding the Palestinian refugees and Jerusalem. This unprecedented Israeli approach in relation to Jordan caused Hussein, perhaps for the first time ever, to demonstrate a degree of aggravation towards an Israeli leader, during his meeting with Prime Minister Rabin shortly after the accords were signed in Washington. That incident allegedly happened in late September 1993 during a meeting between him and Rabin, the prime minister of Israel, which took place on a boat at sea not far from Aqaba.[35] The issues raised at that meeting included Hussein's displeasure with any granting of Palestinian access to the bridges – in other words, Israel would have to make sure that Palestinians would not flood into Jordan. However, regardless of the obvious tension between the two countries the steady move towards peace continued, as did the careful talks aimed at reaching a peace treaty. As part of this process a joint security committee was established – for the first time a public forum, unlike similar teams which had been meeting secretly for decades. Rabin also reiterated the Israeli guarantee to the Hashemite regime and laid the groundwork for the resumption of bilateral strategic cooperation.

Perhaps the public signing of the Israeli–Palestinian Declaration of Principles and the Jordanian expectation to be bailed out of its continued economic troubles paved the way for the public process.[37] Moreover, with the apparent Israeli withdrawal from the "Jordanian option" Hussein needed clear-cut Israeli assurances that Israel would continue to support the existence of the Hashemite Kingdom, and would not support any Palestinian move against it, nor allow any Palestinian demographic movement from the west to the east. These considerations led first to the July 1994 Washington Declaration ending the state of war between the two countries, and in October to the signing of the Israeli–Jordanian peace treaty. Even though Jordan decided in September 1944 to sever its connections with the religious structure in the West Bank it did not relinquish its connection with the Temple Mount.[38] This, to the extreme disapproval of the PLO, which believed that the Jordanian policy, including the preparations for a peace agreement, contributed to Jordanian–Palestinian mistrust since both Jordan and Israel had agreed on issues which the PLO saw itself more fit to negotiate,[39] in the first place the issue of Jerusalem. The refugee issue was not to the satisfaction of the PLO either, since the agreement opened the way to an abandonment of the Palestinian right of return, a major requirement for peace in the PLO's view.[40]

The signing ceremony in the desert on the common border not only highlighted the common Jordanian–Israeli interest in making the desert bloom. It had clear political connotations, perhaps the most important of them being the omission of Yasir Arafat, chairman of the PLO and the Palestinian Authority, from the list of dignitaries invited to the occasion. Moreover, the short but intensive process between the kingdom and Israel led to an agreement on Israel respecting "the present special role of the Hashemite Kingdom of Jordan in Muslim holy shrines in Jerusalem"[41] – a clear snub to Arafat who insisted that these areas should be turned over to the Palestinians and not to Jordan. In a sense this expression indicated a limited Israeli return to the traditional "Jordanian option" aligning the prime minister of Israel and Hussein, as against the Oslo axis aligning the Israeli foreign minister, Peres, with Arafat.[42] Another party to be offended was Saudi Arabia, which had made every effort to renovate the Jerusalem shrines only a few years back in order to establish its own claim to the city. However, the ceremony was more of a tribute to a secret partner that was enjoying a remission from a grave illness, and both the ignoring of Arafat, and the issue of Jerusalem, were much more of a personal gesture than anything else. The Jerusalem issue, at least in Jordanian eyes, was settled with their January 1995 agreement with the PLO recognizing *inter alia* the Israeli–Jordanian peace treaty, thus indirectly accepting at least formally the Jordanian position regarding Hashemite rights in the Holy City. In fact, in spite of this supposed accommodation of the issue, the leading religious figures on the Mount were no longer connected to Jordan, and received their instructions from the Palestinian Authority. It is safe to assume that nothing in Jordan's diplomatic handling of its relations with Israel and the Palestinians indicated any deviation from genuine support of the independent Palestinian track as long as Jordan could accommodate itself to the unfolding Israeli–Palestinian developments. This approach allowed Jordan to appear as the closest party to the Palestinians while providing them with support and yet not involving itself in their affairs.[43]

With the signing of the Jordanian–PLO agreement in January 1995 another chapter in these rocky relations came to an end. Beyond its clauses speaking of several dimensions of mutual relations, it was a document attesting to the mutual recognition of two almost equal partners. In a sense, the Jordanian commitment to open an office in Gaza dedicated to Palestinian interests, which would open in June 1995, indicated a qualified recognition of a distinct Palestinian political entity, a step not taken by Jordan at any point in the past. Just by way of signaling to both sides where Jordanian interests were really placed at that time, Jordanian and Israeli military units held a joint drill in the south a couple of days after the signing of the agreement with the PLO.[44] Judging from past examples of political behavior by Hussein it was not a mere coincidence. One day later Israel concluded its retreat from disputed lands in accordance with the peace treaty.

With the signing of the peace treaty the two countries started a process of accelerated normalization, meaning implementation of the series of understandings arrived at over the years. Almost overnight the image projected was one of two countries long at peace. Thus, contacts between leaders of both sides became frequent and public, usually devoted to mutual updating regarding third parties, and especially, relations with the Palestinians and the ongoing diplomatic process between them and Israel. The respective armies began jointly chasing Palestinians acting against Israeli targets. It is clear that much time during the mutual negotiations was devoted to the Jordanian side expressing its concern over the possible establishment of a Palestinian state, and the possibility that Israel would repeat its Oslo stunt and surprise Jordan with an uncoordinated critical move.[45] Thus, in spite of public condemnations of Israel, as happened during the 1996 Israeli operation in Lebanon, when the media was allowed to use very harsh language against Israel, for the most part relations remained warm and contacts intensive between the leaders. This comfortable picture of relations is somewhat misleading: between the Jordanian economic interest in promoting peace and the concern with the Israeli takeover of the Jordanian economy nothing much had been accomplished. Accordingly, the outcome of the peace process is much more apparent at the higher echelons of the two countries while the grassroots remained indifferent at best, hostile at worst.

Hussein's personality acted like magic on all Israeli leaders and that along with the more than 30 years of *de facto* peace meant that peace between Israel and Jordan was a matter of consensus among Israeli leaders of all political persuasions. An interesting issue relating to Hussein's connections with Israel had to do with his contacts with the center-right-wing Likud Party, and especially the term of Prime Minister Benyamin Netanyahu (1996–1999). Already as the leader of the Israeli opposition prior to his election he had developed close relations with the Hashemite court. The common ground was probably the opposition of the Likud bloc to the Oslo process and accords, and the concern of Hussein regarding possible Israeli concessions to the PLO. Netanyahu and Hussein met several times, twice in August 1996 in London and Amman, when their meetings were devoted to many bilateral issues but basically reflected the special status that Israel accorded to the monarch – that of an ally who can and wants to act as a bridge between Netanyahu and the rest of the Arab world. Bearing in mind this special status never before enjoyed by Hussein, along with the warm relations that had survived several wars and outside challenges and which made the two partners members of one alliance, it is no wonder that the three major tests during Netanyahu's term as prime minister: the tunnel riots, the Hebron agreement, and the Mash'al scandal, did not lead to a rupture in relations (see p. 199).

In late September 1996 Israel decided to open the Western Wall Tunnel, which is sometimes referred to as the "Rabbi's Tunnel." That event was marked by violent riots all over the Palestinian areas due to what they saw as another Israeli infringement of Muslim rights on the Temple Mount. This incident not only highlighted once more the obvious sensitivity of the site, but also caused a rupture in the delicate nature of relations between Israel and the Palestinian Authority. This episode involved several elements close to Hussein: in the first place, there was the issue of Jerusalem with its outstanding significance for the Hashemites, and yet with the eroding Jordanian presence and importance on the Mount, Hussein could not ignore this combination. What is more, with his history of understandings with Israel and his open but cautious dialogue with the PLO he found the issue deserving of his involvement. Perhaps the potential threat of riots, which might get out of hand and spill over in one way or another to Jordan, provided the final incentive for Hussein to get involved in the efforts to find common ground between the two local parties. Indeed, after filing official protest with Israel to the effect that Israel had to get his permission first,[46] Hussein joined with the US in its attempt to convene a summit meeting in Washington with the participation of all relevant parties including, obviously, Jordan. However, in spite of Hussein's participation the outcome of the summit did not promote his role in Jerusalem and thus left the matter in the hands of Israel and the PLO. The summit meeting was also the scene of a tense speech by Hussein voicing his disappointment with Prime Minister Netanyahu.[47] The Amman visit of the policy advisor of the Israeli prime minister a few days before the opening of the tunnel was interpreted by the Palestinians as an indication that the affair had been prepared by Jordan and Israel, and thus the price Jordan had to pay was a further retreat from its position in the Muslim religious institutions on the Mount.

The public crisis and the resulting temporary pause in his diplomatic efforts did not deter Hussein, who continued his dialogue with Israel in spite of increasing pressures not to do so. About the time the crisis was over Hussein paid the first official visit of any Arab leader to the Palestinian Authority, demonstrating his solidarity with the cause of Jerusalem and the Palestinian side in its confrontation with Israel. Shortly after the tunnel episode, Hussein's vigilance and attempt at defining any crack between Israel and the PLO, once again, in early 1997, initiated action regarding difficulties in the peace process. Indeed, after Hussein's visit to Israel and the Palestinian Authority in January 1997, Israel and the PLO signed an agreement regarding Israeli deployment in Hebron.[48] The complex nature of relations was expressed again later that year with the king insisting that so far as a Palestinian state was concerned, it "would not be a threat to Jordan." He added that such a state would have "every reason to consider Jordan, a strong shoulder on which it can lean." The king was upset about Israeli claims that Israel would turn to Jordan to help it keep control over Palestinians, rather than give the Palestinians their own state. "The King insists that he has made it clear to the Israeli government that he will not negotiate on Palestinian issues. 'That's why I am upset,' he says. 'By speculations that suggest we are involved.'"[49]

Another crisis occurred in early 1997 with Israel's insistence on continuing a major building project in East Jerusalem contrary to Hussein's wishes, as expressed in two messages in late February and in early March.[50] The exchange of public reactions between the Israeli and Jordanian leaders at the time created the impression of a crisis in their mutual relations, but the Hashemite court made every effort possible to make sure that Jordan saw the issue as one between the king and the prime minister, definitely not as a confrontation between two countries at peace. However, the crisis was not over, since after the last message was delivered a Jordanian soldier opened fire on a group of Israeli schoolgirls and killed seven of them, while they were visiting Naharayim, an area known as the Island of Peace because of the special regime in that area agreed by both sides at the signing of the peace treaty. That special regime allowed uninterrupted visits by citizens of both countries to the area, which was kept under Jordanian sovereignty and private ownership by Israeli citizens. This tragic incident was transformed by Hussein to serve as a new peak in his success in becoming a welcome visitor to Israel. While visiting the families of the girls who were killed he knelt down before them and begged for their forgiveness. Both countries used this humanitarian gesture to alleviate the tension and resume normal relations. This visit was also used to once again play a mediating role between Israel and the PLO – a position that was essential for Jordan in light of its own concerns in this triangle. To make sure that the message was not lost, Hussein replaced his prime minister, who had publicly snubbed prime minister Netanyahu, with a new one, Abd al-Salam al-Majali, a Jordanian statesman known for his personal involvement and stake in the peace process with Israel. Even though the more substantial reasons for this change had much more to do with the Jordanian domestic scene, Israel noted its significance in this context as well.

In addition to the parliamentary activities of radical Muslims, some of their extra-parliamentarian activities were gathering momentum as well. About the time of the Iraqi invasion the HAMAS organization began laying the groundwork for operating from Jordan, presumably against Israel, but obviously once the infrastructure was laid there was a potential to operate against the Hashemite regime if and when circumstances arose. Two factors enabled HAMAS to operate in Jordan: the open political support which it received from the legitimate Muslim fundamantalist movement in Jordan, and Jordan's long-standing suspicion of the PLO. All this made Amman, during the period after the Iraqi invasion of Kuwait, a center of activity unequalled in any other Arab country.

The Muslim constraint remained in play throughout the 1990s. The road to a public peace treaty was not free of this snag either. In April 1994 Israel warned[51] Jordan that it would not tolerate the freedom which HAMAS was enjoying in Jordan. Later, as part of the final preparations for the signing of the peace treaty, Israel and Jordan agreed to cooperate in curtailing the activities of radical Muslim organizations, including exchanging intelligence material and coordinating operations against the organizations.[52] This understanding did not lead to the closing down of the offices in Amman of HAMAS, and with the wave of bombings against Israeli civilian targets in early 1996 the two countries once again closed ranks. In March 1996 the commander of Jordanian military intelligence visited Israel and met with his Israeli counterpart. One day later, the foreign minister of Israel, himself a former commander of military intelligence, visited Amman and met the Crown Prince and the prime minister. The two countries discussed an exchange of intelligence, and cooperation in curtailing HAMAS activities.[53] About the same time a leading member of the Muslim movement was sentenced to three years in jail for accusing Hussein of betraying his country in signing a peace treaty with Israel. However, these Jordanian activities did not lead to the closure of the HAMAS offices in Amman, a move that might have brought about a change in the rules, that is, no more public warnings but rather an all-out attack on the radical Muslims. If such a move had been made it would have constituted a change in the way Hussein had operated for years, especially with regard to the PLO in the context of the civil war, which was that confrontation should be avoided at almost any price. A confrontation should only be resorted to if all other options failed. With the degree of potential radical Muslim threat to Jordan at this point it was not yet necessary to confront HAMAS. That careful position was not to the liking of Israel and the US, which found both public and less public ways to voice their dissatisfaction with the continued acquiescence of Jordan in these activities.[54] Jordan for its part blamed Syria for allegedly helping HAMAS in smuggling weapons and drugs from its territory to Jordan.[55]

In late September 1997 Israeli agents attacked one of the leaders of HAMAS, Khalid Mash'al, in Amman. The failed attempt and the subsequent apprehension of the Israeli agents not only infuriated Hussein, but, as had already happened under similar circumstances, he turned this crisis into a springboard for further policy accomplishments. Following the negotiations between Hussein and Netanyahu after the Israeli attack, Hussein released the two Israeli agents in exchange for Ahmad Yasin – the HAMAS leader. Once again, Hussein could convince Israel to move ahead in the Palestinian context even under the most difficult conditions – a quality the PLO did not possess. In light of the necessary future steps in Israeli–Palestinian relations and in spite of the changing circumstances, Hussein could still play the role of mediator, to the extreme dissatisfaction of Arafat.[56] This episode brought Israeli–Jordanian relations to their lowest point since the signing of the 1994 accord, though even this public mutual embarrassment did not put an end to the semi-secret contacts on security and anti-terrorist issues between the two countries. What happened was a pattern of political behavior very familiar by now: at time of crisis a reversion to the old secret channels and if necessary leaving them in some "creative ambiguity." Indeed, whatever threatened to sabotage the mutual relations and even led the Jordanian press to vehement attacks on Israel did not have any lasting effect on joint strategic cooperation.

Jordan's last contribution to the peace process under Hussein related to the Middle East peace talks also known as the Wye Summit, convened in mid-October 1998. The ailing Hussein joined the talks and indeed contributed to the signing of an agreement in order to eliminate one more source of concern for Jordan: the continued stalemate between Israel and the Palestinians. The inability of these two parties to implement their prior agreements carried, as always, the potential of a clash between them – a specter to be avoided in Jordanian eyes.

The Domestic Scene

One field in which Hussein's legacy is far from what he desired is the Jordanian economy. Perhaps the food riots, which broke out in southern Jordan in April 1989, spreading to the rest of Jordan and claiming 12 lives, were more than just popular protests against decreased subsidies for basic foodstuffs. The riots came on top of past economic decisions in October 1988, among them a devaluation of the Jordanian dinar and limitations on the import of luxury items. The concentration of the April riots in the south at the heart of the Bedouin area meant that for the first time since the creation of the kingdom, dissatisfaction was voiced by that element of the population which had served for so long as the backbone of the Hashemite regime. The inability of the Desert Police, composed of local Bedouin, to put an end to the unrest and the subsequent calling in of the army served as another ominous indication that even the Bedouin had reached their limits. In spite of this pessimistic picture, the break in the pattern of past close relations between the Hashemites and the Bedouin never developed into a serious threat to the coalition, but it did serve as a reminder that not all economic moves were possible given the inability of the Bedouin-based regime to deal with this element. After all, even the behavior of the police and later the army towards the rioting crowds were clearly different, and much better, than any reaction to similar moves by Palestinian Jordanian citizens. These developments also demonstrated the fragility of the position of Crown Prince Hassan as a substitute for Hussein, who stayed in the US and believed Hassan would perform as the circumstances required. The government response as formulated by Hassan and executed by Prime Minister Zayd al-Rifa'i was rather hesitant and did not prevent the riots spreading quickly from the south to the rest of the country, leading to the early return of Hussein from his overseas trip. Zayd al-Rifa'i lost his position as a result of the riots. Hassan's inefficiency may have contributed to Hussein's disappointment with his brother.

However, the bad news concerning the Bedouin resentment of the regime, especially that of the Huwaytat tribe, traditional participants in the Jordanian security forces, was to some extent balanced by good news on two levels: there was no public demand that the king abdicate – only his prime minister was depicted as the guilty party concerning the deteriorating economic situation; and secondly, neither Palestinian citizens nor the PLO had taken part in the events. This most violent wave of opposition to the regime since the 1970–1 civil war did not attract the large Palestinian population of Jordan, clearly indicating that they had really become part and parcel of the Jordanian political infrastructure and stood to lose their share in the local economy if they participated in the riots. The PLO for its part followed the diplomatic maneuvering regarding possible elections in the territories closely and had no interest in being portrayed as enemies of the peace process.

Those events helped shed some light over the most acute crisis in Jordan: the state of the economy.[57] Perhaps Jordan's most rewarding relations on the regional level were with the oil-producing countries. In the 1970s and until the oil glut of the early 1980s Jordan had enjoyed a steady flow of foreign currency from Jordanian citizens abroad and later from subsidies emanating directly from the oil countries. Those funds enabled Jordan to stabilize its economy, with unemployment under control and inflation at a little over 10 percent annually. Although the improving economic situation spelled good news in the short run it was not used to build a new infrastructure, which would have guaranteed that the improvement continued.

With the 1980s over and the economies of the oil-rich countries in decline as a result of the oil glut, Jordan felt the side-effects of this process. The declining oil revenues caused fewer subsidies to be transferred to Jordan by the oil-rich countries, and the remittances of expatriate Jordanian workers abroad lost ground in their contribution to the national economy and their contributions to their families. Around the mid-1980s these changes caused a gradual decline in the foreign reserves of the kingdom and an increase in the foreign debt. From a peak of around US$ 1 billion in 1981 the reserves shrank to US$ 350 million in 1985 and about 200 million in the first half of 1987. The crisis in the Gulf since the early 1980s had caused tens of thousands of Jordanian workers to return home and thus aggravate the already existing unemployment problem in the kingdom. All these negative economic indicators caused Jordan to borrow about US$ 6.5 billion during the 1980s, which led in 1989 to near bankruptcy.

In early 1989 four Arab countries announced the formation of a new Arab alliance composed of Jordan, Egypt, Iraq and North Yemen, demonstrating that the old animosities of the 1960s were a thing of the past. For Jordan this new alliance signaled hope of improving its economy after several years of continued economic crisis, but such hopes were not realized. This new regional framework did not produce new working opportunities for Jordanians nor did it produce any new subsidies for Jordan. Even the slightest hopes were dashed when the members of this body found themselves on opposing sides during the 1990–1 Gulf War. Jordanian pleas with the International Monetary Fund and the lending countries had produced a demand for economic reforms and a program of economic rehabilitation, which was to be implemented in the period 1989–93. In return for these programs Jordan was given longer to repay its debts. Jordan embarked on a courageous economic plan of austerity and cutting back on subsidies, which was supposed to produce improvement in about six years. However, this did not happen and in 1996 the economy grew[58] by only 0.8 percent and in 1997 by 2.7 percent.

Actually, the April 1989 riots came as no surprise to the king. Already in late 1988 and early 1989 he had spoken of the need for structural changes in the Jordanian economy[59] and blamed the only partial application of the Baghdad subsidies on the economic troubles of his country. Economic constraints were also very much on his mind. On two occasions in June 1989 he spoke of the unjust distribution of economic resources[60] as the major issue taking up most of his time.

In the wake of the Gulf War and crisis it was expected that Jordan would continue its economic decline.[61] The Jordanian GNP, which had begun to rise before the war, was expected to decline by 8 percent with the loss of markets, the rise in unemployment due to the return of expatriates (mainly Palestinians from the Gulf), and the ensuing worsening of the balance of payments.

Perhaps one of the last elements to be added to Hussein's legacy was his expressed wish to become a constitutional monarch. He tried to implement this through a careful and rather slow process of democratization very much in line with his consistent effort to uphold the constitution in spite of sporadic crises.[62] Even though not all studies on the Jordanian elections agree[63] that the three election campaigns so far (1989, 1993, 1997) indicate a true progression towards democracy, an authoritative source like the Freedom House attests to such a process. After many years of declaring Jordan not democratically free, with a ranking of 6.6[64] (the lower the number the more democratic the country), Jordan was declared partly free by Freedom House in 1984/5 with 5.5, and it maintained that ranking (with the exception of 1988/9, the year of the food riots) until 1991/2 when it got 4.4, and a ranking of 3.3 in 1992/3. It is ironic that Hussein, who was so much concerned with the democratic future of his country, was diagnosed with cancer and operated on in 1992, the same year that his country received the highest grade ever for its democratic political behavior. That in a sense gave a glimpse of a significant element of his legacy. From 1993/4 onwards Jordan generally kept the ranking of "partly free" with 4.4. This rather objective assessment indicates that the last ten years of Hussein's rule saw a meaningful advancement towards democracy, in spite of the risks usually associated with such moves in traditionally non-democratic societies and the inherent contradiction between a monarchy in which the king has the decisive say in almost all fields of life and the democratic system. Clearly, the removal of the constant danger to the survival of the country and the regime allowed Hussein, a student of Western political traditions, to try to follow them.

Jordan's road to democracy was indicated by several gradual steps, starting in April 1978 with the creation of a National Consultative Council, since a parliament could not be elected by the West Bankers lest it would be interpreted as a contradiction of the 1974 Rabat resolution, while acknowledging Israeli control over the occupied territories. The three councils convened between 1978 and 1984 consisted of representatives appointed by Hussein. This interim measure, as a substitute for a parliament, came to an end in January 1984. At that time the living members of the 1967 parliament met officially after a short campaign of by-elections in the East Bank and decided which of the members would represent the West Bank.

The response to the changing circumstances was mixed: movement towards democracy along with tactical retreats. Several changes in the system were introduced between 1989 and 1993, including the following. In April 1989, the 1986 election law was modified[65] to reflect the new relations with the West Bank: the 60-seat representation of the West Bank was abolished altogether along with the elimination of the 11 seats for the refugee camps in Jordan, which from then on would be represented in the same way as all other Jordanian citizens. The law gave a clear advantage, in terms of the number of representatives, to voting districts outside Amman and Zarqa, areas with large Palestinian populations. In a series of moves between the parliamentary elections of 1989 and 1993, martial law was revoked; the National Charter was introduced in 1991, pre-empting the elections and adding a more modern, Jordanian and popular dimension to the constitution;[66] and the new 1992 Parties Law[67] was approved by Parliament, renewing the old party politics of the early 1950s in Jordan. After the 1993 elections the process of legislating a press law was begun, with one version passed in 1993, and later in 1997 another, curtailing the large degree of freedom granted to the press by the older version. The processes leading to the adoption of these laws were accompanied by public debate in Jordan in the media and in parliament. Even though the final outcome did not yet conform to accepted Western political norms it was definitely a testimony to Jordan's movement towards democracy. This democratization process was one of the tools with which Hussein demonstrated the political difference between Jordanian nationals and the Palestinians, by pointing out the different political climates in which Palestinians and Jordanians were operating.

The repercussions of these reforms were manifested in the parliamentary elections, especially in November 1989. Giving representation to all East Bank Jordanians under the new law, which practically signaled an open field for all political currents, indicated a calculated risk on the part of Hussein. The same was true of the suspension of emergency decrees, the releasing of political prisoners, and the announced abolition of press censorship – all moves creating a new, freer public atmosphere.[68] These changes did not alter dramatically the nature of the regime, but clearly manifested a Jordanian move towards more democracy. A succession of events and processes around 1988/9 enabled Hussein to embark on that road; perhaps his most pressing need as the father figure to his nation was to renew his bond with his people. During the year or two before the election he had stayed away from Jordan for long periods, leading to a feeling among many Jordanians that he had lost touch with them – a feeling that was magnified by the hesitant response of Hassan to the April riots and the hasty return of Hussein to the kingdom, which probably highlighted the emerging gap. It also affected the level of obedience within the army and other security apparatus, which never went as far as endangering the regime but clearly marked a change compared with the unquestionable loyalty in the past. Several other similar factors should be noted: the resignation of the minister of information in late 1988 over the lack of press freedom,[69] and the food riots of April 1989, which in spite of their severity did not pose a major risk to the regime, and which in retrospect indicated a sort of popular warning to the king not to implement the economic reform program too vigorously. General parliamentary elections were intended, on top of additional political considerations, to reaffirm a degree of popular participation in the Jordanian political system. Other, no less important factors leading to the electoral process were the severance of relations in 1988 between the two banks, and the declaration of the Palestinian state in November 1988, both indicating that Hussein could no longer aspire to represent the Palestinians of the West Bank; the elections were intended to institutionalize the recognition of the East Bank as a separate and independent political entity. All these changes served to highlight the need to provide Jordan with new channels of political expression. With most if not all of the survival crises over, Hussein was much more concerned with his new contribution to the future of Jordan: its path to democracy.

Clearly, the relative advance towards democracy compared with political precedents was reflected in the parliamentary debate leading to the confidence vote in Badran's cabinet (December 1999). Many of the expressions voiced[70] by members of all political persuasions were candid and reflected true criticism of the cabinet and the regime. While Hussein's exercise in democracy was genuine, it failed to forecast the success of the rather dangerous Muslim element. The potential risk was at times reflected, after the campaign, in the speeches by religious figures in Jordan and in the West Bank. In the wake of the impressive showing of radical Muslim candidates in the elections the preacher of the al-Aqsa spoke[71] of the approaching creation of a world Muslim state. He also called for further reforms in the Jordanian regime. Economic constraints were not missing from parliamentary debate either. The victory of the Islamic trend was clear. Since the Muslim Brotherhood – under different names and various organizational forms – had operated for years, unlike most of the political parties it had a rather elaborate system that was put in action before and during the elections. All other parties could be formed only shortly before the elections. Obviously, the success of the Muslim trend was also due to the economic crisis and the spill-over effect of the Palestinian uprising. Still, the Palestinians did not vote in force for the national trend, perhaps because identifying with a loyal Muslim opposition could be more acceptable to the regime than taking a pro-Palestinian opposition stand. The Muslim candidates for their part included, in their campaign propaganda, anti-Israeli slogans reminiscent of the Arab–Israeli conflict of the 1950s and 1960s: calling for *jihad* against Israel, the creation of a *shari'ah* state over all of the former Mandatory Palestine, and a rejection of any compromise in the diplomatic process. The PLO, on the other hand, did not intervene in the elections and did not issue any guidelines to the Palestinians living in Jordan.

The bottom line of the 1989 election indicates a political confrontation between four main groups of candidates: members of the Hashemite school, leftists, the pan-Arab, and the Muslim oriented.[72] Taking a tally indicates that the "loyalists" won 38 seats compared with 42 to the opposition. Apparently, the success of the Muslim candidates emanated from the decline of previously popular ideas like socialism and pan-Arabism. Even the successful showing of the Muslims did not change the clear conclusions of the campaign and its outcome. However, the Muslims' success in the Jordanian political sphere was not only the result of the growing fundamentalist Muslim trend throughout the Muslim world, it was also the result of specific Jordanian political circumstances. Even the Muslim trend, supposedly connected with such movements outside of Jordan, with its use of universal slogans, confined its local propaganda, and later its activity, to Jordanian issues.

If anything, the 1989 elections established a new status quo between the descendant of the Prophet Muhammad, Hussein, and a rather radical Muslim movement calling for the creation of a Muslim religious political entity. Indeed, this particular campaign and its consequences, a significant representation for the Muslim bloc in Parliament, brought to fruition a process which had begun in the 1970s. The political vacuum created by the end of the civil war in 1971 made the Muslim circles the most important opposition element in Jordan, serving as a magnet for Palestinians as well as Trans-Jordanians interested in voicing dissident views under the legal cover of being a semi-legal organization. After all, the outlawing of all parties back in 1957 had not put an end to the activities of the Muslim Brotherhood, it being not only a political body, but a social organization as well. The Israeli–Egyptian peace process and eventually the treaty, along with the spreading phenomenon of the rediscovery of Islam, did not skip Jordan in the late 1970s and later.[73] The gradual retreat from the relatively prosperous 1970s along with the success of the Iranian revolution, which toppled one of the closest friends and allies of Hussein, the Shah, had its effect on the Jordanian public. Until the mid-1980s, concurrent with similar processes in other areas of the Middle East, the Muslim radicals, usually under the leadership of the Muslim Brotherhood, became a power to reckon with. With the success of the three Muslim candidates who stood in the 1984 by-elections, and the subsequent formation of the Muslim bloc in Parliament, this trend became a recognized and represented factor in Jordanian politics.

With this realization Jordan initiated a public campaign against the radical trends embodied in this activity and Hussein and Asad, two rivals united in apprehension of the Muslim threat, met in late 1985. Along with internal legislation intended to curb this activity, and the closure of their training camps, several activists were arrested and extradited to Syria.[74] But these moves were a temporary setback for the radical Muslims, who did not stop their drive. In May 1986 they were at least partly responsible for the riots at Yarmuk University in Irbid.[75] The riots allegedly began as a protest against high tuition fees but the intensity of the violence, which caused several deaths, attested to a larger and more organized protest. Later, as a Reformist movement which "eschewed violence and acted as a social and parliamentary movement" while working within the existing system,[76] members and sympathizers of radical Islam decided to run in the November 1989 parliamentary elections. Out of the 80 elected members, 22 were members of the Muslim Brotherhood and eight more were sympathizers.

Perhaps the main stumbling block holding back the movement towards democracy had to do with the Muslim trend in the Jordanian political scene. Between the elections of 1989 and 1993, members of the Muslim Brotherhood, or people holding views close to theirs, served on Jordanian cabinets, were at times subject to persecution by the regime, and from time to time were engaged in internal infighting regarding the right attitude *vis-à-vis* the Hashemite regime. Yet the Muslim current in Jordanian politics remained as the most coherent power outside the internal circle of politicians close to Hussein. The potential threat of radical Islam was perhaps the main driving force in Jordanian domestic decisions between the two parliamentary campaigns. The possibility of friction became more noticeable with the signing of the Israeli–Palestinian Declaration of Principles in

September 1993, just two months prior to elections. However, this signing did not dramatically change the Jordanian domestic political scene, and the issues on the agenda were mostly of a local nature: economics and the quality of life.

The outcome of the 1993 elections, the first under a law permitting parties to run, proved that the changes in the system harmed the Islamic element while bringing the tribal element back to power in force.[77] Another reason for the radical Muslims' lack of success compared with the 1989 results had to do with the concentration of public debate around local and national issues rather than the more general Islamic message. The change in the system, while allowing the Islamic Action Front Party to run as the main Muslim group, produced a parliament more convenient to Hussein than its predecessor, thus the democratic experiment of 1989 was not abandoned, it was only modified somewhat, similar to the way the press law underwent several changes to reflect the careful movement towards[78] (and sometimes minor retreat from) democracy, instead of unlimited freedom of speech and organization.

In August 1996 another round of food riots took place in southern Jordan and spread to Amman, resulting from another round of economic moves including cuts in subsidies, and a widespread feeling that most Jordanians did not benefit from the peace with Israel.[79] The way the riots were handled served once again to indicate how far Jordan had come since the 1989 disturbances in the same locations: this time foreign TV crews were allowed into the area and the reaction of the security forces was reserved. Even though the usual ritual was repeated – arrests of some opposition leaders and journalists and putting the blame on Iraq – it was evident that no one in Jordan or outside suspected any risk to the regime as a result. Riots, but to a lesser extent, were repeated in Ma'an in February 1998[80] with demonstrators shouting pro-Iraqi slogans. That, resulting from the continued economic difficulties, indicated that the obvious allegiance of the Bedouin was still strong but not as solid as in the past. With the failing health of Hussein, Jordanians probably felt more at ease voicing their grievances towards their government.

Between early 1997 and November, Jordan entered a semi-transitional period. With the replacement of Abd al-Karim Kabariti by Abd al-Salam al-Majali as prime minister, Hussein actually rejected all proposals by the outgoing figure to delay parliamentary elections by two years. The incoming Majali initiated a policy much more in line with the democratic process the king had adopted. In his term, the cabinet ministers would not be members of parliament but technocrats devoted to their professional positions and subject to criticism and votes by Parliament. Moreover, Majali's main concern was to hold the scheduled November elections and make sure the radical Muslims would not repeat their successes. However, with the specter of another successful show by Muslim radicals, in May Hussein decreed new censorship measures on the press, which led to an obvious infringement of freedom of expression. The rule of "one-man, one-vote," which was introduced later, signaled a break with the past when voters could cast a number of votes equal to the number of district representatives in Parliament. That change in the election process deprived people in the more populated areas, namely the capital and Zarqa, mostly suspected as potential voters for the radical Muslims, of some of their power. The result was that the radical Muslims and other parties boycotted the parliamentary elections. In terms of issues on the national agenda, the 1997 campaign went even further in the direction of concentrating on domestic affairs. In spite of the 1994 peace treaty with Israel, and opposition from Muslim circles and the trade unions, the outcome was a clear victory to the traditional tribal representatives.

Succession

When Hussein published his autobiography in 1962 the title given to the photograph of him and his son Prince Abdullah read "My son and heir."[81] While pressure mounteded on the monarchy and on the king personally, it took 37 more years for the succession to be fulfilled.

Two main issues threatened the life of Hussein for many years: his enemies and his health. Out of concern for the future of his kingdom he nominated his brother Hassan, in 1965, to serve as the Crown Prince. In Hussein's words: "I was much younger, and facing a threat as usual, I was very concerned about the future. My own children were very young then."[82] For years Hussein had suffered from a variety of medical problems. He was known to suffer from his back, and from a recurrent heart condition, and eventually in 1992 he was diagnosed with cancer – the disease that led to his death in 1999. With that diagnosis he began to voice his concern over the future of Jordan. On his return to the kingdom on November 5, 1992, he spoke[83] of Jordan continuing after him – in essence the beginning of the road separating this father figure from his country. Thus, even though over the years the danger to his kingdom gradually diminished, his failing health made it critical for Hussein to ensure the continuity of the dynasty: would Hassan, the nominated Crown Prince, succeed him when the time came, or someone else? Within the framework of these considerations, in October 1996 Hussein nominated his son Abdullah to command the special units of the army, after another son, Faysal, was nominated to command the helicopters of the Jordanian air force; in other words, these two princes were placed at the main vital junction enabling them to take care of any domestic threat, or if necessary to change the face of the regime.

Hussein's failing health became more and more noticeable and in February 1998, in a publicized letter to his brother the Crown Prince, he admitted that he had been sick for months. Even though cancer was not mentioned and there was an expressed hope for a full recovery, to go public in this way was a rather unusual episode. Later, in July, it was revealed that Hussein was suspected to be suffering from lymphoma, a cancer of the lymphatic system. Once again, Hussein made all details public in the form of an open letter to his brother. It became clear that Hussein would be absent from Jordan for five months, and even if he recovered he would need a prolonged period of convalescence.[84] This time some public discussion began in Jordan and elsewhere about what would happen when Hussein was gone. Perhaps the foundation of any serious discussion centered on the issue of how well Crown Prince Hassan would handle the country once he succeeded to the throne. The possibility that one of Hussein's sons would succeed was mentioned from time to time but there were no apparent signs that that would be the case. Hassan himself began carefully to prepare the groundwork for his own succession when the time came.[85]

Consequently, one of the last elements of Hussein's political legacy was the settling of a generation-old account: the nomination of his own son as the next King of Jordan instead of the brother who had served in the capacity of Crown Prince for 34 years. The exact circumstances leading to Hussein's decision to remove Hassan from his post and instead nominate his son Abdullah are not yet fully known. However, judging from sketchy press reports, whose authenticity is unknown, it might be assumed that the trigger for Hussein's decision was Hassan's behavior during the last absence of Hussein from the kingdom. It is rumored[86] that Hassan had already begun his preparations to take over the reins of power.

In late January 1999 a gravely ill King Hussein returned home to take care of the succession issue. On January 25 Hussein decided to change the order of succession and make his son Abdullah his heir once again, in line with the Jordanian constitution, conveying in the process a rather harsh message to Hassan for his conduct.[87] The next day he returned briefly to the US for further medical treatment, only to come back to die among his people a few days later. On February 6, on Hussein's doctors' advice, the cabinet decided that the king was incapacitated, and declared Abdullah the regent, and the following day, upon the death of his father, he was proclaimed King of Jordan. Hussein's long and at times risky term was brought to its end through natural causes.

Conclusion

Upon his return in November 1992 from a medical procedure during which Hussein underwent the removal of a cancerous kidney, he delivered[1] a major address to the nation outlining his legacy: Islam, Arabism, Jerusalem and, above all, Jordan as a nation. No mention, however remote, of the Arab–Israeli conflict, no usage of the term "Palestinian" nor "the West Bank" nor "the occupied territories." In short, a speech by a national leader intent on leaving behind a clear political legacy: the survival and preservation of his own nation-state.

There is no way of knowing when exactly the late King Hussein began to devise his way out of isolation and into a future guaranteeing the survival of his kingdom. Suffice it to say that at the time of his death he undoubtedly represented stability and an uncompromising quest for peace. After ruling Jordan for 46 years, during which he witnessed a succession of attempts on his life, and an unending national struggle for survival in an arena with two formidable players, Israel and the Palestinians, he passed away leaving behind a viable nation-state.

Perhaps the heart of his legacy is "Smaller Jordan," the East Bank that remained in the hands of the Hashemite dynasty after the armed confrontation of June 1967. In reality, this term indicates several interwoven processes combining to make Jordan a twenty-first-century country operating on the basis of a unique national identity typical of all developed countries. Jordan is one of the first Middle Eastern nations to demonstrate these characteristics and it is in large measure due to the way the late King Hussein navigated his way around those different challenges. Jordan is also today a legitimate member in the Middle Eastern family of nations and this too is the result of the far-sighted policies of King Hussein. These accomplishments were the accumulated successful response to a series of challenges on all possible tacks. First, the need to define relations with Israel and the Palestinians, thereby bringing about discussion of the ingredients of the Jordanian national interest as different from the Arab interest. Secondly, the urgent need to devise Jordanian nationalism in the face of Palestinian nationalism, and thus build up the basic legitimacy for the existence of a Hashemite Kingdom on part of the former Mandatory Palestine. Finally, there was the hesitant beginning, coupled with some setbacks, of a democratic Jordanian system. All of these against the background of continuous speculations of the imminent demise of the kingdom, which began to fade out in the 1970s in the wake of the so-called 1967 defeat, and eventually totally disappeared in the 1980s.

Since 1967 Hussein had struggled to keep the West Bank outside of Jordanian sovereignty and yet eliminate any danger resulting from its citizens, and that danger's likely magnification by the PLO. The best solution he could envision was that the West Bank, and probably the Gaza Strip, would enjoy security and economic prosperity under Israeli rule and indirect Jordanian influence, both political and economic. That combination worked relatively well until December 1987 and the outbreak of the Palestinian uprising. After December 1987 Hussein had to adapt himself to new realities: Israel could no longer restrain the Palestinian activity on the ground and was basically forced to embark on the Oslo track. In this way Israel abandoned its traditional pro-Jordanian policy, paving the way to new concerns for Hussein. However, this new development not only highlighted the robust nature of the kingdom but also led directly to the legitimization of peace agreements with Israel. Thus, even though the Oslo Accords were only interim agreements, the 1994 Israeli–Jordanian treaty summarizing many years of tacit understandings and agreements was a final and conclusive document.

Still, this is only the tip of the iceberg and the full implementation of the treaty and the winning over of the Jordanian people have been left to the next king of Jordan. The success in legitimizing many years of tacit cooperation still awaits another success: convincing the Jordanian people that they would benefit from it. At the time of Hussein's death that realization was still far away: Jordan still feared being flooded by Palestinians, did not see the economic benefits of full peace, and yet is reserved in cooperating with Israel lest it take over Jordan's economy. On the other hand, the old secret understandings, mainly in the field of military and strategic cooperation, were broadened and made Jordan to some extent a member of a semi-public coalition with Israel and Turkey, backed by the US.

With the future well-being of Jordan involving such issues, it is easy to see how far the kingdom came under King Hussein: from a larger threatened monarchy into a smaller nation-state concerned no longer with its existence, but rather with the quality of that existence.

Notes

Introduction

1 Cf. Ze'ev Schiff, *Security for Peace: Israel's Minimal Security Requirements in Negotiations with the Palestinians,* Policy Paper Series, no. 15 (Washington: Washington Institute for Near East Policy, 1989), 4.

2 Yehuda Lukacs, *Israel, Jordan, and the Peace Process,* Syracuse Studies on Peace and Conflict Resolution (Syracuse, NY: Syracuse University Press, 1999), 5.

3 Yezid Sayigh, "Jordan in the 1980s: legitimacy, entity and identity", in Rodney Wilson, *Politics and Economy in Jordan* (London and New York: Routledge, 1991), 170.

4 Ambassador Findley Burns, Jr. [US ambassador to Jordan, 1966–8], oral history interview, Georgetown University Library, November 3, 1988, 13.

1 The Hashemite–Palestinian Crisis of April 1963

1 In 1960 both countries resumed an exchange of communications on military matters after a ten-year break. Top-level Jordanian–Israeli political negotiations during King Hussein's reign, with his participation, started in 1963. Moshe Zak, *King Hussein Makes Peace* (Hebrew), (Ramat Gan: Begin–Sadat Center for Strategic Studies, 1996), 40, 57–8; Chaim Herzog, *Living History* (Hebrew), (Tel Aviv: Miskal–Yedioth Aharonot, 1997), 196–8.

2 Public Record Office, London/FO371/157766/1015G/July 14, 1961, From: Jerusalem, gives a fascinating account of a variety of Palestinian approaches to the idea of Palestinian entity. In a country such as Jordan, which operates under the close supervision of the ruler, views expressed to foreign diplomats are seldom only private opinions. It is most likely that without being given a green light by the king for the airing of possible alternatives to Jordanian control over the West Bank, no one would dare voice such ideas even in private.

3 United States National Archives [USNA] /RG59/POL25/JORDAN/Circular 1819/April 22, 1963, From: the Department of State.

4 Canada National Archives [CNA] /RG25/7608/11312-40/Pt. 2.2/March 25, 1963, From: Tel Aviv.

5 CNA/RG25/7608/11312-40/Pt. 2.2/March 14, 1963, From: Tel Aviv.

6 USNA/RG59/POL25/JORDAN/Circular 1887/May 3, 1963, From: the Department of State.

7   The summary of the April 1963 events is based on USNA/RG59/
    POL25/JORDAN/Circular 1819/April 22, 1963, From: the Department of
    State; USNA/RG59/POL25/JORDAN/16257/April 22, 1963, From:
    Jerusalem; USNA/RG59/POL25/JORDAN/21019/April 27, 1963, From:
    Amman; USNA/RG59/POL25/JORDAN/Circular 1887/May 3, 1963, From:
    The Department of State. Another source is Moshe Zak, "The change in Ben-
    Gurion's attitude *vis-à-vis* Jordan," in *Studies in the Resurrection of Israel*, 6
    (Hebrew) (1996), 104–7.
8   USNA/RG59/POL25/JORDAN/19310/April 25, 1963, From: Jerusalem.
9   *al-Difa'*, April 21, 22, 1963. On the king's reaction to the parliamentary
    events, see USNA/RG59/POL15/JORDAN/15538/April 21, 1963, From:
    Amman; USNA/RG59/POL25/JORDAN/Circular 1819/April 22, 1963,
    From: the Department of State. One of the Jordanian politicians to be
    arrested during the crisis was Sulayman al-Nabulsi, prime minister during the
    1956 crisis. See USNA/RG59/POL29-1/JORDAN/16421/April 22, 1963,
    From: Amman.
10 On this exchange of letters see: Zak, *King Hussein Makes Peace*, 60–1.
11 Ibid.
12 USNA/RG59/POL1/JORDAN-PAL/A-249/November 26, 1963, From:
    Amman.
13 USNA/RG59/POL26 JORDAN/14524/April 27, 1963, From: the
    Department of State; USNA/RG 59/POL 26 JORDAN/14582/April 28, 1963,
    From: the Department of State.
14 USNA/RG59/POL26/JORDAN/19352/April 25, 1963, From: London.
15 Rumors about such an attempt, however, continued to circulate among
    foreign observers. See USNA/RG59/POL26/JORDAN/14487/April 27, 1963,
    From: the Department of State.
16 CNA/RG25/7608/11312-40/Pt. 2.2/May 7, 1963, From: Tel Aviv.
17 USNA/RG59/POL15/JORDAN/15538/April 21, 1963, From: Amman.
18 USNA/RG59/POL29-1/JORDAN/16421/April 22, 1963, From: Amman;
    USNA/RG59/POL25/JORDAN/16257/April 22, 1963, From: Jerusalem;
    USNA/RG59/POL25/JORDAN/18433/April 24, 1963, From: Amman.
19 This viewpoint was not shared by the British during the first week of the crisis,
    but was adopted by them thereafter. See USNA/RG59/POL26/JORDAN/
    19352/April 25, 1963, From: London; USNA/RG59/POL25/JORDAN/
    19555/April 25, 1963, From: New York; USNA/RG59/POL26/JORDAN/
    20230/April 26, 1963, From: London.
20 USNA/RG59/POL15/JORDAN/A-573/May 1, 1963, From: Amman.
21 CNA/RG25/7608/11312-40/Pt. 2.2/May 7, 1963, From: Tel Aviv;
    USNA/RG59/POL25/JORDAN/19555/April 25, 1963, From: New York.
22 USNA/RG59/POL25/JORDAN/21019/April 27, 1963, From: Amman.
23 USNA/RG59/POL15/JORDAN/A-573/May 1, 1963, From: Amman.
24 During the early stages of the crisis a spokesman for the State Department
    denied Israeli press allegations that the US was encouraging the king to abdi-
    cate, USNA/RG59/POL15-1/JORDAN/Memorandum of Conversation/
    April 19, 1963, From: the Department of State. For other American expres-
    sions of support, see PRO/FO371/170529/ER103180/10/May 7, 1963, From:

Tel Aviv; PRO/FO371/170529/103180/10(A)/May 17, 1963, From: Amman; USNA/RG59/POL25/JORDAN/Circular 1887/May 3, 1963, From: the State Department; this idea was probably denied as well at the meeting of the US and British ambassadors with the prime minister of Jordan, *Filastin* , May 17, 1963.

25 Avner Yaniv, *Politics and Strategy in Israel* (Hebrew), (Haifa: Haifa University, 1994), 156; USNA/RG59/POL15-1/JORDAN/Memorandum of Conversation /April 19, 1963, From: the Department of State; USNA/RG 59/POL 26 JORDAN/14582/April 28, 1963, From: the Department of State; USNA/RG 59/POL 26 JORDAN/266/May 1, 1963, From: Tel Aviv.

26 PRO/FO371/170529/E1074/4/May 1, 1963, From: London.

27 USNA/RG 59/POL 26 JORDAN/575/May 1, 1963, From: Tel Aviv.

28 PRO/FO371/170529/1024/63/April 2, 1963, From: Tel Aviv; USNA/RG 59/POL 26 JORDAN/266/May 1, 1963, From: Tel Aviv.

29 PRO/FO371/170529/1024/63/April 2, 1963, From: Tel Aviv.

30 Cf. PRO/FO371/170529/103180/10(A)/May 17, 1963, From: Amman.

31 PRO/FO371/170529/1024/63/April 2, 1963, From: Tel Aviv.

32 Ibid.

33 The information for this analysis was obtained partly from PRO/FO371/170529/1024/63/April 2, 1963, From: Tel Aviv, and partly from the opinions of the US ambassador to Tel Aviv as conveyed to his British counterpart and reported to London, PRO/FO371/170529/ER103180/8/May 2, 1963, From: Tel Aviv.

34 PRO/FO371/170529/ER103180/4/April 22, 1963, From: Tel Aviv. A military confrontation with Syria with a defense posture on the Egyptian and Jordanian fronts would require about 72 hours. See PRO/FO371/175805/ER103200/2/April 9, 1964, From: Tel Aviv.

35 USNA/RG 59/POL 26 JORDAN/266/May 1, 1963, From: Tel Aviv.

36 PRO/FO371/170529/1024/63/April 2, 1963, From: Tel Aviv.

37 CNA/RG25/7608/11312-40/Pt. 2.2/May 7, 1963, From: Tel Aviv.

38 Message to Ottawa by the Canadian ambassador in Cairo, May 10, 1963, as transmitted to the FO, in PRO/FO371/170537. For Ben-Gurion's letter and the British position, see PRO/FO371/170537/ER1071/22/July 9, 1963.

39 Cf. PRO/FO371/170537/ER1071/22/July 9, 1963.

40 PRO/FO371/170536/ER1041/10/May 10, 1963, From: Tel Aviv. The legal experts at the British Foreign Office studied this argument carefully, but did not concur, holding that only an extremely radical act by a new regime east of Israel would justify declaring the 1949 armistice agreement null and void. This meant that their recommendation to their government would be, under almost all circumstances, to convey to Israel that it had no legal claim to the West Bank. PRO/FO371/170536/May 13, 1963, FO memorandum.

41 USNA/RG59/POL25/JORDAN/16479/April 22, 1963, From: Amman; PRO/FO371/170529/ER103180/4/April 22, 1963, From: Tel Aviv; USNA/RG 59/POL 26 JORDAN/266/May 1, 1963, From: Tel Aviv; PRO/FO371/170529/ER103180/8/May 2, 1963, From: Tel Aviv.

42 PRO/FO371/170529/ER103180/4/April 22, 1963, From: Tel Aviv; CNA/RG25/7608/11312-40/Pt. 2.2/May 7, 1963, From: Tel Aviv.

43   CNA/RG25/7608/11312-40/Pt. 2.2/March 14, 1963, From: Tel Aviv.

44   PRO/FO371/170536/ER1071/20/June   20,   1963;   PRO/FO371/170537/
      ER1071/22/July 17, 1963; PRO/FO371/170537/ER1071/28/July 31, 1963.

45   President Kennedy indicated in a conversation with the Canadian prime
      minister on May 11 that the response to Israeli security demands was linked
      with its nuclear development. See USNA/RG59/POL ISR-JORDAN/
      Memorandum of Conversation/May 11, 1963; cf. PRO/FO371/170537/
      ER1071/22/July 9, 1963.

46   PRO/FO371/170537/ER1071/28/July 31, 1963.

47   The scenarios that follow are based on USNA/RG59/POL JORDAN-US/
      Memorandum of Conversation/April 27, 1963; USNA/RG 59/POL 26
      JORDAN/14524/April 27, 1963, From: the Department of State; CNA/
      RG25/5486/12076-40/Pt. 6/June 3, 1963, From: Tel Aviv.

48   CNA/RG25/5486/12076-40/Pt. 6/June 3, 1963, From: Tel Aviv; cf. USNA/RG
      59/POL 26 JORDAN/21431/April 29, 1963, From: Cairo.

49   USNA/RG 59/DEF 4 ISRAEL-US/3257/May 5, 1963, From: Tel Aviv.

50   PRO/FO371/170529/ER103180/10/May 7, 1963, From: Tel Aviv.

51   Message to Ottawa by the Canadian ambassador in Cairo, May 10, 1963, as
      transmitted to the FO, and as it appears in PRO/FO371/170537; Message to
      Ottawa by the Canadian ambassador in Tel Aviv, May 17, 1963, as trans-
      mitted to the FO, and as it appears in PRO/FO 371/170537;
      PRO/FO371/170529/103180/10(A)/May   17,   1963,   From: Amman;
      USNA/RG59/POL25/JORDAN/Circular 1819/April 22, 1963, From: the
      Department of State.

52   USNA/RG59/POL1/JORDAN/April 26, 1963, "Secret" memorandum for
      the White House from the Department of State.

53   USNA/RG59/POL26/JORDAN/14487/April   27,   1963,   From: the
      Department of State.

54   USNA/RG59/POL JORDAN-UK/Memorandum of Conversation /May 3,
      1963.

55   USNA/RG59/POL1/JORDAN/April 26, 1963, "Secret" memorandum for
      the White House from the Department of State.

56   USNA/RG 59/POL 23-9 JORDAN/21036/April 27, 1963, From: JCS.

57   USNA/RG 59/POL 26 JORDAN/14524/April 27, 1963, From: the
      Department of State.

58   USNA/RG59/POL26/JORDAN/19352/April 25, 1963, From: London; PRO/
      FO371/170577/ER1225/1/May 6, 1963, Foreign Office "secret" minute.

59   PRO/FO371/170529/ER103180/10/May 7, 1963, From: Tel Aviv.

60   CNA/RG25/5486/12076-40/Pt. 6/May 22, 1963, From: New York.

61   This   message   is   clear   despite   its   diplomatic   wording.   See:
      USNA/RG59/POL25/JORDAN/Circular1887/May 3, 1963, From: the State
      Department. Note, for example, the carefully chosen wording by the US act-
      ing Secretary of State in a conversation with the Israeli ambassador: "If
      possible, we will try to keep the Hussein government in control."
      USNA/RG59/POL JORDAN/POL JORDAN-ISRAEL/Memorandum of
      Conversation/April 27, 1963.

62   USNA/RG 59/POL 26 JORDAN/266/May 1, 1963, From: Tel Aviv;

USNA/RG59/POL 1/May 9, 1963, "Secret": The role of the United Nations.

63 PRO/FO371/170536/ER103180/11/May 7, 1963, From: Tel Aviv (1024/63); PRO/FO371/170536/ER1071/11/June 13, 1963.

64 Moshe Zak, *Israel and the Soviet Union* (Hebrew), (Tel Aviv: Ma'ariv, 1988), 255–6.

65 USNA/RG59/POL26/JORDAN/14487/April 27, 1963, From: the Department of State.

66 PRO/FO371/170529/ER103180/8/May 2, 1963, From: Tel Aviv; PRO/FO371/170529/ER103180/10/May 7, 1963, From: Tel Aviv; Message to Ottawa by the Canadian ambassador in Cairo, May 10, 1963, as transmitted to the FO, and as it appears in PRO/FO371/170537; PRO/FO371/170537/ER1071/4/May 30, 1963, FO memo. These thoughts were voiced by President John F. Kennedy in private talks. See PRO/FO371/170536/ER1071/20/June 20, 1963.

67 USNA/RG59/POL15-1/JORDAN/Memorandum of Conversation/April 19, 1963, From: the Department of State; USNA/RG59/POL JORDAN/POL JORDAN-ISRAEL/Memorandum of Conversation/April 27, 1963; USNA/RG59/POL26/JORDAN/14487/April 27,1963, From: the Department of State; USNA/RG59/POL26/JORDAN/14524/April 27,1963, From: the Department of State; USNA/RG 59/POL 26 JORDAN/21431/April 29, 1963, From: Cairo; USNA/RG 59/POL 26 JORDAN/266/May 1, 1963, From: Tel Aviv; USNA/RG59/POL25/JORDAN/Circular 1887/May 3, 1963, From: the Department of State.

68 USNA/RG59/POL 1/May 9, 1963, "Secret": The role of the United Nations. Note the sentence: "The purpose of the [Security Council] meeting would be to dramatize the dangers of the situation and maximize pressures on Israel to refrain from launching an attack."

69 USNA/RG59/POL 33-1/JORDAN-ISRAEL/18532/June 21, 1963, From: London.

70 On the UNEF modus operandi, see Indar Jit Rikhye, *The Sinai Blunder: Withdrawal of the United Nations Emergency Force Leading to the Six Day War, June 1967* (New Delhi: Oxford & IBH Publishing Co., 1978), 1–13.

71 USNA/RG59/POL 1/May 9, 1963, "Secret": The role of the United Nations.

72 CNA/RG25/5486/12076-40/Pt. 6/May 13, 22, 1963, From: New York.

73 CNA/RG25/5486/12076-40/Pt. 6/May 22, 30, 1963, From: New York; USNA/RG59/POL 33-1/JORDAN-ISRAEL/18532/June 21, 1963, From: London.

74 USNA/RG59/POL26/JORDAN/19352/April 25,1963, From: London; CNA/RG25/5486/12076-40/Pt. 6/May 13, 1963, From: New York.

75 PRO/FO371/170529/E1074/4/May 1, 1963, From: London; cf. the views of the US ambassador in Tel Aviv on Israel's determination to seize the West Bank: PRO/FO371/170529/ER103180/8/May 2, 1963, From: Tel Aviv; PRO/FO371/170529/ER103180 /4G(A)/May 7, 1963, From: Tel Aviv.

76 Message to Ottawa by the Canadian ambassador in Cairo, May 10, 1963, as transmitted to the FO, and as it appears in PRO/FO371/170537; Message to Ottawa by the Canadian ambassador in Tel Aviv, May 17, 1963, as transmitted to the FO, and as it appears in PRO/FO371/170537.

77 CNA/RG25/5486/12076-40/Pt. 6/May 13, 1963, From: New York.

78 PRO/FO371/170529/ER103180/8/May 2, 1963, From: Tel Aviv; PRO/FO371/170529/ER103180/10/May 7, 1963, From: Tel Aviv; Message to Ottawa by the Canadian ambassador in Tel Aviv, May 17, 1963, as transmitted to the FO, and as it appears in PRO/FO371/170537; cf. PRO/FO371/170529/ER103180/10(A)/May 17, 1963, From: Amman; USNA/RG59/POL 33-1/JORDAN-ISRAEL/18532/June 21, 1963, From: London.

79 CNA/RG25/7608/11312-40/Pt. 2.2/May 7, 1963, From: Tel Aviv.

80 USNA/RG 59/POL 26 JORDAN/14582/April 28, 1963, From: the Department of State; USNA/RG 59/POL 26 JORDAN/266/May 1, 1963, From: Tel Aviv; USNA/RG 59/POL 26 JORDAN/266/May 1, 1963, From: Tel Aviv.

81 Israel State Archives/A 7230/4, May 13, June 14, 25, 1963. From: Washington, to Jerusalem.

82 ISA/A 7230/4, June 25, 1963, From: Washington, to: Jerusalem.

83 CNA/RG25/7608/11312-40/Pt. 2.2/May 7, 1963, From: Tel Aviv.

84 CNA/RG25/5486/12076-40/Pt. 6/May 30, 1963, From: New York; cf. PRO/FO371/170537/ER1071/4/May 30, 1963, FO memo.

85 USNA/RG59/POL26/JORDAN/19352/April 25, 1963, From: London; USNA/RG59/POL1/JORDAN/April 26, 1963, "Secret" memorandum for the White House from the Department of State. These ideas were echoed at the meeting between the US ambassador in Tel Aviv and the director-general of the Israeli Foreign Ministry. See USNA/RG 59/POL 26 JORDAN/575/May 1, 1963, From: Tel Aviv; CNA/RG25/5486/12076-40/Pt. 6/May 22, 1963, From: New York.

86 USNA/RG 59/POL JORDAN/2364/May 3, 1963, From: London; CNA/RG25/5486/12076-40/Pt. 6/May 22, 1963, From: New York; PRO/FO371/170537/ER1071/22/July 17, 1963.

87 "Tripartite Declaration Regarding Security in the Near East: Three-Power Statement released May 25, 1950, and Statement by President Truman released May 25, 1950," in John Norton Moore, *The Arab–Israeli Conflict: Readings and Documents* (Princeton: Princeton University Press, 1977), 987–9.

88 Cf. Richard B. Parker, *The Politics of Miscalculation in the Middle East* (Bloomington: Indiana University Press, 1993), 52–3.

89 USNA/RG 59/POL 26 JORDAN/14691/April 29, 1963, From: the Department of State; PRO/FO371/170537/ER1071/36/August 28, 1963; cf. PRO/FO371/180871/ER1071/92/March 10, 1965, FO memorandum.

90 PRO/FO371/170529/ER103180/10/May 7, 1963, From: Tel Aviv. These views were shared by the Canadian government as well; cf. message to Ottawa by the Canadian ambassador in Cairo, May 10, 1963, as transmitted to the FO, and as it appears in PRO/FO371/170537; cf. CNA/RG25/5486/12076-40/Pt. 6/June 3, 1963, From: Tel Aviv.

91 USNA/RG59/POL26/JORDAN/19352/April 25, 1963, From: London.

92 Ibid.

93 USNA/RG 59/POL 26 JORDAN/21415/April 29, 1963, From: Cairo.

94 USNA/RG59/POL26/JORDAN/20230/April 26, 1963, From: London.

95 Rifa'i's analysis was accepted to a large extent by the State Department. See USNA/RG 59/POL 26 JORDAN/21415/April 29, 1963, From: Cairo.

96 See PRO/FO371/vols. 151207-8; CNA/RG24, RG25; and ISA/FM2314, 2339 and 2340 and passim.

2 The Israeli–Jordanian Military Confrontation of November 1966: A Prelude to the 1967 War

1 Cf. PRO/FO371/186818/ER103180/1/May 4, 1966, From: the Foreign Office.
2 USNA/RG59/POL JORDAN-PAL/July 7, 1966, Memorandum of Conversation with the First Secretary, Israeli Embassy; and see: USNA/RG59/POL18 JORDAN/October 14, 1966, from: Jerusalem.
3 PRO/FO371/186830/ER1071/4/March 23, 1966, From: Tel Aviv.
4 USNA/RG 59/AID (US) 8-7 JORDAN/4263/December 6, 1966, From: Amman.
5 PRO/FCO17/208/ER1071/53/Jordan: annual review for 1966.
6 USNA/RG59/POL 32-1 ISR-JORDAN/11201/November 12, 1966, From: Amman; ISA/A 7230/4/December 16, 1966/From: Washington, to: Jerusalem.
7 Colonel Avraham Ayalon, "Grinding mill operation," *Ma'arkhot* [official organ of the Israeli army] (Hebrew), issue 261–2, 27.
8 Interview with General Indar Jit Rikhye, former commander of the United Nations Emergency Force prior to the 1967 war. Charlottesville, Virginia, October 25, 1997.
9 Moshe Zak, *Israel and the Soviet Union: A forty years dialogue* (Hebrew) (Tel Aviv: Ma'ariv, 1988), 141; Yosef Guvrin, *Israeli–Soviet Relations* (Hebrew), (Jerusalem: Magnes, 1989/90), 248.
10 USNA/RG59/POL32-1 ISR-JORDAN/12343/November 14, 1966, From: Amman; USNA/RG59/POL 32-1 ISR-JORDAN/21193/November 23, 1966, From: Amman.
11 USNA/RG59/POL32-1 ISR-JORDAN/12343/November 14, 1966, From: Amman; USNA/RG 59/POL 32-1 ISR-JORDAN/13051/November 15, 1966, From: Amman.
12 USNA/RG59/POL32-1 ISR-JORDAN/12343/November 14, 1966, From: Amman; USNA/RG59/POL32-1 ISR-JORDAN/22273/November 23, 1966, From: Amman.
13 USNA/RG59/POL32-1 ISR-JORDAN/12343/November 14, 1966, From: Amman.
14 USNA/RG 59/POL 32-1 ISR-JORDAN/13051/November 15, 1966, From: Amman; Yizhaq Rabin, *Yoman Sherut* [Service memoirs] (Hebrew), (Tel Aviv: Ma'ariv library, 1979), vol. 1, 126; Zak, *King Hussein Makes Peace*, 70–1.
15 State Department cable 90603, Immediate Secret, November 23, 1966 as quoted by, Zak, *King Hussein Makes Peace*, 102, footnote 94; and USNA/RG59/Entry5190/Box 1/Chronology of US–Jordan consultations on the Middle East, May 18–June 10, 1967/Based on Amman telegram 3612 (control 019078), May 18, 1967.
16 USNA/RG59/POL23-9 JORDAN/9500/December 10, 1966, From: Amman.
17 Ibid.
18 Official text of his proposal: *al-Majmu'ah al-Kamilah li-Khutab Jalalat al-Malik al-Husayn bin Talal al-mu'azzam* (Arabic) [the full collection of HM

King Hussein bin Talal's speeches], [Amman: 1985?], vol. 3. 357–65.

19 USNA/RG59/POL23-9 JORDAN/December 6, 1966, From: Amman (1406).

20 USNA/RG59/POL23-9 JORDAN/18053/November 19, 1966, From: Amman; USNA/RG 59/POL 23-9 JORDAN/December 6, 1966, From: Amman (1406).

21 USNA/RG 59/POL 32-1 ISR-JORDAN/21193/November 23, 1966, From: Amman.

22 PRO/FO371/186830/ER1071/53/December 1, 1966, From: Washington; USNA/RG 59/POL 23-9 JORDAN/9500/December 10, 1966, From: Amman; USNA/RG59/POL JORDAN-US/9559/December 11, 1966/From: Amman; PRO/FCO17/226/EJ2/5/April 26, 1967, From: Amman; cf. USNA/RG59/POL23-9 JORDAN/18053/November 19, 1966, From: Amman.

23 ISA/A 7230/4/December 20, 22, 1966/From: Washington, to Jerusalem.

24 Colonel Ayalon, "Grinding mill operation," *Ma'arkhot*, issue 261–2, 36–7.

25 Jordanian press; USNA/RG59/POL23-8 JORDAN/91452/November 25, 1966/From: Department of State.

26 Cf. USNA/RG59/DEF4 ARAB/14710/December 16, 1966, From: Cairo.

27 USNA/RG59/POL23-8 JORDAN/91452/November 25, 1966/From: the Department of State; USNA/RG59/POL23-9 JORDAN/December 6, 1966, From: Amman (1406); USNA/RG59/POL23-9 JORDAN/9500/December 10, 1966, From: Amman.

28 USNA/RG59/POL23-9 JORDAN /December 6, 1966, From: Amman (1406).

29 USNA/RG59/POL32-1 ISR-JORDAN/21544/November 23, 1966, From: Cairo.

30 USNA/RG59/POL23-8 JORDAN/91452/November 25, 1966/From: the Department of State.

31 USNA/RG59/POL JORDAN-PAL/July 7, 1966, Memorandum of Conversation with the First Secretary, Israeli Embassy.

32 Ibid.

33 PRO/FO371/186431/ER1075/20(A)/March 2, 1966, From: Cairo.

34 PRO/FO371/186547/E1198/2/Annual report for Jordan for 1965.

35 *al-Majmu'ah*, vol. 2, 399–406; Jordanian press, January 6, 1966, and PRO/FO371/186431/ER1075/5/January 5, 1966, From: Amman.

36 USNA/RG59/POL 23-9 JORDAN/9500/December 10, 1966, From: Amman.

37 USNA/RG59/POL18 JORDAN/October 14, 1966, From: Jerusalem; USNA/RG59/POL ISR-JORDAN/November 10, 1966, from: Jerusalem; USNA/RG59/POL 32-1 ISR -JORDAN/December 6, 1966, From: Amman (1406).

38 USNA/RG59/POL ISR-JORDAN/November 10, 1966, From: Jerusalem.

39 USNA/RG59/POL18 JORDAN/October 14, 1966, From: Jerusalem

40 Cf. Jordanian press coverage of King Hussein's June 14, 1966 speech deploring the activities of Ahmad al-Shuqayri, head of the PLO and the official text: *al-Majmu'ah*, vol. 2, 435–48.

41 USNA/RG59/POL32-1 ISR-JORDAN/5909/December 7, 1966/From: Cairo.

42 PRO/FO371/186547/E1198/2/Annual report for Jordan for 1965; CNA/RG25/8864-222/20-ISR-1-3/Vol. 4/Internal External Affairs memo-

randum on the foreign policy of Israel/F3633/33/[First quarter of 1966?];
USNA/RG59/POL ISR- JORDAN/November 10, 1966, From: Jerusalem.

43   USNA/RG 59/POL 32-1 ISR-JORDAN/22466/November 24, 1966, From:
     Amman; USNA/RG 59 /POL 23-9 JORDAN /December 6, 1966, From:
     Amman (1406).

44   USNA/RG 59/POL 23-9 JORDAN/December 6, 1966, From: Amman (1406).

45   USNA/RG 59/POL 32-1 ISR-JORDAN/22466/November 24, 1966, From:
     Amman; USNA/RG 59/POL 23-9 JORDAN /December 6, 1966, From:
     Amman (1406).

46   See Daniel Dishon (ed.), *Middle East Record* (Jerusalem: Israel Universities
     Press, 1971), vol. 3, 401.

47   USNA/RG59/POL 23-9 JORDAN/7550/December 8, 1966, From: Jerusalem.

48   PRO/FO371/186431/ER1075/20(A)/March 2, 1966, From: Cairo

49   USNA/RG59/POL23-9   JORDAN/18053/November   19,   1966,   From:
     Amman.

50   USNA/RG59/POL32-1 ISR-JORDAN/13051/November 15, 1966, From:
     Amman.

51   USNA/RG59/POL JORDAN-ISR/9566/December 11, 1966/From: Amman.

52   The US valued this channel highly as a means of influencing the two parties;
     cf. 1399, USNA/RG59/POL 32-1 ISR-JORDAN/4875/December 6, 1966/
     From: Amman ("in Jordan we have an ace in the hole . . . ").

53   USNA/RG59/POL32-1 ISR-JORDAN/11368/November 13, 1966/From: Tel
     Aviv; USNA/RG59/POL ISR-JORDAN/83785/November 13, 1966/From:
     the Department of State.

54   USNA/RG59/POL ISR-JORDAN/83785/November 13, 1966/From: the
     Department of State.

55   USNA/RG59/POL ISR-JORDAN/November 18, 1965/From: Tel Aviv.

56   USNA/RG 59/POL 32-1 ISR-JORDAN/66870/October 15, 1966, From: the
     Department of State.

57   PRO/FO371/186818/ER103180/1/May 4, 1966, From: the Foreign office.

58   USNA/RG59/POL ISR-JORDAN/March 4, 1966/From: Tel Aviv.

59   USNA/RG59/POL ISR-JORDAN/November 18, 1965/From: Tel Aviv.

60   USNA/RG59/POL ISR-JORDAN/4042/December 5, 1966/From: Tel Aviv;
     cf. CNA/RG25/8864-222/20-ISR-1-3/Vol. 4/January 30, 1967/From: Tel
     Aviv

61   USNA/RG 59/POL 32-1 ISR-JORDAN/12343/November 14, 1966, From:
     Amman.

62   USNA/RG59/POL ISR-JORDAN/93317/November 29, 1966/From: the
     Department of State.

63   USNA/RG 59/POL 32-1 ISR-JORDAN/22273/November 23, 1966, From:
     Amman; Brig. S. A. El-Edross, *The Hashemite Arab Army, 1908–1979*
     Amman: The Publishing Committee, 1980), 391.

64   USNA/RG 59/POL 23-9 JORDAN/18053/November 19, 1966, From:
     Amman;   PRO/FO371/186830/ER1071/53/December   1,   1966,   From:
     Washington.

65   USNA/RG59/POL 32-1 ISR-JORDAN/4875/December 6, 1966/From:
     Amman.

66 USNA/RG 59/POL 32-1 ISR-JORDAN/13051/November 15, 1966, From: Amman.

67 USNA/RG 59/POL 32-1 ISR-JORDAN/6233/December 7, 1966, From: Tel Aviv.

68 PRO/FO371/180871/ER1071/92/March 10, 1965, and draft of March 17, 1965.

69 USNA/RG 59/POL JORDAN-PAL/July 7, 1966, Memorandum of Conversation with the First Secretary, Israeli Embassy.

70 USNA/RG59/POL ISR-JORDAN/83785/November 13, 1966/From: the Department of State.

71 CNA/RG25/7608/11312-40/Pt. 2.2/May 7, 1963, From: Tel Aviv.

72 USNA/RG59/POL ISR-JORDAN/Circular, Department of State/August 1, 1964.

73 USNA/RG59/POL 23-7 ISR/March 17, 1967, from: Jerusalem.

74 PRO/FO371/186830/ER1071/22/June 1, 1966, From: Tel Aviv.

75 USNA/RG59/POL ISR-JORDAN/83785/November 13, 1966/From: the Department of State.

76 USNA/RG59/POL 32-1 ISR-JORDAN /October 19, 1966/From: Amman.

77 Cf. TASS report of May 28, 1966: "not only are Americans and Israelis more active [against Syria], but reactionary quarters in Jordan and Saudi Arabia are also hatching plans," as quoted by CNA/RG25/8864-222/20-ISR-1-3/Vol. 4/January 30, 1967/From: Moscow.

78 USNA/RG59/POL 32-1 ISR -JORDAN /October 19, 1966/From: Amman.

79 Cf. US Cairo ambassador's analysis of Jordanian–Egyptian relations before and after the raid: USNA/RG59/POL 32-1 ISR-JORDAN/5909/December 7, 1966/From: Cairo; PRO/FCO17/226/EJ2/5/April 26, 1967, From: Amman.

80 PRO/FO371/186431/ER1075/1/December 31, 1965/From: Amman.

81 USNA/RG59/POL ISR-JORDAN/87250/November 18, 1966/From: Department of State; USNA/RG59/POL 23-8 JORDAN/17596/November 25, 1966/Department of State, information memorandum; USNA/RG59/POL 32-1 ISR-JORDAN/5909/December 7, 1966/From: Cairo.

82 PRO/FO371/186437/ER1073/1/January 18, 1966/From: Jerusalem.

83 USNA/RG59/POL 32-1 ISR -JORDAN /October 19, 1966/From: Amman.

84 Cf. USNA/RG59/POL 32-1 ISR-JORDAN/5909/December 7, 1966/From: Cairo.

85 USNA/RG59/POL 32-1 ISR-JORDAN/3194/December 3, 1966, From: Amman.

86 USNA/RG59/POL32-1 ISR-JORDAN/13320/December 15, 1966, From: Cairo.

87 USNA/RG59/POL32-1 ISR-JORDAN/5909/December 7, 1966/From: Cairo.

88 USNA/RG59/POL32-1 ISR-JORDAN/13320/December 15, 1966, From: Cairo.

89 *Al-Ahram*, December 2, 1966.

90 USNA/RG59/POL32-1 ISR-JORDAN/13320/December 15, 1966, From: Cairo.

91 PRO/FO371/186830/ER1071/38/December 29, 1966, From: Tel Aviv, quotes Israeli press reports.

92 See USNA/RG 59/POL 32-1 ISR-JORDAN/13051/November 15, 1966, From: Amman.
93 ISA/A 7230/4/December 14, 16, 20, 22, 1966/From: Washington, to Jerusalem.
94 USNA/RG59/POL 23-8 JORDAN/17596/November 25, 1966/Department of State, information Memorandum; PRO/FO371/186830/ER1071/53/December 1, 1966, From: Washington; USNA/RG 59/POL 32-1 ISR-JORDAN/December 16, 1966, memorandum of Conversation with the Counselor, Canadian Embassy; PRO/FCO17/226/EJ2/5/April 26, 1967, From: Amman.
95 Cf. USNA/RG59/POL 32-1 ISR-JORDAN/4875/December 6, 1966/From: Amman.
96 Cf. P. J. Vatikiotis, *Politics and the Military in Jordan* (New York: Praeger, 1966), 139.
97 USNA/RG59/POL JORDAN-ISR/9566/December 11, 1966/From: Amman.
98 USNA/RG 59/POL 23-9 JORDAN/18053/November 19, 1966, From: Amman.
99 USNA/RG 59/POL 32-1 ISR-JORDAN/21193/November 23, 1966, From: Amman.
100 USNA/RG 59/POL 32-1 ISR-JORDAN/13051/November 15, 1966, From: Amman.
101 See USNA/RG 59/POL 23-9 JORDAN/9500/December 10, 1966, From: Amman.
102 USNA/RG59/POL JORDAN-US/9559/December 11, 1966/From: Amman.
103 ISA/A 7230/4/December 12, 1966/From: Washington, to Jerusalem.
104 See USNA/RG59/DEF 4 ARAB/14710/December 16, 1966, From: Cairo.
105 ISA/A 7230/4/December 16, 1966/118/from: Washington, to Jerusalem; The Israeli Minister of Labor, a former general, warned Jordan on December 16 at a public political meeting against the deployment of any Arab forces, PRO/FO371/186818/ER 103180/5/December 19, 1966, From: Tel Aviv; Israel repeated these public warnings in the following days, PRO/FO371/186818/ER 103180/5/December 29, 1966, From: Tel Aviv.
106 USNA/RG59/DEF 12-5 JORDAN/19208/December 22, 1966/From: Amman.
107 USNA/RG59/POL 32-1 ISR-JORDAN/10376/December 12, 1966/From: Amman.
108 USNA/RG 59/POL 32-1 ISR-JORDAN/13051/November 15, 1966, From: Amman.
109 USNA/RG59/POL 32-1 ISR-JORDAN/10376/December 12, 1966/From: Amman.
110 Ibid.

3 Jordan in the 1967 War: A Political Victory which Guaranteed the Survival of the Kingdom

1 "A message to Nasser," *al-Watha'iq al-'Urduniyyah 1967*, 99; Interview with *al-Nahar*, August 24, 1971.
2 *al-Majmu'ah*, vol. 3, 359.

Notes to pp. 49–53

3   USNA/RG 59/General foreign policy files, 1967–9, Political and defense, Box 2080, Airgram A-1513, November 4, 1967 from: London; Summary of the king's interview on November 1, 1967, with David Frost; Message to Arab leaders of November 1970, Amman Home Service, March 31, 1971, 9:00 p.m. as quoted by the Israeli BBC, April 2, 1971; "A message to Jordanian officers," *L'Orient Le Jour*, May 31, 1973; October 30, 1992, Interview, *FBIS*, November 5, 1992.
4   ISA/FM 4092/13, Minutes of the committee's session of December 12, 1966.
5   ISA/FM 4092/14, recommendations of the committee as presented on January 9, 1967, to the foreign minister of Israel.
6   The following discussion is based on ISA/FM 4092/13, minutes of the committee's session of December 19, 1966.
7   A similar Israeli action in April 1973 in Beirut ended with the assassination of the three leaders of the PLO. The 1973 action, unlike the one in 1997 in Amman, was intended as a warning to the government of Lebanon while eliminating some of the leaders, and to curtail the PLO's ability to carry out its activities; the action was much larger and Israel did not take any particular measures to hide its involvement.
8   Avner Yaniv, *Politics and Strategy in Israel* (Hebrew), (Haifa: Haifa University Press, 1994), 156.
9   PRO/FO371/170529/1024/63/2 April 1963, From: Tel Aviv.
10 See PRO/FO371/170529/103180/10(A)/17 May 1963, From: Amman.
11 PRO/FO371/170529/1024/63/2 April 1963, From: Tel Aviv.
12 Richard B. Parker (ed.), *The Six Day War: A retrospective* (Gainesville: University Press of Florida, 1996), 159.
13 Zak, *King Hussein Makes Peace*, 119.
14 USNA/RG59/Entry 5190/Box 1/Chronology of US–Jordan consultations on the Middle East, May 18–June 10, 1967/Based on Amman telegram 3612 (control 019078), May 18, 1967; see also, "A message to Jordanian officers," *L'Orient Le Jour*, May 31, 1973.
15 Amman Radio, April 3, 1971, Itim/Mizrah news service.
16 Amman Home Service in Arabic, September 15, 1971, Itim/Mizrah news service and BBC Monitoring Service, September 17, 1971.
17 Cf. USNA/RG59/POL32-1 ISR-JORDAN/10376/December 12, 1966, From: Amman.
18 USNA/RG59/POL ISR-JORDAN/93317/November 29, 1966, From: the Department of State; PRO/FO371/186830/ER1071/53/December 1, 1966, From: Washington; USNA/RG59/POL 32-1 ISR-JORDAN/4875/December 6, 1966, From: Amman; USNA/RG59/POL32-1 ISR-JORDAN/10119/December 12, 1966, From: Amman.
19 PRO/FCO17/226/EJ2/5/May 12, 1967, FO internal correspondence (overtaken); PRO/FCO17/225/EJ2/4/January 20, February 27, 1967, From: Washington and the Foreign Office, respectively.
20 USNA/RG59/POL 32-1 ISR-JORDAN/10376/December 12, 1966, From: Amman.
21 USNA/RG59/POL JORDAN-PAL/July 7, 1966, Memorandum of Conversation with the First Secretary, Israeli Embassy.

22 USNA/RG59/POL 23-9 JORDAN/18053/November 19, 1966, From: Amman.
23 USNA/RG59/POL JORDAN-PAL/July 7, 1966, Memorandum of Conversation with the First Secretary, Israeli Embassy.
24 PRO/FO371/175810/ER1071/11/April 1, 1964, From: Amman; PRO/FO371/175810/ER1071/8/May 17, 1964, FO memorandum.
25 PRO/FO371/175810/ER1071/30/October 8, 1964.
26 CNA/RG25/7608/11312-40/Pt 2.2/May 7, 1963, From: Tel Aviv.
27 PRO/FO371/175810/ER1071/14/April 10, 1964; From: Jerusalem; USNA/RG 59/POL 32-1 ISR-JORDAN/13320/December 15, 1966, From: Cairo.
28 A succinct summary of the British position can be found in a memorandum prepared on the eve of the Israeli prime minister's visit to London: PRO/FO371/180871/ER1071/92/March 10, 1965, FO memorandum.
29 USNA/RG59/POL ISR-JORDAN/83785/November 13, 1966, From: the Department of State.
30 PRO/FO371/186830/ER1071/53/December 1, 1966, From: Washington.
31 USNA/RG59/POL ISR-JORDAN/90603/November 23, 1966, From: the Department of State; USNA/RG59/POL 23-8 JORDAN/17596/November 25, 1966/Department of State, information memorandum.
32 PRO/FCO17/208/ER1071/53/Jordan: annual review for 1966; PRO/FCO17/205/EJ1/1/Telno. 6/January 2, 1967, From: Amman.
33 PRO/FCO17/209/EJ1/6/February 8, 15, 1967, From: Amman.
34 PRO/FCO17/206/1014/March 21, 1967, From: Amman.
35 PRO/FCO17/209/EJ1/6/March 1, 1967, From: Amman; PRO/FCO17/206/1603/67/June 22, 1967, From: Jerusalem, to the Foreign Office.
36 PRO/FCO17/205/EJ1/1/1012/67/March 15, 1967, From: Amman, to the Foreign Office.
37 Parker (ed.), *The Six Day War*, 159.
38 Cf. PRO/FCO17/226/EJ2/5/May 12, 1967, FO internal correspondence (over-taken).
39 Parker (ed.), *The Six Day War*, 157.
40 Parker (ed.), *The Six Day War*, 159.
41 USNA/RG59/Entry 5190/Box 1/Chronology of US–Jordan consultations on the Middle East, May 18–June 10, 1967/Based on Amman telegram 2699 (control 23768), May 23, 1967; Daniel Dishon (ed.), *Middle East Record 1967* (Jerusalem: Israel Universities Press, 1971), 127; *al-Watha'iq al-'Urduniyyah 1967*, 14.
42 USNA/RG59/Entry 5190/Box 1/Chronology of US–Jordan consultations on the Middle East, May 18–June 10, 1967/Based on Amman telegram 3612 (control 019078), May 18, 1967.
43 Ibid.
44 *Al-Watha'iq al-'Urduniyyah 1967*, 10; *Radio Jordan*, May 21, 1967.
45 USNA/RG59/Entry 5190/Box 1/Chronology of US–Jordan consultations on the Middle East, May 18–June 10, 1967/Based on Amman telegram 3711 (control 023914), May 23, 1967; *al-Watha'iq al-'Urduniyyah 1967*, 14; Brig. S.

A. El-Edross, *The Hashemite Arab Army, 1908–1979* (Amman: The Publishing Committee, 1980), 390.

46　USNA/RG59/Entry 5190/Box 1/Chronology of US–Jordan consultations on the Middle East, May 18–June 10, 1967/Based on State telegram 198902, May 20, 1967.

47　PRO/FCO17/206/EJ1/2/1039/67/May 22, 1967, From: Jerusalem, to the Foreign Office.

48　USNA/RG59/Entry 5190/Box 1/Chronology of US–Jordan consultations on the Middle East, May 18–June 10, 1967/Based on Amman telegram 3690 (control 023277), May 23, 1967; Brig. S. A. El-Edross, *The Hashemite Arab Army, 1908–1979*, 391.

49　USNA/RG59/Office of the Executive Secretariat Middle East Crisis files, 1967/Entry 5190/Box 4/control 26248/May 25, 1967, From: Amman; Box 9/control 29303/May 27, 1967, From: Amman; Box 7/control 32201, 32466/May 31, 1967, From: Amman; USNA/RG59/Office of the Executive Secretariat Middle East Crisis files, 1967/Entry 5190/Box 1/June 15, 1967/Chronology of US–Jordanian consultations on the Middle East, May 18–June 10, 1967, citing Amman telegrams, control 028118, of May 26, 1967, control 029305, of May 27, 1967.

50　PRO/FCO17/290/ER5/15/May 16, 1967, From: Tehran; ISA/FM6444/5/371, May 29, 1967, From Jerusalem to Israeli delegations, based on the British ambassador to Israel's conversation with an Israeli foreign ministry official reporting the king's conversation with the British ambassador; USNA/RG59/Office of the Executive Secretariat Middle East Crisis files, 1967/Entry 5190/Box 1/June 15, 1967/Chronology of US–Jordanian consultations on the Middle East, May 18–June 10, 1967, citing Amman telegram, control 027020, of May 25, 1967; cf. Brig. S. A. El-Edross, *The Hashemite Arab Army, 1908–1979*, 394.

51　Ambassador Findley Burns, Jr [US ambassador to Jordan, 1966–8], oral history interview, Georgetown University Library, November 3, 1988, 8, 9, 11.

52　USNA/RG59/Entry 5190/Box 9/control 30529/May 29, 1967, From: Amman.

53　*Al-Watha'iq al-'Urduniyyah 1967*, 18.

54　For the full text of the joint defense treaty, see *al-Watha'iq al-'Urduniyyah 1967*, 19–21.

55　USNA/RG59/Entry 5190/Box7/control 32201, 32466/May 31, 1967, From: Amman; Findley Burns, Jr, oral history interview, 8.

56　PRO/FCO17/206/1603/67/June 22, 1967, From Jerusalem, to the Foreign Office.

57　Interview with *Le Monde*, November 21, 1967, as quoted by USNA/RG59/General foreign policy files, 1967–9, Political and defense, Box 2080, November 20, 1967, From: Paris, telegram 316.

58　USNA/RG59/Entry 5190/Box 7/control 32201/May 31, 1967, From: Amman.

59　USNA/RG59/Entry 5190/Box 7/control 32497/May 31, 1967, From: Amman.

60　USNA/RG59/Entry 5190/Box 7/control 32466/May 31, 1967, From: Amman.

61　*Al-Watha'iq al-'Urduniyyah 1967*, 11.

62　USNA/RG59/Entry 5190/Box 7/control 32472/May 31, 1967, From: Amman; USNA/RG59/Office of the Executive Secretariat Middle East Crisis files,

1967/Entry 5190/Box 1/June 15, 1967/Chronology of US–Jordanian consultations on the Middle East, May 18–June 10, 1967, citing Amman telegrams, control 028832, of May 27, 1967, control 204891, of May 30, 1967, control 3885, of June 2.

63   ISA/FM6444/5, from the Foreign Ministry to Israeli embassies, no. 477, June 1, 1967; *al-Watha'iq al-'Urduniyyah 1967*, 40.

64   Cf. USNA/RG59/Office of the Executive Secretariat Middle East Crisis files, 1967/Entry 5190/Box 4/control 2773/June 2, 1967, From: Amman.

65   ISA/FM6444/6, from the Foreign Ministry to Israeli embassies, no. 553, June 3, 1967; PRO/FCO17/27/5/June 23, 1967, From: Amman; Dispatch no. 2 on the Jordanian army, 1967.

66   Parker (ed.), *The Six Day War*, 160.

67   Samir A. Mutawi, *Jordan in the 1967 War* (Cambridge and New York: Cambridge University Press, 1987), 132.

68   Findley Burns, Jr, oral history interview, 11.

69   Brig. S. A. El-Edross, *The Hashemite Arab Army, 1908–1979*, 379, 396.

70   *Al-Majmu'ah*, vol. 2, 595; interview with *al-Nahar*, August 24, 1971.

71   PRO/FCO17/27/5/June 23, 1967, From: Amman; Dispatch no. 2 on the Jordanian army, 1967.

72   Ibid.

73   Colonel Efraim Kam, "Operating the Eastern Front during the Six Day War," *Ma'arkhot*, issue 325 (1992), 17.

74   ISA/FM6444/6, from the Foreign Ministry to Israeli embassies, nos. 643, 687, June 5, 1967; Parker (ed.), *The Six Day War*, 157; Zak, *King Hussein Makes Peace*, 112; Moshe A. Gilbo'a, *Six Years – Six Days: Origins and History of the Six Day War* (Hebrew) (Tel Aviv: Am Oved, 1968), 223; PRO/FCO17/54/E2/52/February 3, 1968, quoting Jordan's foreign minister's speech at the European assembly.

75   USNA/RG59/Executive Secretariat/Box 4/United States policy and diplomacy in the Middle East crisis, May 15–June 10, 1967/Based on Amman telegram 5623, June 5, 1967.

76   Colonel Avraham Ayalon and David Eiger, "The battle for Jerusalem," *Ma'arkhot*, issue 223 (1972), 5.

77   It should be noted that even Syria could have got away with artillery barrages during these early stages of the war. Only the continued shelling after the June 8 cease-fire and the domestic pressures on the Israeli government produced the Israeli assault on the Syrian Heights on June 9–10.

78   ISA/FM6444/6, from the Foreign Ministry to Israeli embassies, no. 653, June 5, 1967.

79   USNA/RG59/Entry 5190/Box 6/control 4927/June 5, 1967, From: Amman; PRO/FCO 17/206/1603/67/June 22, 1967, From: Jerusalem, to the Foreign Office.

80   *Al-Watha'iq al-'Urduniyyah 1967*, 37.

81   *Al-Majmu'ah*, vol. 2, 595; *al-Watha'iq al-'Urduniyyah 1967*, 41.

82   ISA/FM6444/6, From: the Foreign Ministry to Israeli embassies, no. 653, June 5, 1967.

83   Brig. S. A. El-Edross, *The Hashemite Arab Army, 1908–1979*, 363.

84 USNA/RG59/Entry 5190/Executive Secretariat/Box 8/June 5, 1967, From: Amman, 4572.
85 USNA/RG59/General foreign policy files, 1967–9, Political and defense, Box 2080, August 26, 1967, From: Amman, 1106.
86 Parker (ed.), *The Six Day War*, 157.
87 Ibid., 158.
88 PRO/FCO17/27/5/June 23, 1967, From: Amman; Dispatch no. 2 on the Jordanian army, 1967.
89 *Al-Majmu'ah*, vol. 2, 597–8; *al-Watha'iq al-'Urduniyyah 1967*, 43.
90 PRO/FCO17/27/5/June 23, 1967, From: Amman; Dispatch no. 2 on the Jordanian army, 1967.
91 Samir A. Mutawi, *Jordan in the 1967 War*, 134.
92 *MER*, 1967, 242; Brig. S. A. El-Edross, *The Hashemite Arab Army, 1908–1979*, 398.
93 USNA/RG59/Office of the Executive Secretariat Middle East Crisis files, 1967/Entry 5190/Box 4/control 5519/June 6, 1967, From: Amman.
94 USNA/RG59/Office of the Executive Secretariat Middle East Crisis files, 1967/Entry 5190/Box 4/control 5497, 5559/June 6, 1967, From: Amman; Box 8/control 6288/June 6, 1967, From: Tel Aviv.
95 USNA/RG59/Office of the Executive Secretariat Middle East Crisis files, 1967/Entry 5190/Box 8/control 7135/June 7, 1967, From: Amman.
96 USNA/RG59/Office of the Executive Secretariat Middle East Crisis files, 1967/Entry 5190/Box 4/control 5519/June 6, 1967, From: Amman.
97 USNA/RG59/Office of the Executive Secretariat Middle East Crisis files, 1967/Entry 5190/Box 8/control 5662/June 6, 1967, From: Amman.
98 Samir A. Mutawi, *Jordan in the 1967 War*, 138–9; *al-Watha'iq al-'Urduniyyah*, 1967, 51–3.
99 USNA/RG59/Office of the Executive Secretariat Middle East Crisis files, 1967/Entry 5190/Box 8/control 6288/June 6, 1967, From: Tel Aviv.
100 *Al-Watha'iq al-'Urduniyyah 1967*, 49.
101 Ibid.
102 Samir A. Mutawi, *Jordan in the 1967 War*, 139.
103 USNA/RG59/Office of the Executive Secretariat Middle East Crisis files, 1967/Entry 5190/Box 4/control 6306/June 6, 1967, From: Amman.
104 USNA/RG59/General Records of the Department of State; Executive Secretariat, Historical Office Research Projects, 1969–74/Box 4 – US Policy and Diplomacy, p. 129, based on Washington telegram 208748 to Tel Aviv, June 6, pp. 129–30 based on Amman telegram 4112, June 6.
105 USNA/RG59/General Records of the Department of State; Executive Secretariat, Historical Office Research Projects, 1969–74/Box 4 – US Policy and Diplomacy, p. 130, based on Amman telegram 4119, June 7, 1967.
106 USNA/RG59/Office of the Executive Secretariat Middle East Crisis files, 1967/Entry 5190/Box 4/control 6434/June 7, 1967; Box 8/control 6553/June 7, 1967, From: Amman; Box 6/control 6603/June 7, 1967, From: Tel Aviv; Box 4/control 208800/June 7, 1967, From: Washington, to Amman and Tel Aviv; Gilbo'a, *Six Years – Six Days*, 228.
107 USNA/RG59/Office of the Executive Secretariat Middle East Crisis files,

1967/Entry 5190/Box 1/June 15, 1967/Chronology of US–Jordanian consultations on the Middle East, May 18–June 10, 1967, citing Tel Aviv telegram,
control 208787, of June 7, 1967.

108 *Al-Watha'iq al-'Urduniyyah 1967*, 57.

109 USNA/RG59/Office of the Executive Secretariat Middle East Crisis files,
1967/Entry 5190/Box 9/control 6873/June 7, 1967 From: Amman; Box
8/control 6951/June 7, 1967 From: Amman.

110 USNA/RG59/Office of the Executive Secretariat Middle East Crisis files,
1967/Entry 5190/Box 8/control 208985/June 7, 1967, From: Washington,
toTel Aviv; ISA/FM6444/6, from the Foreign Ministry to Israeli embassies,
no. 687, June 7, 1967.

111 USNA/RG59/Office of the Executive Secretariat Middle East Crisis files,
1967/Entry 5190/Box 1/June 15, 1967/Chronology of US–Jordanian consultations on the Middle East, May 18–June 10, 1967, citing Amman telegram,
control 7399, of June 8, 1967; Zak, *King Hussein Makes Peace*, 119.

112 "A message to Jordanian officers," *L'Orient le Jour*, May 31, 1973.

4 The Emerging Elements of Jordanian Composite Nationalism

1 The sources quoted in the following notes represent a sample of the overall
body of documents consulted; the full list would have occupied a much larger
space. An excellent article analyzes the formation of Jordanian identity from
different starting points: see Laurie A. Brand, "Palestinians and Jordanians:
A Crisis of Identity," *Journal of Palestine Studies*, 24 (Summer 1995), 46–61
and especially 50–2.

2 Another approach to the issue of "Transjordanian nationalism" is presented
by Adnan Abu-Odeh, *Jordanians, Palestinians and the Hashemite Kingdom*
(Washington, DC: United States Institute of Peace Press, 1999), 237–61.

3 Broadcast by Amman Radio, November 1970 Message to Arab leaders,
Amman Home Service, March 31, 1971, BBC, April 2, 1971.

4 Address to the nation, *al-Ra'i*, *al-Dustur*, April 27, 1989; November 5, 1992.

5 *Al-Majmu'ah*, vol. 3, 345.

6 February 19, 1986, Itim/Mizrah, *al-Ra'i*, *al-Dustur*, February 20, 1986;
October 30, 1992; Interview, *FBIS*, Novemeber 5, 1992.

7 *Al-Majmu'ah*, vol. 3, 519; *al-Dustur*, January 29, 1982; November 21, 1983;
Speech, BBC, November 23, 1983 and *FBIS*, November 22, 1983; Speech to
the European Parliament on December 15, 1983, *FBIS*, December 16, 1983.

8 PRO/FCO17/247/EJ3/20/May 13, 1968, King Hussein of Jordan press conference.

9 *Selected Speeches of King Hussein* (Amman: Royal Hashemite Bureau, 1995),
Qur'an, chapters 2 (143), 16 (125), 6 (32), 21 (107), 3 (159).

10 *Al-Dustur, al-Ra'i*, October 13, 1991; Qur'an, chapter 106 (1–4).

11 *Al-Ra'i*, November 6, 24, 1992; quoting Qur'an, chapters 93 (1–5), 33 (33), 16
(127), 2 (249, 285), 35 (10).

12 *Al-Majmu'ah*, vol. 3, 359; *al-Dustur*, August 12, 1982, English version: BBC,
August 13, 1982, quoting Amman Home Service, August 12, 1982; *al-Ra'i*,
October 12, 1991.

13 *Al-Majmu'ah*, vol. 2, 538; Amman Home Service in Arabic, December 15, 1983, *FBIS*, December 16, 1983; *Sawt al-Sha'b*, April 28, 1988; cf. *al-Ra'i*, November 23, 1992.

14 Amman Home Service in Arabic, April 5, 1989, Itim/Mizrah news service; *al-Majmu'ah*, vol. 3, 202; cf. his expressions of friendship with Syria: *al-Majmu'ah*, vol. 3. 579; *al-Dustur*, August 12, 1982, English version: BBC, August 13, 1982, quoting Amman Home Service.

15 *Al-Majmu'ah*, vol. 3, 251.

16 January 23, 1984, BBC Domestic TV interview, *FBIS*, January 24, 26, 1984.

17 March 31, 1982, Interview, *FBIS*, April 1, 1982.

18 *New York Times*, November 6, 1992.

19 See Brand, "Palestinians and Jordanians: A Crisis of Identity," 46–7.

20 PRO/FCO17/247/EJ3/20/May 13, 1968, King Hussein of Jordan press conference; Interview with French TV, Amman domestic service, *FBIS*, August 13, 1982.

21 PRO/FCO17/830/1/NEJ26/1/April 23, 1969, Hussein's speech before the Royal Institute of International Relations, London; *al-Ra'i*, September 15, 1971; Amman Home Service in Arabic, November 21, 1983, BBC, November 23, 1983; Same speech: *FBIS*, November 22, 1983; *al-Ra'i, al-Dustur*, separation speech, August 1, 1988.

22 BBC, May 16, 1978; *al-Hawadith*, April 13, 1979; *US News and World Report*, March 15, 1982; *L'Espresso*, May 23, 1982.

23 November 2, 1985 speech, *al-Ra'i*, November 2, 1985.

24 For example: PRO/FCO17/830/1/NEJ26/1/Speech before the Royal Institute of International Affairs, London, April 23, 1969; Message addressed to all Arab leaders and published by Amman Radio, March 31, 1971, Itim/Mizrah news service; November 1970 Message to Arab leaders, Amman Home Service in Arabic, March 31, 1971, BBC, April 2, 1971; April 3, 1971 speech, *al-Majmu'ah*, vol. 3, 251–3; November 1, 1972 speech, *al-al-Majmu'ah*, vol. 3, al-*Majmu'ah*, vol. 3, 382–4.

25 *Al-Majmu'ah*, vol. 3, 21.

26 The audience for this message is the Arab leaders, this association between Israel and international Zionism is made in a message addressed to all Arab leaders, in November 1970, Amman Home Service in Arabic, March 31, 1971, BBC, April 2, 1971; *al-Majmu'ah*, vol. 3, 355; February 19, 1986 speech, *al-Ra'i, al-Dustur*, February 20, 1986; cf. *al-Ra'i*, April 26, 1988.

27 *Time*, July 26, 1982.

28 June 8, 1988 Algiers summit conference speech, *al-Ra'i, al-Dustur*, June 9, 1988; CBS interview, *al-Ra'i*, November 21, 1988; Interview with *al-Ra'i* and *al-Siyasah*, January 29, 1989.

29 *Al-Ahram*, May 6, 1982.

30 *Nouvelle Observateur*, May 18, 1984; *al-Hayat*, interview, October 28, 1988; cf. CNN interview, *al-Ra'i*, February 26, 1989.

31 March 23, 1968, *al-Majmu'ah*, vol. 3, 33.

32 King Hussein's July 9 [1968] interview, USNA/RG 59/General foreign policy files, 1967–9, Political and defense, Box 2080, Airgram A-408, July 22, 1967 from: Amman; "King Hussein's London Press Conference 19 March" *FBIS*,

March 21, 1983; *L'Express* interview, February 12, 1988; *al-Ra'i*, February 10, 1988.

33 *Al-Mustaqbal*, September 5, 1981.

34 February 28, 1982 ABC interview; Jordanian press, March 1, 1982; January 28, 1984 press conference, Jordanian press, January 29, 1984.

35 June 8, 1988 Algiers summit conference speech, *al-Ra'i, al-Dustur*, June 9, 1988.

36 Speech before the 28th class of graduates of the General Staff College, Amman Radio, *al-Dustur* and *Sawt al-Sha'b*, December 15, 1987.

37 *Wall Street Journal*, November 11, 1982; *Los Angeles Times*, August 21, 1983; *Le Figaro*, May 22, 1984.

38 *Al-Hayat, Daily Star*, August 29, 1974; August 22, 1982 address, BBC, August 24, 1982, quoting Amman Television.

39 February 19, 1986 speech, *al-Ra'i, al-Dustur*, February 20, 1986; *al-Ra'i*, October 27, 1974; *al-Nahar al-'Arabi w-al-Dawli*, December 26, 1981; *al-Dustur*, April 27, 1982.

40 *al-Majmu'ah*, vol. 3, 382; *al-Dustur*, February 10, 1988.

41 *Daily Star*, August 29, 1974.

42 *Al-Dustur*, May 27, 1981.

43 February 7, 1977, interview with *Time* magazine, *FBIS*, February 9, 1977.

44 *Al-Ra'i*, March 22, 1988.

45 January 2, 1984, interview, *FBIS,* January 4, 1984.

46 USNA/RG 59/General foreign policy files, 1967–9, Political and defense, Box 2080, Airgram A-1513, November 4, 1967, from: London; summary of the king's interview on November 1, 1967 with David Frost; *al-Majmu'ah*, vol. 3, 136 (November 1, 1969), 254 (February 5, 1971); TASS interview, July 7, 1987; Amman Home Service in Arabic, May 1, 25, 1989.

47 *Al-Majmu'ah*, vol. 3, 357; Amman Home Service in Arabic, September 15, 1971, *FBIS*, September 16, 1971, BBC, September 17, 1971; *Time*, January 23, 1978; *al-Anbaa*, September 6, 1988; Press conference, May 30, 1989, Amman Home Domestic Service in Arabic, May 30, 1989, *FBIS*, June 1, 1989.

48 Amman Home Service *in Arabic,* September 15, 1971, BBC; *al-Dustur*, March 28, 1976.

49 Hussein interview, Amman Domestic Service, November 24, 1980, *FBIS*, November 23, 1980.

50 November 5, 1992 Address to the nation, *al-Ra'i, al-Dustur,* November 6, 1992.

51 *Al-Majmu'ah*, vol. 3, 360.

52 *Al-Majmu'ah*, vol. 3, 104; King Hussein's July 30, 1969 speech, USNA/RG 59/General foreign policy files, 1967–9, Political and defense, Box 2080, Telegram 173, August 1, 1969, from: Amman.

53 Cf. Arthur Day, "Hussein's Constraints, Jordan's Dilemma," *SAIS Review* 7 (Winter 1987), no. 1, 87.

54 *Al-Ra'i*, August 30, 1974; *al-Hawadith* interview, Amman Domestic Service, July 10, 1975, Itim/mizrah news service; *al-Ra'i al-'Amm*, February 13, 1982; ABC interview, Amman Domestic Television service in English, March 1, 1982, *FBIS*, March 2, 1982.

55 April 27, 1982 Speech to the new national Consultative Council, *al-Dustur*, April 28, 1982, and BBC, April 29, 1982.
56 *Al-Majmu'ah*, vol. 3, 560; *al-Dustur*, April 11, 1983.
57 *Al-Hawadith* interview, Amman Domestic Service, July 10, 1975, Itim/mizrah news service; *FBIS*, February 11, 1977, quoting his *Die Zeit* interview; BBC November 4, 1982 interview, *FBIS*, November 5, 1982; Cf. Amman Domestic Service, January 28, 1984, *FBIS*, January 30, 1984.
58 *Ma'ariv*, January 28, 1972, interview with the Rome correspondent.
59 *New York Times*, November 5, 1974; *al-Anwar*, January 26, 1977; interview with Japan TV, December 10, 1982, BBC December 13 1982; Amman Home Service in Arabic, January 10, 1983 speech, *FBIS*, January 11, 1983; January 23, 1984, London BBC domestic TV interview, *FBIS*, January 24, 26, 1984.
60 April 3, 1971, *al-Majmu'ah*, vol. 3, 252, 458–9, 560, 580; *al-Dustur*, November 6, 1976; *FBIS*, February 11, 1977, quoting his *Die Zeit* interview; ABC interview, Amman Domestic Television Service in English, March 1, 1982, *FBIS*, March 2, 1982; Amman Home Service in Arabic, January 10, 1983 speech, *FBIS*, January 11, 1983; January 23, 1984, London BBC domestic TV interview, *FBIS*, January 24, 26, 1984.
61 See, for example, November 1, 1972, *al-Majmu'ah*, vol. 3, 384; *al-Anwar*, January 26, 1977; *al-Ahram*, May 7, 1982.
62 Amman Television Service, January 2, 1984, *FBIS*, January 4, 1984; January 23, 1984, London BBC domestic TV interview, *FBIS*, January 24, 26, 1984.
63 Amman Home Service in Arabic, speech, January 10, 1983, *FBIS*, January 11, 1983; January 23, 1984, London BBC domestic TV interview, *FBIS*, January 24, 26, 1984.
64 *Al-Majmu'ah*, vol. 3, 445; *al-Ra'i*, February 15, 1974.
65 Amman Home Service in Arabic, January 10, 1983 speech, *FBIS*, January 11, 1983.
66 December 1, 1971, *al-Majmu'ah*, vol. 3, 346–7; September 1, 1980 *Der Spiegel* interview, *FBIS*, September 8, 1980; *al-Ra'i al-'Amm*, February 13, 1982; *al-Ahram*, May 6, 1982; Aaron, D. Miller, "Jordan and the Palestinian Issue: The Legacy of the Past," *Middle East Insight*, 4, no.4 (1986), 24; Amman Radio, March 21, 1988, speech before the conference of the foreign ministers of the Muslim countries, Jordanian Press, March 22, 1988; *al-Quds*, April 24, 1994.
67 *Al-Majmu'ah*, vol. 3, 357; *The Times*, April 17, 1971; January 29, 1978; *Der Spiegel*, February 1, 1988.
68 December 18, 1974, *Guardian* interview, *al-Ra'i*, December 19, 1974; November 28, 1976, *al-Majmu'ah*, vol. 3, 616; September 1, 1980, *Der Spiegel* interview, *FBIS*, September 8, 1980; *al-Dustur*, November 5, 6, 1981.
69 French TV Channel 2, interview, as broadcast by Amman Radio, February 4, 1988.
70 *Al-Rai*, February 14, 1974, ; May 1, 1974, speech, Amman Home Service, Itim/Mizrah; *Middle East News Agency*, October 9, 1978; *al-Ra'i al-'Amm*, February 13, 1982.
71 See, for example, *al-Rai*, April 23, 1975.
72 April 3, 1971, *al-Majmu'ah*, vol. 3, 252.
73 April 3, 1971, *al-Majmu'ah*, vol. 3, 253.

74 *Al-Hawadith*, July 10, 1975.

75 November 1, 1969 speech before Parliament, *al-Majmu'ah*, vol. 3, 139; PRO/
FCO17/806/NEJ1/4/[November 2, 1969], From: Amman.

76 Speech before the 28th class of graduates of the General Staff College, as
broadcast by Amman Radio, December 16, 1987; Address to the nation, *al-
Ra'i, al-Dustur*, April 27, 1989.

77 June 7, 1967, *al-Majmu'ah*, vol. 2, 597 (June 7, 1967), vol. 3, 254 (April 3, 1971),
364 (March 15, 1972); Amman Home Service in Arabic, September 15, 1971,
BBC; September 1, 1980 *Der Spiegel* Interview, *FBIS*, September 8, 1980;
Hussein's interview with Jordanian press, published in all Jordanian newspapers on June 13, 1989.

78 Address to the nation, *al-Rai, al-Dustur*, April 27, 1989.

5   Is Peace Without the Territories Possible? Hussein's Reading of the Palestinian Issue between the Six-Day War and UN Resolution 242

1   *al-Watha'iq al-'Urduniyyah 1967*, 68-71.

2   USNA/RG59/Office of the Executive Secretariat Middle East Crisis files,
1967/Entry 5190/Box 4/control 9949/June12, 1967, From: Amman.

3   PRO/FCO17/93/EJ3/8/Telno. 643/June 12, 1967, From: Amman, to the
Foreign Office.

4   Ibid.; PRO/FCO17/242/EJ3/12/Telno. 975/August 7, 1967, From: Amman, to
the Foreign Office.

5   PRO/FCO17/279; 242/Telno. 984/August 8, 1967, From: Amman, to the
Foreign Office.

6   PRO/FCO17/212/EJ1/12/Telno. 670/June 15, 1967, From: Amman, to the
Foreign Office.

7   PRO/FCO17/93/EJ3/8/Telno. 643/June 12, 1967, From: Amman, to the
Foreign Office.

8   PRO/FCO27/1/August 1, 1967, Points arising from Secretary of State's
meeting on 27 July and Permanent Under-Secretary's morning meeting on 28
July.

9   Yezid Sayigh, "Jordan in the 1980s: Legitimacy, Entity and Identity," in
Rodney Wilson, *Politics and Economy in Jordan* (London and New York:
Routledge, 1991) 172.

10 PRO/FCO17/212/Telno. 605/June 9, 1967, From: Amman, to the Foreign
Office; USNA/RG59/Office of the Executive Secretariat Middle East Crisis
files, 1967/Entry 5190/Box 1/June 15, 1967/Chronology of US–Jordanian
consultations on the Middle East, May 18–June 10, 1967, citing Amman
telegram, control 8608, of June 9, 1967.

11 PRO/FCO17/219/[1967], a note on the economy of Jordan; June to December
1967; Daniel Dishon (ed.), *Middle East Record* (Jerusalem: Israel Universities
Press, 1971), 411.

12 PRO/FCO17/219/[1967], a note on the economy of Jordan, June to December
1967.

13 PRO/FCO17/279/Telno. 984/August 8, 1967, From: Amman, to the Foreign
Office.

14 Ibid.
15 Mahmoud Riad, *The Struggle for Peace in the Middle East* (London and New York: Quartet Books, 1981), 46.
16 PRO/FCO17/212/Telno. 605/June 9, 1967, From: Amman, to the Foreign Office; PRO/CAB133/364/July 3, 1967, Visit of King Hussein of Jordan, London, 1967; Record of a meeting held at No. 10 Downing Street; USNA/RG59/General foreign policy files, 1967–9, Political and defense, Box 1843, First Special meeting, July 16, 1967, From: Amman, 13806.
17 USNA/RG59/General foreign policy files, 1967–9, Political and defense, Box 1843, First Special meeting, July 18, 1967, From: Amman, 15640; interestingly enough this position would be repeated years later, indicating Hussein's consistent position on this issue, CBS interview, Amman Radio, *al-Ra'i*, November 20, 21, 1988.
18 USNA/RG59/Entry 5190/Box 17/July 6, 1967, From: Lucius D. Battle.
19 Sami Hakim, *al-Quds wa-al-taswiyah* (Bayrut: Dar al-Nidal, 1987), 261–2.
20 PRO/FCO17/279/Telno. 984/August 8, 1967, From: Amman, to the Foreign Office.
21 USNA/RG59/General foreign policy files, 1967–9, Political and defense, Box 1843, July 19, 1967, From: Washington, 9614.
22 Interview with *Le Monde*, November 21, 1967, as quoted by USNA/RG59/General foreign policy files, 1967–9, Political and defense, Box 2080, November 20, 1967, From: Paris, telegram 316; Jordan's foreign minister's speech at the opening of the Madrid Conference, *Federal News Service*, October 31, 1991.
23 PRO/FCO17/212/EJ1/12/Telno. 670/June 15, 1967, From: Amman, to the Foreign Office.
24 PRO/FCO17/93/EJ3/8/Telno. 643/June 12, 1967, From: Amman, to the Foreign Office; PRO/FCO17/212/EJ1/12/Telno. 670/June 15, 1967, From: Amman, to the Foreign Office.
25 PRO/FCO17/93/EJ3/8/Telno. 643/June 12, 1967, From: Amman, to the Foreign Office; PRO/FCO17/212/EJ1/12/Telno. 670/June 15, 1967, From: Amman, to the Foreign Office.
26 Reuven Pedatzur, "Coming Back Full Circle: The Palestinian Option in 1967," *Middle East Journal*, vol. 49 (Spring 1995), no. 2, 271; Zak, *King Hussein Makes Peace*,151.
27 Riad, *The Struggle for Peace*, 46.
28 Yair Hirschfeld, "Jordanian–Israeli peace negotiations after the Six Day War, 1967–1969: The view from Jerusalem," in J. Nevo and I. Pappé (eds.), *Jordan in the Middle East: The Making of a Pivotal State* (London: Frank Cass, 1994), 234.
29 PRO/FCO17/246/EJ3/18/October 13, 1967, From: Washington.
30 USNA/RG59/General foreign policy files, 1967–9, Political and defense, Box 1843, First Special meeting, July 15, 1967; Interview with *Le Monde*, November 21, 1967, as quoted by USNA/RG59/General foreign policy files, 1967–9, Political and defense, Box 2080, November 20, 1967, From: Paris, telegram 316.
31 Reuven Pedatzur, "Coming Back Full Circle," 273.

32 Amman Radio, July 9, 1967 – BBC, July 11, as quoted by *MER*, 1967, 259.
33 USNA/RG59/Entry 5190/Box 17/July 14, 1967, 12476, Memorandum of Conversation between Secretary Rusk and Mr Tuqan.
34 USNA/RG59/Entry 5190/Box 9/June 14, 1967, From: US embassy Amman, to Washington, 11960.
35 USNA/RG59/General foreign policy files, 1967–9, Political and defense, Box 1843, August 9, 1967 (composed on July 31, 1967), From: Washington, 17947.
36 Ibid.
37 See, for example, *The Times*, April 17, 1971.
38 This approach is very carefully alluded to in USNA/RG59/General foreign policy files, 1967–9, Political and defense, Box 1843, First Special meeting, July 16, 1967, From: Amman, 13806.
39 USNA/RG59/General foreign policy files, 1967–9, Political and defense, Box 1843, August 9, 1967 (composed on July 31, 1967), From: Washington, 17947.
40 *Al-Nahar*, August 29, 1967.
41 USNA/RG59/General foreign policy files, 1967–9, Political and defense, Box 1843, Memorandum of Conversation, London, September 15, 1967.
42 Riad, *The Struggle for Peace*, 80–1.
43 *al-Dustur*, November 3, 1967; USNA/RG59/General foreign policy files, 1967–9, Political and defense, Box 2080, Airgram A-1513, November 4, 1967, From: London; Summary of the king's interview on November 1, 1967 with David Frost.
44 Interview with *Le Monde*, November 21, 1967, as quoted by USNA/RG59/General foreign policy files, 1967–9, Political and defense, Box 2080, November 20, 1967, From: Paris, telegram 316.
45 USNA/RG59/General foreign policy files, 1967–9, Political and defense, Box 1843, July 19, 1967, From: Washington, 9614.
46 PRO/FCO17/243/EJ3/13/Telno. 1373/December 29, 1967, From: Amman, to the Foreign Office.
47 PRO/FCO27/2/1273, 1274/November 18, 1967, From: Amman; *al-Dustur*, September 3, 1978.
48 A message to Arab leaders, *Amman Radio*, March 31, 1971, Itim/Mizrah news service; November 1970, Message to Arab leaders, Amman Home Service *in Arabic*, March 31, 1971, BBC, April 2, 1971.
49 *Al-Nahar al-'Arabi w-al-Dawli*, December 26, 1981; February 28, 1982, ABC interview, *FBIS*, March 2; March 17, 1982 Hussein's speech as read by Queen Nur, al-Rai, March 17, 1982; Hussein's speech, June 8, 1988, at the Algiers Arab summit conference, *al-Ra'i, al-Dustur*, June 9, 1988; October 30, 1992, interview, *FBIS–NES*, 92-215, November 5, 1992.
50 USNA/RG59/General foreign policy files, 1967–9, Political and defense, Box 1843, July 19, 1967, From: Washington, 9614.
51 Amman radio, July 9, 1967, BBC, July 11, 1967.
52 Riad, *The Struggle for Peace*, 46; February 6, 1972, interview with *al-Siyasah*.
53 USNA/RG59/Entry 5190/Box 17/July 18, 1967, memorandum for the special NSC committee from the control group, entitled "Resumption of limited grant military assistance to Jordan."

54 USNA/RG59/General foreign policy files, 1967–9, Political and defense, Box 1843, July 22, 1967, From: Amman, 19737.

55 *Al-Jumhuriyyah*, September 2, 1967; *al-Watha'iq al-'Urduniyyah 1967*, 216; *Washington Post*, October 22, 1967.

56 USNA/RG59/General foreign policy files, 1967–9, Political and defense, Box 2080, Memorandum of Conversation, September 6, 1967, Washington, 15624.

57 PRO/FCO17/212/EJ1/12/Telno. 670/June 15, 1967, From: Amman, to the Foreign Office.

58 USNA/RG59/Entry 5190/Box 17/July 6, 1967, From: Lucius D. Battle.

59 Zak, *King Hussein Makes Peace*, 151.

60 USNA/RG59/Entry 5190/Box 17/July 14, 1967, 12476, Memorandum of Conversation between Secretary Rusk and Mr Tuqan.

61 Interview with *Le Monde*, November 21, 1967 as quoted by USNA/RG59/General foreign policy files, 1967–9, Political and defense, Box 2080, November 20, 1967, From: Paris, telegram 316.

62 PRO/CAB 133/364/July 3, 1967, Visit of King Hussein of Jordan, London, 1967; Record of a meeting held at No. 10 Downing Street.

63 PRO/FCO17/93/EJ3/8/Telno. 643/June 12, 1967, From: Amman, to the Foreign Office.

64 Amman Radio, April 3, 1971, Itim/Mizrah news service.

65 Interview with *Le Monde*, November 21, 1967, as quoted by USNA/RG59/General foreign policy files, 1967–9, Political and defense, Box 2080, November 20, 1967, From: Paris, telegram 316.

66 USNA/RG59/General foreign policy files, 1967–9, Political and defense, Box 1843, First Special meeting, July 16, 1967, From: Amman, 13806.

67 PRO/CAB133/364/July 3, 1967, Visit of King Hussein of Jordan, London, 1967; Record of a meeting held at No. 10 Downing Street.

68 PRO/CAB133/364/July 3, 1967, Visit of King Hussein of Jordan, London, 1967; Record of a meeting held at No. 10 Downing Street, p. 2: "Half his country was occupied, the losses of war had been heavy."

69 John Norton Moore, *The Arab–Israeli Conflict, Readings and Documents* (Princeton: Princeton University Press, 1977), 1062–3.

70 USNA/RG59/General foreign policy files, 1967–9, Political and defense, Box 1843, July 22, 1967, From: Amman, 19737.

71 USNA/RG59/Entry 5190/Box 17/July 14, 1967, 12476, Memorandum of Conversation between Secretary Rusk and Mr Tuqan.

72 USNA/RG59/General foreign policy files, 1967–9, Political and defense, Box 2080, Memorandum of conversation, September 6, 1967, Washington, 15624.

73 Ibid.

74 USNA/RG59/General foreign policy files, 1967–9, Political and defense, Box 2080, Airgram A-1513, November 4, 1967, From: London; Summary of the king's interview on November 1, 1967, with David Frost.

6 The Israeli and Palestinian Challenge

1 USNA/RG59/Box1843/Telegram 3122Q/March 13, 1968, From: Amman; PRO/FCO17/807/NEJ1/6/April 2, 1968 [*sic!* should be 1969], From: Amman;

Amman Radio, September 15, 1971, Itim/Mizrah news service and BBC, September 17, 1971.

2 Ambassador Findley Burns, Jr [US ambassador to Jordan, 1966–8], oral history interview, Georgetown University Library, November 3, 1988, 12; PRO/FCO17/212/EJ1/12/July 7, 20, 1967, From: Beirut; PRO/FCO17/272/ EJ10/14/December 30, 1967, From: Amman.

3 PRO/FCO17/212/EJ1/12/Telno. 670/June 15, 1967, From: Amman.

4 USNA/RG59/Entry 5190/Box 17/July 6, 1967, resumption of arms shipments to Jordan; PRO/FCO17/272/EJ10/14/December 30, 1967, From: Amman; PRO/FCO17/247/EJ3/20/January 2, 1968, From: Amman; PRO/FCO17/ 248/January 20, 1968, From: Amman.

5 PRO/FCO17/279/Telno. 984/August 8, 1967, From: Amman.

6 PRO/FCO17/248/January 20, 1968, From: Amman; PRO/FCO17/ 806/[November 1968], "The position of King Hussein."

7 PRO/FCO17/248/January 20, 1968, From: Amman; PRO/FCO17/219/EJ1/16 January 24, 1968, "Jordan in the Doldrums"; PRO/FCO17/221/EJ1/20 (Crawford) February 19, 1968, From: Amman; PRO/FCO17/221/EJ1/20 (Adams) February 19, 1968, From: Amman; PRO/FCO17/247/EJ3/20/March 7, 1968, From: Amman; al-Hawadith, March 8, 1968; USNA/RG59/Box 1843/Telegram 3131Q/March 13, 1968, From: Amman; Kull Shay, March 30, 1968; PRO/FCO17/207/EJ1/3/April 26, 1968, From: Amman.

8 Al-Watha'iq al-'Urduniyyah 1967, 219–20; PRO/FCO17/93/E4/1/September 5, 1967, From: Amman.

9 PRO/FCO17/807/NEJ1/6/April 2, 1969, The Premiership of Bahjat Talhouni, From: Amman.

10 PRO/FCO17/221/EJ1/20/February 26, 1968, From: London.

11 PRO/FCO17/221/EJ1/20/March 3, 1968, From: Amman.

12 PRO/FCO17/54/E2/52/June 7, 1968, From: Amman; Amman Radio, April 3, 1971,Israeli Itim/Mizrah news service; CBS interview, Amman Radio, November 20, 1988; French TV interview, December 13, 1988, as quoted by the Middle East News Agency; King Hussein's speech, The Xinhua General Overseas News Service, May 22, 1991; King Hussein's speech at the European Parliament, Inter Press Service, Strasbourg, September 11, 1991; cf., for example, Jordan's foreign minister's speech at the opening of the Madrid Conference, Federal News Service, October 31, 1991.

13 Cf. USNA/RG59/General foreign policy files, 1967–9, Political and defense, Box 2080, Memorandum of Conversation, December 17, 1968.

14 Hussein's NBC interview, January 31, 1981, FBIS, February 3, 1981.

15 PRO/FCO17/209/EJ1/6/December 12, 1967, Foreign Office memorandum.

16 PRO/FCO17/250/EJ3/23/January 5, 1968, From: Amman; USNA/RG59/Box 1843/Telegram 3131Q/March 13, 1968, From: Amman.

17 Abba Eban, An Autobiography (London: Futura, 1977), 446.

18 PRO/FCO17/250/EJ3/23/January 5, 1968, From: Amman.

19 PRO/FCO17/248/EJ3/21/January 20, 1968, From: Amman.

20 A most knowledgeable and accurate analysis of the Israeli position is to be found in the above mentioned article by Hirschfeld, "Jordanian–Israeli Peace Negotiations after the Six Day War, 1967–69: The View From: Jerusalem," in

Joseph Nevo and Ilan Pappé (eds), *Jordan in the Middle East: The Making of a Pivotal State, 1948–1988* (London: Frank Cass, 1994), 239–40; Reuven Pedatzur, "Coming Back Full Circle," 274.

21 Reuven Pedatzur, "Coming Back Full Circle," 277.
22 *Al-Dustur*, February 20, 1968; PRO/FCO17/211/EJ1/11/February 20, 1968, From: Washington; PRO/FCO17/221/EJ1/20/March 5, 1968, "Effects in Jordan of Israel's attack of 15 February" (From Amman); PRO/FCO17/247/EJ3/20/March 7, 1968, From: Amman, to the Foreign Office; Bakr Khazir al-Majali, *al-Milaff al-Watha'iqi lima'arakat al-karamah* (Arabic) [The documentary file of the Karameh battle] [Amman], 1996, 28–37.
23 PRO/FCO17/211/EJ1/11/February 22, 1968, From: Amman.
24 PRO/FCO17/221/EJ1/20/February 28, 1968, From: Tel Aviv; *Financial Times*, March 29, 1968.
25 PRO/FCO17/211/EJ1/11/January 30, 1968, From: Washington; PRO/FCO17/221/EJ1/20/March 3, 1968, From: Amman.
26 PRO/FCO17/221/EJ1/20/February 28, 1968, From: Tel Aviv, and March 1, 1968, internal FO memorandum ("Mr Eban's remarks about Jordan"); PRO/FCO17/308/EJ22/15/May 8, 1968, Summary of the king's meeting with the PM of the United Kingdom.
27 PRO/FCO17/247/EJ3/20/March 7, 1968, From: Amman; USNA/RG59/Box 1843/Telegrams 3122Q and 3131Q/March 13, 1968, From: Amman.
28 PRO/FCO17/54/E2/52/March 16, 1968, From: Amman, and March 18, 1968, From: Washington.
29 PRO/FCO17/633/ET2/8/March 20, 1968, telegrams 216, 218, 369, From: Amman and Tel Aviv.
30 PRO/FCO17/247/EJ3/20/March 7, 1968, From: Amman to the Foreign Office.
31 Zak, *King Hussein Makes Peace*, 246–7.
32 Riad, *The Struggle for Peace*, 80.
33 PRO/FCO17/633/[ET2/8]/March 24, 1968, "Report on operations in Karama . . . ," PRO/FCO17/633/ET2/8/April 1, 1968, "The Karama raid."
34 MER, 1968, 371, quoting: *Weltwoche,* March 29, 1968.
35 PRO/FCO17/633/ET2/8/March 23, 1968, From: Amman.
36 PRO/FCO17/221/EJ1/20/March 28, 1968, From: Washington.
37 Abu Iyyad, *Without a Homeland* (Hebrew translation), (Tel Aviv: Mifras, 1979), 89; PRO/FCO17/222/EJ1/21/March 25, April 2, 1968, From: Amman.
38 USNA/RG59/Box 1843/June 7, 1968/Memorandum for the files.
39 PRO/FCO17/221/EJ1/20/March 28, 1968, From: Amman.
40 PRO/FCO17/633/ET2/8/March 20, 1968, From: Tel Aviv; PRO/FCO17/633/ET2/8/April 1, 1968, "The Karama raid."
41 PRO/FCO17/222/EJ1/21/March 26, 1968, From: Amman.
42 USNA/RG59/Box 1843/Telegram 2081Q /April 8, 1968, From: Amman.
43 Reuven Pedatzur, "Coming Back Full Circle," 274, 282.
44 PRO/FCO17/54/E2/52/April 13, 1968, From: Amman; PRO/FCO17/247/EJ3/20/May 13, 1968, Record of conversation between the Foreign Secretary and His Majesty King Hussein of Jordan.
45 PRO/FCO17/308/EJ22/15/May 8, 1968, Summary of the king's meeting with

the PM of the United Kingdom; cf. Rifa'i's remarks, PRO/FCO27/1/July 12, 1968, From: the Foreign Office, to Amman; PRO/FCO17/ 308/EJ22/15/[August 24, 1968], FO memorandum: Mr Roberts' call on King Hussein; and cf. Rifa'i's complaint regarding the Israeli refusal to discuss their substantive position regarding borders, USNA/RG59/Box 1843/10372Q/ August 31, 1968, From: Amman.

46   PRO/FCO17/54/E2/52/and ER2/15/March 21, 1968, From: Amman.

47   USNA/RG59/Box 1843/June 4, 1968/Memorandum of Conversation between the Under-Secretary of State and Ambassador of Israel, Washington.

48   PRO/FCO17/54/E2/52/July 19, 1968, From: Washington.

49   King Hussein's July 9 [1968] interview, USNA/RG59/General foreign policy files, 1967–9, Political and defense, Box 2080, Airgram A-408, July 22, 1968 From: Amman; USNA/RG59/Box1843/Telegram 1056Q /August 5, 1968, From: Amman.

50   Reuven Pedatzur, "Coming Back Full Circle: The Palestinian Option in 1967," 283.

51   PRO/FCO17/221/EJ1/20/1, From: Amman, June 7, 1968; USNA/ RG59/General foreign policy files, 1967–9, Political and defense, Box 2080, Memorandum of Conversation with Ben-Aharon, Israeli Embassy, August 19, 1968; PRO/FCO17/810/NEJ3/408/2/December 3, 1968, From: Tel Aviv; Reuven Pedatzur, "Coming Back Full Circle," 275.

52   Riad, *The Struggle for Peace*, 81; PRO/FCO17/54/E2/47/April 9, 10, 1968, From: Amman; PRO/FCO17/54/E2/52/April 13, 1968, From: Amman; PRO/FCO17/247/EJ3/20/May 13, 1968, Record of conversation between the Foreign Secretary and His Majesty King Hussein of Jordan.

53   PRO/FCO17/247/EJ3/20/May 13, 1968, Record of conversation between the Foreign Secretary and His Majesty King Hussein of Jordan, para. 6.

54   PRO/FCO17/308/EJ22/15/May 8, 1968, Summary of the king's meeting with the PM of the United Kingdom; PRO/FCO17/247/EJ3/20/May 13, 1968, Record of conversation between the Foreign Secretary and His Majesty King Hussein of Jordan.

55   PRO/FCO27/1/July 12, 1968, From: the Foreign office.

56   Hirschfeld, 242, quoting Gideon Rafael, *Destination Peace – Three Decades of Israeli Foreign Policy: A Personal Memoir* (London: Weidenfeld and Nicolson, 1981), 197; USNA/RG59/Box 1843/June 4, 1968/Memorandum of Conversation between the Under Secretary of State and Ambassador of Israel, Washington; USNA/RG59/Box 1843/June 5, 1968/internal note.

57   USNA/RG59/Box 1843/June 4, 1968/Memorandum of Conversation between the Under-Secretary of State and Ambassador of Israel, Washington.

58   PRO/FCO17/809/October 22, 1968, From: London, to Amman; October 23, 1968, From: Washington; October 24, 1968, From: London; USNA/RG59/Box1843/Telegram 9156Q /October 28, 1968, From: Amman; PRO/FCO17/809/NEJ3/408/1/October 31, 1968, From: Amman, to London

59   Reuven Pedatzur, "Coming Back Full Circle," 274.

60   *Al-Difa', al-Dustur*, September 14, 1968; USNA/RG59/General foreign policy files, 1967–9, Political and defense, Box 2080, Tel. 444, September 14, 1968,

From: Amman; PRO/FCO17/219/EJ1/16 September 16, 1968, From: Amman.

61 PRO/FCO17/219/EJ1/16 September 15, 1968, From: Amman.

62 PRO/FCO17/809/NEJ3/408/1/October 31, 1968, From: Amman, to London; King Hussein's October 31, 1968 interview, USNA/RG59/General foreign policy files, 1967–9, Political and defense, Box 2080, Tel. 639, November 1, 1968 from: Amman.

63 Zak, *King Hussein Makes Peace*, 247–8.

64 USNA/RG59/Box1843/Telegram 0192Q/November 1, 1968, From: Amman.

65 PRO/FCO17/805/NEJ1/3/November 6, 1968, From: Amman.

66 USNA/RG59/Box1843/Telegram 6090Q/January 23, 1969, From: Tel Aviv; PRO/FCO17/830/1/NEJ/3/414/1/January 23, 1969, From: London; *New York Times*, March 25, 1969.

67 Zak, *King Hussein Makes Peace*, 160; PRO/FCO17/830/ 1/NEJ/3 /414/1/January 23, 1969, From: London.

68 Henry Kissinger, *White House Years*. Boston and Toronto: Little, Brown [1979]), 357.

69 USNA/RG59/Box1843/Telegram 1754Q/March 6, 1969, From: Tel Aviv; Telegram 21174Q/March 7, 1969, From: Amman; Telegram 2014Q/March 7, 1969, From: Tel Aviv.

70 USNA/RG59/Box1843/Telegram 3012Q/March11, 1969, From: Tel Aviv.

71 USNA/RG59/General foreign policy files, 1967–9, Political and defense, Box 2080, Memorandum of Conversation, April 8, 10, 1969; PRO/FCO17/ 831/NEJ26/4/April 14, 1969, King Hussein's visit to the United States, From: Washington; Henry Kissinger, *White House Years*, 362–3; PRO/FCO17/ 830/1/NEJ26/1/April 23, 1969, From: London.

72 PRO/FCO17/831/NEJ26/4/April 14, 1969, King Hussein's visit to the United States, From: Washington.

73 CNA/RG25/8854/20–Israel–1-3/14 April 1969, From: Tel Aviv.

74 USNA/RG59/Box1843/Secret memorandum/June 5, 1969/Next steps towards Israel–Jordan settlement – action memorandum; Amman telegram 2515Q of June 11; Tel Aviv Telegram 5694 of June 24.

75 PRO/FCO17/807/NEJ1/6/July 5, 1969, From: Amman; PRO/FCO17/827/ NEJ22/4/July 24, 1969, From: Amman.

76 USNA/RG59/General foreign policy files, 1967–9, Political and defense, Box 2080, July 29, 1969, From: Amman.

77 PRO/FCO17/807/NEJ1/6/July 5, August 15, 1969, From: Amman; FCO17/ 806/NEJ1/4/November 14, 28, 1969, From: Amman.

78 USNA/RG59/Box1843/Telegram 7204Q/August 30, 1969, From: Amman.

79 PRO/FCO17/808/Telegram 2686/December 12, 1969, From: London; USNA/RG59/Box1843/Telegram 4180Q/September 17, 1969, From: Tel Aviv; /Telegram 209556/December 18, 1969, From: Washington to Tel Aviv and Amman; Telegram 5535Q/December 31, 1969, From: Tel Aviv; Telegram 213942/December 31, 1969, From: Washington.

80 November 1, 1969, speech before Parliament, *al-Majmu'ah*, vol. 3, 139; PRO/ FCO17/806/NEJ1/4/[November 2, 1969], From: Amman; USNA/

RG59/General foreign policy files, 1967-9, Political and defense, Box 2080, November 3, 1969, From: Amman.

81 See, for example: *al-Difa'*, *al-Dustur*, April 8, 1970.

7 The 1970s: From a Survival Struggle to the Consolidation of the Political Success

1 PRO/FCO17/223/EJ1/22/June 7, 1968, From: Amman; PRO/FCO17/804/NEJ1/2/November 29, 1968, From: Amman.

2 PRO/FCO17/805/NEJ1/3/November 9, 1968, From: Amman; PRO/FCO17/806/NEJ1/4/November 15, 1968, From: Amman; PRO/FCO17/808/NEJ3/304/1/December 20, 1968 From: Washington; PRO/FCO17/805/NEJ1/3/November 28, 1969, From: Amman.

3 PRO/FCO17/831/NEJ26/4/April 14, 1969, King Hussein's visit to the United States; From: Washington.

4 PRO/FCO17/248/EJ3/21/January 20, 1968, From: Amman, to the Foreign Office; *al-Majmu'ah*, vol. 3, 22–3; PRO/FCO17/221/EJ1/20 (Crawford) February 19, 1968, From: Amman, to the Foreign Office; PRO/FCO17/830/1/Telegram 312/October 3, 1969, From: London.

5 PRO/FCO17/830/1/NEJ1/3/October 9, 1969, From: London; PRO/FCO17/805/NEJ1/3/November 28, 1969, From: Amman.

6 February 6, 1972, interview with *al-Siyasah*, *FBIS*, February 8, 1972 .

7 November 1, 1969, speech before Parliament, *al-Majmu'ah*, vol. 3, 139; PRO/FCO17/806/NEJ1/4/[November 2, 1969], From: Amman; USNA/RG59/General foreign policy files, 1967–9, Political and defense, Box 2080, November 3, 1969, From: Amman.

8 Kissinger, *White House Years*, 599.

9 See his interview with the London *Times*, April 17, 1971.

10 Mahmoud Riad. *The Struggle for Peace in the Middle East* (London; New York: Quartet Books, 1981), 159–60; William B. Quandt, *Decade of Decisions: American policy towards the Arab–Israeli conflict, 1967–1976* (Berkeley: University of California Press, 1977), 134–5.

11 Riad, *The Struggle for Peace*, 161–3; Henry Brandon, "Were we masterful . . .", *Foreign Policy* (Spring 1973), 168.

12 Arthur Day, "Hussein's Constraints, Jordan's Dilemma," *SAIS Review*, 7 (Winter 1987), no. 1, 85.

13 Brandon, "Were we masterful . . . ", 158–70; David Schoenbaum, " . . . Or Lucky?", 171–1; Kissinger, *White House Years,* 606, 610, 618–9 and *passim*. to p. 631; Nabeel A. Khoury, "Leadership in crisis: a comparative study of Lebanon (1975–1979) and Jordan (1970–1971)," in Fuad I. Khuri (ed.), *Leadership and Development in Arab Society* (Beirut: Center for Arab and Middle East Studies, Faculty of Arts and Sciences, American University of Beirut, 1981), 109.

14 Zak, *King Hussein Makes Peace*, 45–6.

15 Riad, *The Struggle for Peace*, 196; November 1970 Message to Arab leaders, Amman Home Service in Arabic, March 31, 1971, BBC, April 2, 1971.

16 Interview to Jordanian television, January 22, 1971, Itim/Mizrah news service.

17 November 1970 Message to Arab leaders, Amman Home Service in Arabic, March 31, 1971, BBC, April 2, 1971.

18 Hussein's Interview with *al-Nahar,* August 24, 1971; *New York Times*, August 25, 1971.

19 First indications of his new approach are to be found in an interview on February 6, 1972, *al-Siyasah, FBIS*, February 8, 1972; the text of his United Kingdom speech is in al-*Majmu'ah*, vol. 3. 357–65.

20 *Al-Majmu'ah*, vol. 3, 383.

21 *Die Zeit* interview, *FBIS*, February 11, 1977.

22 *Los Angeles Times*, August 21, 1983.

23 Cf. his analysis of the Palestinian status in Jordan and the West Bank, see his expressions of friendship with Syria: *al-Majmu'ah*, vol. 3, 458–9.

24 February 19, 1986 speech, *al-Ra'i, al-Dustur*, February 20, 1986.

25 Cf. Zak, *King Hussein Makes Peace*, 165–6.

26 February 5, 1997, interview with the French *France-Soir*, *FBIS*, February 8, 1977.

27 *Die Zeit* interview, *FBIS*, February 11, 1977.

28 "A message to Jordanian officers," *L'Orient le Jour*, May 31, 1973.

29 This secret visit has become public knowledge in recent years. A senior Israeli figure who was privy to all policy contacts at the time, Mr M. Gazit, publicly confirmed the existence of this meeting and its significance. *Ha'aretz*, May 26, 1998; Lukacs, *Israel, Jordan, and the Peace Process*, 1.

30 February 19, 1986 speech, *al-Ra'i, al-Dustur*, February 20, 1986.

31 Published by Amman Radio, March 31, 1971, Itim/Mizrah news service.

32 Shimon Peres, edited by David Landau, *Battling for Peace: A Memoir* (New York: Random House, 1995), 260.

33 Riad, *The Struggle for Peace*, 279.

34 June 17, 1976, interview, Vienna Domestic Television Service, *FBIS*, June 21, 1976.

35 March 16, 1977, Teacher's day speech, *FBIS*, March 17, 1977

36 February 5, 1997, interview to the French *France Soir*, *FBIS*, February 8, 1977.

37 Shmu'el Ben Zvi, *Jordan's economy* (Hebrew), (Tel Aviv University: Armand Hammer Foundation for Middle Eastern Economic Cooperation, 1993), 16–17.

38 Lawrence Tal, "Peace for Jordan?" *The World Today* (August–September 1993), 169.

39 January 23, 1978, BBC interview, *FBIS*, January 24, 26, 1978.

40 September 23, 1978, Press conference, *FBIS*, September 27, 1978.

8 The Palestinian Decade and the Final Closing of the West Bank Issue

1 June 8, 1988, Algiers summit conference speech, Amman Radio, *al-Ra'i, al-Dustur*, June 9, 1988.

2 For an historical review of this concept, see Daniel Pipes and Adam Garfinkle, "Is Jordan Palestine?," *Commentary* (October 1988), 35–42.

3 *Ha'aretz*, March 22, 1968.

4 A former senior *Mossad* official, Dr Eliyah Ben Elissar, went as far as publicly promoting this line, *Ha'aretz*, September 4, 1970; Shlomo Avineri (ed.), *Israel and the Palestinians* (New York: St. Martin's Press, 1971), 150–2.

5 For example, Hussein's Interview with *al-Nahar*, August 24, 1971; *New York Times*, August 25, 1971.

6 *Ma'ariv*, November 29, 1974.

7 *US News and World Report*, March 15, 1982.

8 *Yediot Aharonot*, October 28, 1981; *Ha'aretz*, October 28, 30, 1981; Yitzhak Shamir, "Israel's Role in a Changing Middle East," *Foreign Affairs*, no. 1, 60 (Spring 1982), 789–91, *Ma'ariv*, September 3, 1982; *Yediot Aharonot*, September 3, 1982.

9 *Ha'aretz*, August 15, 1982.

10 *Middle East Policy Survey*, Confidential bi-weekly Washington report, August 13, 1982.

11 Sharon's interview, *Ma'ariv*, September 17, 1982.

12 *Ha'aretz*, June 21, 26, 1983; *Jerusalem Post*, June 28, 30, 1983.

13 Amman Home Service in Arabic, February 19, 1986 speech, Itim/Mizrah, February 20, 1986.

14 *Ma'ariv*, February 15, 1989; cf. *Ma'ariv*, August 22, 1997.

15 *Ha'aretz*, August 14, 1997.

16 *Ha'aretz*, February 3, 1991; *Davar*, May 22, 1991; Adam Garfinkle, *Israel and Jordan in the Shadow of War* (New York: St Martin's Press, 1992), 171–2; Lukacs, *Israel, Jordan, and the Peace Process*, 12; Joseph Alper, "Israel: The Challenge of Peace," *Foreign Policy*, 101 (Winter 1995–6), 138.

17 Dore Gold, interview, Jerusalem, November 30, 2000; Lukacs, *Israel, Jordan, and the Peace Process*, 13.

18 Arthur Day, "Hussein's Constraints, Jordan's Dilemma," *SAIS Review*, 7 (Winter 1987), no. 1, 87.

19 *Tishrin*, October 11, December 27, 1980; *Monday Morning*, November 17–23, 1980; *al-Hadaf*, December 27, 1980.

20 Accordoing to 'Adnan Abu Udah, a close advisor to Hussein, *Jordan Times*, May 9, 1981.

21 *Al-Safir*, April 14, 1981; Kuwait News Agency, April 19, 1981; *al-Qabas*, May 1, 1981; *al-Mawqif al-'Arabi*, June 22, 1981.

22 Cf. Alexander M. Haig, Jr, *Caveat: Realism, Reagan, and Foreign Policy* (New York: Macmillan, 1984), 342–52.

23 Sharon's interview, *Ma'ariv*, January 28, 1983.

24 Hussein's speech, interview with *US News and World Report*, March 15, 1982.

25 *Al-Nahar*, May 1, 1983; Amman Home Service in Arabic, February 19, 1986 speech, Itim/Mizrah, February 20, 1986, Aaron D. Miller, "The PLO and the Peace Process: The Organizational Imperative," *SAIS Review*, 7, No. 1 (Winter 1987), 97; cf. *The Times*, January 11, 1984.

26 Cf. Hassan Bin Talal, "Jordan's quest for peace," *Foreign Affairs* 60 (Spring 1982), no. 4, 802–13.

27 January 10, 1983 speech, Amman Domestic Service in Arabic, *FBIS*, January 11, 1983.

28 *Wall Street Journal*, November 11, 1982.

29 *New York Times*, March 15, 1984.

30 *Shu'un Filastiniyyah*, no. 140–1 (November–December 1984), 146–74; no. 166–7 (January–February 1987), 75–88; Aaron D. Miller, "Jordan and the Palestinian Issue: The Legacy of the Past," *Middle East Insight*, 4, no. 4 (1986), 28–9.

31 *Filastin al-Thawrah*, January 4, 1986; Amman Home Service in Arabic, February 19, 1986 speech, Itim/Mizrah, February 20, 1986.

32 New York representative Stephen Solarz's interview with *al-Hawadith*, June 7, 1985; cf. *al-Bayadir al-Siyasi*, February 1, March 8, 1986.

33 Cf. *al-Bayadir al-Siyasi*, January 4, February 1, 1986; for the July–September developments see: *Shu'un Filastiniyyah*, 150–1 (September–October 1985), 131–40; Amman Home Service in Arabic, February 19, 1986 speech, Itim/Mizrah, February 20, 1986; on the US perspective: "Robert G. Neumann: A Failure to Negotiate," *Journal of Palestine Studies* 15, no. 3 (1986), 3–11; Aaron D. Miller, "The PLO and the Peace Process: The Organizational Imperative," *SAIS Review* 7, No. 1 (Winter 1987), 109.

34 Amman Home Service in Arabic, February 19, 1986 speech, Itim/Mizrah, February 20, 1986.

35 *New York Times*, May 23, 1986.

36 *Al-Dustur*, October 25, 26, 1986; *Christian Science Monitor*, October 31, 1986.

37 *Al-Quds*, July 11, 1987.

38 Edmund Ghareeb, "Interview with El Hassan Bin Talal," *American Arab Affairs*, 16 (Spring 1986), 112–13; *Los Angeles Times*, September 17, 1986.

39 *Financial Times* interview, February 18, 1987; *al-Ra'i*, February 19, 1987, March 6, 1987; *al-Dustur*, March 26, 1987; *al-Qabas*, April 8, 1987.

40 Cf. *al-Hurriyah*, October 5, 1986.

41 See, for example, *al-Ra'i*, January 1, 17, 1988; *Sawt al-Sha'b*, January 6, 1988.

42 *Der Spiegel*, February 1, 1988, cf. *al-Fikr al-Dimuqrati*, Spring–Summer 1988.

43 French TV Channel 2 interview, Amman Radio, February 4, 1988.

44 Cf. an article rejecting the idea put forward by Israel's Peres to transfer the Gaza Strip to Jordanian responsibility, *al-Ra'i*, January 14, 1988.

45 Speech before the 28th class of graduates of the General Staff College, Amman Radio, December 16, 1987; *al-Dustur*, *Sawt al-Sha'b*, December 15, 1987, as quoted by Amman Home Service in Arabic, December 17, 1987; June 8, 1988 Algiers summit conference speech, Amman Radio, June 8, *al-Ra'i, al-Dustur*, June 9, 1988.

46 See random expressions regarding the autonomy issue: Amman Radio, February 4; *L'Express* interview, February 12, 1988.

47 Amman Home Service in Arabic, September 18, 1997, BBC Monitoring Service, Summary of world broadcasts, September 20, 1997.

48 *Der Spiegel*, February 2, 1988.

49 April 24, 1988, Irbid speech, *al-Ra'i*, April 25, 1988.

50 *Al-Quds, al-Sha'b, al-Nahar*, July 29, 1988; *al-Fajr*, July 30, 1988.

51 *Al-Shark al-Awsat*, July 27, 1988.

52 *Al-Quds*, July 31, 1988.

53 *Al-Nahar, 'Ukaz*, July 29, 1988.

54 *Al-Fikr al-Dimuqrati* (Spring–Summer 1988).
55 Jordanian press, August 1, 1988.
56 CBS interview, as broadcast by Amman Radio, November 20, 1988.
57 Schiff, *Security for Peace*, 10.
58 Shimon Peres and Robert Littell, *For the Future of Israel* (Baltimore and London: Johns Hopkins University Press, 1998), 94.
59 *Al-Fajr, al-Nahar, al-Sha'b, al-Quds*, August 1, 2, 1988.
60 *Al-Ittihad*, August 1, 1988.
61 *Al-Watan*, November 13, 1989.
62 *Al-Nahar*, December 6, 1989.
63 *Al-Nahahr, al-Quds*, December 21, 1989.
64 Amman Home Service in Arabic, March 7, 1989, Itim/Mizrah news service.
65 *Ha'aretz*, March 1, 1990.
66 Robert B. Satloff, *Troubles on the East Bank: Challenges to the Domestic Stability of Jordan*, The Washington Papers, no. 123 (New York: Praeger, 1986), 40–6.
67 Kuwait News Agency, April 19, 1981.
68 *The Times*, January 11, 1984.
69 *Ha'aretz*, October 20, 1983.
70 *Al-Majallah*, May 26, 1984.
71 Edmund Ghareeb, "Interview with El Hassan Bin Talal," *American Arab Affairs*, 16 (Spring 1986), 116–17; Interview with H.R.M. King Hussein of the Hashemite Kingdom of Jordan, ibid., 156–7; *al-Bayadir al-Siyasi*, March 1, 8, 1986; Arthur Day, "Hussein's Constraints, Jordan's Dilemma," *SAIS Review*, 7 (Winter 1987), no. 1, 92.
72 *Shu'un Filastiniyyah*, no. 166–7 (January–February 1987), 80, 85.
73 *Jerusalem Post*, May 11, 1987.
74 For Rifa'i's statement denying any agreements, see *Jerusalem Post*, May 5, 1987; Zak's articles in *Ma'ariv*, April 9, 15, 1990; for the text of the agreement see Shimon Peres, edited by David Landau, *Battling for Peace: A Memoir* (New York: Random House, 1995), 314–15; Interview with Yitzhak Shamir, former Israeli prime minister (1983–4; 1986–92), Tel Aviv, February 20, 2001. Zak based his articles on data received from Shamir.
75 *Al-Dustur*, February 15, 1988.

9 From the Gulf War to Peace, and the Road to Democracy

1 Reuters news agency, June 1, 1990.
2 Anonymous, "The Temptation of Mecca: King Hussein and the Gulf Crisis," unpublished manuscript (1999), 27.
3 Ibid., 32.
4 *Al-Sha'b*, August 8, 1990; Shmu'el Ben Zvi, *Jordan's Economy*, 18.
5 "The Temptation of Mecca," 29.
6 Bruce Maddy-Weitzman, *The Inter-Arab System and the Gulf War: Continuity and Change* (The Carter Center of Emory University, 1991), 16; Asher Susser, "Jordan," *Middle East Contemporary Survey*, 14 (1990), 457–99; Adam Garfinkle, "Jordanian Policy from the *Intifada* to the Madrid Conference," in

Robert O. Freedman (ed.), *The Middle East after Iraq's Invasion of Kuwait* (Gainesville: University Press of Florida, 1993), 298–9.

7 "The Temptation of Mecca," 14.

8 Moshe Zak, "Thirty Years of Clandestine Meetings," *Middle East Quarterly*, 2 (March 1995), 53; Interview with Yitzhak Shamir, February 20, 2001.

9 Robert Satloff, "The Confounding Strategy of King Hussein," *Peacewatch: Analysis of the Arab–Israeli Peace Process from the Washington Institute*, no. 29 (March 12, 1992), 69; Aharon Klieman, "The Israel–Jordan Tacit Security Regime," in Efraim Inbar (ed.), *Regional Security Regimes: Israel and its Neighbors* (Albany: State University of New York Press, 1995), 138–9.

10 "The Temptation of Mecca," 15, 16.

11 Muslim Brotherhood, Jordan, "A *communiqué* from the Association of Muslim Brotherhood in Jordan regarding current events in the Arab Field," August 5, 1990.

12 Nasser Eddin Nashashibi, "Palestine and Jordan," in Barry Rubin *et al.* (eds.), *From War to Peace: Arab–Israeli Relations, 1973–1993* (Brighton and Portland: Sussex Academic Press [published in association with New York University Press], 1994), 184.

13 Jordanian press, November 18, 26, 1990.

14 *Al-Quds*, July 12, 1991.

15 Yann Le Troquer and Rozenn Hommery al-Oudat, "From Kuwait to Jordan: The Palestinian's Third Exodus," *Journal of Palestine Studies*, 28 (Spring 1999), no. 3, 37–51.

16 Associated Press, August 7, 1991.

17 NBC, March 21, 1991; *Le Monde*, November 6, 1991.

18 Nasser Eddin Nashashibi, *Palestine and Jordan*, 185.

19 *Al-Quds*, May 20, 1991.

20 *Al-Sharq al-Awsat*, May 31, 1991; denied by Jordan: AFP News Agency, June 1, 1991; *al-Nahar*, June 30, 1991.

21 *Al-Quds*, August 13, 1991; AFP News Agency, August 15, 1991.

22 Interview with *Le Point*, June 1, 1991.

23 Address to the Jordanian National Congress, Amman, October 12, 1991, http://www.kinghussein.gov.jo/speeches_letters.html

24 Shimon Peres, edited by David Landau, *Battling for Peace: A Memoir* (New York: Random House, 1995), 277.

25 Jordan TV in Arabic, January 1, 1994, BBC Monitoring Service, Summary of world broadcasts, ME/1886MED/5[17], January 4, 1994; Amman Home Service in Arabic, January 4, 1994, BBC ME/1886MED/3[5], January 6, 1994; Jordan TV in Arabic, April 25, 1994, BBC ME/1982MED/5[9], April 27, 1994; Jordan TV in Arabic, January 25, 1995, BBC ME/2215MED/16[37], January 28, 1995; Jordan TV in Arabic, July 10, 1997, BBC ME/2969MED/5[16], July 12, 1997.

26 Ghanim Habib Allah, *'Alaqat Munazzamat al-Tahrir al-Filastiniyah bi-al-nizam al-Urduni, 1964-1976: bayna al-tansiq wa-al-sidam* [PLO relations with the Jordanian regime, 1964–1976: between coordination and confrontation] (Arabic) (Akka: Dar al-Aswar, 1987), 13.

27 January 4, 1994, before army commanders; February 14, 1994, Senate speech.

Cf. David Makovsky, *Making Peace with the PLO; The Rabin Government's Road to the Oslo Accords* (Boulder, CO : Westview Press, 1996), 124.

28 January 1, 1994 speech before army commanders, BBC, January 4, 1994; speech to members of the Senate's Foreign affairs Committee, BBC, February 15, 1994.

29 *Ha'aretz*, January 23, February 12, 20, 26, March 1, 1990.

30 Interview with Yitzhak Shamir, February 20, 2001.

31 *Jerusalem Post*, May 31, 1991.

32 *Le Point*, June 1, 1991; all Israeli newspapers, June 2, 1991.

33 Shimon Peres, edited by David Landau, *Battling for Peace: A Memoir* (New York: Random House, 1995), 304.

34 Ibid., 294.

35 *New York Times*, July 31, 1994.

36 *Ha'aretz*, April 6, 1994, March 19, 1997.

37 Jawad al-Anani, "Special Policy Forum Report: Jordan and the Peace Process," *Peacewatch: The Washington Institute's Special Reports on the Arab–Israeli Peace Process*, no. 29 (July 29, 1994); *New York Times*, July 31, 1994, March 3, 1995.

38 *Ha'aretz*, September 28, 1994.

39 Hanan Ashrawi, *This Side of Peace: A Personal Account* (New York: Simon & Schuster, 1995), 13.

40 Cf. Robert B. Satloff, "The Jordan–Israel Peace Treaty: A remarkable Document," *Middle East Quarterly*, March 1995, 49–50.

41 *Peace between the State of Israel and the Hashemite Kingdom of Jordan* (Jerusalem: Ministry of Foreign Affairs, 1994), p. 15, article 9.

42 *Ha'aretz*, October 28, 1994; *New York Times*, October 30, 1994.

43 Cf., for example, *Address by His Royal Highness, Crown Prince el-Hassan Bin Talal, of the Hashemite Kingdom of Jordan, at the Dinner hosted by HE Mr Benjamin Netanyahu, Prime Minister of Israel*, Tel Aviv, March 10, 1998 [np, nd].

44 *Ha'aretz*, January 30, 1995.

45 Cf., *Ha'aretz*, January 3, 4, 1996.

46 *Ha'aretz*, October 9, 1996.

47 *New York Times*, October 10, 1996.

48 *Yediot Aharonot*, June 13, 1997; *Ha'aretz*, September 22, October 1, 2, 4, 1996, January 13, 1997.

49 *Jordan Times*, December 26, 1997.

50 *Ha'aretz*, March 12, 13, 1997; *International Herald Tribune*, March 13, 1997; *The Economist*, April 12, 1997.

51 *Ha'aretz*, April 17, 1994.

52 *Yediot Aharonot*, October 25, 1994.

53 *Ha'aretz*, March 13, 1996.

54 *Ma'ariv*, March 22, 1996.

55 *Ha'aretz*, May 5, 1996.

56 Regarding Arafat's reaction, see *New York Times*, October 10, 17, 1997.

57 Ben Zvi, *Jordan's Economy*, 17–18.

58 *The Economist*, July 4, 1998.

59 CBS interview, Amman Radio, November 20, 1988; *al-Ra'i*, *al-Siyasah*, January 29, 1989; Amman Home Service in Arabic, March 7, 1989, Itim/Mizrah news service.

60 Hussein's interview with the Jordanian press published in all Jordanian newspapers on June 13, 1989; Amman Radio, June 12, 1989.

61 *Al-Nahar*, May 9, 1991.

62 Cf. October 30, 1992 interview, *FBIS*, November 5, 1992.

63 Kamel S. Abu-Jaber and Schirin H. Fathi, "The 1989 Jordanian Parliamentary Elections," *Orient*, 31, no. 1 (1990), 67–86; Linda Shull Adams, "Political Liberalization in Jordan: An Analysis of the State's Relationship with the Muslim Brotherhood," *Journal of Church and State*, 38, no. 3 (Summer 1996), 507–28; Laurie A. Brand, "Economic and Political Liberalization in a Rentier Economy: The Case of the Hashemite Kingdom of Jordan," in Iliya Harik and Denis J. Sullivan (eds.), *Privatization and Liberalization in the Middle East* (Bloomington, IN: Indiana University Press, 1992), 167–88; Rex Brynen, "Economic Crisis and Post-rentier Democratization in the Arab World: The Case of Jordan," *Canadian Journal of Political Science*, 25, no. 1 (March 1992), 69–97; Curtis R. Ryan, "Elections and Parliamentary Democratization in Jordan," *Democratization*, 5, no. 4 (Winter 1998), 176–96.

64 www.freedomhouse.org/ratings/iceland.htm

65 Hanna Yousif Freij, "Liberalization, the Islamists, and the Stability of the Arab State," in *The Muslim World*, vol. 86, no. 1 (1996), 12–13; *al-Hurriyyah*, July 9, 1989.

66 Cf. the Speaker of Parliament, Sulayman Arar's interview, *al-Watan al-'Arabi*, March 30, 1990.

67 *Al-Ra'i*, August 21, 1992; *Filastin al-Muslimah*, August 1992.

68 Cf. *al-Quds*, December 4, 1989.

69 Interview with former minister Layla Sharaf, *al-Minbar*, October 1988.

70 *Al-Ra'i*, December 31, 1989, January 1, 2, 3, 1990, cf. *Sawt al-Sha'b*, January 11, 1990.

71 *Al-Nahar*, November 25, 1989.

72 Cf. *al-Dustur*, November 19, 29, 1989.

73 Satloff, *Troubles on the East Bank*, 39–40.

74 November 2, 1985 speech, *al-Ra'i*, November 2, 1985; *Jordan Times*, November 11, 29, 1985; *Washington Times*, August 13, 1986.

75 Robert Satloff, "Repression in Irbid: Raising the Stakes in Jordan," *Middle East Insight*, 5 (January 1987), 31–7; *Washington Times*, August 13, 1986.

76 Barry Rubin, "Islamic Radicalism in the Middle East: A Survey and Balance Sheet," *MERIA Journal*, vol. 2, no. 1 (May 1998).

77 Tim H. Riedel, "The 1993 Parliamentary Elections in Jordan," *Orient*, 35, no. 1 (March 1994), 58.

78 Cf. *al-Yawm al-Sabi'*, April 9, 1990.

79 US Department of State, *Jordan Country Report on Human Rights Practices for 1996* (Washington: Bureau of Democracy, Human Rights, and Labor), January 30, 1997.

80 US Department of State, *Jordan Country Report on Human Rights Practices*

for 1998 (Washington: Bureau of Democracy, Human Rights, and Labor), February 26, 1999.

81 King Hussein of Jordan, *Uneasy Lies the Head* (London: Heinemann, 1962), facing p. 197.

82 October 30, 1992, interview, *FBIS*, November 5, 1992.

83 November 5, 1992, Address to the nation, Amman Jordan television network in Arabic, *FBIS*, November 6, 1992.

84 *The Economist*, August 1, 1998.

85 Cf. *International Herald Tribune*, November 2, 1998.

86 Yosef Bodansky, "After King Hussein, What?", *Defense and Foreign Affairs Strategic Policy* (January 1999), 16–17.

87 *Al-Ra'i, al-Dustur*, January 26, 1999.

Conclusions

1 Address to the nation, Amman Jordan television, *FBIS*, November 6, 1992.

Index

Index

Arab–Israeli war (1973), 148–9
  autonomous area in Gaza Strip, 170
  Camp David accords, 155, 158, 162
  cease-fire with Israel (1970), 113
  change in US foreign policy towards, 19
  confederation idea, 177
  declaration of new Arab union (1963), 3,
    9, 10, 24
  deployment of technicians to Jordan, 40
  diplomatic relations with Jordan, 148
  directing of Palestinian activity, 34, 47
  al-Fatah military activities, 47
  hostility to Israel, 24, 25
  hostility to Jordan, 2, 8, 12, 13–14, 24–5,
    32, 41–3, 57
  improved relations with Jordan (1970s),
    156
  interim talks (1974–1975), 150–1
  Israeli invasion threat (1963), 21
  Jordanian civil war, 140, 141
  Jordanian–Israeli post-war (1967) peace
    moves, 126–7, 129–30, 132, 133
  Jordanian–PLO relations, 146
  June 1967 war, 53, 58–9, 60, 62–3, 68
  military agreement with Jordan (1967),
    52, 53
  military tension with Israel (1960), 56
  Palestinian military force in West Bank,
    33
  peace treaty with Israel (1979), 146, 156,
    160
  and the PLO, 41–2, 155
  post-war (1967) policies, 99, 100, 101
  Samu' crisis (November 1966), 29, 32
  Soviet support for, 17
  subsidies from oil-rich countries, 107
  see also United Arab Republic
Eilat, 15
Eshkol, Levi, 29, 103, 121, 133

al-Fahum, Khalid, 145
family reunification, 122
al-Fatah
  beginning of activities (1965), 30, 33, 48
  expelled from Jordan (1986), 168
  future cooperation formula between
    Arafat and Hussein (1985), 167
  headquarters location, 40–1
  Hussein's support for, 128
  and Jordan, 34–5, 36, 47–8, 56, 124, 128,
    168, 176
  Karameh incident, 124–5
  military activities, 28–9, 34–5, 36, 39,
    47–8
  monitoring of, 36, 47–8
  Nasser's connections with, 129

Palestinian military force in West Bank,
  33
reopening of offices in Jordan (1989), 176
Samu' crisis (November 1966), 28–9
Faysal, King of Saudi Arabia, 15
Faysal, Prince of Jordan, 208
Fez Arab summit (1982), 165, 167
fidayin, 12, 16, 121–2, 139
France
  April 1963 crisis, 23–4
  Tripartite Declaration, 23–4, 25
Freedom House, 202

Gaza Strip, 77, 100, 134, 135, 170
Gazit, M., 50, 241*n*
Geneva Conference, 149, 151, 157
Golan Heights, 148, 149, 154
Goldberg, Arthur, 105
Gulf crisis, 183–6, 187, 191–2
Gulf states, 178

Haig, William, 163
Halhul, 56
al-Hamah, 178
HAMAS, 51, 198–9
Hashemite Broadcasting Service (HBS), 55
Hashim, 77
Hassan bin Talal, Prince, 9, 163, 164, 187,
  200, 204, 208–9
Hebron mountain area, 14
Herzog, Jacob, 102
Hizb al-Tahrir, 139
Hussein bin Talal, King
  alliance with Syria (1970s), 153–7
  Allon plan, 120, 129, 135, 151
  April 1963 crisis, 3–4, 9, 11, 13–15, 25–6,
    27, 53
  Arab historical legitimacy, 75, 79–81
  Arab–Israeli war (1973), 147–50, 154
  armistice lines, 109
  at cease-fire (1967), 94
  becomes king, 8
  Cairo summit with Arafat (1977), 145,
    146
  civil war, 88–9, 140–2
  concept of Jordanian people, 76, 89–91
  confederation idea, 176
  confrontation of *fidayin*, 121–2
  demilitarization of West Bank proposals,
    22
  democratization process, 202–8
  diplomatic campaign against Egypt, 14
  direct negotiations with Israel, 3–4, 9, 26,
    27, 29, 36–7, 43–4, 47
  domestic Palestinian challenge (1967–71),
    112–13, 115–17, 120, 124–6, 140–3
  food riots (1989), 200–1, 204

Index

Index

deployment of Egyptian technicians, 40
diplomatic relations with Egypt, 148
direct negotiations with Israel, 3–4, 9, 26, 27, 29, 36–7, 43–4, 47
domestic Palestinian challenge (1967–71), 112–13, 115–17, 120, 124–6, 138–9, 140–3
economic agreement with PLO (1994), 191
Egyptian hostility towards, 2, 8, 12, 13–14, 24–5, 32, 41–3, 57
and *al-Fatah*, 34–5, 36, 47–8, 56, 124, 128, 168, 176
food riots (1989), 200–1, 204
food riots (1996), 207
future cooperation formula between Arafat and Hussein (1985), 166–9
Gulf crisis, 183–6, 187, 191–2
Hamas activities, 51, 198–9
immediate post-war (1967) circumstances, 96–100
improved relations with Egypt (1970s), 156
interim talks (1974–1975), 150–1
international conference proposal (1987), 170–1
Intifadah uprising, 171–3, 182
Iraqi expeditionary forces, 43, 45, 60, 65, 101–2, 120, 140
Iraqi hostility, 12, 149
Iraqi reliance on, 179, 183–4
Israeli challenge (1967–71), 112–13, 117–37
Israeli concern (1990), 191
Israeli policy (November 1966–June 1967), 50–2
Israeli–Palestinian Declaration of Principles, 189
June 1967 war, 48–9, 53, 58–72
legitimacy of the Hashemite dynasty, 75, 77–86
London agreement (1987), 180–1
Madrid conference (1991), 187–9, 190, 192–3
military agreement with Egypt (1967), 52, 53
military contacts with Israel, 9, 212*n*
military cooperation with United States, 142, 178
Naharayim shootings, 197–8
nation-state legitimacy, 75–6, 86–91
national economy, 97–8, 152, 200–2
nationalist feelings, 4–5, 51, 73–93, 113–14, 141–2
Oslo Accords, 187, 190, 193
Palestinian assimilation, 51

Palestinian refugees due to Gulf crisis, 187
peace treaty with Israel (1994), 1, 80, 86, 91–2, 194–6, 211
and PLO, 33, 34–5, 51, 96, 115–16, 139, 142–7, 164–78, 179–82, 186–200
PLO–Hashemite coalition, 113, 124–5
post-Gulf war peace moves with Israel, 192–4
post-war (1967) peace moves with Israel, 94–5, 96, 100–1, 102–11, 117–20, 121–4, 125–37
post-war (1967) policies to Egypt, 99, 101
rapprochement with Syria (1986), 179–80, 182
resumption of parliamentary life, 160–1, 173
Samu' crisis (November 1966), 27–46, 53–4, 55, 56
Saudi expeditionary forces, 43, 45, 60, 101–2
Soviet warning, 41
status of women, 78
subsidies from oil-rich countries, 107, 183
Syrian military deployment (1980), 156–7
tension with Syria (1980s), 178
territorial legitimacy, 76, 86–7
threat from Syria, 12, 139, 149, 160
threat from West Bank Palestinians, 9, 12, 13, 55–7
US financial support, 153
use of US as channel to Israel, 36–7
West Bank development plan (1986), 170, 175
West Bank disengagement process, 5, 33, 48, 56–7, 160–1, 211
West Bank open bridges policy, 96–7, 98, 117
Jordan River, 15
Jordanian Arab Army, 52, 53, 83
Arab–Israeli war (1973), 150
as attribute of sovereignty, 76, 92–3
June 1967 war, 58, 65–7, 68
lessons of the Arab–Israeli war (1973), 149–50
loyalty to Hussein, 13, 115
rehabilitation after June 1967 war, 97–8, 114–15, 139
Samu' crisis (November 1966), 31–2, 35, 58
Jum'ah, Sa'd, 64

Kabariti, Abd al-Karim, 207
Karameh incident, 83, 113, 123, 124–5
Katzenbach, Nicholas, 131
al-Kaylani, Rasul, 119

Index

Index

Index

Intifadah uprising, 160, 161, 169, 171–3, 182
Israeli invasion threat (1963), 9–10, 14, 16–18, 19, 20–3, 54
Israeli open bridges policy, 96–7, 98, 117
Israeli retaliatory actions in, 37, 39
Jordanian development plan (1986), 170, 175
Jordanian disengagement policy, 5, 33, 48, 56–7, 160–1, 211
Jordanian–Israeli post-war (1967) peace moves, 119–20, 127–8, 132, 134–5
June 1967 war, 48–9, 65, 68–72
refugees as result of 1967 war, 96, 107
sensitivity prior to June 1967 war, 57
US reassurance to Hussein after cease-fire (1967), 94
West Bank Palestinians

April 1963 crisis, 9–11, 13, 26
conscription law, 35
growing alienation of, 34
Samu' crisis (November 1966), 27–8, 31
threat to Jordan, 9, 12, 13, 55–7
unity on issues, 35
use of Jordanian passports, 176
Wilson, Harold, 109
Wye Summit, 199–200

Yarmuk River, 26
Yarmuk University, 206
Yasin, Ahamd, 199
Yemen, 15, 19, 24, 178, 201

Zarka conspiracy (1957), 8
Zayd bin Shaker, Sharif, 163
Zionist movement, 75, 81–6